CALIFORNIA ROCK & ROLL

SMART ASS

THE MUSIC JOURNALISM OF JOEL SELVIN

Ricky Nelson

Monterey Pop (with Jim Marshall)

Summer Of Love

San Francisco: The Musical History Tour

Sly and the Family Stone

Photopass: The Rock & Roll Photography of
    Randy Bachman

Treasures Of the Hard Rock (with Paul Grushkin)

Nagle, Ron

CALIFORNIA ROCK & ROLL

SMART ASS

THE MUSIC JOURNALISM OF JOEL SELVIN

PARTHENON

SLG BOOKS

Smart Ass I The Music Journalism of Joel Selvin

First Published in 2011

Parthenon Books
A division of SLG Books
P.O. Box 9465, Berkeley, CA 94709
Tel: 510-525-1134
Email: smartass@slgbooks.com
Publisher's URL: www.slgbooks.com
Author's URL: www.joelselvin.com

Color Separations and printing by
Snow Lion Graphics, Berkeley/Hong Kong

Library of Congress Cataloging-in-Publication Data

Selvin, Joel.
    Smart ass : the music journalism of Joel Selvin.
      p. cm.
    ISBN 978-0-943389-42-4
    1. Popular music—United States—History and criticism. 2. Musical
criticism—United States. I. San Francisco Chronicle. II. Title.
    ML3477.S45 2011
    781.640973—dc22
                                        2010033861
    ISBN 10:   0-943389-42-4
    ISBN 13:   978-0-943389-42-4

Printed in Hong Kong
10 9 8 7 6 5 4 3 2 1

To Carla

All is possible.

Foreword

By Greil Marcus

YEARS AGO I READ AN INTERVIEW WITH JOEL SELVIN where he said, in essence, it's a privilege for me to interview James Brown, but it's also a privilege for James Brown to be interviewed by me. That wasn't merely the most arrogant statement I'd ever heard from a critic – it struck me as unbelievably arrogant. Even though I'd been reading Selvin for years, I couldn't imagine what sort of person could say such a thing – for that matter, I couldn't imagine how such a person could get through an interview with James Brown without Brown having his bodyguards throw the guy out. Smart ass didn't come close to covering it.

Years later, when along with Roy Blount, Jr., Dave Marsh, and Matt Groening, we were fellow members of the benighted Critics Chorus in the all-author band the Rock Bottom Remainders – "This is the nadir of western civilization," our band director Al Kooper, himself a published author, said after one rehearsal for our big number, an execution of the Swingin' Medallions' "Double Shot (Of My Baby's Love)." "Right here, in our show" – I discovered that with Joel, what seemed like arrogance was a big sense of life. It wasn't simply that, alone among we five (one of the few San Francisco bands not covered in this book), Joel could sing: loudly, with delight, bravado, and, the one quality we all shared, shamelessness. It was that in Joel's company, anything seemed possible. There was no door that couldn't be talked open, no obstacle that didn't reveal a short cut, no refusal that wasn't topped by a story of a better one.

What *Smart Ass* captures completely is the expansive and generous spirit of a writer who cannot take no for an answer. If the subject of a given piece isn't talking—Sly Stone, for example, in "Lucifer Rising," a shattering account of the making of *There's a Riot Goin' On*, or Phil Spector in the deadline-yesterday "Over the

Wall" – Selvin will tease out the story from other people, from the ambiance of place and time, a feel for dead ends and locked rooms, an ear for truth and lie, and his own vast knowledge of who was where, when, and why, until rather than sensing the absence of a subject, the reader can sense that figure standing on the outside of the piece, looking in, wishing he'd had the nerve to talk while there was still time.

There is perhaps less of Joel's humor, his sarcasm, his ability to unmask a fraud with a sentence of that person's own words, perfectly placed, than there might have been here – but this is the record of a man covering a beat, knocking on the same doors again and again, until they seem to open without a touch. The story here is not only the story of music in California over the last forty years or so. It's also the story of one man earning the trust of other people, to the point where, at the end of a tribute to a colleague, the late Ralph J. Gleason, his widow, the late Jean Gleason, will tell Selvin, "He was not a good writer. He wrote about interesting things," and it can seem like the finest epitaph a writer could ask for, and most of the people in these pages speak that plain language, because Joel knows how to hear it.

TABLE OF CONTENTS

California Rock & Roll

WHEN I STARTED, THEY USED TO SQUEEZE MY PIECES between the adult theater ads and the edge of the page. It was more than a year before so much as a one-column mug shot ran with one of my stories. Now they call it *music journalism* and teach courses about it at the universities.

The '60s party was almost over when I first began writing for the *San Francisco Chronicle*. There were still some people who had stayed too late and enough wreckage around to indicate what kind of a bash it had been. On Thanksgiving night in 1972, I left my parents' dinner table in the Berkeley hills and drove down to a toilet called Keystone Berkeley, where a sweaty, steamy, beered-up mob waited for Commander Cody and his Lost Planet Airmen and the Elvin Bishop Group to play a benefit for ailing harmonica ace Charlie Musselwhite, who'd been injured in an auto accident and needed to pay some bills. That was where I walked in.

I'd been around before. As a Berkeley High School student, I frequented the Fillmore, Avalon, the Jabberwocky, the New Orleans House, the Berkeley Folk Festival at the Greek Theater, anywhere there was music and, in San Francisco and Berkeley in 1965-7, there was music everywhere. After failing to make it across the finish line at high school, I ended up joining the copy boy crew at the Chronicle, where I earned $55 a week and could get on the guest list at the Fillmore. No greater aspiration occurred to me until I found myself writing about rock music for my college newspaper and started getting free records in the mail from record companies. Then I was done. When *Chronicle* columnist John L. Wasserman hired me to substitute for jazz singer Jon Hendricks, while he took a six-week engagement at a nightclub in London, I couldn't envision any greater rewards in life. But I was 22 years old – what did I know?

Over the course of the years, from my post as the *Chronicle*'s pop music man,

I have been able to pursue my rather single-minded fascination with American music up close and personal. I have met the people who could answer the questions I wanted to ask. When I first got the bug, there was no Rolling Stone magazine or books about rock. I stood for hours after school and weekends reading the backs of album jackets in record stores along Telegraph Avenue. I checked out old folk and blues records from the public library. In a sense, my journalistic enterprises have been a series of post-graduate papers on my studies in the field.

Although I have spent my career writing for a San Francisco daily, California has always been my beat. I have always seen myself as a Californian. In Europe, when people ask me if I'm American, I always tell them, no, I'm from California. They understand. Growing up in California in the '60s, the Beach Boys told my story as much as the Grateful Dead did. I know Southern California well – I went to school there and have spent many happy hours pursuing the good life in Hollywood and beyond. I lived in L.A. while I wrote a book about Ricky Nelson, one of Hollywood's golden sons.

To find country music immortal Merle Haggard nestled in his irascible dotage in the scrubby hills outside Redding comes as no surprise to anybody who understands the way a boy growing up poor in Bakersfield would see the state. Just as it's easy to understand why the dark bard of Sunset Boulevard, Tom Waits, would retreat to raise his family in the quiet fields of western Sonoma, but still want to meet for his interview in the midst of San Francisco's bustling Mission District. I've seen Elvis in Tahoe and Sonny Bono in Palm Springs. California encompasses multitudes.

Five thousand years of the western march of civilization ended here – from Mesopotamia to the Gold Rush, a bunch of crazed and desperate zealots out to make it rich on the far end of the continent. California – the final resting place of western civilization – has brought the world movies and computers, oranges and avocados, hippies and Hells Angels, Mickey Mouse and Charlie Manson. The kind of fearless, crazed individuals driven to make music in California have provided a steady source of subjects for vulgar entertainment by the jackal press in the Datebook pages of the daily *Chronicle*.

There wasn't much of a tradition of rock critics in the newspaper game when I first showed up. Ralph Gleason cast a long shadow. He started writing about jazz and pop at the Chronicle around 1950. He covered everything – he caught Hank Williams and Fats Domino in the early '50s. Louis Armstrong and Duke Ellington thought of him as a hero. Gleason, almost alone among his generation, figured out the new rock scene of the '60s and directed its course from his pulpit in the *Chronicle*, eventually helping Jann Wenner start *Rolling Stone*. He wore trench coats and deerstalker hats, smoked a pipe and held strong views, unreservedly expressed, on subjects far and wide. He left the *Chronicle* in 1970 to work for Fantasy Records, although he continued to loom over the paper until his death five years later.

My boss, John L. Wasserman, was not as hip as Gleason. He had a *Playboy* magazine sense of cool – bachelor apartment, chilled martinis, low-lights, jazz on the hi-fi – and didn't really dig the rock beat the kids so enjoyed. That was where I came in. As long as I was out there, slogging through those three-act weekends at Winterland, hitting the clubs during the weeknights, he could write his facetious commentaries on the eccentric nooks and crannies of pop culture that interested him (porno movies, Latin jazz, Clint Eastwood, female supper club vocalists), confident that the news of the day, those tawdry rock bands with their smelly audiences, would be handled by his trusty assistant. He never checked on me. As long as the mail was opened by eleven in the morning, he didn't care what I did.

When you look back on the club calendars from those days, it's hard to believe what was going on out there in any given week. Herbie Hancock, the Doobie Brothers, Tower of Power playing the Keystone Berkeley. Asleep At the Wheel or Sylvester and the Hot Band at the Longbranch. Van Morrison at the Lion's Share in Marin County. If he wasn't on the road with the Dead, Jerry Garcia would be playing all night in some dump like the Matrix with Howard Wales or, later, Keystone Korner with Merl Saunders. Elvin Bishop was jamming in North Beach clubs every night, literally wandering the streets with a guitar in hand. Mike Bloomfield used to love to work this tiny little neighborhood bar out on California Street.

Music was more than entertainment. It was an all-consuming passion. Nothing else really mattered. My early stuff wasn't very good. But at least I was there. That counted. And there was something in the paper, no matter how cogent and incisive it may or may not have been.

The features have always been the backstory to the hit parade. Over the years, with long-lived institutions such as the Grateful Dead or the Beach Boys, the coverage takes on the character of a running story. Following the disintegration and eventual dissolution of the once mighty Dead after the death of Jerry Garcia was a ten-year soap opera, culminating in a series of legal stories and obits. During the band's actual existence, the Dead had been a non-stop fountain of great stories and lore and the band members all – well, almost all – treated me like gentlemen. As one of the few non-Deadheads to write consistently about the band, I've always felt like my perspective is skewed somewhat differently than the usual viewpoint you see represented. And with the band members and their extended families all *Chronicle* subscribers, it has been an interesting relationship at times.

Like the time I attended – and reviewed – the first show of two shows over the weekend the Dead did with the Who at the Oakland baseball stadium. It wasn't that great a show, something I made mention of in the review. But when I showed up at the *Chronicle* office Monday morning, somebody had hand-delivered a stack of reel-to-reel tapes to my desk. How they got past the front desk to drop them off directly at my desk was always part of the mystery. The note attached read "Yeah, but you should have been there Sunday."

Some artists can be tracked through their entire careers in my clip files. My first Sunday pink section interview with Bonnie Raitt, for instance, was setup by the Warner Brothers publicity office back when I was still flattered just to be getting a phone call from a record label. She was passing through town on a publicity tour for her first album. When I mentioned to Bonnie some twenty, thirty years later that I had conducted one of my first interviews for the Sunday paper with her on the occasion of her debut album, she brightened right up. "And we both still got our same jobs," she said.

I long ago got over being impressed with the fact that I have a job at the newspaper (although I still do find it funny). When I started out, there were still underground newspapers with rock critics who wouldn't so much as capitalize their names in their bylines and it was the golden age of the "conversational" style of writing practiced by *Rolling Stone*. I chose instead to take my pointers from newspaper sports writers, even if I never cared much for the sports themselves. Sports writers had long before established a common language with their readers and they weren't shy about sharing their opinions or airing locker room topics in the sports pages. I saw a lot of parallels.

The first time my work appeared on the front page was in 1984, when a hot-shot city desk editor thought we should jump the *New York Times* by a year and declare rock and roll thirty years old a year ahead of schedule, provided I could make a case for it. I could and did and "Rock Music: The Wild Child Turns 30" brought rock and roll for the first time since the Beatles landed at SFO out of the

Datebook, which in those days very few people even gave a glance if they weren't looking for the TV listings.

Without realizing it at the time, we had successfully identified a growing audience among newspaper readers, who wanted to read about rock music in their morning paper. Editors were asking me for tickets to concerts that weren't for their kids. Photographers were getting assigned to shoot the shows with me. They started running my interviews on the cover of the pink section, where my weekly Lively Arts column was making me semi-famous. A punk band, the Fried Abortions, made a record called "Joel Selvin" ("I want to kick the shit out of you," went the catchy chorus). For seventeen years, I was the lone rock and roll soldier stationed in the *Chronicle's* Sunday paper, where I earned a reputation for writing about nothing but Journey and Huey Lewis and the News.

A couple of things happened next. One, the San Francisco music scene cooled off quickly after the brief, sputtery flash of new wave and punk. It had been a good run, but the laws of diminishing returns were taking hold and, outside of sporadic, die-hard pockets, nobody cared. When Bill Graham died in 1991, the scene's last strong man disappeared. San Francisco, once center of the pop music universe, would soon revert to its demographic destiny as just another secondary market. The pop music stories would retreat from the nightclubs, as the tech boom swept through San Francisco and technology became the new rock. If you wanted to write about the old rock – they called it "classic rock" by now – you had to look elsewhere.

Second, after starting to write non-fiction books, my direction as a writer began to move strongly in favor of longer, more complex narratives. I grew more interested in musicians and the process of making music than the music itself. Before long, I was writing about everything from Courtney Love's estranged (and strange), biological father to the grim, sordid story of Kevin Gilbert, a dismal tale of Hollywood greed and ambition behind the rise of Sheryl Crow that could have been written by Nathaniel West. By the time I managed to unwind the serpentine plotline of the Bill Graham probate case over three days and several thousand words in *The Chronicle*, I had drifted far afield from my beginnings as a churlish nightclub reviewer.

Growing up in Berkeley was a little weird from time to time. It offered certain cultural advantages – as a child I watched Charlie Chaplin movies at a theater, excuse me, cinema repertory house run by Pauline Kael in her pre-*New Yorker* days – but they came at a definite cost. You needed to account for yourself politically. You needed to contribute. It was a credo of the '60s – if you weren't part of the solution, you were part of the problem. Justine and Larry were classic Berkeley – he an unpublished playwright, she a successful Jungian therapist. I was explaining to them at a party about my new life as a cultural commentator for the pig establishment press, as useless to the social revolution as tits on a priest. I told them I felt like I'd grown up to run away and join the circus.

"Well, anything that helps make life possible," said Justine, ever the problem-solving, reality-oriented therapist.

"Yes, but beware the difference between 'diversion' and 'divergence,'" said Larry the playwright.

I always wondered what he meant.

This is what I wanted to do, nuts as it is to say that. I have devoted what we might laughingly refer to as my adult life to covering the pop music panorama for the readers of *The Chronicle*. It took me a long time to figure out what I was doing and anybody who writes about pop music for the same paper as Ralph J. Gleason would have a hard time thinking they left much of an impression by comparison. But I wrote a lot of stories. Some of them weren't bad.

January 2008

Chapter 1

California Breed

Merle Haggard

Tom Waits

Phil Spector

Bill Graham

Ralph J. Gleason

The Last True Cowboy

Real country music may be dead, but Merle Haggard carries on the original sound

Before Haggard would allow a reporter to visit his home outside Redding, he wanted to meet me at a concert appearance in Santa Rosa so he could look me over, sort of a cool check to see if I could hang. A corpulent Cajun named Rodney brought me to the bus. "You don't have a problem with marijuana?" he asked. Merle and his guitarist were each smoking their own pipe – no unhealthy cigarette papers for Merle; that stuff will kill you. I pulled out a joint and tore it open on the table. We got along fine.

COUNTRY MUSIC IS OVER. There are lots of rock singers wearing cowboy hats these days, but genuine country music is all but dead and gone. Willie Nelson is still doing his thing - which has as much to do with country music as the Grateful Dead has to do with rock. Johnny Cash is suffering from some mysterious debilitating illness. Buck Owens lost half his tongue to cancer. George Jones is out there . . . somewhere. Merle Haggard is one of the last damn cowboys left.

Country music used to stand for something. It was country music, not city music, the farmer's friend, the voice of the people, the white man's blues. The men who made this music were truly men to be reckoned with – towering figures of imperfect character who looked over the abyss and brought back their tales.

Hank Williams was the archetype - the tortured-genius country boy who wrote simple, direct, heartfelt songs that touched people's lives. He died at 29 on New Year's Eve in 1952, full of booze and pills, roaring down the highway in the backseat of a Cadillac on his way to another gig. These were desperate men. They made this music because there wasn't really anything else they could do.

Today's country superstars grew up listening to Lynyrd Skynyrd, wondering if they could borrow dad's car for a Friday-night date only to wind up hanging out with their buddies at the mall. Country music was a career decision, a "direction." Predictably, their records are puerile confections, full of chintzy drum machines and processed vocal sounds, and every one of them would need a ladder just to kiss Ernest Tubb's butt.

2

Merle Haggard

Haggard, long one of country music's most resolute traditionalists, is going backward. He is going back to the past to see if he can find something that was lost along the way. Haggard, who turned 64 years old April 6, is the living repository of country music's great traditions.

This is not some empty platitude; he lives among CD boxed sets of old-time country music and museumlike memorabilia, from instruments that belonged to the music's greats to old 78s framed and mounted on the walls.

He says he is tired and speaks of quitting the road, maybe settling in for some long-term residency at a Reno hotel. But really, he is a man at the peak of his powers. His latest album, "If I Could Fly," is easily one of the best of his nearly 40-year recording career. His voice has aged like fine leather. But he is far from the Nashville crowd these days.

The new album was released by Epitaph Records, a successful punk rock label that had never put out anything remotely like the Haggard record before. But like the punk rockers, Haggard, too, has always been an outsider.

He is hurtling down the highway in his Ford Expedition, the Eddie Bauer model, toward Redding, past new roadside businesses like a self-storage lot. The sight doesn't make him happy. "It's exploded the past five years," he says disdainfully. "Look at it – it's just like the edge of L.A."

Haggard smiles his trademark teeth-baring grin that tightens the lines roadmapping his face. His hawk eyes bear down, and he raises an eyebrow questioningly. He is short, compact, a tightly coiled spring in a pair of seven-dollar granny glasses with blue lenses. His salt-and-pepper beard may give him a stately Lincolnesque air, but the blue ovals over his eyes and the black fedora he plunked on his head make him look more like an escapee from a '60s biker movie. Plus, he's stoned. His ever-present pipe is clutched between the fingers of one hand and an M&Ms tube full of buds is nearby.

Haggard obviously has no use for any big city, even a backwater one like Redding. He stays away from Los Angeles. And he stays away from Nashville, too.

He has spent the last 22 years living around Lake Shasta in the foothills at the north end of California's Central Valley. There isn't another country star living within a hundred miles. Hell, two hundred miles.

Haggard first saw Lake Shasta on one of his early tours in 1963. He bought a lakeside cabin sight-unseen and spent an idyllic Memorial Day weekend there in 1969 with his second wife, Bonnie Owens, who still sings in his band. He moved north full time from Bakersfield in 1978.

During the '80s, in between marriages, he owned a place called the Silverthorn Resort, a marina, some houseboats, a few cabins and a bar and grill. He lived on his houseboat. "We had a new set of women renting houseboats every Wednesday, and every Friday we held a wet T-shirt contest to take a look at the competition," he said.

He is a long way from that kind of debauchery now. He met Theresa, his fifth wife, while he was still married to his fourth. She was a wild child who came to a Merle Haggard concert in 1984 with the guitar player and left with the bandleader. They lived on the houseboat together for years. But after Theresa got pregnant with their daughter, she and Merle sobered up, moved out of the houseboat and haven't looked back.

They have two children; Jenessa, 11, and Ben, 8. An attractive, younger blonde, she was planting vegetables in the garden next to the chicken coop – a Daisy Mae in shorts and overalls. She also is running their business and recently closed a deal to sell Merle Haggard-brand oranges to the military from their citrus ranch in Porterville. A proof of the orange crate promotional art – Merle holding an orange and giving the thumbs-up sign – was hanging on the wall above her desk in the upstairs living room.

They have just moved into one of the many houses on the dozens of acres he owns about 15 miles east of Redding. The home he refurbished when the kids were born was recently condemned because of black mold. It sits on the edge of the hill above, out of sight, surrounded by ponds Haggard built on the property. Tally Studios, his 48-track professional studio, is on top of the hill, too, attached to yet another vacant home, where he lived with his third wife when he first moved to the property.

Now the rest of that house is mostly empty, although the walk-in closet in the abandoned master bedroom is still filled with his clothes from the era – like the nice brick-red suit bought off the rack at J.C. Penney. The studio remains an obvious nerve center on the compound. Outside the door of the studio hangs a framed Bob Wills 78 rpm record. A Grammy Award is tossed inconspicuously in a corner. Engineer Lou Bradley is out from Nashville to do some work.

Haggard has turned the living room in the new family home into another recording studio. He found an acoustic sweet spot under the slanted ceiling and semicircular staircase and put shades over the windows on the outside of the house. He parked an inexpensive Tascam 12-track mixing board on a card table in the adjacent poolroom and fed it to an old two-track, 1/4-inch tape recorder. He hung photos of his heroes on the walls – Lefty Frizzell and Bob Wills. A Stradivarius violin that western swing great Wills left him in his will, probably Haggard's most valuable possession, sits in its case. The upright bass lying on the floor belonged to Nashville session player Bob Moore and was used on many hit records of the golden era.

Haggard likes mementos. In a stand in the poolroom is a guitar that belonged to Wynn Stewart, the now mostly forgotten, late country singing star who gave Haggard his first break. An antique radio in the corner of the room once sat in the home of Jimmie Rodgers, "The Singing Brakeman" himself.

In March, between tour dates, Haggard convened a group of his musicians under the staircase around his new discovery, guitarist Norm Stephens. The 69-year-old retired civil engineer belonged to Lefty Frizzell's band when he was an 18-year-old hotshot and while Frizzell had seven consecutive Top 10 hits on the country charts in 1950, before the draft interrupted his musical career. Frizzell is never far from Haggard's mind – he was his boyhood idol, the singer he modeled himself after and someone who might be all but entirely forgotten today if it weren't for Haggard continually recording his old songs. When he discovered that Frizzell's old guitarist was living down the road in Cottonwood, it called for some very special recording sessions.

Using this low-fidelity setup in his front room, Haggard wanted to re- create the sound of the Jim Beck Studio in Dallas where Frizzell cut all his roadhouse hits a half-century ago. Haggard, his band and Lefty's old guitarist sat downstairs for days and ran through Frizzell songs Haggard remembered from his childhood. They were not using any modern studio technology. There would be no fixing mistakes or postproduction polishing; only complete, unedited takes would be used. Haggard was turning back the technological clock. In its own way, this is a profoundly rebellious act, but Haggard has always been a rebel.

He grew up in a converted railroad boxcar in Oildale, a bump in the road on the other side of the Kern River from Bakersfield. He and his parents were part of the Dust Bowl migration of the '30s, real "Grapes of Wrath" stuff, and he has known the sting of being called an Okie all his life. His father died when he was 9 years old. He was a troubled kid who only excelled at truancy in school. He ran away from home, riding the rails like a hobo. He did time in a reformatory.

He landed in San Quentin at age 20 after a badly bungled burglary of a neighborhood tavern went haywire. While his pregnant wife and their infant child waited in the car outside, Haggard and an equally drunken friend broke into a restaurant owned by someone who knew them, only to discover the place was still open and that they'd been recognized.

He made a run for it, but the cops nabbed him minutes later driving away without his lights, burglary tools by his feet on the floorboard. He escaped from jail the next morning, just slipped away while he was being escorted down a hallway, and spent Christmas Eve 1957 eating a furtive baloney sandwich with his wife in a seedy motel before the cops grabbed him later that night at his brother's house. He served almost three years in prison and, on release, he headed back to Bakersfield to try his hand playing music in the town's thriving country and western bars. Many years later, he would receive a pardon from Governor Ronald Reagan.

His 1963 cover of a Wynn Stewart song, "Sing a Sad Song," launched his Country Music Hall of Fame career (one that Haggard characterized as "a 35-year bus ride"). It was his 1969 antiprotest song, "Okie From Muskogee," that vaulted Haggard into nationwide controversy, although his country career had already long been established. His "Today I Started Loving You Again" had been recorded some 70 times. But with "Okie From Muskogee" serving as a battle cry for the so-called Silent Majority, President Richard Nixon declared Haggard his favorite country singer. It is a song he has never stopped apologizing for, even though he has to perform it at every show. ("I must have been as dumb as a rock when I wrote this," he told a Santa Rosa audience a week earlier.)

Even then, he was an outsider. He kept his headquarters in Bakersfield - not Nashville, big difference - and represented the maverick spirit of West Coast country music, which always maintained an uneasy peace with the often dogmatic Nashville country music establishment. These distinctions are not slight in the field. Haggard is talking about the dichotomy to this day. He cites the theory that players on the east side of the Mississippi River come from entirely separate traditions than players from the west side.

Today, the onetime Frizzell guitarist, Stephens, and his wife, Verna, have driven up from Cottonwood, and Chester Smith is up from Modesto to put some final touches on the record he is making with Haggard. Smith is a fascinating character himself. Haggard remembers hearing him on Modesto radio station KTRB when he was a young boy spending summers with his aunt. Smith's 1954 hit, "Wait a Little Longer Please Jesus," led to his being voted best new "sacred singer" the following year by country and western disc jockeys. But Smith glimpsed the future and left music almost 40 years ago to start Spanish language television stations He owns six stations and three large communications-transmitting sites, and is one of the biggest stockholders of Univision, the Spanish-language network.

At age 71, he has decided to return to country music in what would be one of the most remarkable comebacks in the history of country. He looks every bit the billionaire industrialist – with the Rolls-Royce parked in the lot outside – elegantly groomed and attired, an almost delicate, soft-spoken gentleman who still lives up to his old stage nickname of "Stringbean." ("We try not to swear around him," says Haggard.)

Talk turns, as it often does around Haggard, to Frizzell. Haggard repeats a story Frizzell told him before his death from a stroke at age 47 in 1975. Frizzell, according to Haggard, played Hank Williams some lines he had written but not yet included in a song – Haggard then sings the middle eight bars from Williams' "Your Cheatin' Heart." Everybody nods somberly. Nobody reacts in shock or amazement that Haggard suspects the great Hank Williams of song-swiping. Norm Stephens even allows that the bridge sounds like something Lefty might have written.

"You know, Hank told me he and Lefty tried to write some songs together," says Chester Smith. "He said they went away together, got all sequestered and nothing came of it. Lefty drove him crazy, Hank said."

"I don't know if it was the time you're talking about," says Stephens, "but I was with them when they tried to write one. It was in a hotel room after a show. Nothing happened."

As quietly as a breeze, the ghost of Hank Williams has slipped into the room and he doesn't feel the slightest bit out of place. These fellows are talking about an old friend, not just country music history. This is not a conversation that would be held in Nashville. They ran ol' Hank out of that town. Not many people left there knew him anyway. But at Tally Studios outside Redding, the ghosts of country music's past are always welcome. It's not just the photos of the Maddox Brothers and Rose hanging in the studio or septuagenarian Smith (who Haggard says he respects for "not going with the Nashville softball") using the place to make his unlikely comeback record.

Haggard treats country music's time-honored values like the endangered species they are. An hour or so later, Haggard sits outside his home in his SUV with the engine idling (this guy has spent way too much time living on buses) and contemplates the point.

"We're talking about an art form," he says, "so dear to me. I am so involved with it that I am the art form; the art form is me. My family knows that. My friends know that. Anybody who ever cared about talent has got to know I've been given a double serving. Any wrong moves I've made have come from when I tried to pick it up without laboring for it, without studying.

"With these musicians these days, there's a lot of catering to the bubblegum side of life rather than paying tribute to the older guys whose music they used before they had any of their own. I don't see that happening, more from a lack of thought than a lack of desire. Mostly I hear people want to know how much money does it generate and does the desired age bracket like it. We've got to give them their pablum, y'know.

"It is going away, and it is worthy of being passed down. But the quality of the things we did compared with what's going on today . . . " His voice drifted off.

"All the patterns have been laid and cut, and all the trails blazed, I guess," he continued. "They just take the beaten paths and make them electronically perfect." The last two words are spoken with utter contempt.

"Everybody's always wanting to know how to get into country music," Haggard said. "I want to know how to get the f- out of country music."

San Francisco Chronicle Magazine | *Sunday, June 3, 2001*

Barroom Bard's Next Round

Tom Waits is a hothouse orchid who wilts at celebrity events

Waits stops to admire a suit in the Mission Street thrift store window. "They say lime green is coming back," he says. "I say it never went away." Two days later, Chronicle columnist Leah Garchik runs the quote in her column – some other passer-by overheard him and phoned it in. Only time I've ever been scooped on my own interview.

TOM WAITS SIPS COFFEE AT THE FORMICA COUNTER of the Chinese takeout and doughnut shop, looking out on the intersection of Mission and 24th streets. A truck selling watermelon out of the back is doing brisk trade. An impatient ambulance pushes through the congested traffic, and the throngs making their way along the sidewalk pay no attention to the screaming siren. Waits smiles.

"Where I live," he says, "I can hear the birds' wings."

The brilliant songwriter doesn't appear in public much. Waits is a hothouse orchid who wilts at celebrity events such as the opening last month of his American Conservatory Theater musical "The Black Rider" – which he did not attend.

Over his 30-year career, Waits, 54, has proved to be not only one of the most original voices in American music but also one of the most enduring talents of his generation, the rare recording artist whose recent work is as fresh and challenging as anything he's done before.

He is an uncomfortable performer who plays only sporadic concerts. Unlike the dispirited, disturbed and dubious characters in his noirish songs, he spends most of his time living happily in rural Sonoma with his wife and their three children, emerging only occasionally from his semi-seclusion, in this case to talk about his new album, "Real Gone."

He prepared notes for the interview and consults the well-used notebook he always carries in his pocket. He speaks quietly, in a throaty rasp. He wears a black T-shirt, tattoos peeking out from the bottom of both short sleeves, long black pants and large, black boots with scuffed toes.

"For years, every time I went to St. Louis, there were so many people wearing red pants, I couldn't get it," he says, looking up from his notes. "I didn't get it for years. So many guys wearing red pants in St. Louis, and it takes a lot of guts to wear red pants. I mean really, really red pants. Then it all hit me – the Cardinals. Red pants, not a red shirt, red pants. Believe me, it takes a lot of courage to wear red pants."

Old-time show business is on his mind. He looks down at the notebook again and comes back with the name of the 19th century French stage star who did vaudeville late in life.

"Sarah Bernhardt," he says. "She was playing Juliet in her 70s and had one leg. Barnum and Bailey bought her leg, the leg that was amputated, and they had it in a tank with some formaldehyde and fish. It was being displayed as the leg of Sarah Bernhardt, and at one point her leg was making more money than she was when she was playing joints. I always think of that when I get depressed. I think that's got to really hurt."

He sips his coffee and checks his notes.

"Why are theaters dark on Monday?" he says. "There are people who say it's because in the old days Monday was hanging day. Everyone wanted to be at the hanging, especially if you're an actor. Is there a better show than a hanging for an actor? They knew they couldn't compete. It's the beginning of the week. Of course, if you're being hanged, it's the end of your week. It's the beginning of everyone else's. That's a terrible thing to say, but it's true. We can't get to it until Monday – how many times have you heard that?"

"Real Gone," Waits' fourth album in five years, comes in a period of relative productivity. His 1999 album, "Mule Variations," ended a seven-year hiatus from recording. He simultaneously released two albums, "Alice" and "Blood Money," in 2002. The same year, he contributed two songs to the soundtrack for the Debra Winger film "Big Bad Love," one of which, "Long Way Home," was recorded by Norah Jones on her recent album "Feels Like Home."

His records sell only modestly, but his songs have been done by the biggest names in the business – Bruce Springsteen, Bette Midler, Rod Stewart, the Eagles – and Waits is everybody's favorite party guest, having made more than 100 appearances on other people's records, from old-time West Coast bebopper Teddy Edwards to modern classical composer Gavin Bryars. Waits once recorded a duet with Keith Richards.

With his zealous cult following stampeding the stores the week of release, his past three albums have all made midchart premieres. Never destined for MTV stardom or Top of the Pops success, Waits can nonetheless make releasing a new album a cultural event.

He recorded "Real Gone," his 19th album – in stores Tuesday – in what he called a "legitimate studio" in woodsy Forestville, as opposed to the abandoned schoolhouse in the Sacramento delta ghost town of Locke, where he recorded previously with a remote truck.

He recruited longtime associate Larry Taylor on bass, a journeyman whose resume extends back to '60s boogie kings Canned Heat, and drummer Brain, who used to bang away behind San Francisco thrash-punk band the Limbomaniacs, but most recently has been playing with Axl Rose in the current edition of Guns N' Roses. Bassist Les Claypool of Primus, who also plays on three tracks from the new album, introduced Brain to Waits. On guitar is downtown New York avant-gardist Marc Ribot, who adds a lot of funky, Cuban-flavored playing to the spare, gritty sound. Ribot, who has recorded with Elvis Costello, played on Waits' 1985 landmark, "Rain Dogs," and did some overdubs for "Mule Variations."

"You have to be careful with certain musicians because they're idiosyncratic," Waits says. "You have to dial them in very carefully. If you ask him for a little feedback, for example, you'll get an automobile accident. You have to qualify everything you ask for. It comes only in large."

Waits shares songwriting and production credits with his wife of 24 years, playwright Kathleen Brennan, his partner in every realm of his life. He's ready for the question about her role in their collaboration.

"She's like a heavy equipment operator and a clairvoyant – it's rare you get that together," he says, flipping pages in his notebook to find his place. "She's something else – tree surgeon and a ventriloquist, astronaut and private eye. You're always looking for those two things. A newspaperman and a bathing beauty. It's a combination that works for us, 'cause a lot of times, I'm in a stroller waiting to be pushed out into traffic. She's the one that'll do it."

He says he did not suffer over the recording process, finishing the album in a couple of months. Vocals were recorded live and many of the final versions were first takes. He ended up not using any keyboards on the record, although he brought everything he thought he might possibly use.

"My theory is if you don't bring it, you'll definitely need it," Waits says. "So I tell them to bring everything. Then we don't use it. I brought a piano and never even sat down on it. It didn't seem to fit."

The tracks groan and clang with a burglar's bag of strange percussion instruments and other mysterious, almost stray sounds. Waits gets his barnyard soundscape by overloading tape, slamming vintage microphones with information and singing the often bizarre "mouth rhythms" that fill the backgrounds of his songs.

Waits' 18-year-old son, Casey Waits, plays some percussion and scratches some turntables on "Real Gone." The college student has introduced the world of skateboard rap to Waits' already panoramic musical world view. Waits rattles off names from the graffiti underground such as Sage Francis, Aesop Rock, Vast Aire, Ol' Dirty Bastard, Weakerthans, Atmosphere, KRS-One. "He delves," Waits says. "All that stuff gets played around the house because that's what happens when you have kids. You stop dominating the turntable. I haven't had that kind of sway around here for years. 'Put on that Leadbelly record one more time, Dad, and I'm going to throw a bottle at your head.' "

Waits did offer one piece of songwriting advice that he tries when he finds himself stuck. "Take out your favorite line," he says. "It's hard to do. What you're doing is, you've only got one line and you're trying to hang everything on it. What you need is a better line."

Some songs need work; some write themselves. "Came out of the ground like a potato, always the best ones," Waits says. "Most of my songs are contraptions. Take the head off that doll and screw it onto the side of that washing machine. But the best ones come out just like a litter. I usually start with two tunes, put them in a room together and they have kids. There are usually two songs that are the parents of the rest. That's my theory."

He downplays his highly personal approach to music. "I'm not original," he says. "I'm doing bad impersonations of other people. I like to sound like Ray Charles. Who wouldn't? So you're hearing my poor, failed attempt at a Ray Charles impersonation."

Waits grows extraordinarily fevered fans. One fellow stood up and ran out of a Mission Street coffeehouse when Waits walked in, only to return a few minutes later, huffing and puffing and carrying a program from "The Black Rider" he fetched from his apartment for Waits to sign. Because of the personal nature of his work, these people often think they know him.

"People want to drink with you," says Waits, who has been sober for 14 years despite continued references to drinking in his writing. "Immediately. But I think it's good to have 'em think you're down here when you're really over there. I'm kind of a ventriloquist. You don't want to get confused with the dummy. It's easily done."

In his youth, he may have more closely resembled the characters in his songs, living in a sleazy $9-a-night Hollywood motel called the Tropicana and eating breakfast in the coffee shop late every morning. He is no longer that guy, but he carefully keeps his private life separate from his public persona.

He used to own big old American cars like his '64 champagne-colored Cadillac, but now he drives an anonymous black Chevy Suburban. He is an accomplished pizza chef who, as a teenager in San Diego, spent five years working in a pizza parlor ("I thought I was going to go into the restaurant business," he says). He grows his own heirloom tomatoes and sends homemade canned tomato sauce to his friends for Christmas.

"People want to believe that they feel you're sincere," he says. "That part's important. They want to know they've got the real thing or at least a dead ringer for it. I dunno how it works. I'm lucky. Not like Liberace or those guys who can live in the business. I don't think there's anything there to eat. Your life is ultimately something else. So I usually go upstream. That's where I get my ideas. I get songs for nothing and I sell them to you. Don't cost me anything. No overhead. Growing by the side of the road."

The next morning, Waits phones. There were some points he feels needed elaboration. He'd taken some more notes. He was thumbing through the pages of his notebook.

"Family and career don't like each other," he says. "One is always trying to eat the other. You're always trying to find balance. But one is really useless without the other. What you really want is a sink and a faucet. That's the ideal. Sometimes you do want it to fill up. Other times you want it to go down the drain. You usually don't get that luxury."

He wanted to reflect on some of his influences, although it's hard to see what doesn't influence someone whose work encompasses the dirty blues of Howlin' Wolf and the Broadway operettas of Bertolt Brecht, the detective fiction of Raymond Chandler and the burlesque dancing of Lily St. Cyr.

"Yeah, it all goes in, most of it melts, so it's really rather invisible, " he says. "I still listen to Mabel Mercer, James White, Captain Beefheart, Big Mama Thornton, Willie Dixon, Johnny Cash, Big Joe Turner ..." His voice trails off.

"My wife says I can run on anything when it comes to what I put in my creative tank," he says. "I can run on anything, but don't get stuck behind me."

San Francisco Chronicle | Sunday, October 3, 2004

Over The Wall!

The Mad Past and Strange Present of
Mr. Wall of Sound

A dicey assignment – slash and burn, five days to work the phones and file the copy after the magazine's regular American guy bobbled the story. With almost three months between deadline and publication, you have to kind of hold your breath. It turned out my guys made a pretty good stab at predicting Spector's eventual defense, but I was just glad not to be embarrassed by some further development that emerged before the magazine hit the stands.

LEGENDARY RECORD PRODUCER PHIL SPECTOR ATE a $55 midnight snack of salad and downed a couple of Bacardi rum drinks at his customary corner table in the darkest recesses of Dan Tana's, long a tony restaurant that caters to the flashy Hollywood show business crowd. His dining companion was a blonde waitress at a Beverly Hills restaurant, a singer-songwriter on the side who would occasionally don a French maid's uniform and play the sexy servant for Spector's Saturday afternoon boys club that met regularly at his castle home in remote Alhambra, almost 45 minutes away from the Sunset Strip. He left a $500 tip, a not uncommon act of largesse by Spector at his favourite restaurant.

He repaired alone to the House of Blues, where he often frequented the elite hideaway Foundation Room, a private enclave on the top floor of the $9 million niterie, and ordered a Bacardi 151 drink. Lana Clarkson, a blonde B-movie actress who started work that month as a hostess at the VIP room of the sprawling bar-restaurant-club complex, joined the Spector party on the blue-and-purple sofas for a glass of vintage champagne, soon switching to bourbon highballs. Shortly after closing at 2am, she and Spector left in his chauffeur-driven Mercedes S430.

Three hours later, at the crack of dawn, Los Angeles police were summoned to Spector's bizarre castle on the hill in the largely Mexican-American community east of downtown Los Angeles by Spector's driver, who dialled 911 after he heard gunfire coming from the mansion. Police found Clarkson, shot in the face, lying

**Phil Spector (left)
with Bill Russell**

dead in a pool of blood in the grand entranceway guarded by suits of armour. A pistol was recovered nearby and Spector, who was subdued by a taser gun, was handcuffed, arrested and taken to jail. He was released 12 hours later after posting $100,000 bond on his million-dollar bail.

Phil Spector, 62, has been so weird for so long that in rock'n'roll circles his outrageous behaviour was accepted fact. But with the Clarkson murder splashing on front pages around the world, all the old tales were instantly trotted out – the karate boasts to journalist Tom Wolfe ("I could literally kill a guy like that"); the bullet hole he put in the ceiling of A&M Studios during a session with John Lennon; the twisted husband stuff from ex-wife Veronica's tell-all biog a few years back; the drunken public displays at the Rock and Roll Hall of Fame dinners; and, over and over, the dubious remark invariably attributed to Dee Dee Ramone ("He's a good shot – I've seen him hit a fly at 50 yards"), as if a lifelong junkie dead last year from an overdose qualified as a credible witness.

Spector himself even contributed unwittingly to the deepening portrait of despair and doom. By eerie coincidence, the day before the shooting the Daily Telegraph ran an interview with writer Mick Brown, one of the first in-depth interviews Spector has conducted in a long while (although not quite as long as the Telegraph claimed), in which Spector obsessively mused about his mental condition. He admitted to be taking drugs to treat personality disorders, pondered the elusiveness of happiness ("temporary") and waxed unfortunately Gothic about his condition.

"I have not been well," said Spector, in what has already become one of the most famous interviews in rock journalism. "I was crippled inside. Emotionally. Insane is a hard word. I wasn't insane, but I wasn't well enough to function as a regular part of society, so I didn't. I chose not to. I have devils inside that fight me."

His friends, however, told a different story; they saw a man getting his demons under control. The people who were in the Spector orbit – a handful of wiseacre music business types that Spector seemed to congregate occasionally for company, while still maintaining a lonely, isolated life with no real close friends – uniformly expressed their amazement, not that it happened, but that it happened now. The Spector they've been seeing in the resent past gave up the booze more than three years ago. "Phil completely stopped drinking," said drummer Hal Blaine, who played on virtually every record Spector made, "not that he was a drunk. But he liked his wine."

The new Spector was a witty, charming host of regular Saturday afternoon salons at his wacky faux-Moorish castle on the outskirts of Los Angeles. "There was a youth movement going on with him," said Denny Bruce, a longtime Hollywood scenester who attended the Saturday luncheons. He constantly forwarded jokes to his pals via e-mail and, for all appearances, was coming out from under a half lifetime's cloud of darkness and gloom.

Last August, Spector returned to the studio for the first time in nearly a decade, in London with young British rockers, Starsailor, a band brought to his attention by his 22-year-old daughter, Nicole, a college student in New York. He amused his pals with typically acerbic post cards ("Do you know why Jesus couldn't have been born in England?" he wrote. "Where would they find three wise men and a virgin?"). He was excited about working with Starsailor – and was talking to other young bands (Coldplay, The Hives) about more producing – and he was telling his friends he was going to make hit records again. He had not been behind a control board since a few days of disastrous sessions in 1995 trying to record Celine Dion singing "River Deep – Mountain High."

But as the new year dawned, bad news piled up on Spector's doorstep. His romance with Nancy Sinatra ended after months of steady dating. Only recently, he had been diligently accompanying her to daily recording sessions in which he did not otherwise participate. The Telegraph noted photos of the couple together in Spector's home. The long-running lawsuit by his loathed ex-wife for unpaid royalties came back to life. The $3m verdict had been overturned on appeal and sent back to the original court for recalculation. The news was that the recalculation of money the court found he owed Ronnie Spector and her two cousins – who recorded gloriously for Spector in his Philles Records heyday as The Ronettes – may cost him as much, if not more, than the original judgment. For Spector, such a loss represented something far greater than the mere money. He reserves special rage for his second wife. He can't bring himself to mention her by name. He faxed people asking them not to vote for her in the Rock and Roll Hall of Fame ballot. "His concern is to cause as much economic damage as he can to Ronnie," said attorney Chuck Rubin, who has represented the ex-Mrs Spector on this suit since 1988.

Instead of the triumph Spector anticipated with the Starsailor album, the band decided to use only one of the four or five tracks he produced. Comments in the English press by lead vocalist James Walsh hinted at a vast gulf between Spector and the band. "It was worlds colliding," he told a British music weekly. "He's not done much for a long time. He's learned from us about how studios work these days, and we learned from him about older techniques."

"Did you see what the kid from Starsailor said about him?" said Denny Bruce. "It was almost like, 'Out of the way, old man.'"

Then Paul McCartney announced that The Beatles would be releasing a new version of the group's final album, *Let It Be*, a mix made by engineer Glyn Johns before Spector became attached to the project. In March 1970, while The Beatles were rancorously dissolving, Spector waded into the mess that was the group's unfinished album and pulled together a finished record from the miles of tape and hours of recordings. He stripped McCartney's ballad, "The Long And Winding Road," of everything except the vocal part and swathed it in lush, florid strings. McCartney never made a secret of his disgust for Spector's production, although Spector enjoyed the full support of George Harrison and John Lennon at the time.

"I knew Phil was being brought in," said McCartney. "But I didn't go to the sessions. When I got the finished record there were loud ladies' voices wailing. It wasn't terrible... I preferred it the way it was. I never really had vicious arguments with [the other Beatles] before that, we'd never hated each other before that. That's when it got heavy"

But when Spector stepped up to finish the last Beatles album, help John Lennon launch his solo career with "Instant Karma" and give George Harrison a Wall of Sound makeover – including the first post-Beatles Number 1 hit, "My Sweet Lord" – he may well have been the most famous record producer in the world, but he was also a man that time had already left behind. It had been three long years since Spector had even set foot in a studio.

He'd long been a music business legend when he met The Beatles in 1964. He joined the group on their first flight to the USA to play The Ed Sullivan Show. Spector, a nervous flier, felt sure The Beatles were going to make it in America, so he thought the flight would be safe. He must have loomed large to the young British chart-toppers headed off to try their luck in a country Phil Spector had already conquered. He was coming off a streak of five consecutive Top 10 hits in the previous 15 months, all on his own Philles Records.

Back then he dressed like an Edwardian dandy with Prince Valiant hair and purple wire-rim shades and was widely regarded as a genius. His records were phenomena – extravaganza events with interchangeable singers that were each stamped with the grandiose personality of their creator. He invented the rock'n'roll record producer and played the part to the hilt, the mad genius of 45s, the prince of pop. He was riding the absolute apex of the booming, earth-shaking American rock'n'roll industry. He was 23 years old.

But Spector was already seeing a psychiatrist – he immortalised his therapist in the Philles B-side instrumental, Dr Kaplan's Office – and worried about his mental health. His parents, after all, were first cousins. His steelworker father attached a hose to the exhaust pipe of his car and killed himself when Spector was nine years old, growing up in the Bronx. His domineering, seamstress mother moved the teenager and his older sister to Los Angeles. Insecure, pint-sized Spector went to Fairfax High School and buried himself in music, recording in his senior year a song with a couple of classmates which took its title from his own father's tombstone. "To Know Him Is To Love Him" by The Teddy Bears was the 1958 Number 1 record that auspiciously started his career.

Telling his mother he wanted to be a translator at the United Nations, Spector moved to New York in May 1960 and ingratiated himself with some of the big guns in the Broadway rhythm and blues world. With Atlantic Records' Jerry Wexler, Spector made a mess of the first version of "Twist And Shout," before songwriter Bert Berns took it over to Scepter Records and gave it to The Isley Brothers. With Jerry Leiber and Mike Stoller, he served a kind of apprenticeship, sleeping on their office couch, making demos for Hill & Range music publishers in the Brill Building penthouse, writing Spanish Harlem with lyricist Leiber, even playing the guitar solo on the Leiber & Stoller record, On Broadway, by The Drifters. Leiber also remembers a phone call from his partner Stoller, who found some Spector songwriting contracts missing from the office files. "Jerry, did you give Phil Spector a key to the office?" Stoller asked.

He was a millionaire before he turned 21 years old. Spector quickly earned a reputation. He was ambitious and could be unscrupulous. He was a fastidious dresser in cut velvet and bad toupees. He threw tantrums, screamed at people over perceived slights. He practised caustic, often insulting humour. He drove people crazy with his obsessive attention to detail in the studio. He could spend hours going over the same eight bars of music, but the records sounded like records never had before.

"He kept us on our toes," said session bassist Carol Kaye. "We never knew what was coming. He wasn't hard to work for, but the dates were long. We'd work the whole time on one side and then jam real fast on the B-side. Phil was very intense."

"He could be almost unbearable with the vocalists," said veteran session pianist Don Randi. "He heard something he wanted and, until he got it, he was relentless. The mannerisms of getting there were sometimes a little crude. But he got there."

It was all over in a few short years. At 26, he would be retired. Spector always maintained that he left the business because of American radio's failure to embrace his greatest work, "River Deep – Mountain High" by Ike And Tina Turner. But signs of his growing uncertainty were already showing. He told the Telegraph a long, fanciful story about his doubts before the release of his previous high-water mark, "You've Lost That Lovin' Feelin'" by The Righteous Brothers.

But even as he produced these final masterpieces, Spector was never able to finish the follow-up to his lady love's magnificent "Walking In The Rain" by The Ronnettes. Spector laboured for more than a year on "Paradise," obsessively mixing and remixing, editing and re-editing, unable to come up with a version he felt was powerful enough to release, much to the frustration of neophyte songwriter Harry Nilsson, who saw the song as his first big break. "Phil psyched himself out on that one," Nilsson told me in a 1975 interview.

Life was closing in on Spector, dubbed 'The Tycoon of Teen' in the 1965 New York Herald Tribune profile by Tom Wolfe that helped cement his growing reputation an uncontrollable weirdo. He retreated behind electronically-controlled gates to a 21-room Beverly Hills mansion, living like the desolate protagonist of his favourite movie, *Citizen Kane*, in his own Xanadu. He married his teen queen vocalist, surrounded himself with bodyguards and lived vampire hours and dark insomniac days, Ronnie Spector recounted chillingly in a 1990 autobiography, *Be My Baby*. It was not by accident that Spector played a cameo role in the 1969 film, *Easy Rider*, as the cocaine dealer who starts the whole journey in the first place. That Christmas, he sent out cards with a still from the film showing him holding a spoon to his nose and reading, "A little snow at Christmas never hurt anyone".

Through the '70s, Spector took on isolated projects. His gifts were clearly diminished. He was more madman than genius. When Lennon left Yoko in New York and moved to Los Angeles in 1974 on an extended alcoholic binge, Spector was a favourite partner in crime. They started an album at A&M Studios, but were thrown out, not after Spector fired a handgun during a session, but when somebody – Spector was among the suspects – took a dump in the elevator. The album was never finished. Spector started his first label since Philles, although nobody even noticed the oddly out-of-step singles that trickled out of the Warner/Spector imprint – strange, lifeless, lumbering productions with Philles survivor Darlene Love, early '60s golden oldie Dion, former Gold Star Studios background vocalist Cher (who once cut a Beatles novelty for Spector, "Ringo, I Love You," under the name Bonnie Jo Mason) and a duet between Cher and Nilsson.

He made an album with songwriter Leonard Cohen, *Death Of A Ladies' Man* in 1977 that Cohen immediately disowned ("There's nothing about it I like," he told the New York Times). He tortured an album out of the Ramones two years later, although Dee Dee Ramone claimed in his 1997 memoirs to not remember a thing.

"I still to this day have no idea how they made the album," he wrote, "or who played bass on it." "I was produced by Phil Spector," remembered Kim Fowley. "In 1979 I got a call saying 'Phil's got to put out a greatest hits package for Polydor in England and we need to fill some space.' I went to this studio off of Hollywood Boulevard, and they had a small group of musicians assembled. Then Phil arrives with beefy bodyguards in tow, saying, 'Hi everyone, I'm here to produce some rock'n'roll. Note the technique I will use.' We were all waiting breathlessly to learn what this stroke of genius would be, when he stands up and pulls the fire alarm, setting it off. 'As you can see, I've just set off the fire alarm. I'm leaving now but I'm gonna lock all you guys inside the studio so the fire department will have to come and break down the door to free you. But you'll start recording right now, and amid the chaos, the noise and the clamour, you'll find the motivation to cut a great record. That's how I'm producing this session! Goodbye.' We somehow cut the track which is on *Phil Spector 1974-79*. It charted in England and, of course, I never got paid."

Spector acted as if he was still the greatest record producer in the world, not some rich has-been Norma Desmond in a Charles II wig who hadn't had a hit record with someone who didn't belong to the Beatles since before colour TV. He enjoyed the company of people who would support that illusion and didn't put his reputation to the test. Occasionally, Spector would audition a promising young talent, entertain another project, but - except for the Celine Dion debacle - not outside the electronic fence that encircled his home.

Spector bought the Pyrenees Castle in 1991 for a mere $1.1m, modest considering southern California real estate values. Built in 1926, the 40-room turreted edifice rests out of sight on top of an unlandscaped, overgrown hill reached by private driveways. Just the servants' quarters and four-car garage (with his 1964 white Silver Cloud with the Phil 500 license plates) alone measures more than 10,000 square feet. The place had once been used as a monastary. It sits surrounded incongruously by a distinctly unglamorous, lower middle-class, mostly Hispanic neighbourhood, far removed from Beverly Hills or even Pasadena, where Spector lived previously in the same kind of secluded splendor as he did during the '70s in Beverly Hills. Many of his Alhambra neighbours told reporters they didn't even know the place was there.

Suits of armour flank the red-carpeted, oak-panelled entrance hall. John Lennon's old guitar rests on a stand in the music room. A Lennon sketch hangs next to a Picasso drawing. A photo of Spector shooting pool with Minnesota Fats looks over the billiard room. Classical music plays from hidden speakers.

His third marriage ended in divorce 10 years ago, but his ex-wife Janice came to work at his home as his personal assistant every day until last fall, when she was replaced by Michelle Blaine, daughter of Spector's loyal session drummer Hal Blaine. Her first job was to book private jet transportation for Spector and his party (which included his best friend, big shot Hollywood divorce attorney Marvin Mitchelson) to London for the Starsailor sessions. Around the same time, Spector felt confident enough of his newfound sobriety to dismiss his bodyguards, a round-the-clock presence in his life since George Brand first came to work at Bel Air in 1968.

Last August, he threw his third annual bowling party at the Montrose Bowl, an old-fashioned set of lanes in a remote, downscale section of town up in the hills past Glendale. Although Spector played affable host to around 200 guests, the crowd was hardly A-list Hollywood. Clem Burke of Blondie and rockabilly singer Billy (I Can Help) Swan were among the luminaries. But Spector's luncheons also revolve around a set of music journalists and record company types who are as much fans as friends. They sit around and swap music business stories over lunch at Spector's impressive home, while he holds forth from a chair slightly larger and slightly higher than his guests'. After his arrest, all Spector associates were swarmed over by the media. Many refused to talk to the press. Nobody wanted to miss out on the next bowling party.

Although he maintains a relationship with his 22-year-old daughter from his third marriage, Nicole (whose twin brother, Phillip, died of leukemia at age 10), Spector is estranged from the three children he adopted with his second wife, Ronnie (and whose custody he retained after their divorce). Donte, 33, a production assistant in Hollywood, and Gary, 36, who works as a cable TV technician in Colorado, both told American network television after the shooting that their father kept them locked in their rooms and subjected them to sex acts when they were children. Gary Spector told NBC-TV's Katie Couric about being blindfolded and molested at age nine by one of Spector's girlfriends. His brother Donte, who is trying to sell his story, told an English newspaper his father should be locked up for what he did to him. "He's a sick man," his son said.

"Donte hasn't had a good life," said Jonathan Greenfield, married to Ronnie Spector since 1982.

Mental illness is a delicate issue for Spector, who has been treated by psychiatrists since 1960. His sister has been in and out of mental institutions all her life. He told the Telegraph that he was currently under medication for a bi-polar personality disorder.

Part of Spector's coming out in the sunshine has involved reclaiming his past. He has become an active participant in the selection process for the Rock and Roll Hall of Fame, regularly attending the annual nominating committee meetings in New York, every year hosting an elite after-party in his upstairs suite at the Waldorf Astoria following the induction dinner (he sought special permission from Los Angeles courts to attend this year's event). Director Cameron Crowe and actor Tom Cruise contemplated a movie about Spector's life that would star Cruise, ultimately giving up the project because they couldn't find a satisfying ending.

Raechel Donahue, widow of Spector's close friend, FM DJ Tom Donahue, produced an authorised documentary on Spector's life – including a filmed interview with the reclusive producer – for cable TV's Discovery Channel, only to have Spector turn characteristic at the last minute and refuse to sign the releases for the finished hour-long TV show.

Everybody who knows Spector, knows the weirdness. Even when he is the urbane, witty and articulate host, it lurks in the background. Quick, hip and acerbic, Spector can make it obvious in an instant why people like Lenny Bruce and John Lennon wanted to be his friend. He is a gifted, hilarious mimic whose impressions range from Ike Turner to Mr Ed the talking horse. But the intensity never leaves him. His friends and associates all know how volatile he can be. They just didn't think he was capable of murder.

They all also expressed surprise to hear Spector had been drinking again. Even the bartender who took his order at Dan Tana's that night came out from behind the bar to Spector's table to double-check the order.

"It's a tragic accident," said attorney Marvin Mitchelson, in his kind of unofficial press spokesman role for his friend. Spector was immediately represented legally by attorney Robert Shapiro, the heavy duty player who called the shots on the O.J. Simpson defence. Shapiro swung into action instantly and sent former New York City coroner Michael Baden to attend the Clarkson autopsy. Both police and defence have been utterly silent about what happened that night, but scenarios have surfaced in whispers suggesting Spector shot Clarkson mistaking her for an intruder after she left and returned for something she forgot, or that Clarkson shot herself in a drunken misadventure with one of Spector's many guns. Of course, he may have shot her, too... but no one wants to say that.

Mojo, May 2003

Bill Graham's Tangled Legacy

This series was the talk o' the town the week it ran. I was invited to appear on a public TV show where the reporters that wrote the big stories of the week talked about them with the show's host. There was a Sacramento correspondent who had been covering important legislation and a city hall reporter who was talking about significant changes in police policy and they all wanted to know about Bill Graham's will. I couldn't find any deeper social significance in this long, tangled account of the millionaire rock concert promoter's will marching through probate, but it did make a fascinating story.

1. Battle Over Rock Impressario's Riches

Rock concert producer Bill Graham strode into the 42nd-floor offices of Greene, Radovsky, Maloney and Share in the spring of 1991 wearing an uncharacteristic suit – one of two he owned, he told attorney Dick Greene. They were gifts from film director Barry Levinson, part of Graham's wardrobe from the film "Bugsy," where he played gangster kingpin Lucky Luciano.

"Forty-five minutes – no stories," barked Graham, who immediately relaxed into several stories. He was meeting with Greene at the top of the Market Street skyscraper on the subject of estate planning. Except for two slight revisions, he had not considered the subject since writing a will 15 years earlier.

"I really have no idea how much money I have," the multimillionaire concert producer told the lawyer. "All I know is that whatever I want, I can buy."

One week later, Greene sent Graham a draft of a new will, but Graham did not respond. Greene called. He wrote. But he never heard back.

Spring turned to summer and summer to fall. Finally, on October 17, Graham phoned and made an appointment to sign the document. "It's absolutely perfect," he told Greene.

A week later, before he could keep the appointment, Graham, 60, was dead, swept out of stormy skies when his helicopter exploded into a PG&E tower outside Vallejo. He was on his way home from a Concord Pavilion concert by Huey Lewis and the News. Graham's girlfriend, Melissa Gold, and pilot Steve (Killer) Kahn were also killed.

For 25 years, Graham had been a monumental figure in the rock world. From a modest beginning throwing benefit concerts for the San Francisco Mime Troupe at the Fillmore Auditorium in 1965, Graham rose to become the most dominant character in the realm of rock concert production, the man who single-handedly ushered the field into the modern era.

He headed a music business empire that managed successful artists, produced a hit movie about the Doors, manufactured millions of dollars' worth of T-shirts and sold $100 million worth of tickets to concerts annually. There were six companies and 80 full-time employees in the main office in San Francisco.

Under Graham's charismatic, often manic leadership, his company produced national and international tours by acts such as the Rolling Stones; Crosby, Stills, Nash and Young; George Harrison and Bob Dylan. It also presented historic events such as the Live Aid concert and the global rock concert trek on behalf of Amnesty International.

Graham's sudden death not only threw the future of his multimillion-dollar enterprise into doubt but also left a muddled three-year trail of battling heirs, embittered relatives and legal bills that mounted to more than $2 million before the estate was finally brought to rest in January.

His attorneys and executor had to contend with a bewildering tangle of bank accounts, foreign investments, real estate and secret safe deposit boxes in a $36 million estate. The contest over the will pitted his two sons against his four sisters and left the future of his beloved company, Bill Graham Presents, hanging in the balance.

Graham lived life on a grand scale and left behind an equally extravagant drama in his wake. The curtain lifted almost as soon as his casket was lowered into the ground.

Nicholas Clainos stretched out on the floor as family members filled the sofas and chairs in the small den off the living room. Son of an Army colonel and graduate of Princeton and Stanford, Clainos – short, trim, always a little better groomed and dressed than the typical rock and roll executive – had been overseeing Graham's affairs since he joined the company almost 20 years earlier as general counsel.

He had been president for the previous five years and could now add executor to his responsibilities. Clainos felt numb from five wrenching days of exhausting duties, from dealing with body bags in the Sonoma County marshlands to overseeing the details of a $60,000 funeral held two days earlier before an overflow crowd at San Francisco's Temple Emanu-El.

They had buried Graham and repaired to sit shivah in the Mill Valley hilltop home he called Masada, an 11-acre estate crowned by a rough-hewn, simple ranch-style building with beamed ceilings, marble floors and large rooms open to the sweeping vistas.

Attorney Greene and executor Clainos had assembled the heirs in the cozy den to read them the original will.

Graham's sister, Ester Chichinsky, then 66, who was especially close to her brother, was there with her husband, Manny. A strong-willed woman with a kind face, Chichinsky never lost her German accent, unlike her brother. She had cooked the hamburgers during the early days at the Fillmore Auditorium and lived rent-free at Graham's old house in Mill Valley.

(Despite repeated requests to her and her attorney, Chichinsky has refused to be interviewed for this article.)

Graham's other sisters were in town from all over the world: Sonja Szobel, 67, from Vienna; Evelyn (Echa) Udry, 69, from Geneva; and Rita Rosen, 73, and her husband, Eric, from the San Fernando Valley.

It was a family that already had survived the extraordinary adversity the Third Reich wreaked upon Jews during the Second World War.

Ten-year-old Bill Graham, then named Wolfgang Grajonza, was sent to Paris from his Berlin home to escape the lengthening shadow of the Nazis. He survived a tortuous walk across France to safety. Sixty-three children started that walk. All but 11 died, including his sister, Tolla. Their mother was killed in a concentration camp; Chichinsky survived Auschwitz. It was amazing that they even found one another after the war.

Also in the room that afternoon were Graham's two sons.

Gangly, tall David Graham, 23, grew up with his mother and stepfather in rural Pennsylvania and attended Quaker private schools before finishing Columbia University the previous year. He had been living at Masada for months. David Graham was trying to establish himself in the music business. His own firm, Music Unlimited, had signed a promising band called Blues Traveler, although David Graham managed the act under the wing of his father's firm, Bill Graham Management.

The turbulence of David's recent relations with his father had died down in the months before Graham's death, and the two were edging toward a companionable relationship.

David Graham

Younger brother Alexander Graham-Sult, 14, attended the meeting with his mother, Marcia Godinez. With his dark hair and chiseled features, Alexander closely resembles his mother, but the intensity in his eyes comes from his father. Godinez and Alexander have lived in Maui since his birth, and his contact with his famous father was limited to vacations and a $3,000 monthly support payment. The only absent heir was Roy Ehrenreich, Graham's foster brother, who was traveling in Tibet and did not change his plans to attend the funeral.

Greene read the original will and its two codicils and discussed the terms of the unexecuted document, copies of which were passed out. He said death taxes would consume at least 55 percent of the estate.

Sonja Szobel told David Graham's mother later that afternoon that she felt the heirs must stick to the signed will, but Clainos hoped that at least some aspects of the unsigned will could be instituted. Marcia Godinez entertained no such delusions.

"We quickly divided into two camps," she said during a brief visit to the Bay Area last month. "There were those who were thinking and looking at Bill's estate as, 'What does he want to have happen?' Then there were those who were interested in making sure they were getting every penny they were due."

The will that Graham never signed was drastically different from the earlier document, which was the one Greene and Clainos had to submit to the Marin County probate court. The new plan created a trust for his two sons and, for his older sisters, structured a modest annual allowance, ranging from $50,000 a year for his closest sister, Ester Chichinsky, to $30,000 a year for Rita Rosen. The other three siblings, including foster brother Ehrenreich, were to be given $40,000 each year.

In addition, the unsigned will also included more than $1.25 million in specific bequests to nieces and nephews, Alexander Sult-Graham's older brother, the concert producer's ex-wife and three other women in his life, as well as generous gifts to three men who worked for him personally, including the man who cleaned his office for nearly 20 years.

But even assembling the assets proved to be difficult. Greene and Clainos found a safe deposit box key among Graham's effects and, in the presence of a bank officer, opened the box at the Bank of America's Market and Van Ness branch, one block from the site of the Fillmore West, where Graham held weekly concerts for three years until he shut down the operation in an emotional pique in June 1971.

What they found was more than a half million dollars in cash – old, worn small bills, the rubber bands rotted away after so many years in storage. The secret stash came as a complete surprise to his most trusted associates and financial advisers at the office. Only his former personal secretary, Jan Simmons, seemed to know anything about the safe deposit boxes. She drove around town fruitlessly to see whether she could recognize any of the banks she and Graham used to visit on their runs.

An account in the Jersey Islands off the coast of England contained more than $1.7 million. Letters from heir hunters who had located assets and would supply the information for a commission began arriving. Although attorneys were able to find almost all the funds the heir hunters discovered, one stack of several thousand dollars' worth of stocks was obtained only through one of these free-lance investigators.

Before they were done, his attorneys had searched every bank in the Bay Area and every bank within a reasonable radius of his New York residence.

But other problems for the estate quickly accumulated. Graham's longtime lover Regina Cartwright, who lived in New York with Graham's financial support, vigorously insisted that he was the father of her 3-year-old daughter, Caitlin, and wanted money.

A voluptuous, doe-eyed brunette who came to work at Graham's office as a 19-year-old receptionist in 1973, Cartwright claims to be the illegitimate daughter of comedian Lenny Bruce.

Shortly after she started working for Graham, the two began an on-again, off-again affair that lasted until his death. While he attended Columbia University, David Graham had ample opportunity to watch the couple in action.

"I was fully submerged in the psychosis," he said last month at his Marin County home. "I was completely aware of my dad's infatuation with her, which I had no understanding of. "He knew it was not his child. He said to me he knew the father was one of two men. I was the one person my dad didn't shield a lot of this personal weirdness from. I know firsthand how crazy she is and how much he was concerned and cared for her. She was a fly that wouldn't go away."

After Graham's death, Cartwright unflinchingly detailed her version of their relationship to a Graham biographer. "Bill believed that the only reason I was put on this Earth was to run into him when I was a kid and be there for him," she told author John Glatt. "Sex was his first bond with me. But I soon fell in love with him. He liked to tell me that God had designed my body especially for him, and I was the only woman who really knew how to love him."

31

Throughout his tenure as the estate executor, Clainos felt torn between his fiduciary duty to act on behalf of the best interests of the heirs and his moral obligation, as he saw it, to carry out Graham's wishes.

Since Graham left a $100,000 bequest to Cartwright under the terms of the unsigned will, Clainos decided to make an equally generous settlement with Cartwright, although he was under no legal obligation to give her anything.

A few months after Graham's death, Clainos arrived at an arrangement he thought would both legally remove any claims Cartwright might make on the estate and honor Graham's intended gift.

Clainos lost his temper during a heated conference call with attorney Greene and Cartwright, her child crying in the background, but eventually offered her $300,000 (approximately $140,000 to the heirs after taxes, or $40,000 more than Graham's intended bequest). As a condition, he insisted that she sign an agreement that, among other things, called for Cartwright and her daughter to submit to blood testing.

At first, according to Clainos, Cartwright balked, but finally relented, although she had the actual blood tests videotaped. In order to create a sample of Graham's own genetic structure, all four of his sisters also submitted to blood tests, as well as his two acknowledged sons. The results conclusively excluded Graham as the child's father, information that was not shared with Cartwright. Clainos felt confident that they would not hear from her again.

Ester Chichinsky often hovered over official Bill Graham events like a queen bee during her brother's lifetime. Her matronly presence in his harsh, rock and roll bachelor life occasionally spilled over into his business.

Chichinsky attended the first meeting at Greene's office without a lawyer, and Clainos and Greene helped her find her own attorney. She expressed reservations about the Cartwright settlement, but sitting together in Clainos' car outside the Graham office, the two agreed to take the solution to the other heirs together.

Apparently some simmering resentments lay hidden, because they soon boiled into view.

When the Rock and Roll Hall of Fame announced that Graham would be a special inductee at the annual dinner in January 1992, Marcia Godinez could not face the ordeal. She confidently sent her teenage son Alex to New York in the care of his "auntie," Ester Chichinsky, and her husband, Manny.

"Ester was very comforting," said Alex Graham during a recent visit to the Bay Area. "She helped me write my speech. I had a lot of fun with Ester on that trip."

But tensions erupted at the dinner. David Graham and his half-brother exchanged angry words, and Alex spent some time sulking in his hotel room. By the time the award was presented, however, the family made a united front, with David, Alex and their aunts Ester and Sonja appearing together onstage.

Threads began to unravel again on the flight back. In the car riding home from the airport, Manny Chichinsky came unglued at young Alex.

"He was hurling stuff at me," Alex Graham remembered. "He was screaming and yelling, saying things like, 'That's why your father never loved you – that's why he treated you like a dog.'"

"The next time we saw Ester, things had totally changed," said Godinez.

II. Dividing a Lifetime's Bounty
Long, painful negotiations over fate of promoter's estate

Six months after Bill Graham died in October 1991 in a fiery helicopter crash outside Sears Point, the unveiling of his gravestone brought together the rock concert producer's heirs for the first time. Tension and anxiety filled the event, as his bitterly divided family were struggling over the will Graham had left behind.

The night before, Marcia Godinez, mother of Graham's teenage son, Alex, had confronted Graham's sister Ester Chichinsky at Masada, the promoter's 11-acre Mill Valley hilltop home.

Godinez had heard that Chichinsky, the family matriarch, had been insinuating that Graham was not the father of Godinez's child. Godinez asked to speak with her privately, and the two adjourned to the deck outside the house.

"Immediately she started backpedaling," said Godinez. "I had to ask her several times and she never really answered me. I started crying. She left in a huff. I was mind-blown."

That night, David Graham was awakened suddenly from a deep sleep in his father's bed by a loud crash. A lithograph in the adjoining bathroom had exploded out of the frame and off the wall for no apparent reason, the glass breaking on the floor. He woke up the next morning jangled and spooked.

The next day, at Eternal Home Cemetery in Colma, a crowd gathered for the traditional Jewish unveiling rite. But the sisters and the sons stood on opposite sides of the grave. When it came time for David Graham to speak to the mourners, he was standing on his father's grave.

He tearfully begged estate executor Nicholas Clainos not to sell Masada, so he could continue living in his father's home. His girlfriend gently led him away from the stunned crowd.

"That was the one time I didn't appear with the grace I wanted," he said last month at his Nicasio home, "the one time I just wasn't ready to be there. There were times I was down on everybody. On that morning, I wasn't very happy."

These were troubled days for David Graham, then 23. He had expressed his puzzlement when a plan was announced at a Bill Graham Presents staff meeting earlier in the month for a group of key employees to purchase the company from the estate.

"I don't understand the legality of this," he said.

David Graham never fit in at his father's firm anyway. He had never been directly involved in the company's day-to-day operations, and the close-knit group that runs the business, whose members remember him as an awkward teenager spending his summer vacations tagging behind his busy and important father, didn't carve out a place for him.

He was even growing remote from his one legitimate role in the business, managing Blues Traveler, leaving most of the work to a partner.

"I was so unknowledgeble and uncomfortable that my body language would react," he said. "I wanted to be there and show everybody that I felt the company should be with the Grahams. I wanted to show them I was a team player. I wanted to be a little more consulted in business decisions."

At the same time, Clainos and estate attorney Dick Greene had concluded that David Graham could not afford to live at Masada. For an estate that owed more than $16 million in taxes, the property represented too valuable a liquid asset. And running it was too expensive.

Graham had also owned property in San Mateo County, San Francisco, New York, Colorado and Hawaii; the estate put virtually everything up for sale. His spectacular home in Telluride, Colo., quickly sold for more than $1.75 million.

Despite David Graham's tearful plea, the hammer fell on Masada in June 1992: It was sold for more than $5.7 million, the highest price ever paid for a piece of real estate in Marin County.

After Masada, the largest single asset on the books of the estate was Graham's company. And selling that would prove one of the most difficult tasks of the probate.

Graham had informally discussed the idea of selling the company to his executives with Clainos, Greene and a few other close associates, but no steps had been taken to write up a plan.

Drawing from lists compiled by both Clainos and Greene during Graham's lifetime, Clainos put together a group of key employees to purchase Graham's companies from his estate.

Buyers included co-presidents Clainos and Gregg Perloff, chief financial officer Franklin D. Rockwell and vice presidents Steve Welkom, Stan Feig, Danny Scher and Sherry Wasserman.

Graham's holdings included six wholly owned corporations, starting with the umbrella, Bill Graham Enterprises. Bill Graham Presents is the concert-producing wing of the operation, responsible for the bulk of the revenues. Bill Graham Management is an artist management firm that handles artists such as Eddie Money, Joe Satriani and the Neville Brothers.

Shoreline Ltd. is the general partner in Shoreline Amphitheatre Partnership, a limited partnership that includes investors Ann Getty, Apple Computer mogul Steve Wozniak and San Jose Sharks owner George Gund. AKG is the nightclub division of the company and operates the restored Fillmore Auditorium, the Warfield Theater and the Punch Line comedy clubs. Fillmore Fingers is the catering company that serves food and beverages at these various sites.

The will allowed Clainos to buy and sell assets of the estate. But putting a price on the package proved difficult, and Chichinsky was suspicious of company employees.

"Ester wanted to know, 'Why should (they) get a cut rate on the company when he treated you so well?' " David Graham said. "She wanted to know who should benefit more from my father's passing."

Chichinsky has refused to comment for this series.

"There was this incredible level of distrust," Godinez said during a visit to the Bay Area last month.

"Suddenly people who had always been on Bill's side, in Ester's mind, they turned overnight into a pack of thieves. Everything was suspect. Everything was scrutinized."

According to Godinez, Chichinsky sent accountants into the office to check the phone bills David Graham was running up at Masada to make sure his personal bills weren't being paid by her portion of the estate.

When Clainos asked that any royalties from Graham's posthumously published autobiography be donated to the charitable Bill Graham Foundation, Chichinsky allegedly insisted that the money should go to the estate instead.

When Gary Orendorf, Graham's majordomo since 1977, was stricken with AIDS, Clainos, mindful of a $100,000 bequest to Orendorf in the will Graham left unsigned at his death, asked the heirs to make a contribution. Only David Graham and Alex Graham-Sult did.

Into this cauldron of contention walked Kevin Johnson, a man living in upstate New York. His biological mother had given him up for adoption at birth in the mid-'50s and, after Graham died, she told him Graham was his father.

Johnson came to San Francisco curious about the father he never knew. Godinez met him and invited him and his wife to celebrate Thanksgiving with her and Alex in Hawaii.

Clainos again asked the heirs for money, believing that Graham would have wanted to give some to the son he never met. Again, only David and Alex contributed.

Meanwhile, according to court documents, Stephen Chichinsky, Ester's son, raised questions about the legitimacy of the 1981 second codicil to Graham's original will, which removed his gift of 5 per cent of the estate to Stephen. He hired forensic experts to investigate the will and, according to family members, accused Clainos of forging the document; he demanded samples of Graham's handwriting.

His uncle had given him money over the years and, feeling the irony of the situation, the company supplied Chichinsky with copies of the checks Graham had written him.

Stephen Chichinsky could not be reached for comment for this story.

Rockwell, the treasurer of the Bill Graham operation who spent 19 years with a lumber and paper company before joining Graham in 1986, conducted most of the negotiations over the purchase of the company.

He tried various approaches to determining the company's value – a multiple of earnings, an average of the previous three years, "a myriad of sophisticated analyses," he said.

His problem was always the same; a great deal of the company's worth rested in the experience of the employees, who functioned without contracts. These employees, now trying to buy the company, did not think it made sense to include their own value in the purchase price. "We didn't want to buy ourselves," said Rockwell.

Negotiations moved slowly. "It was starting to get frustrating to me," said Rockwell. "I was making offers against myself."

The protracted probate process began to take a toll on the participants. In addition to legal haggling over the estate, David and Alex filed a wrongful-death suit against PG&E, charging, among other things, that the utility was negligent and in violation of Federal Aviation Administration regulations for not properly marking the tower into which Graham's helicopter crashed. (The case is scheduled to come to trial in September. PG&E attorneys have declined to comment.)

High school freshman Alex Graham-Sult found himself pulled out of school in Hawaii and sent to the mainland virtually every month after his father's death.

"I'd miss school for three days or a week," he said last month, in town to attend a memorial service for Orendorf.

"I'd come over here and go to meetings or depositions. I'd just call it 'legal stuff' and find out about the details when I get here. I'd never dealt with anything like that – the loss of my dad, starting high school, going through all this legal stuff, all at the same time. I don't think there are too many ninth-graders that go through what I was going through."

In an effort to break the stalemate over selling the company, lawyers for all the heirs hired an independent appraiser to put a price on the Graham operation. Benton Levy, a Manhattan-based entertainment attorney, conducted interviews at five companies involved in concert promotion, some privately held and some public.

He also interviewed key executives of Bill Graham Presents. In the end, Levy estimated the company was worth $8.75 million with employment contracts and $2.75 million without the existing executives in place.

Rockwell said three-quarters of the heirs were persuaded to accept a second offer, after a previous offer was turned down, of $4.75 million. He felt confident that the court would order the sale when presented with the petition at a hearing in June 1993.

A contingent of Bill Graham Presents employees attended the Marin County court hearing, along with the customary complement of heirs and attorneys. But when Ester Chichinsky showed up with a brand-new attorney, the smiles disappeared.

The first thing Chichinsky's new lawyer did was move to disqualify the probate commissioner who had been hearing the case since its inception.

On impulse, returning to the courtroom from the bathroom, Godinez walked over to Chichinsky and hugged her.

"I said, 'This is so stupid,'" she recalled. "'Can't we talk this over and work it out?' Ester started crying. I did, too."

With court in recess, family members asked the lawyers to leave the room so they could talk. All agreed, except Chichinsky's new representative. Chichinsky, seated in the jury box, received members of the company and the other heirs one by one.

David Graham and his aunt began to exchange angry words. When Graham brought up her accusations over his half-brother's paternity, Chichinsky began to defend herself, Godinez exploded and Chichinsky started yelling, too. The scene quickly disintegrated into a shouting match.

"I remember people screaming and yelling," said BGP production assistant Rita Gentry. "I remember David going off, I remember Marcia going off. It was ugly."

A judge from an adjoining courtroom came in and ordered the ruckus to halt. The judge left, but posted a bailiff in the courtroom in her absence.

The settlement that seemed so close only hours before suddenly never seemed farther away.

III. Fallout From Estate Finally Settles
AFTER DISPUTES, HEIRS RESIGNED, COMPANY STRONG

David Graham lives in a house remarkably like his father's. The sprawling, ranch-style home sits on a breathtaking 30 acres across the road from George Lucas' Skywalker Ranch in northern Marin. The front door opens onto an indoor swimming pool, and the walls are covered with framed memorabilia from his father's career as the industry's top rock concert producer. Graham himself notes the resemblance to Masada, his father's Mill Valley mountaintop home.

Graham, 25, grew up in the shadow of a dynamic father, a rich and powerful captain of the music industry who died in October 1991 when his helicopter exploded into a PG&E tower near Sears Point. For the next 3 1/2 years, Bill Graham's family was embroiled in an angry, divisive battle over his estate that left the young prince caught between his father's sisters and his father's closest business associates.

"I had to contend with some people telling me this and some people telling me that," he said at his home last month. "At times, I wondered who was working in my best interests."

Graham is a hyperkinetic young man, all knees and elbows. His hands fly around as he talks, and his legs wiggle and shake while he sits. At least for now, he has given up his interest in joining the music business.

Two days after his father died, David Graham visited the scene of the crash with the three children of Bill Graham's girlfriend, Melissa Gold, who also died that stormy night. It would have been her 48th birthday.

A coroner showed them around. They sang "Happy Birthday" to the charred spot where Gold's body landed. Graham retrieved a piece of the helicopter, which he keeps in his living room. That night at the Oakland Coliseum Arena, he made a short speech at a sold-out Grateful Dead concert, sounding nervous and unsteady.

Under the terms of a will Bill Graham first signed in 1976, David and his half-brother, Alexander Graham-Sult, equally share 55 percent of their father's $36 million estate. They retained a 10 percent ownership in Bill Graham Presents after it was sold to key executives in January.

Graham's sister Ester Chichinsky received 15 percent of the estate. His three other sisters and foster brother divided the remaining 30 percent.

If Graham had lived to execute a new will that was prepared and simply awaiting his signature, the entire estate would have been placed in trust for his sons, with the four sisters and foster brother getting only a modest annual allowance, substantially less than their share under the probate will.

While estate executor Nicholas Clainos and Graham's sons believed that the intent of the unsigned will should be honored, not all the heirs agreed. Under California law, there was no legal obligation to follow an unsigned will. According to Marcia Godinez, mother of Alex Graham-Sult, if heirs had agreed to put the second will into effect, Graham's sons gladly would have increased the siblings' annual allowance.

"I think it's a sacred thing when someone you love (dies) and you have a list of instructions, signed or unsigned," said Godinez. "Everybody knew that was a valid will because it was so quintessentially Bill – the people who were on that will and the amounts. I was just horrified that they didn't want to honor that."

After Chichinsky derailed plans to sell the company to a group of 15 Bill Graham Presents executives at a dramatic court hearing in June 1993, negotiations to buy the company continued, but without much progress.

Resigned that he could not strike a deal to sell the company as Nick Clainos, president of Bill Graham Presents and the executor of the Bill Graham estate, in his office part of the estate, executor Clainos decided that to close probate he had only one choice. He would have to distribute stock to the heirs and make individual deals to purchase it, even if it meant not being able to acquire the entire company.

Hoping to close the already protracted, draining and complex probate case, Clainos asked the court to let him parcel out the stock in October 1993. BGP executives quickly obtained options to purchase three-quarters ownership and were arranging the financing when another bomb dropped on the estate.

At a routine court hearing in November 1993, estate attorney Dick Greene and Clainos learned that the court had received a letter from a new lawyer representing Regina Cartwright. Graham's ex-lover had accepted $300,000 shortly after his death to drop any claims she may have had against the estate.

Asserting that she had signed the January 1992 agreement under coercion and fraud, Cartwright planned to file suit in federal court in New York, which would pose grave consequences for the California probate case. If Cartwright's daughter was held to be Graham's child, she would be entitled to a share of the entire estate.

Clainos believed Cartwright's claims were unfounded because he had seen the results of blood tests conducted after Cartwright signed the original deal. But it turned out those were informal tests, not admissible in court.

A second round of blood tests was begun, their legality clearly established this time. Technicians were flown to Europe to collect samples from two of Bill Graham's four sisters. Experts from the University of Kansas and Johns Hopkins University were consulted. Once again, the results ruled out Graham as the father of Cartwright's child. They also proved that Alex was Bill Graham's child.

"The blood tests were really hard for me emotionally," said Alex. "The reason I was there – that had me flying thousands of miles just to prove I'm my dad's son – that p– me off. It's like `What do you want, blood?' They said, 'yes.' "

Neither Cartwright nor her attorney attended the June 1994 Marin County probate hearing, where it took only a few hours for a judge to rule that Graham was not the father, clearing the way to close probate. When presented with this evidence, however, the New York federal judge nevertheless ordered the case to continue and depositions to be taken.

Cartwright waived her right to attorney-client privilege with her previous lawyer, who was one of those deposed. This attorney testified that Cartwright had admitted that her child might not be Graham's.

The Graham estate's request for a summary judgment has not been decided yet, although in October 1994, Cartwright's new attorney wrote the federal judge that even his own expert witness agreed with the results of the tests. A ruling is expected soon.

Meanwhile, BGP executives, who had already made deals for 75 percent of the company, made one last offer to the two holdout sisters. Sonja Szobel capitulated, but Chichinsky still refused to sell.

In December, according to Clainos, Chichinsky offered to sell her stock, but for more money. He refused. She finally agreed to sell anyway. In January, around the same time probate closed, the executives closed the deal for ownership of the company.

Company officials refuse to divulge the purchase price. However, an analyst hired to evaluate the company's worth estimated that BGP was worth $8.75 million with employment contracts and $2.75 million without the existing executives. In June 1993, court documents show, the employees were prepared to offer $4.75 million.

Now only one legal issue remained – Chichinsky objected to the legal fees. Superior Court Judge Michael Dufficy ordered them paid; Clainos got more than $600,000 as executor.

During his 3 1/2 years as estate executor, Clainos had wrestled with troubling conflict-of-interest charges from various factions in the family, particularly Graham's sisters.

"The more I did to take care of the conflicts, the more the allegations bothered me," said Clainos recently. "No matter what I did, they didn't care. It was irrational fear."

Wrote Dufficy in the ruling ordering the fees paid, "'This was an unusually difficult estate to administer. . . . The deceased's business interests in the music and entertainment business required a special expertise to manage and operate after (Graham's) death."

Bill Graham so totally dominated the public face of his company that many industry observers speculated it would disintegrate into feuding factions and destroy itself without its powerful father figure. "It's a cesspool of competitive angst over there," said one local rock band manager.

Graham's management style often pitted executives against one another. "Bill was a master of having two people go into his office and debate an issue," said Gregg Perloff, co-president of Bill Graham Presents. "He set up a situation where you had to defend your position. It kept people on edge."

But Graham also built a skillful and loyal 80-person office that could keep his empire running when he took off to tour Southeast Asia with Mick Jagger or run around the world with Bruce Springsteen and Peter Gabriel on behalf of Amnesty International.

"Let me ask a question: When did Bill Graham leave the company?" said Perloff. "The answer is 1982, when he returned from the Rolling Stones European tour and found everything had been running smoothly while he had been gone for the past year and a half."

Since his death, the company has flourished. Eight days after Graham died, employees pulled off a massive memorial. The free concert, "Laughter, Love and Music," was at the Polo Field in Golden Gate Park before more than 300,000 people and featured acts such as the Grateful Dead, Crosby, Stills, Nash and Young, John Fogerty, Journey, Santana, Robin Williams and Bobby McFerrin.

The company went ahead with plans to underwrite a $1 million retrofit and seismic upgrade of the Fillmore Auditorium, a business move perhaps more sentimental than practical. The famed hall, the first place Graham put on shows, reopened in April 1994. They still give away apples there the way Graham did back in the '60s.

Today, Bill Graham Presents continues to rule the Northern California concert scene. New Jersey- based producer John Scher, who has battled the Graham operation for years, thinks the company might be stronger than ever.

According to Perloff, 1994 was the most successful year in the company's 30-year history, thanks to shows by the Rolling Stones, the Eagles, Barbra Streisand and Pink Floyd.

Only one major figure, promoter Queenie Taylor, has left since Graham's death. The people who worked for Graham during his lifetime have learned to get along without Graham there to resolve their disputes.

"It came down to 'How do we keep this thing going?' " said Perloff. "If that meant some petty arguments had to go away, that's what it meant."

Said BGP vice president Sherry Wasserman, "We discovered this incredible framework called Bill Graham Presents that nobody understood until he was gone."

"Candidly, I think the fact that they were willing to buy it at all was an act of sentimentality and kindness," said Scher. "They could have opened an office down the street, called it Bay Area Concert Co. and not missed a beat."

Clainos has a theory that Bill Graham had two families. One was his blood relatives and the other was his company, which Graham frequently referred to as "the Bill Graham family." He certainly spent more time with his working colleagues than his family.

Bill Graham rarely took any time off. David Graham remembers a 1990 trip to Crete, Cairo, Tel Aviv and other Mediterranean ports of call as the only time he ever spent alone with his father and his half-brother. Wasserman recalls babysitting for Alex in concert box offices.

"Bill Graham Presents is my extended family," said Alex. "I grew up with a great deal of them. I stayed with them. I have eaten dinner with them. I have helped them work at the concession stands and run errands at the office."

With the probate case closed and the company sold, the heirs were left to go about their lives, all fundamentally changed by the events of the previous 3 1/2 years.

Alex and his mother live in a house in Maui deeded to them as part of the estate settlement. He is a dance music disc jockey and plans to attend college next fall in San Francisco.

Chichinsky, 68, a multimillionaire from her inheritance, lives with her husband in her brother's old house in downtown Mill Valley. Despite repeated requests to both her and her lawyer, she declined to be interviewed for this story.

"I have seen no fairness or completeness in 3 1/2 years," she said of her decision not to comment.

Of Graham's four sisters, only she and Sonja Szobel continue to enjoy the fruits of their inheritance. Szobel, 70, is a widow who splits her time between homes in Vienna and Majorca. Evelyn (Echa) Udry died in July at age 71.

Rita Rosen, 76, who has Alzheimer's disease, recently entered an institution in Southern California.

David Graham hasn't spoken to his aunt Ester in many months.

"I love Ester, but we are definitely far apart on this. She feels there is a pot of gold somewhere that someone hid. She was the matriarch and was always treated with respect. All that went away when he died. I understand how she feels. I shared the same thing."

To Graham, his peace of mind was more important than picking apart the deal.

"Why would I want to deconstruct the most impressive company in the music industry?" he asked. "I couldn't live with the guilt if I did bring the company down, which certainly could have happened if Alex and I hadn't been the majority."

Said Clainos, "The boys won. In front of us all, they grew up fast, but they grew up straight. In the end, I think that's probably the only thing that would have mattered to Bill."

San Francisco Chronicle | Tuesday, April 4, 1995,
Wednesday, April 5, 1995, Thursday, April 6, 1995

From Jazz to Rock

Don't let the tweed jackets, trench coat and pipe fool you – Ralph J. Gleason was an apostle of jazz and rock with few peers

I've never done a more personal piece of journalism. Ralph was a distant figure on my horizon, but his presence surrounded me; from reading him in The Chronicle from my earliest interest in the subject to seeing his handwriting on the back of old publicity photos in the files. I used to see him around the office – he would drop by to pick up mail on his way out for the evening – from time to time when I worked the night shift as a copy boy. I had spent a long, loathsome year off the beat and, almost soon as I was back, I dug into this piece, spending days reading old Gleason clips in a windowless basement room, as a means of reconnecting with something important in my life.

RALPH J. GLEASON'S BERKELEY HILLS HOME LOOKS as if he left last week, even though the great jazz and rock critic has been dead for nearly 30 years. His epic LP record collection covers one wall of the living room and a pile of 45 RPM singles sits by the door. A poster from the first San Francisco rock concert at the Longshoreman's Hall hangs in the center of the living room. It was one of three silk-screened by Jefferson Airplane vocalist Marty Balin.

A couple of dozen old friends gathered there one night after attending a screening at Fantasy Studios. It was a night like many long ago, when the house rang with music and laughter and seemed to be the center of the world for the people who were there. It hasn't been like that in a long time, but this more recent night was special.

Kehala Gleason, 21, and her college pal Jennica Murray spent their junior year making a movie about the grandfather Gleason never knew. At Fantasy, they screened an hour-long rough-cut of the class project for friends and family. Young Gleason, a petite blonde who grew up in a log cabin without electricity or telephones in eastern Washington, was leaving the next day to spend six months with an agitprop street-theater troupe in Mexico.

The sweet student film, which may never screen again, mixed vintage footage from the Gleason family archive – photos of him with the Beatles, Coltrane; film footage of him with Sonny Rollins – with tributes from friends and associates. Her grandfather's name was still good enough for the young Gleason to land interviews with Rolling Stone publisher Jann Wenner, rock critic Dave Marsh, journalist Studs Terkel and others (including myself). Kehala Gleason's voiceover

John Lennon and Ralph Gleason

narrative, in her reticent little girl's voice, gave the whole thing a sentimental wash.

"We came to this house expecting to find answers and found questions," she intones over a sequence of shots taken at the Spruce Street house. "We came to the past and found hope for the future."

Among the friends at the party was an artist who once ran off to Hawaii with one of the Quicksilver Messenger Service. Also attending, coincidentally, was Ron Polte, the man who used to manage the group. Ralph was much in the air. "He was a really cool father," said his oldest daughter, Brigitte, 53, whose 24-year-old son, Kelly, is living with his grandmother these days. "He took us to the Fillmore and everything. But he always wore a tie."

Music critics are a dime a dozen these days. Virtually everyone who can score advance CDs from the labels seems to be out there hawking commentary in print or on the Internet.

But there was a time, not that long ago, when there were only a few and they all knew each other. Today's pop music critics, who cut their teeth on Pearl Jam and Nirvana, will never have the chance to leave behind a legacy like Gleason's. In an age of the information superhighway and media overload, the era of E! Television and Entertainment Weekly, how do you explain one lone writer working for a daily newspaper in a provincial backwater changing music history? But it was never easy to explain Gleason, even when he was alive.

He started one of the first magazines about jazz. He was the first full- time jazz critic on a daily newspaper in this country. At a time when there were practically no books on the subject, he wrote the history of jazz on the back of album covers, writing literally hundreds of liner notes in the golden age of long-playing albums.

He was the cofounder of the Monterey Jazz Festival and cofounder of Rolling Stone magazine. When Lou Adler and John Phillips of the Mamas and Papas wanted to throw the Monterey Pop Festival, they traveled north to kiss the Gleason ring, knowing they couldn't hope to pull it off without his approval.

He was the defender and friend of Lenny Bruce, the chronicler and confidant of Duke Ellington, a man who wrote poetry for Miles Davis albums, hosted John Coltrane and Bob Dylan on television and produced one of the best country and western movies ever made. He was a vigilant defender of free speech and an outspoken lefty who understood that music and politics were inextricably linked. He made Nixon's enemies list.

His trademark trench coat hangs in the Rock and Roll Hall of Fame in Cleveland. He was a natty dresser who favored tweed jackets, deerstalker hats, wore a handlebar mustache and smoked a pipe. He was also a diabetic who drank only milk at nightclubs and always carried a Hershey bar in his pocket in case of emergency.

"He did a wonderful job of living in his world," said veteran jazz producer Orrin Keepnews, who worked across the hall from Gleason at Berkeley's Fantasy Records in the '70s. "He might partake of your world, but he lived in his world."

The movie, "Remembering Ralph J. Gleason," begins, as it should, with his writing. The clattering of his Underwood typewriter fills the black screen and his words appear typewritten on the screen, letter by letter:

Form and rhythm in music are never changed without producing changes in the most important political forms and ways."

Plato said that.

The quote comes from the essay "Like a Rolling Stone" that Gleason wrote for American Scholar magazine in 1966. The student filmmakers include the rest of his introduction to that essay later in the film:

There something happenin' here. What it is ain't exactly clear. There's a man with a gun over there, telling me I've got to beware. I think it's time we STOP, children, what's that sound? Everybody look what's going down."

Buffalo Springfield said that.

"For the reality of politics, we must go to the poets, not the politicians."

Norman O. Brown said that.

"For the reality of what's happening today in America, we must go to rock 'n' roll, to popular music."

I said that.

Old black-and-white footage from a 1965 British Broadcasting Corporation program about people with unusual jobs shows Gleason in his attic office, wearing a checkered shirt, fiddling with his pipe and tapping away at the keyboard. His reedy, pinched voice fills the room: "Well, this is Gleason high in the Oakland/Berkeley hills, as usual, bringing all the latest news from Never-Neverland, which, if you think about it, is where we all really live."

The idea that popular arts deserved serious commentary emerged in 1924, a mere 10 years before Gleason wrote his first record reviews for his college newspaper, the Columbia Spectator. The publication of "The 7 Lively Arts" by Gilbert Seldes, an East Coast Brahmin and editor of the long-defunct Dial magazine, was greeted by an uproar among the high-brows. He dared to extol the virtues of such prosaic fare as jazz, Charlie Chaplin movies, Flo Ziegfield musicals and "Krazy Kat" cartoons. "Newspaper Comics, Circus, Slapstick Films, Jazz Are Art, Says Editor Of 'Dial,' " sniffed an indignant Chronicle headline of the day.

In 1934, both jazz and Gleason were in the full bloom of youth. He discovered the music during a case of the measles, when the doctor prescribed bed rest in a dark room and his mother let him listen to the Atwater Kent. "I lay there, wide awake in the night, picking up those strange sounds in the night – Duke Ellington, Louis Armstrong, Cab Calloway, Earl Hines, Fletcher Henderson," he wrote in the introduction to "Celebrating the Duke," his posthumously published collection of jazz writing.

As with all schools of art, as jazz grew, the music developed a critical elite. Otis

Ferguson, also one of the first film critics, wrote about jazz for the New Republic, starting in 1936. The music's new scholars soon began to document the history. French discographers Hughes Panassie and Charles Delaunay published their error-riddled but nevertheless landmark works in the mid-'30s. Two important books on jazz history – Wilder Hobson's "American Jazz Music" and "Jazzmen" by Frederic Ramsey Jr. and Charles Edward Smith – were published in 1939, the same year Gleason left Columbia to start what may have been the first magazine devoted to the music, Jazz Information.

In 1939, New York was the unquestioned jazz capital of the universe and Columbia University was only blocks from Harlem, home to Duke Ellington, Fats Waller, Billie Holiday, Lionel Hampton, Cab Calloway. The Count Basie Band had just moved to New York. The entire world of jazz was swinging in uptown Manhattan, and Gleason used to go door-to-door in the black neighborhoods, looking to buy old jazz records. He also haunted the clubs and theaters where bands played by night.

"And when I got to the Big Apple," he wrote in a set of Jimmie Lunceford album notes, "and found that you could actually get to see a band like this in person at the Apollo or the Savoy Ballroom or the Renaissance or the Strand or Paramount theaters, I simply couldn't believe it. It was just too good to be true."

San Francisco in the '40s was the world headquarters of the New Orleans jazz revival. Lu Watters and the Yerba Buena Jazz Band started playing in 1939, soon settling into residency at the Dawn Club, a basement in an alley off Market Street, its site marked today by a brass plaque. In 1943, jazz enthusiasts bought a new set of false teeth for old-time New Orleans trumpeter Bunk Johnson and brought him to San Francisco for a series of historic concerts.

In September 1945, Gleason, who spent the war years working for the Office of War Information, booked the old Dixieland jazzman into the Stuyvesant Casino on New York's Lower East Side. The following year, Gleason and his wife, Jean, moved to San Francisco to produce concerts by New Orleans tailgate trombonist Kid Ory, then living in Los Angeles, only recently rescued from obscurity and his job in the poultry business by appearances on the Orson Welles radio program.

Gleason soon found sympathetic ears at The Chronicle in executive editor Scott Newhall and managing editor Gordon Pates, music fans whose taste tended toward Earl Hines and Edith Piaf, respectively. He started at $15 per review. In 1950, they hired him full-time, about the same time he started contributing regularly to the bi-monthly bible of jazz, Downbeat magazine. By 1954, the Gleason family and its three children could afford a modest home on busy Ashby Avenue in Berkeley's Elmwood district.

At The Chronicle, Gleason became the first daily newspaper critic in the country to cover jazz and pop music openings like theater or opera openings. Although his main topic was jazz, he was no snob. He picked up stories across the pop panorama. He interviewed Hank Williams and covered his show in 1952 at San Pablo Hall in the far reaches of the East Bay. Gleason gave early glowing reviews to Nat King Cole ("the top balladeer of his time") and Frank Sinatra ("far and above anybody by a country mile").

He kept an ear cocked toward other sounds and frequently lectured his readers on the musical qualities of rock 'n' roll and rhythm and blues. He interviewed Elvis Presley, Fats Domino, Louis Jordan, Ivory Joe Hunter, Big Joe Turner and Ray Charles in The Chronicle. He even paused to scorch the unspeakably square Pat Boone ("pretentious and a bit of a phony").

From the pulpit of the daily newspaper, Gleason's jazz criticism penetrated mainstream culture. He gave early coverage to Miles Davis and described Louis Armstrong in 1954 as "one of the most important people alive today." Gleason and Davis became close friends. Gleason once returned from visiting the trumpeter during a nightclub engagement where the diabetic Gleason discovered that he and Davis used the same-sized hypodermic needles. Davis was not diabetic.

But Gleason never limited his contributions to the printed page. He played a crucial role in founding the Monterey Jazz Festival. It was Gleason's idea to take the music out of the dark, smoky, smelly nightclubs and into the fresh air and sunshine. Disc jockey Jimmy Lyons, who ran the festival for the first 34 years, located the horse show arena on the Monterey County Fairgrounds. "Ralph was essential to the festival," said the late Grover Sales, publicist on the first festival. "He suggested the whole concept of the festival."

They certainly got the cast they wanted for that 1958 weekend – Louis Armstrong, Dizzy Gillespie, Billie Holiday, Dave Brubeck, Modern Jazz Quartet, Sonny Rollins. But serving the festival behind the scenes made little difference to his coverage. He was equally capable of cheering or criticizing the event in the paper the next day. When Los Angeles Times jazz critic Leonard Feather complained about Gleason having better seats, Feather was informed that Gleason had paid for his tickets.

A contentious Irish American who read extensively on topics ranging from the Civil War to civil rights, Gleason took a put-up-your-dukes attitude about anything he thought smacked of injustice, intolerance or ignorance. He took up the Lenny Bruce cause when nobody else did. He testified eloquently in Bruce's trials about his social significance as a comedian and wrote passionate defenses of Bruce's work in the press.

Bruce sent Gleason presents; he borrowed Gleason's name in his routines ("and here he is, that silver master of the airwaves, Ralph J. Gleason ..."). And, as Bruce's legal problems with obscenity busts intensified, Gleason grew ever more emphatic in his columns.

"Truly it is Kafka's 'The Trial' brought to life," he wrote, "to real life. And if the closing walls do, in the end, bring silence, we will be the guilty, all of us, not Lenny Bruce."

He saw some of the same rebel qualities in Bob Dylan, just not at first. He caught Dylan's West Coast debut at the 1963 Monterey Folk festival and dismissed him. A year later, he repented. "When I first heard Bob Dylan at Monterey I did not like him," Gleason wrote. "I was deaf."

His endorsement of Dylan came from a major, well-credentialed spokesman. Gleason had become widely recognized as the country's top jazz critic. His Chronicle column was syndicated to more than 60 papers across the nation. In addition to his contributions to Variety, Downbeat, Hi-Fi/Stereo Review and other national magazines, he brought jazz to network television.

From 1961 to 1968, Gleason, who looked like a casting director's dream of a professorial jazz critic, produced and hosted a half-hour television show, "Jazz Casual," hovering over the pianos, puffing his pipe and drawing out such figures as Count Basie, Louis Armstrong, John Coltrane, Carmen McRae, Dizzy Gillespie, Dave Brubeck, Modern Jazz Quartet. "He got Count Basie to talk more than I ever heard before," said fellow jazz critic Nat Hentoff, "more than I ever did."

The close-focus, intimate programs were broadcast across the country on what was then called educational TV, the precursor to PBS, long before jazz musicians were accustomed to seeing themselves on television. He produced landmark specials with Duke Ellington. With his connections at the television station KQED, Gleason arranged and hosted a remarkable press conference with Dylan in 1965.

Gleason leads Dylan through the crowded room and makes the introduction while Dylan settles into a seat behind a table. "Welcome to KQED's first poet press conference," Gleason said. "Mr. Dylan is a poet. He will answer questions on everything from atomic science to riddles and rhymes. Go."

The Gleason home, less than a mile from campus, was action central. Student leaders sought his advice and held meetings in the living room. When the four long-haired artists who called themselves the Family Dog planned to throw a dance at Longshoreman's Hall featuring new rock groups with crazy names such as the Charlatans, Jefferson Airplane and the Great Society, they came over to discuss their ideas. "San Francisco can be the American Liverpool, " Family Dog's Luria Castell told Gleason.

That night at Longshoreman's, Gleason stood on the balcony and watched the birth of the San Francisco scene. When he came down to the dance floor, a 19-year-old college student named Jann Wenner, who wrote a rock music column for the Daily Cal, walked over and introduced himself. "I knew exactly who he was," Wenner said in a phone interview from his Midtown Manhattan offices.

As the San Francisco rock scene exploded, Gleason was there, night after night, reporting each latest development in the pages of The Chronicle. He covered the first public performance by the Jefferson Airplane. He quickly became the band's biggest booster, wrote the liner notes for the first album and followed the Airplane intensely in the paper.

Band member Paul Kantner later cribbed some lyrics from a piece Gleason wrote about a concert in Golden Gate Park. Gleason wrote a paperback book, "The Jefferson Airplane and the San Francisco Sound," and then handed over his column to a guest reviewer who panned the book.

Wenner accompanied Gleason to shows and spent long hours at Gleason's home. "It was always easy to scrounge a free meal," said Wenner. "I was predictably there around dinner time."

Gleason found the fledgling rock critic a job at Sunday Ramparts, a new broadsheet newspaper started by the publishers of Ramparts, a left-wing San Francisco magazine where Gleason was contributing editor. A framed blank page from Sunday Ramparts hangs in the Gleason home to this day, a handwritten message scrawled in marker pen: "Thanks for the job, the advice and the start. Love, Jann."

Gleason didn't simply encourage Wenner. He invested $1,500 in the magazine Wenner wanted to start and, when the first issue of Rolling Stone was published in November 1967, Gleason was listed as consulting editor and introduced his long-running column in that magazine with a sermon on race relations in pop music: "Sound Is Without Color."

At age 48, he was substantially older than both his audience and the people he was writing about. Gleason can't decide, the joke went, whether he's two 24-year-olds, three 16-year-olds or four 12-year-olds.

Gleason's relationship with Wenner turned stormy at Rolling Stone. He battled with his protege over editorial issues and personnel matters. Gleason fumed when Wenner spent precious funds for metal filing cabinets when cardboard boxes would do. He briefly quit the magazine weeks before its first anniversary.

In June 1970, Gleason left his full-time post at The Chronicle. He kept a Sunday column and continued to write a column for Rolling Stone. His old friend Saul Zaentz, owner of Fantasy Records, sold a few million records by a rock band called Creedence Clearwater Revival and built a spanking-new Berkeley headquarters for the label, complete with recording studios and a grand, sweeping staircase leading to the second-floor executive suites. He brought Gleason onboard as a kind of minister without portfolio.

In early 1975, Gleason began frustrating, infuriating negotiations with Wenner to sell back his stock in Rolling Stone. "Do me a favor," Gleason said to a mutual associate he bumped into on the streets of Berkeley. "The next time you see him, punch him in the nose for me."

On Monday, June 2, Wenner returned to his office from flying around the state with Tom Hayden – then campaigning for U.S. Senate and married, at the time, to Jane Fonda – and learned that Gleason had suffered a massive heart attack. Wenner burst into uncontrollable sobs. By nightfall, Gleason was dead at age 58.

Within a year, Wenner folded the Rolling Stone tent in San Francisco and slipped off to New York. "It seemed like a good time to get out of Dodge," he said.

Gleason's 83-year-old widow, Jean, is sitting on her front porch, smoking a cigarette, waiting for her visitor.

Her eyesight is going but her peripheral vision is strong, so she tilts her head when she talks, looking out of the corner of her eye.

She lives in the Berkeley hills home she and Gleason bought in 1970, sharing the panoramic view with her grandson Kelly, Kelly's dog, and two other young people who worked with her granddaughter, Kehala, on the documentary. The two college students continue to work on the film, trying to raise money and film more interviews. Ralph Gleason's books still line the shelves and his papers are stowed in the attic. It doesn't look like Jean Gleason has bought a single piece of new furniture since they moved in.

Ralph Gleason first met her older brother in a crap game. The brother said his younger sister was a jazz fan. His interest piqued, Gleason took the provincial young lady from out of town to see the jazz bands on 52nd Street. "It was one of those setups you think you're going to hate, but I didn't," says Jean Gleason. "We really grooved."

They married in 1940. Throughout his career, she was his support team – typing, clipping columns, sending out clippings to record companies and pals across the country, taking his finished copy to the bus stop and convincing the AC Transit driver to take it to the East Bay Terminal where a Chronicle copy boy would pick it up.

Gleason did not keep a desk at The Chronicle office. He worked out of his home and occasionally dropped by the city room at night, on his way out to the clubs, to pick up the mail. The BBC caught Gleason making one of his nighttime visits to The Chronicle in 1965.

Wearing his trench coat, pipe in mouth, Gleason pauses at the entrance by the phone booths at the top of the office to exchange words with city editor Abe Mellinkoff. He drops a column off at the copy desk and he walks back to speak with Datebook editor Judy Stone. "He didn't like to be edited, I can tell you that," said Stone in an interview.

The only time his editors cut him off was when he wrote about the anniversary of the attempt to assassinate Hitler (Gleason, a World War II buff, had been reading up on the Third Reich). Managing editor Gordon Pates thought that had gone too far astray for the boundaries of an entertainment section. Pates always told him that the publisher would read the first few sentences of his column to see if he had gotten subversive, so Gleason needed to start tame. That may explain why Gleason developed a habit of what they call in journalistic circles "burying the lead."

"He was not a good writer," says his widow. "He wrote about interesting things."

San Francisco Chronicle | Thursday, December 23, 2004

CHAPTER 2

Rock & Roll Noir

Kevin Gilbert

Bill Bottrell

Sly Stone

Vince Welnick

More Than `The Piano Player'

Dumped by Sheryl Crow after propelling her to success, brilliant musician **Kevin Gilbert** *died before finding his own*

This story benefitted greatly from me being the first person to turn up asking questions. Everybody was still hurt and angry. After they got it off their chests, they shut up (Bottrell did later give a reluctant, terse interview to *Rolling Stone* for a Sheryl Crow cover story). There was so much more than I could get into in a Sunday Datebook cover story – the tale of how Chappell Music screwed the poet in the woods out of his publishing rights for "All I Wanna Do" alone is a show business classic – but there's more than enough here to sour your stomach.

LOS ANGELES – A BLACK HOOD COVERED HIS FACE. He wore a black skirt. His head was slumped against a leather strap chained to the headboard of the king-size bed in the sparsely furnished living room.

Kevin Gilbert, 29, was dead. That much his manager could see peering in at the front door that morning last May.

The Los Angeles County coroner's office sees four or five such deaths a year – "autoerotic asphyxiation," caused when people go one small step too far in depriving their brains of oxygen while they reach orgasm. It was a death without dignity, a random fall through the cracks of a secret life.

Gilbert was a prodigy musician from San Mateo who could play any instrument; colleagues invariably called him "the most talented musician I ever met." To the rest of the world, though, his only real claim to fame lies in the credits to "Tuesday Night Music Club," the 1993 debut album by Sheryl Crow.

"I saw something in Entertainment magazine that said Kevin Gilbert, the piano player on Sheryl Crow's record, had died," said songwriter David Baerwald, a member of the Tuesday club of the album's name. He paused, sadly shaking his head. "He hated that Sheryl Crow record and that's all he's going to be known for. The piano player? Roll over, Kevin Gilbert."

56

Kevin Gilbert

When Gilbert first brought his girlfriend Sheryl to informal Tuesday night songwriting sessions with his friends, he played a pivotal role in shaping an $85 million megahit. For her, the album brought three Grammys, stardom and an industry buzz that makes her forthcoming CD one of the most eagerly anticipated releases this fall. But for him, it was hardly a triumph. "I don't know if I can ever forgive her," he wrote in his journal. "I don't hate her – I'm just soooo disappointed."

In a way it's a classic Hollywood tale: Gifted boy artist meets girl artist, mentors her to success and is left in the dust – equal parts "Sunset Boulevard," "A Star Is Born" and "All About Eve." By any measure, Gilbert's career was a fitful tumble of brilliance and happenstance, a series of near misses and one hit that wasn't his. And his Tuesday night cohorts describe Crow – who refused to be interviewed for this story – as a marginally talented singer who exploited his skills and theirs in a ruthless grab for success.

But this wasn't a movie, and so the real story is inevitably messier and more complex. As the circumstances of his death suggest, Gilbert had a dark side, a hidden face making him an enigma to his friends. There was a history of antidepressants, a string of journal entries registering acute self-loathing and doubt. Once, he wrote about feeling intimidated when meeting a well-known session musician at a concert. "I suck," he wrote, circling the words for emphasis.

He had a promising start. As a South Bay teenager, Gilbert was given the run of Sunnyvale's Sensa Sound studio after hours; there, he recorded tracks with his progressive rock group, Giraffe. In 1988 he won the U.S. and worldwide finals of a talent contest run by the Yamaha piano company. One of the judges – Pat Leonard, a producer for Madonna – invited Gilbert to make a record in Los Angeles.

That album, "Toy Matinee," sold nearly 200,000 copies in 1991, thanks in part to an MTV video featuring actress Rosanna Arquette (whom Gilbert had dated). Gilbert put together a road version that included his then current girlfriend on background vocals and second keyboard – Sheryl Crow.

Making that album, Gilbert, at 21, met another record producer, Bill Bottrell, who became a kind of father figure. Bottrell brought him to sessions for Madonna and Michael Jackson; before long, Gilbert had sublet the space adjacent to Bottrell's Pasadena studio, Toad Hall. From there he set about recording his solo debut.

Drawing on all his perfectionist instincts, along with his ingrained self-doubts, Gilbert didn't just work on his record; he suffered over it, recording and rerecording, polishing, tweaking, rethinking, redoing.

"It was a long process," said Bottrell, who used to hear Gilbert thumping away through the common wall. "He sat over there endless nights."

In August 1992, Bottrell convened Gilbert and other musicians at Toad Hall with the simple agenda of collaborating for the fun of it every Tuesday night. "We were all good, not to be immodest," Baerwald said. "We were also all cynical, embittered by the process of pop music. We were trying to find some joy in music again."

A party atmosphere predominated – "Bill would sift through (the music) the next morning while we were all nursing hangovers," drummer Brian MacLeod recalled. Then Bottrell introduced a project he thought might force a little focus onto the freewheeling, chaotic sessions.

Crow had finished an album for A&M Records, but despite the $500,000 spent on it, nobody at the label was thrilled with the results. Hoping for a quick fix, A&M hired Gilbert to remix the album, which was, in the immutable illogic of the record industry, already scheduled for release. Crow's manager asked Bottrell to step in as well.

On Crow's first Tuesday night with the club, Baerwald showed up with musical sidekick David Ricketts (from the 1986 David and David album), both of them high on LSD, with the first verse already written to a song, "Leaving Las Vegas." Baerwald picked up a guitar, Ricketts the bass, and the band fell together to pick up where it had left off.

Baerwald "couldn't function," said Bottrell. "Sheryl started to get drunk. I was looking for that moment when the good take would happen."

For most of that year, Bottrell and his Tuesday crew – now working all week long – scrupulously fashioned and reshaped Crow's album. Because everything was a collaboration, songwriting credits were equally shared. "Everybody was equal," said Baerwald, "except Sheryl. She wasn't one of us. We helped her make a record."

Gilbert's name wound up on seven of the 11 songs; he sang and played keyboards, guitar, bass and drums.

His relationship with Crow was kept separate and even a secret from the group. "I'd see long conversations in the parking lot," Baerwald said.

"Kevin challenged her," MacLeod said. "He was trying to get her to be honest and sing from her heart."

Unsure of herself, professionally in over her head, Crow went home with Gilbert after sessions and listened to him rant about the industry's failings. "She had Kevin filling her with doubts," Bottrell said.

When he wasn't with Crow or the club, Gilbert struggled with his solo album, playing most of the instruments on his supple but powerful pop-rock tracks – polished productions that showed the gleam of countless studio hours. A proposed deal with a major label fell apart, so he made do with a tiny custom label.

After nearly a year of working together, all for one and one for all, the Tuesday Night musicians were shocked to learn they didn't figure into any more of Crow's plans. Bottrell got the news when he met her to hand over the finished master in a Sunset Strip coffee shop. Although there had been much talk of hitting the road together to promote the record – bassist Dan Schwartz even bought a new bass for the tour – "she essentially told me to get lost," Bottrell said.

"I add Sheryl Crow to a long list of people in Hollywood who told me they were my friend until they got what they wanted from me," Schwartz said.

As Crow's relationship with Gilbert deteriorated – apparently she turned her attentions to an executive at the record label, Baerwald said – an increasingly bitter Gilbert threw himself deeper into his own album.

"I think I'm a tinge jealous over her upcoming release," he wrote in his journal. "It's probably going to be huge so I have to prepare myself mentally for that. If she gets what she wants after behaving this way, she'll be absolutely intolerable."

For Gilbert, the final straw came when Crow sang "Leaving Las Vegas" on the David Letterman show. Afterward, when Letterman asked her if the song was autobiographical, a flustered Crow blurted out, "Yes."

"I've never been to Las Vegas," continued Crow, who nobody remembers having contributed greatly to the writing of the song. "I wrote it about Los Angeles. It's really metaphorical."

The next day, she and Gilbert exchanged angry words over the phone. He wasn't the only one furious. Author John O'Brien – who wrote the novel that inspired both Baerwald's early song lyrics and the movie starring Nicolas Cage – was still grumbling about Crow's gaffe to his literary agent on the day he blew his brains out, a scant few weeks before the movie deal was complete.

As Crow's album soared on the charts (her nod to Gilbert in the liner notes says, "I owe you big for two years of musical and emotional support. Thanks"), Gilbert's solo album, a masterful but underpromoted effort titled "Thud," disappeared almost immediately on release. At the same time, ironically, a tape he recorded for the Led Zeppelin tribute album, dropped from the disc at the last minute, exploded on Los Angeles radio, leaving his label ineptly scrambling to capitalize.

Despite its new prominence, the Tuesday Night Music Club never could quite regroup. The members did play one guest appearance with Crow at an out-of-town club, but the record company made it clear they would not be included in the more prestigious Hollywood show.

Gilbert threw himself into other projects: helping Baerwald produce a solo album by Susannah Hoffs of the Bangles, working with Bottrell on an album by Linda Perry of 4 Non Blondes (the Tuesday night gang dubbed her "the anti- Sheryl"), writing and recording scores for TV shows under a pseudonym. He even produced a movie soundtrack song for which Crow sang vocals – a version of Steve Miller's "The Joker" – although they were never in the studio at the same time.

In November 1994, Gilbert met playwright Cintra Wilson at a party in San Francisco; two months later she moved to Los Angeles to live with him. "He was massively depressed over the whole Sheryl debacle," Wilson said. "I was a basket case. We were perfect for each other."

Despite the tension with Crow, most of the Tuesday Night Music Club attended the Grammy Awards in March 1995. To show irreverence, Wilson rented

19th century funeral regalia for Gilbert and her to wear: a morning coat and top hat for him, ostrich plumes and a bustle for her. Crow sat in the row in front of them. "They were not on good terms," Wilson said. "She was tensely gracious. It was a furtive, tense, real glitzy night."

Crow picked up three awards, including Record of the Year for "All I Wanna Do," a Tuesday Night instrumental with lyrics borrowed from verses in a little-known volume by a poet in Vermont. A week later, Gilbert was still wearing his Grammy medallion around his neck like a badge of valor.

From there, he set out to recapture the creative anarchy he felt was the authentic legacy of the club. He and MacLeod produced some startling recordings, far removed from anything either of them had ever done.

They were scary, dense, pop-industrial recordings, with Gilbert whispering ominous, almost threatening processed vocals. "They gave me nightmares," Bottrell said.

Gilbert envisioned a new band, Kaviar, clad in fetish rubber gear. He pulled other musicians into the plan. At the same time, Gilbert could toss off simple, beautiful, sentimental tunes. In Baerwald's last memory of Gilbert, the pianist was noodling around on the keyboard, plaintively singing Randy Newman's "Marie." Baerwald had briefly dozed off. "I woke up crying," he said.

Bottrell, who played perhaps the largest role in Gilbert's career, doesn't think he ever really knew him. "There were tremendous areas of his life I was not privy to," he said. "There were motives I could never quite figure out."

But Bottrell's wife, Elizabeth, remembers sensing a powerful mood of peace and reconciliation in a phone conversation with Gilbert the afternoon before he died. They talked about attending an industry dinner together; Gilbert kidded her about wearing rubber. They never spoke again.

On an afternoon this summer, several hundred of Gilbert's friends and associates gathered for a memorial service at the Bottrells' Glendale home. Wilson, dressed in white, sat next to MacLeod as Crow walked up to say hello. "I barked at her," Wilson recalled. Wilson knew the titles of the album's songs well enough. "Run, baby, run," she yelped at Crow, who fled in tears.

Although Crow is reluctant to discuss Gilbert, she has been openly vocal in interviews about the rift over the album with the Tuesday Night Music Club. "There were guys in the group who were feeling bitter about the record doing so well," she recently told Billboard magazine. "Maybe I should have called it something else."

Later this month, she will release her follow-up album, titled, not insignificantly, perhaps even defiantly, "Sheryl Crow" – a two-word title that speaks volumes. Clearly, this singer wants to prove that she's an act and a talent all her own – not the smoke-and-mirrors creation of a savvy, multitalented backup band.

She did mention Gilbert to a Dutch journalist in an interview last month. "I wasn't surprised by his death," Crow told Edwin Ammerlaan of Orr Magazine. "Kevin was one of the most self-destructive people I've ever met. I don't want to go into this too much, but it wasn't a nice story."

San Francisco Chronicle | Sunday, September 15, 1996

Reborn as a Rocker

Producer Bill Bottrell finds balm for family tragedy, career troubles in playing in a band

The Stokemen will never be rewarded the band's just due as one of the great Mendocino rock and roll legends, but Bill Bottrell deserves every bit of peace he can find for himself. I first visited Bottrell at that old schoolhouse on the coast as he was just getting ready to move his family to Albion to talk to him about Kevin Gilbert. He impressed me, if only because he was one of the few interview subjects in my experience to think about his entire answer before starting to speak.

BILL BOTTRELL, WHO PRODUCED MULTIPLATINUM RECORDS for Michael Jackson and Madonna, was sick of the music business. He decided to leave Hollywood for the town of Albion on the rugged Mendocino coast. In 1997 he brought recording equipment into an old schoolhouse on a hill above the cliffs overlooking the ocean and moved in with his wife and three kids.

The day after his family settled into its new home, his 7-year-old son, William, fell off the cliff and died. Six months later, his wife of 24 years, his high school sweetheart, left him.

But Bottrell, 48, swears he is through singing sad songs. "There's almost nothing I could face that would be worse than the last three years," he said. "In a way, I'm glad to know the worst is over." Now that he's leading a rock band, which plays the Sweetwater tonight, life is looking a lot happier.

Bottrell, who discovered Sheryl Crow and produced her 1994 premiere album, the Grammy-winning "Tuesday Night Music Club," has stayed busy, even though he lives more than three hours from a major airport. Tom Petty and the Heartbreakers made the trek to have Bottrell produce a recent recording. Jewel has been with Bottrell at the studio he built in nearby Caspar, "just messing around," he said. He is working with Los Lobos. He produced last year's breakthrough album by country singer Shelby Lynne.

"I Am Shelby Lynne" earned Lynne a Grammy as best new artist, although she no longer speaks to Bottrell. "All I will say is that my wife is now her manager," said Bottrell.

The Crow project also ended bitterly for Bottrell. When he went to New Orleans to start work on the singer's follow-up, he wound up leaving within hours of landing. They did not speak again until Bottrell ran into her at the Grammys last month. "I'm not sitting here a victim," he said. "I think these women are victims of their own egos and ambition. I feel fine. I'm laughing in the face of disaster."

Lynne, in accepting her award at the Grammys, failed to mention Bottrell, even though he co-wrote the songs in addition to producing the record. Bottrell called that "a jab – a glaring omission."

"I cannot have this," he said backstage at the Great American Music Hall last month, where he made his San Francisco debut with his band, the Stokemen. "I cannot go another 10 years with some rock star dissing me that I created. Why does this happen? It's unfathomable.

"The only thing I can figure is that there is something in the process that just pisses the women off, and they hold it in until the record's done. . . . I get with these women, go deep and get into their lives, sort of channel them into songs. It's a deep, hard psychological experience for them. When it's done, they breathe a sigh of relief, and they don't want to see my face."

For Bottrell, playing well has been the best revenge. He started working nightclubs around the Mendocino and Humboldt area with the Stokemen – guitarist Roger Fritz, bassist Birdie Hanson, drummer Dana Miller and Bottrell on vocals and rhythm guitar. Playing music outside of recording studios is not something he has done since high school.

At the Music Hall last month, opening for Box Set, Bottrell led the crack unit through a happy rave-up built around brilliantly crafted rock songs such as the reggae-lilted "That Killer Weed," a rollicking "Can't Cry No More," the crunching "What Do You Want? (And for That What Would You Give?)" and the band's driving ska theme song, "Stokin' My Life Away."

There was wit and passion, a buzz running just beneath the surface. Bottrell happily hammed it up. At one point the rhythm section dropped the band into a repeating figure that tape-looped as the band members left their instruments to stand shoulder to shoulder center stage for some happy foolishness they called "dance lessons." They may have been the opening act for a half-filled house, but the Stokemen made it their party.

Bottrell said the band packs the Caspar Inn, where the Stokemen have been road-housing for a year and a half, and plays three-hour sets to sheer pandemonium among roadhouses in the redwoods.

Bottrell has recorded the band, "but nothing we've done blows my mind," he said. When he first moved to Mendocino, he spoke about trying to support himself as a local musician, without even recording his songs, but now he thinks he would like to try to take the Stokemen out for a run in the real world.

He is still the savvy professional who knows the obvious drawbacks – "I'm a 48-year-old something, certainly not what radio wants to play." But he feels obligated to the other musicians.

"They are not interested in my social experiments," he said.

Bottrell is single father to two older daughters who he says have pulled through the family's turbulent years.

"If they hadn't," he said, "I wouldn't feel right. But they have, so I feel fine. See the songs I'm writing? They're full of optimism, daylight, stokin'. It's a good life."

San Francisco Chronicle | Saturday, April 7, 2001

Sly & The Family Stone

Lucifer Rising

Hamp Banks wasn't easy to find. But when I did finally reach him, he wanted to talk. Nobody had ever asked him about Sly Stone before and he had plenty to say. He went further and arranged for me to talk with other people. A onetime pimp and ghetto hustler, he is a proud man who wields considerable authority behind an easy smile. Without him, nobody would have ever heard the true story of Sly and the Family Stone. Taken from interviews conducted for a 1997 oral history, this account of the making of "There's a Riot Goin' On" ran as a cover article for England's Mojo magazine.

THE ENGLISH TUDOR MANSION AT 783 BELAIR ROAD had been built for Jeanette MacDonald, the Hollywood screen actress who starred in all those '30s operettas with boy tenor Nelson Eddy.

Situated on two acres of terraced, landscaped gardens, the house was still on those maps of the stars' homes they sold on Hollywood Boulevard when John and Michelle Phillips of The Mamas And The Papas bought the place in 1967, two years after Jeanette MacDonald died. It was record producer Terry Melcher, Doris Day's son, who called Phillips and told him that Sly Stone might be interested in renting the Beverly Hills estate, especially since Phillips had installed a recording studio. He had the cedar-lined walk-in closet where Jeanette MacDonald kept her extensive wardrobe ripped out and built a sitting room for the recording studio. The studio itself was in the attic, reached through a secret passageway behind a bookcase on the main stairway. Behind the house a path through a grape arbour led down to a slate swimming pool and the pool house, a smaller version of the main house with a large fireplace in the living room. Melcher brought Sly over and they all stayed up all night, playing music, doing dope. He couldn't afford to buy the expensive property from Phillips but Sly did agree to rent the place for $12,000 a month while he recorded an album in the fall of 1970.

"It was havoc," said Sly And The Family Stone saxophonist Jerry Martini. "It was very gangsterish, dangerous. The vibes were very dark at the point. There was

PSA

Fly OAKLAND
It's Easier Than Ever

Sly Stone

a cloud flying over that place. There was a cloud flying over Sly from the time he moved down to Los Angeles to this day, same cloud."

The earth had cooled considerably in the 18 months since the release of the previous Sly And The Family Stone album, *Stand!*. That album made the band stars. 'Everyday People' zoomed to the top of the charts. The group all but stole the show before Woodstock's fabled half-million with the anthemic finale, 'I Want To Take You Higher'. The songs on *Stand!* drew an optimistic portrait of harmony among the races, the triumph of spirit and a whole social agenda playing to liberal sentiments in vogue at the time. Sly Stone watched with great amusement the outbreak of flower power and acid rock in San Francisco's Haight-Ashbury, while he and his band drove cherried-out Thunderbirds, dressed Mod and worked an after-hours gig for the suburban car crowd down the peninsula. He plundered the prevailing thinking, converted it into zippy slogans ("Different strokes for different folks"), and managed to perfectly capture a mood among the new young, white American rock crowd.

Little had been heard since from Sly And The Family Stone other than a couple of hit singles. 'Hot Fun In The Summertime' was a summer record that, typically enough from Sly, showed up late. Epic Records rush-released the track to radio stations in August 1969, just as summer was on the wane.

In January 1970, Sly And The Family Stone simply exploded with the chunky, cheeky 'Thank You (Faletinnme Be Mice Elf Agin)'. As fresh as a slap in the face, the single became the band's second Number 1 hit. The one-chord romp was an ominous masterpiece with plenty of attitude lurking beneath the smug chorus line. Sly And The Family Stone, annointed at Woodstock (and the subsequent concert film), were not just the hottest soul-rock band on the scene, they were redefining boundaries in pop music. A *Greatest Hits* album was pumped out and sold millions. There was a lot of interest in more records, and the only thing answering that demand from Sly's end was silence.

Sly stone's life had changed enormously since Woodstock. He moved from San Francisco to Los Angeles. He renewed some old associations and began to indulge high-living appetites. The scene he assembled at Bel Air resembled nothing so much as a twisted, deranged royal court, full of sexual intrigue, family feuds, double-dealing, backstabbing, chicanery and knavery. Sly was the unquestioned despot, drug-addled to the point of dementia.

"There was no real separation between life and drugs," said Stephani Swanigan Owens, who was trying to handle what could laughingly be referred to as the logistics of Sly's personal and professional life at the time. "Life was drugs, and it was music. They would spend so many hours collectively, 36-48 hours at the Record Plant, wearing out the engineers. But they were doing drugs, too."

Sly's creative powers had not entirely evaporated, but it took a great effort to marshall any concentration. He started showing up to concerts late or missing them entirely. The band was dissolving in rancour under his increasing control over every aspect of their lives. He was spending money like a Persian pasha. He was surrounded by thugs with guns. The police were keeping watch. Making a new album was only of incidental interest to Sly. There was already a riot going on and it was his life.

The mansion was a mess when they moved in. Stephani Swanigan, Sly's on-again, off-again girlfriend but always efficient administrative assistant, found a ouija board and, somehow that led everyone to believe the place was haunted. Moving out in a hurry, the Phillips had left behind items like their children's birth certificates, an ounce of cocaine, things that other people wouldn't have forgotten. At Sly's insistence, saxophonist Jerry Martini closed down his Mann County home, and moved down to Bel Air with his wife Lynne. Back in the rock'n'roll days, Martini played with SF duo George And Teddy, headliners on Broadway in North Beach when Sly was a young boss soul DJ on KSOL. Martini used to visit Sly at the station during his shift and smoke weed.

His wife Lynne went to work cleaning up the pool house, which was completely trashed. Martini was hopeful that the move would restore some of the bonhomie and camaraderie that had been such a big part of the group's climb to success – those long, late after-hours sessions at Winchester Cathedral in Redwood City, the grueling nights at the Pussycat A Go Go in Las Vegas, riding the subway together to work at the Electric Circus in New York.

"He talked me into literally boarding up my house in Marin County and coming down when he moved to Bel Air," said Martini. "He tried to pull it together with him and I as friends again – 'Come on down and let's do it again, let's make it like the old days.' I went for it."

Showing up late to concerts just started to sneak up on the group. At first, Sly liked to heighten the dramatic tension by keeping an audience waiting. Then it became a power trip he needed to pull – they would have him on his time, not the other way around – but soon he began to not show up at all. Yes, there were drugs involved, but nothing was quite that simple in Sly Stone's increasingly twisted world. Soon he would be philosophising about the irrelevant nature of time ("I make time," he would tell his people), and it would become a psychological battle between the audience and Sly. Getting Sly to every single concert soon became a huge struggle, a convoluted, malevolent little game that he insisted on playing over and over again.

"He was never on time," said Stephani Swanigan. "It was always an effort to get the band to the gig and get them on-stage on time. It was a whole series of things. It was mostly Freddie and Sly because even when the rest of the group would catch a commercial flight and do what they were supposed to do, with Freddie and Sly I would be trying to find a private plane for them to go on. A lot of times the group would be there, waiting, when they showed up."

Sly did show for his headline appearance at the Newport Jazz Festival that summer, but he incited a full-scale riot. With Sly singing 'You Can Make It If You Try', several hundred fans outside the concert crashed through the cyclone fence and rampaged down into the elite front row boxes. Newport police, in full mask-and-shields riot gear, responded. The city fathers decided not to allow the festival again. When Sly showed up five hours late for a concert at Washington DC's Constitution Hall, the crowd outside the oversold venue exploded into a rock-and-bottle throwing fracas, where police arrested 18 people and windows were broken for blocks in every direction. The Daughters Of The American Revolution, owners of the hall, banned subsequent rock concerts in the room.

The Chicago police shot three rioters when thousands of angry youths stormed the streets downtown after a free concert by Sly And The Family Stone had been cancelled at the last minute. Although, for once, it wasn't his fault, it was still no-show Sly who got his name in the headlines. The riot lasted more than five hours and police arrested over 150 people. It all started two hours before the band was even due to hit the stage but, by this point, Sly was known for showing up late and skipping concerts entirely. On one swing through the South in February 1971, Sly missed five concerts in a row.

It was hard to put your finger on where things began to change. Sly And The Family Stone manager David Kapralik thought it was the Fillmore East show where Sly didn't allow any individual solos. Martini thought it had been the move to Los Angeles. Other people suspected things went awry once he started smoking that nasty horse tranquilliser, PCP. Other people saw things change after Hamp 'Bubba' Banks made the scene.

"Bubba and Sly and some of their other friends came from what I call a ghetto pimp mentality, where they ran women," said Swanigan. "They had a different attitude of what a woman's role was."

Bubba Banks had turned up the previous year after finishing a jail term. Bubba always claimed he went down on a debt of honour, pleading guilty for something he didn't do to avoid suspicion that he had rolled over on a fellow desperado, but who knows? He knew Sly Stone the young San Francisco disc jockey and record producer, the former church kid from the sticks just getting his taste of big city life. Banks was a pimp who ran a hair salon at the corner of Geary and Fillmore Streets, dead centre of San Francisco's ghetto. Almost immediately on arriving in Hollywood, Banks started taking responsibility for Sly's personal and professional life and assumed a position of authority. He took Sly's sister Rose, keyboard player in the band, as his woman, and he brought in some of his friends to serve in ill-defined, vaguely sinister positions.

He was the door guard; if you wanted to speak to Sly, you first had to talk to Bubba. He was in charge of invitations. And he was also in charge of ejections. Like the king's favourite courtier, he was installed in a bedroom suite adjacent to Sly. Band members – including Sly's younger brother Freddie – were forced to seek slightly less regal accommodations in the house. "I was sitting at Sly's house in what used to be my room, but he took it away and gave it to Bubba," said Jerry Martini. "I was sitting on the floor talking about something and one of the guys – it wasn't Bubba – came up behind me and grabbed me by the hair and neck and drug me out of the room and said, 'Get the fuck out of my friend's room'"

Bubba Banks knew his role. "I was his pit bull that lived good," he said. "Whatever he was saying, it got handled, I don't care what it was. It was handled. It wasn't nobody else but me. The girls, they had to check with me. Stephani was there when I got there, but once I got there, from that point on I had not one problem. I called the shots and nobody double-checked me. Nobody had to check with Sly if I said something."

Bub handled business affairs differently than they had been run in the past. Kapralik, the band's official manager, never knew where he stood with these new faces on the scene. He was told they were on hand to help out with the concerts, and Kapralik didn't manage Sly long before he learned not to ask certain questions. Banks quickly started representing Sly in many important matters. Banks was a no-nonsense ghetto cat and he, along with his associate – another ex-con named James Brown but universally known as J.B. – brought the street right into the highest levels of showbusiness.

Sly was also growing distant from Kapralik, the elfin extrovert who didn't manage Sly so much as lead the crusade. Kapralik left his job running Epic Records to join forces with Sly after seeing the band once at the Winchester Cathedral. Sly still wore the Star of David necklace Kapralik gave him, but Kapralik was no longer sure of his position with Sly. Loretta, Sly's older sister, came down to run the Stoneflower office and she made it clear she did not approve of Kapralik.

Some members of the Black Panthers had taken Sly aside and poured poison in his ear about his honky Jew manager. Still, Kapralik dutifully moved his base of operations to Los Angeles with Sly He never questioned Sly about the guns, the drugs, the thugs. He was also developing a taste for cocaine himself.

"Cocaine is a well-known antidote to pain," Kapralik said, "and I started to do a lot of drugs. So my behaviour was hardly reassuring to anyone around me."

Sly was living at Bel Air with the beautiful, young Debbie King, daughter of the distinguished blues singer Saunders King. Her sister Kitsaun, had moved south with her sister to keep her company, but soon struck up a relationship herself with his brother Freddie. Like everybody else in the band, Freddie kept his home in Oakland but stayed at Bel Air often for weeks on end. Their mother and father, K.C. and Alpha, were often around, too. They would stay in the pool house and Alpha would cook while K.C. tried to make himself useful. K.C. had spent his life working as a custodian. The family stayed close to the church, the Church Of God In Christ, and all five Stewart kids grew up singing gospel music as the Stewart Four (sister Loretta only played piano) They even made a 78, 'On The Battlefield Of The Lord', when Sly was about 11 years old. When he landed his first big payday in the music business – writing and producing the US Top 5 hit 'C'mon And Swim' for rock'n'roller Bobby Freeman at age 19 – Sly bought his parents a huge house in a nice residential neighbourhood of San Francisco and moved into the basement apartment himself They shared in his success from day one and enjoyed the glamorous life. Like everyone else around Sly they learned well to turn a blind eye.

A small arsenal was kept in the pool house: antique firearms, briefcase rifles, everyday handguns. There were expensive cars parked everywhere – from a fully restored yellow and black '36 Cord roadster to a Winnebago, a party pad on wheels. Sly kept a pharmacy in his safe in the master bedroom. "There was a guy in LA," said Stephani Swanigan, "he was like a psychologist who lived up in the hills and we could go there and buy bottles of pills at 500 quantity a shot. Sly had a safe in his upstairs bedroom that had these pills in them. All downers. The only upper that they ever dealt with was the cocaine."

Sly doled out the lines. He sat behind a desk in the darkened library and served a line of people with their nostrils extended. When Sly went upstairs, the store was closed. There were no clocks anywhere. Sly lived on his own time – there was only right now for Sly Stone. "Sly was the controller," said Bubba Banks. "Nobody was allowed to have blow. Nobody had their own blow. He was the man."

Gun was Sly's *real* pit bull terrier and was every bit as nuts as the humans he was around. Gun would go off without warning. He had a thing about hats. He tore up singer Joe Hicks once because Hicks was wearing a hat. Sly had a baboon, but Gun killed the baboon and then fucked it. Gun used to chase his tail and Sly thought he might stop if the vet cut his tail off. Gun came home from the surgery and started chasing his butt. Sly liked to occasionally liven up recording sessions by letting Gun in and watching everybody dive for cover. There was also a pair of hostile peacocks, left over from the Phillips. They would drop off the roof onto unsuspecting visitors.

Musically, Sly was moving away from the sound he refined to near-perfection over the course of the band's first three albums. For one thing, he wasn't even recording with the band any more. His first release after the smash success of 'Thank You' wasn't even a Sly And The Family Stone record. It was a single by Little Sister, the gospel girl group his youngest sister Vaetta had belonged to for years. The three girls all went to high school together and sang in church. They had also been sweetening background choruses on Sly And The Family Stone albums from the first.

Kapralik, who had been the head of artist and repertoire at Columbia Records before signing Sly, arranged a label deal for their Stoneflower Productions with Atlantic Records. But the Little Sister records weren't like Sly And The Family Stone records. Sly had discovered one of the very first drum machines, Rhythm King, and he was using that instead of drums. He was also playing bass himself, instead of using Larry Graham. Sly produced a slowed-down version of 'Somebody's Watching You', the darkly paranoid track from *Stand!*, the production emphasising the scornful lyrics ("Sunday school don't mean you're cool..." – who was he talking to?). The overall sound was deadened, flat and dry, far from the intense, highly compressed production of *Stand!*. He produced another, even more stark Stoneflower single with Joe Hicks, 'Life And Death In G and A', a percolating collection of burps and pops over which Hicks occasionally shrieks, "If it feels good, it's all right." Hicks was a friendly guy everybody liked and he used to hang around Bel Air quite a bit, until Sly took his woman. After that, he still came around, just not as frequently. But Sly was living life like a madman in a demolition derby, careening around the track just to watch the wreckage pile up. Like *The Dick Cavett Show*.

If sly didn't make *The Dick Cavett Show*," said J.B., "he was history – that was the statement. So we did everything to get him there." It began with an uneventful concert at Cherry Hill, New Jersey. It was the first Sly And The Family Stone show produced by Ken Roberts, a showbusiness entrepreneur who worked with Frankie Valli and The Four Seasons and would later prove to be very important to Sly. But at this stage he was just a new promoter who brought gifts of portable TV sets to the band backstage that night. After the concert, however, the band had been invited to the home of Muhammad Ali. Kapralik knew Ali from back when he was Cassius Clay, He had signed Ali to a record deal at Columbia and put out some idiotic spoken-word pieces ('I Am The Greatest'), alongside a credible singing job on Ben E. King's 'Stand By Me'. But the champ was not just an admired sports figure, he was the most famous black man in the world. An invitation to his home was the sign of having arrived in black American aristocracy.

The next morning, still glowing from the experience the night before, Bubba Banks woke up in his New York hotel room to discover that Sly had flown the coop. He'd taken a plane back to Los Angeles to score some dope but was due to appear on *The Dick Cavett Show* in a few hours. With the entire band on the road, Banks didn't have many options on the West Coast so he turned for help to Bobby Womack. He sent Womack over to Bel Air to get Sly to the airport and bring him back to New York. "Sly just found every excuse to not go on that show," said Womack. "You take him downstairs and he says, 'I gotta go back upstairs.' This goes on for two hours."

At Butler Aviation in New York, Banks, realising time was tight, had a helicopter waiting to rush Sly downtown to the TV studios for the live broadcast. Sly disappeared in the bathroom and Banks couldn't find him when he first looked. "I go back into the bathroom," said Bubba, "and I look up under the toilet door and Sly has got both feet up on the commode and he's kneeling down, snorting cocaine."

Because the 'copter only had room for two passengers, Banks put Sly and Womack on board and headed downtown himself by car. He happened to look back over his shoulder as he drove off to see the helicopter circling back. He hurried back to see what was happening. The air in the front seat, it turned out, was blowing Sly's dope around, so he insisted the pilot return to the terminal so he and Womack could switch seats.

By the time Banks reached ABC-TV studios, Sly had sequestered himself in the dressing room, door locked. The band was waiting. The show was already on the air. Banks broke down the door and brought Sly down the circular staircase to the edge of the show's set, where he stood alongside the band members. Across the set, Cavett looked at Sly. Sly looked at Cavett. Cavett looked into the camera and solemnly announced, "Ladies and gentlemen, Sly And The Family Stone..."

"Bub, I got diarrhoea," whispered Sly into Banks' ear. "I gotta go." And he disappeared back up the circular staircase.

Cavett never took his eye off the camera. He vamped openly, hanging there, twisting in front of the unblinking camera and the nation's TV audience. Debbie Reynolds, his other guest, offered to sing Tammy. Cavett stuttered and spluttered, but he never took his eye off that camera.

"We'll be right back after this," he said finally, cutting to a commercial. When he returned, another entertainer was performing.

The band did finally take over the show, rampaging through a nine-minute version of 'Thank You' as if they were trying to burn the place down. Sly ambled across the set to take his place on the couch for the post-performance interview. Cavett looked as if he was sitting on an arrow. Sly stumbled over some electrical cords on his way from the stage. He fell into the chair, eyes like slits under one of Stephani's knitted caps, laughing and whooping. He held Cavett's extended hand as he continued to laugh it up. "Oh, Dick, man," he gulped between laughs. "You're the greatest." This sent him into another gale of laughter, and he continued to hold Cavett's hand as the TV host turned nearly crimson. Sly was not invited back.

The next day, the party flew from a midtown Manhattan rooftop heliport to Boston, where they were granted a police escort. Sly handed one of the policemen a violin case where he carried his drug stash. Sly laughed as the officer carried his stash into the limo. Taking this all in was J.B., someone who actually did time in jail as opposed to this grown-up church kid pretending to be bad-ass. He watched the stupid fool with a mixture of fear and disgust. "If they had just opened that, he would be so far in the jailhouse you couldn't even imagine it."

Sly was also beginning to plot secretly against members of his court. He was particularly leery of Larry Graham. Like Sly, Graham had availed himself of the laurels of stardom. He travelled with his own retinue. Alone among the other members of the group, Graham rivalled Sly onstage. He was also something of a playboy and had a way with women. When Bubba Banks first came back on the scene, Graham was conducting an affair with Sly's sister Rose. He had previously carried on with Freddie's wife Sharon for a considerable time before Sly's brother finally found out.

Graham also contributed a signature bass style. His thump-and-pluck thumb-picking style would change the way people played the instrument, a technique he developed as a teenager playing nightclubs with his mother, Del Graham. She sang like Dinah Washington, played piano like Erroll Garner and worked all over the Bay Area with her young son on bass until Sly Stone walked into one of their shows looking to put together a band. Not only did he play bass like nobody else, he could sing. His gravelly baritone added another dimension to the group's vocal sound ("I'm gonna add some bottom..."). But he was still a candy-ass mama's boy and he was beginning to get on Sly's nerves.

Sly would call sessions and Graham would fly down a day or two later. The band would not play the tracks together. Graham would show up, overdub his bass parts and leave. Now Sly started putting on the bass parts himself. It increasingly appeared as if he was trying to make Larry Graham seem superfluous. He even erased Graham's playing and put his own bass part on 'You Caught Me Smilin'.

"I would fly down if Sly wanted me to come and do my parts," said Graham, who kept his residence in Oakland, an hour's flight away "At that time he was doing a lot of tracks himself. *Riot* was recorded a totally different way than we had recorded in that I didn't play anything with the rest of the band. All of my stuff was overdubbed."

Drummer Greg Errico was getting some of the same treatment. Sly was using the drum machines and playing the drums himself. Errico was recalcitrant, growing disenchanted with all the concert cancellations and Sly's patronising attitudes. The money wasn't even that good. He would fly down to LA, sit around Bel Air for days, play on some tracks and never hear them again.

"He started using that drum machine because I wouldn't come down," said Errico. "So he started writing with the drum machine and turned it into an asset. That was 'Family Affair'. That is when he would play the bass on it, the guitar on it. For the horns, Cynthia and Jerry...days on end going in and working on the horn parts. A lot of the other stuff, he started doing himself."

But the whole Bel Air scene was so different. His horn players, Cynthia Robinson and Jerry Martini, were always around.

"I became a coke addict, drug addict, vegetable, sitting around waiting for my line like the rest of the assholes," said Martini.

Sly kept Martini under his thumb and Robinson was so in love with him, she would literally have done anything Sly asked. Freddie didn't have anything else to do with his life. Sister Rose was safely tucked away under Banks' wing. While the band certainly served an important purpose on the road, the other musicians were no longer as important to Sly in the studio as they once were. Sly began to expand his circle of musical associates.

Bobby Womack was around. This slick, R&B veteran came up with his brothers in group called The Valentinos, who were discovered, signed and produced for his own label by Sam Cooke. 'It's All Over Now' was almost a hit for The Valentinos, though it is better remembered for a version by The Rolling Stones. Womack played guitar in Cooke's band. Almost immediately after Cooke's mysterious shooting death, 20-year-old Womack was seen wearing Cooke's old suits and keeping company with his widow. They married less than three months after Cooke's funeral. Womack cut much of his 1971 breakthrough album, *Communication*, upstairs at Bel Air. He would spend endless hours through the night locked away with Sly and the other musicians, whoever they happened to be, cutting track after track. Tape boxes would just pile up. It was how Sly liked to work.

"I played on *Riot*," said Bobby Womack, "and I probably played on a lot of other things. But you come back and tapes have moved and no one has seen them but him. There was some shit that never came out. I hear myself on that. It was one of them nights that I didn't want to go home and I was just there and we just kept cutting. He'd say, 'Bobby, you gotta sing on this, gotta do this.' He was very creative into that and I was off into that whole trip. To be into that, you had to live it. There was a riot going on up at his house."

These long, chemically fuelled sessions could stretch into days. When it was done, there were musical ideas scattered throughout hours of tape and engineer Jimmy Conniff, son of MOR orchestra leader Ray Conniff, would expertly splice pieces together.

Jim Ford was another musician who spent a lot of time writing songs and recording with Sly. A large, goofy white country boy, Ford was a Southern singer cut from Tony Joe White/Joe South cloth. He was best known for 'Harlan County', a soulful pop song about growing up poor in the South that was produced by *Shindig* TV host and LA DJ Jimmy O'Neill. He wrote 'Harry Hippie' and brought it to Womack, who touched it up, put his name on the writers' credits and recorded it.

"Jimmy Ford would come around a lot," said Vernon 'Moose' Constan, the band's technical expert since the earliest days. "He was a very gifted songwriter, a white Southern Tennessee type of guy, I think he contributed. Joe Hicks too. Joe Hicks was right there, along with Jimmy Ford. Generally, it was pretty low profile. Terry Melcher would come around. That was after the Tate/La Bianca murders. Those murderers were after him. He didn't go out in public, but he did come around Sly's house."

Billy Preston was someone Sly had known for many years. When Sly was a young DJ and record producer in San Francisco, he was smitten with Ray Charles. Preston, a former child actor who played with Nat King Cole in the movie *St Louis Blues*, was the organist in Ray Charles' band. The pair became fast friends. Preston spent a lot of time in San Francisco, hanging out at the station with Sly, helping him on sessions at Autumn Records, where Sly worked as house producer and made brilliant British Invasion soundalikes with The Beau Brummels (like 'Laugh Laugh'). In those days, Sly was a burgeoning hipster in a Prince Valiant hairdo who avidly admired The Beatles, Dylan and Lord Buckley. He played piano on Preston's 1965 Capitol album, *The Wildest Organ In Town*, and co-wrote some of that record's tracks, including a piece titled 'Advice' that Sly would eventually retitle several years later when he recorded it as 'I Want To Take You Higher'.

Bel Air was a revolving door for musicians. Ike Turner hung out. Miles Davis started coming around, mostly jamming on keyboards and doing blow, not playing trumpet. It was not hard to detect traces of Sly on *Bitches Brew*, Davis's new sound at the time. Herbie Hancock was another one of the jazz greats who had to check out Sly first-hand. Hancock, who spent time upstairs at Bel Air, was also profoundly influenced by Sly's music. The key track on his 1973 landmark, *Headhunters* – still the biggest-selling jazz album in history, is not titled 'Sly' by accident.

But it wasn't just musicians. J.B. had to play tough one night when some dumb-ass pulled a gun on him somewhere comic Richard Pryor took him and Sly. Pryor loved to spend time at Bel Air; as did Redd Foxx. Errico and Sly visited Foxx in the little office behind his nightclub on La Cienaga in Hollywood. Sly passed Foxx a small vial of blow – as it happened, his entire stash at the moment. Foxx put a straw in his nose, looked up at Sly and Errico, said, "I hope y'all brought some for yourselves," and sucked the entire contents of the vial into his nasal membranes with one quick snort. "Whoa, hose nose!" said Sly.

Money problems began to surface. The deal Sly made with Phillips to rent Bel Air, in addition to the $12,000 monthly rent, called for Sly to make additional $25,000 payments into an escrow account every three months.

Sly wasn't playing many concerts – he cancelled 26 out of 80 shows in 1970. In January 1971, Kapralik took the rather unusual step of filing suit against his client to collect $250,000 in back commissions and unpaid loans. Kapralik had been advancing Sly money for years and, between the gusher of money Sly was spending and his reduced income from not playing concerts, there weren't enough funds to go around. With the prospect of having his box office proceeds attached, Sly's response to the suit was to just skip the next six concerts. He was also growing resentful over his publishing deal with Kapralik. When Kapralik first signed Sly, they formed a 50/50 partnership to publish Sly's music and Sly wanted that income back. With the success of 'Thank You' and *Greatest Hits*, Kapralik, on behalf of Sly, was able to favourably renegotiate his deal at Columbia Records and draw some more advances. But that money, too, was soon gone. Booking agent Al DeMarino was running out of concert promoters who would book the band. The pressure was on Sly to complete an album.

"My vision had disintegrated by this point," said manager Kapralik. "Sly's productivity was suffering, to put it mildly. I had no influence on what Sly was doing. I never had control. I never tried to have control. I was managing the unmanageable."

Sly had been recording all along, in between road trips. He spent days on end in the studio, doing who knows what with who knows who. Sometimes he'd book sessions at the Record Plant and move the party down the hill in the Winnebago. He would park the RV outside the studio and spend days cutting tape and partying. So many different songs were being worked on at any one time, all in different stages, it's doubtful that anyone knew what was going on. Especially Sly. Tape boxes routinely disappeared. The engineers were all on drugs, too. Nobody was immune to the madness.

Slowly an album began to take shape. Much of the material sounded autobiographical but, like his hero Dylan, Sly had long before learned how to hide in the holes. Sly grafted lyrics on top of his simmering, supple grooves, bursts of half-finished thoughts that fused with the percolating instrumental tracks. The feel was very dry, the vocals sounded as if Sly was singing over your shoulder, straight into your ear. The tracks chugged along invisible grooves that guided the careful chattering of guitars and electric keyboards. No more punchy horn builds. No big dramatic panoramas. No more sloganeering. This was stripped-down funk, raw as an exposed nerve, shadowy, mumbled, electronic voodoo.

"He'd get women he wanted to sleep with and ask if they wanted to be on his album," said Martini. "They'd lay down some terrible vocal, Sly would get the goods and then erase it. That's why *Riot* is a lo-fi record. The tape was worn out."

Sly's record company had not heard any new music from him for more than a year – a long time to wait for the follow-up to a Number 1 record. Sly was broke and needed money. He phoned Columbia president Clive Davis at his home in New York to try to convince him to have the company pay him for his home audio time. Davis may have been privately appalled by Sly's abysmal attendance record at his own concerts and concerned about the obvious drug abuse and reckless living, but the only issue he ever pressed with Sly was, When is the next record going to be ready? Davis did not want to rattle the goose that laid the golden egg. He finally suspended Sly's contract because Sly was so far behind schedule.

Kapralik was so distraught – not to mention so far gone on cocaine that he attempted suicide three times. "Exterminate my pain," he said. J.B. broke down the door to a hotel room on one attempt and carried naked Kapralik out of the room where he had swallowed a bunch of pills, rambling incoherently about how much he loved Sly. He could not get Sly to deliver the album. He could not find promoters willing to book the band. Kapralik was a desperate man when he found Ken Roberts, who decided to take on the challenge of producing Sly And the Family Stone concerts. He booked three nights at Madison Square garden in September 1971.

The band barely worked that summer (outside the Newport Jazz festival fiasco) while Sly stayed home and concentrated on finishing the new album. Also, there weren't many promoters willing to risk his appearance. The lack of work especially affected the band members who had to depend on performing for income. Nerves were frayed. Sly gave Martini and Errico hell for some imagined slight after a show in Puerto Rico. When Martini asked why he left them waiting two hours in a limousine in the hot sun, Sly snapped, "Because you're dogs." Drummer Errico was the first to quit. He had been the drummer in Sly's brother's band, Freddie And The Stone Souls, and he had been here that first afternoon in the basement apartment underneath the home on Urbana Street that Sly bought his parents. But that was a long time ago. He was quickly replaced by Jerry Gibson, a big, naive Texan and former drummer in cartoon rock band The Banana Splits. He played with marching drum mallets. He was not going to last long.

Days before the Madison Square Garden shows, Sly delivered the finished album. Kapralik swung into action. He took a couple of dozen publicity photos of the band and scrawled across them in magic marker "Two Years Is A Short Time To Wait". He posted the photographs on walls, desks, everywhere he could find around Columbia Records' offices in time for the weekly meeting of the label executives. On the morning of the first show, Sly missed six flights in Los Angeles before finally getting on board.

He arrived in New York late in the afternoon. "We're so into our new album," Sly told the capacity Garden crowd that night, "we want to play it exactly right. If you're a janitor; clean up the best you can. If you're a musician, play it the best you can."

Stephen Paley had been Sly's A&R man at Columbia since he signed with the label. He hadn't heard anything from the sessions before Sly turned in the master tape. He hadn't heard from Sly at all, in fact, for more than a year.

Paley, who was also the photographer who shot the band for the cover of *Greatest Hits*, had been the one to convince Columbia president Clive Davis to let Atlantic Records have Sly And The Family Stone for the live Woodstock album, a record that ultimately sold millions and, along with the film, was consequential in breaking Sly nationwide. Now, Paley was astonished at what he heard. He knew this was brilliant music, unlike anything anyone had ever heard before, a truly original creation. To Paley, the album's most vivid track was not a group effort. It was Billy Preston on Rhodes piano, a drum machine, sister Rose repeating the song title between cupped hands, Sly's extraordinary vocal pinballed from anger to indifference in a single breath. Called 'Family Affair'; Paley knew this would be the single that would sell the album. Sly wanted to release 'Luv N' Haight' as the first single, but Paley engaged in a mild piece of subterfuge by sending out some acetates of 'Family Affair' to radio stations and telling Sly he didn't know how it happened. The single was released in November and scorched up the charts to Number 1.

"The *Riot* album went so far away from what he was doing," said Paley. "It was almost like brinksmanship. He wanted to see how far from commercial records he could go and still be commercial."

There were very few group efforts on the album. The long, slowed down version of 'Thank You', retitled 'Thank You For Talkin' To Me Africa', was an old track and the only real group performance. It was the only place Greg Errico could hear his drumming.

Sly used drum machines on many tracks (often in combination with his own hi-hat playing). There were very few horn parts, so saxophonist Martini and trumpet player Cynthia Robinson spent hundreds of hours sitting around Bel Air waiting to be called upstairs to play. Freddie played guitar on a lot of the tracks, but so did Sly.

Larry Graham, whose thumb-plucking touch on the bass was such a distinctive feature of the band's sound, was only playing on a few tracks and he overdubbed all his parts by himself. On the other hand, Bobby Womack is all over the album, as are Jim Ford, Billy Preston, even Miles Davis – all uncredited. Many of the LP's secret contributors are pictured in the photo collage on the back cover (the flag on the front cover hung in the living room above the fireplace at Bel Air). It was a circus and Sly was the undisputed ringmaster. "He had pieces of this, pieces of that," said Martini. "He had stuff finished, then changed his mind and redid it. Did stuff in different tempos. He was in the studio every day of his life. Sometimes he would get shit done, and sometimes he wouldn't."

Group harmony vocals, a hallmark of the three previous Sly And The Family Stone albums, all but disappeared. Either Sly ganged up vocals in an indistinct mass (featuring members of the group, the three Little Sister vocalists and whoever was around at the time) or he sang solo. His vocals are scary. Recorded largely without effects, Sly sings naked fear, anxiety, anger and paranoia. He lets his voice roam free, from rumbling, belching baritone to airy, crisp falsetto, often both in the same breath. Nobody ever sang like this on records before. It was clearly the kind of recording that could not have been made without extensive experimentation in the studio, almost justifying the countless hours Sly spent noodling on guitar and otherwise goofing off at $140 an hour. There were other unfinished productions lying in tape boxes, waiting to be brushed up for future albums – a skeletal 'If You Want Me To Stay', a mumbly, incomprehensible 'Skin I'm In'. With *There's A Riot Goin' On*, Sly pushed the boundaries of soul music past the horizon. James Brown may have the title, but it was now Sly who was actually Soul Brother Number 1.

Columbia lifted the suspension and, after the phenomenal success of the three nights at Madison Square where the band broke existing box office records and grossed an astonishing sum in excess of $100,000, Ken Roberts stepped up to the plate with 30 more concert dates with more to come. The money was rolling back in. But there was still Kapralik. Sly asked Al DeMarino to invite Roberts to fly to a concert with him on a private plane. Roberts met DeMarino, Sly and his girlfriend *du jour* at LaGuardia Airport. Standing on the airstrip outside the plane, Sly came to terms with Roberts and asked DeMarino to work out a deal to buy out Kapralik. With a huge hit album, Sly was riding at the top. After another highly favourable renegotiation of his contract, the label contributed heavily toward buying out Kapralik, who went away willingly, a defeated man, a wreck who left the business and moved to Hawaii.

Sly was in total charge now. With Bubba to execute his every whim, he could run rampant. He was soon arrested in a stereo store in midtown Manhattan wearing a cowboy suit and toy gun and holster. Police came racing to Harvey's Radio on 45th Street, off 5th Avenue. "Hey, everybody, I'm from Fort Worth, Texas and I'm a cowboy," said this obviously strange individual waving a gun and wearing buckskin jacket, jeans, Afro hairdo and his silver-studded holster and gun set. Police confiscated his toy pistol. He was arrested driving down Santa Monica Boulevard in the middle of the day, partying in the Winnebago RV with his new girlfriend, her sister and a few others. Banks stuffed the stash into the chemical toilet and told the police he was Sly's brother Freddie. Freddie wasn't there.

The new girlfriend was a 19-yearold Hawaiian beauty named Kathy Silva, who had been Billy Preston's girlfriend. Sly swept her away in a part-romantic, part-kidnap scenario in which she was held prisoner at Bel Air for a couple of days after she met Sly. Nothing untoward happened to her. A large black gent, in fact, had been posted outside her quarters to ensure nothing happened to her. She had an equally striking older sister, a professional golfer, and before long they were sleeping in Sly's master bedroom like bookends.

Unresolved still was the matter of Larry Graham, but his time was coming. Graham could tell. He found himself sharing a limousine ride with J.B. through the mid-South, an hours-long caravan of six black cars streaming down the highway through the night. He kept asking J.B. what was going on in Sly's camp. "This is not getting too cool," he said. Sly was focusing increasing hostility on "that Larry Graham". The affair with brother Freddie's wife still left a bad smell in the air. Sly suspected Graham of trying to upstage him. The guy just made Sly mad.

It was thanksgiving weekend 1972. The band played a successful Madison Square Garden concert on Friday, only to have to turn around and fly across the country to play in Los Angeles the following night. The group was due to headline the KROQ 'Woodstock Of The West' at the LA Coliseum, an event expected to draw more than 100,000 fans. A private plane was hired to fly the band back to California in the middle of the night.

"I was the cat that fired Larry Graham and made him break out of Los Angeles," said Bubba Banks. Banks had an unpleasant encounter with Graham before the Madison Square Garden show. When he called Larry's hotel room to tell him the cars were waiting downstairs, Banks reached Larry's henchman and the cat gave Banks some jive that just pissed him off. He sent the cars ahead without him and went down to Graham's room himself. He gave Graham some serious intimidation, but it wasn't enough. He knew it was time for Graham to go. He decided to have him shot when the band reached Los Angeles.

"I call my man and tell him to meet me at the airport and bring your pistol," said Banks. "I had two dudes around me that if they were here, you would feel uncomfortable. I was at all the wrong places for the right reasons. So he gets there and he is ready."

Banks called his man, a large, ominous fellow people had seen around but had never asked what he did. It was easy enough to guess. The guy looked every inch like the killer thug he was. He was called, appropriately enough, Black. Banks was eagerly looking forward to setting matters straight with that punk Larry Graham after the show.

The KROQ concert couldn't have gone worse. Stevie Wonder opened and he simply wiped the stage clean. He handed Sly And The Family Stone their asses before they even set foot on-stage. Then there was the equipment. The road crew had ordered brand new equipment sent direct from the factory to the gig. These guy's knew what they were doing.

Moose had been with the band since the very early days. Robert Joyce lived with Sly at Bel Air and knew the drill. There were some brief technical problems at the onset of the performance, but nothing Moose and Joyce couldn't fix. The equipment wasn't the problem; Sly was. He was so stoned on downers, he couldn't tell if his keyboard was turned on. He was carried to the stage in a semi-comatose condition. And when he tried to operate the Farfisa organ he had never played before, it didn't seem to be working. He called Moose out over the microphone. "Moose, get out here and fix this organ," Sly told the crowd. "Here he is – this is the guy. It's all his fault this is not working."

It didn't matter that Moose switched on the organ and crept back off-stage as quickly as he did. Sly's steely gaze followed him into the darkness of the wings. The set went downhill from there. The band stumbled over the music. They didn't finish songs. The crowd booed Sly. As he walked off the stage at the end of the debacle, he caught Robert Joyce's eye and pointed his finger. "Hey, it wasn't my fault," said Joyce, but Sly just levelled an evil grimace at Joyce and moved on.

"He played and he was mumbling and he was, obviously, too fucked up to be out there," said Moose. "We packed up all the gear and it wasn't even our gear. Then we went back to the room. Larry was packing up and had his bags with the sleeves all hanging out and running out of the place. He says, 'I got word that Sly is going to come over here with some guys and force me to sign some papers.'"

Banks and Black missed Larry after the concert. He got out of there so fast that Banks was sure he'd smelled a rat. But if he could run, he couldn't hide. Banks knew he'd find Graham back at the Cavalier Hotel.

Since Sly was in Los Angeles, many of his crowd showed up at the Cavalier, where Sly and the band booked rooms – Bobby Womack, Jim Ford, Joe Hicks. Eddie Chin was there, too. Chin was a career criminal who knew Bubba Banks when they were both pimping in the Fillmore district and Eddie had all the Asian hookers. He was another ex-Marine and he could be a bad man. He liked the glamour and action around Sly and had developed a romantic interest in Sly's little sister Vaetta. They'd all recently watched *A Clockwork Orange* with considerable enthusiasm and were carrying walking sticks, prepared for a little ultraviolence. They were also all smoking PCP.

Moose, Joyce and his girlfriend were recovering from the traumatic events of the concert in their room at the Cavalier. There was a knock on their door and a half-dozen crazed black men stormed into the room. Sly walked in behind and pointed his finger at Moose, who was sitting on the edge of his bed. "Why did you stick me with those broken-down organs?" Sly demanded.

"They weren't broken," said Moose and before the last words were out of his mouth – boom. Eddie Chin kicked him in the head from behind. They were all over Moose and Joyce in a sick moment, using their karate kicks and walking sticks. Moose just lay back on the bed and took his pasting, mostly blows to the head. Joyce struggled, but all he got for his trouble was a worse beating. They grabbed his girlfriend and dragged her off with them as they left. Moose and Joyce were badly bleeding and beaten.

"I was almost knocked unconscious by the first blow," said Moose. "They probably went through their karate shit and fucked me up a little bit. Mainly to the head and I didn't have any broken ribs or anything. I was just sitting down, so I just fell back on the bed. I don't even know who it was. I never even saw the guy, he just kicked me from behind. Then they left. They took Rob's girlfriend."

They went looking for Larry Graham. Someone told Banks that Graham's henchman was down in the lobby, fixing to leave.

They got to the lobby in time to see Graham's hapless associate and, in full view of a shocked lobby, they wailed on him with their walking sticks. They beat him to the ground and kept beating on him.

"We heard a rumour that Larry Graham had got a hitman to do Sly" said Eddie Chin. "Me and Bub come outta the streets and the Marine corps. Hitman? This is getting good. We're in the lobby. We look up and here comes Larry and some dudes coming down the stairs. I got behind the stairs and they came down and we worked them. We put the street on 'em. Their mouth got them in trouble. If somebody says that they are going to do you, that's serious.

"'What did you say? Do you know what you just said?' If it was a joke...You don't joke certain things. If you say that you're going to do me, I'm going to do you first. You said that, so I believe that you meant that. That is what that was. We worked them so good. There's no getting away from us. We left some of them laying out."

In the meantime, saxophonist Pat Rizzo, who had joined the band to play alongside Martini scant weeks before, realised that Larry Graham's life was in jeopardy. He found Larry and his girlfriend, Patryce, huddled in their room and sneaked them down the back stairs into his rented Ford Falcon and off to safety. They did not look back.

A couple of weeks later, Ken Roberts flew up to the Bay Area to see if he could put the pieces back together. He met with Jerry Martini at his home and with Cynthia Robinson at her place. He went over to the Oakland Hills to talk with Larry Graham. Roberts knew there had been some sort of a fight. He thought it might be over a girl. He quickly realised that Graham was not coming back. But Roberts wasn't clear just how scared Larry was until they left his house for Graham to drive him to the airport. Before Larry got behind the wheel, he went around to the front of the car and opened the hood.

He was checking for bombs.

Mojo, August 2001

Veering Along the Edge

Vince Welnick lived the dream, playing music with the Grateful Dead, but depression dogged him to his final days

His wife hated the piece. Who can blame her? She hired a lawyer, who drew up an impressive detailed letter of complaint. When all the smoke was cleared, the only thing I had to correct was her Indian tribe name (oops). If anybody asked me, the golden age of Vince Welnick, a lovely fellow, was when he belonged to the Tubes, not the Dead.

Vince Welnick

WHEN VINCE WELNICK SIGNED ON TO PLAY KEYBOARDS for the Grateful Dead, some people said it probably saved his life. He had five good years with the band, five fat years. But then Jerry Garcia died and the Dead was no more. Welnick spent the next 11 years dreaming that the band would reunite, with him, once again, at the keyboards.

That dream died on the cloudless morning of June 2, when the 55-year-old musician stood on a hillside behind his Forestville home and drew a knife across his throat in front of his wife.

Welnick's suicide caught many of his more casual friends by surprise. A fixture in the Bay Area music scene for nearly 40 years and known to thousands of fans of the Dead – and in the '70s, the Tubes – Welnick was always an upbeat kind of guy, with twinkly eyes and a lopsided smile. But his cheery exterior was deceptive. Those who knew him better recognized that even during the last years of the Grateful Dead's long strange trip, Vince Welnick was veering along the edge and battling demons that would eventually alienate many musical colleagues.

In the weeks before his death, several old friends who hadn't heard from him in a while were surprised by phone calls from a cheery, optimistic Welnick, talking about plans for the future. On June 1, the day before he killed himself, he called pianist George Michalski, who invited Welnick to join him at his weekly restaurant job in San Francisco that weekend. The two had debuted their four-handed piano act in February at Mardi Gras in New Orleans and had just received an invitation to return next year.

"He was all excited about it," Michalski said. "And he told me he was going to come by the restaurant and jam Saturday night."

But Michalski had also seen Welnick's dark side and knew he was a troubled soul, especially in recent years as he struggled with deep depression over the demise of the Dead.

Michalski said Welnick talked about committing suicide in February when they flew to New Orleans. "He told me he was going to kill himself," Michalski said. "That's all we talked about all the way to New Orleans. He had no qualms about it."

Grateful Dead computer programmer Bob Bralove, one of Welnick's closest friends, traveled the country playing improvisations with Welnick and another former Dead keyboardist, Tom Constanten. They appeared together last month in Las Vegas.

"He was very, very depressed," said Bralove, "even though he was headed for a gig, which usually cheered him up. We were talking. He said he couldn't stop the bad feelings. He was looking for some way this would change. I guess it didn't. He had hoped to pull something off."

After an earlier suicide attempt about 10 years ago, Welnick started taking antidepressants, but lately, he had been telling friends the pills didn't seem to be working anymore. When he died, according to friends, he was trying to wean himself from the old medication and begin a new drug regimen.

Nobody knows whether there was a direct link between his suicide and the change in his medication, but two years ago the Food and Drug Administration asked antidepressant manufacturers to add a warning on pill bottles about potential suicide risk during changes in dosage.

Welnick was not in the best health anyway. Just before the start of the Dead's final summer tour in 1995, he was diagnosed with throat cancer and emphysema. He beat the cancer, but the respiratory disease left him increasingly weak and often out of breath, although he continued to smoke cigarettes and pot. He carried inhalers with him wherever he went. "He was on the spray can all day long," said one associate.

Welnick was born and raised in Phoenix, Ariz., where the scene in the late '60s was so small, everybody knew each other from hanging out at the VIP Room, the town's sole rock club. Welnick moved to Los Angeles to make it in music, but wound up paying his rent selling office supplies over the phone. Guitarist Bill Spooner brought him back to Phoenix and formed a group called the Beans. Relocating to San Francisco in 1970, the Beans merged with another band of Phoenix refugees and renamed themselves the Tubes.

The Tubes would become one of the few authentic San Francisco rock phenomena of the '70s. Although the band never earned similar acceptance outside of town, the Tubes could draw capacity crowds at Bimbo's 365 Club for weeks-long runs. Known for outrageous staging, tungsten-hard progressive rock and elaborate set pieces for songs such as "Mondo Bondage," "White Punks on Dope" and "What Do You Want From Life?," the Tubes drew deeply from the decadent San Francisco demimonde of the day. But they were never hippies. Welnick was regarded by his bandmates as a highly skilled musician, the most musically trained of the group, and a relaxed, agreeable colleague. He dressed neatly, often wearing satin shirts and even ironed his T-shirts.

"I can see him sitting around in those wraparound shades, that orange suit, a joint hanging out of his lips," said Tubes vocalist Fee Waybill.

The Tubes recorded eight albums and finally scored a Top Ten hit with "She's a Beauty" in 1983. By that time, however, the group had been reduced to a laboratory for experiments by Hollywood session musicians and producers such as David Foster and Steve Lukather. Todd Rundgren, who produced "Love Bomb," the final Tubes album, took drummer Prairie Prince and keyboardist Welnick for his own band when the Tubes broke up in 1985. Welnick toured with Rundgren's band and can be heard on two Rundgren albums, "Nearly Human" and "Second Wind."

When Welnick auditioned for the Dead in 1990, he was sleeping in a barn, separated from his wife, their home rented out, and planning to move to Mexico and homestead. The Dead, in the band's singularly dysfunctional manner, tried out just four or five candidates for the job vacated by Brent Mydland, who died of a drug overdose. Only a handful of keyboard players who lived nearby were called in for the million-dollar post. All the auditions were held in a single day at the Dead's San Rafael rehearsal hall.

"I remember Vince sitting waiting his turn when I got out," said Pete Sears, then fresh off the Starship. "I think the decision had already been made."

Welnick's keyboard skills did not win him the job with the Dead, though; it was his ability to hit the high harmonies on vocals.

"We had no stomach for the amount of work it would have taken to find the right guy," said Dead guitarist Bob Weir. "We took the guy who could sing high and had pretty decent chops. That was good enough."

Bruce Hornsby, a longtime Dead fan who stepped in at piano on an interim basis, put his own thriving solo career on hold for a year to stay with the band while Welnick found his footing. The famously egalitarian band offered Welnick almost full participation in the concert revenues, merchandise and other partnership holdings, rather than simply taking him on as a sideman. At the time, the Dead was the most popular rock group in the country, pulling down more than $50 million a year at the box office. His earnings soared. He started wearing tie-dye. He bought a Mexican vacation home.

He met his future wife on a photo shoot for Rolling Stone magazine in the mid-'70s in Los Angeles. During their first date at the '70s San Francisco fern bar Henry Africa's, the stunning half-[Native American] model and Welnick decided to spend their lives together. Theirs would be a turbulent relationship. Guests at the Mexican vacation home overheard all-night battles. The Tubes once put the couple out of the tour bus on a Texas freeway because they wouldn't stop fighting. People in the Dead crew remember Lori Welnick as a terrified flier. "She was a real contentious person," said Tubes guitarist Spooner.

"They saw themselves as this epic romance," said Michael Cotton of the Tubes, who interviewed the couple last year for a planned Tubes documentary.

Lori Welnick declined to make a statement about her husband's death, although she did say one thing for the record. "You say one foul thing about me," she said, "and you'll regret it the rest of your life. I have been nothing but good to the only man I ever loved. And you can put that in the newspaper."

Only days before departing for the final 1995 Grateful Dead tour, Welnick received a double diagnosis from his doctor. He needed an operation for throat cancer that could possibly affect his singing voice, and he had emphysema. He postponed the surgery until after the tour. When Garcia died Aug. 9, shortly after the band returned home, and the band members announced that they would no longer continue to perform as the Grateful Dead, Welnick felt his world collapse and he sank into depression.

That December, on the RatDog tour bus before a show in Santa Barbara, Welnick spilled out the contents of a Valium bottle and counted 57 pills. He took them all, climbed in his bunk and waited to die. The tour manager accompanied him to the hospital, while the rest of the band played the show. After he recovered, Welnick sought psychiatric treatment and began taking antidepressants. He never played with RatDog again.

The Grateful Dead has always been very much a man's world with a strict code of behavior, carefully developed over the many years of the band's history. Many insiders privately found Welnick's dramatic grieving out of proportion for someone who had belonged to the band as briefly and late in the day (Mydland, his predecessor, was still known as "the new guy" 11 years after he joined the band). The other four members had been with the Dead since the beginning, more than 30 years before. Welnick was the last "new man," the sixth player to the keyboard slot.

He bombarded the Dead's office with phone calls, proposals to put the band back together, always with himself on keyboards. He wrote new songs to already published lyrics he found in the book by Dead lyricist Robert Hunter. He reserved special anger for Dead drummer Bill Kreutzmann, who moved to Hawaii right after Garcia's death, effectively removing himself from the scene and barring any reunion efforts, in Welnick's mind. Tubes drummer Prairie Prince found him depressed and miserable in early 1996.

"He was moping around," Prince said. "I took it on myself to bring him around."

Prince and Welnick went into Cotati's Prairie Sun Studios to work on one of Welnick's new original songs, "True Blue," about friends who stayed the course and others left behind. The sessions evolved into the Missing Man Formation, a band that featured Dead acolytes Steve Kimock on guitar and Bobby Vega on bass. The band made its debut in July 1996 at the Fillmore Auditorium before a packed house of Deadheads. Before long, Kimock and Vega were gone and Prince and Welnick, friends since Phoenix, had a falling out. All were replaced by a new set of musicians.

"We lost touch with each other," Prince admitted. "It wasn't a really pretty scene when we broke up. I distanced myself a little bit from Vince and Lori."

Welnick was frustrated at every turn. He could not use the band's rehearsal hall for his group. He was not allowed to borrow equipment from the Dead when he went into the studio to record some demos in April 2000. He did play a summer 2000 tour with the Mickey Hart Band on the condition that his wife stay home. "He never went crazy on my watch," Hart said.

But an announced reunion of all four remaining original members of the

Dead at a two-day rock festival in Alpine Village, Mich., in August 2002 sent Welnick overboard. He fixated on certain phrases – "Grateful Dead family reunion" and "surviving members of the Dead" – wondering how he could have been excluded, according to his friend Mike Lawson. Welnick went to the festival, Lawson said, played the night before at a local Thai restaurant and performed a campground show the night of the event, hoping there would be a last-minute call that never came.

The members of the Dead were uncomfortable with Welnick and his obsessive behavior. There were certain kinds of craziness the Dead circles would not tolerate. "It was getting bigger and bigger," Weir said. "We could all feel that and we chickened out. Yes, we did. We all had lives to lead and we all had bands to play with.

"I'm sorry," he continued. "I'm sorry for Vince. But stuff doesn't always work out the way people want. And he became more and more difficult to work with as his disease progressed."

Welnick was reduced to playing as special guest with Dead cover bands such as Gent Treadly, Jack Straw or Cubensis, performing for small crowds at holes-in-the-wall where he was sometimes paid with bad checks. "He hated it," Lawson said. "He was miserable because it was embarrassing."

He attended the annual board of governors' awards dinner of the local National Association of Recording Arts & Sciences chapter last year, at the insistence of friends. Hart was there as well. "Should I go over to him?" he said to his booking agent, Linda Yelnick, who watched as Welnick walked across the room, shook hands with his former bandmate and returned.

"It probably lasted all of 10 seconds," she said. "I felt bad. I tried."

When members of the Dead and their extended family gathered to celebrate the 10th anniversary of Garcia's death in September at UC Berkeley's Greek Theatre, Welnick again found himself excluded. "If he came out onstage to play," said Weir, who served as music director for the event, "I don't know how we would have got him off. He was unstable."

The Dead bought out his interest in the band and he reclaimed what little music he wrote with the band from its publishing company. He and his wife lived on a 10-acre parcel of land with a small three-bedroom home worth less than a million dollars, according to Web sources, in Sonoma County. He kept a prized Bösendorfer grand piano in his music studio and a couple dozen cats wandered the place. The couple's home was covered with memorabilia from his days with the

Dead, but contained little or nothing from his much longer stint with the Tubes.

The Tubes, in fact, had been planning a full-scale reunion and Welnick was enthusiastic about it, according to his former bandmates. He played in the band's impromptu Santa Cruz reunion last year.

But getting back together with the Tubes wasn't enough. He still brooded over the fate of the Grateful Dead. He was convinced that his suicide attempt on the RatDog bus was the only thing that kept his former bandmates from bringing him back. The phone calls to band management began again. As recently as a week before he died, he posted a note on his Web site about his continued hopes for a reunion, saying he had discussed the issue with band management.

"Here and now," Welnick wrote, "I want to appeal to the other members of GD to come together for such a worthy cause. Hope you all will pass the message onto the rest of the guys. More then ever, the world needs love and the Gratefuldead!"

According to friends and band insiders who spoke with family members, Welnick woke the morning of June 2 and told his father-in-law, who was staying at the house, that he had slept well. A little later, when his wife found a prohibited bottle of liquor, she went looking for him. She spotted him in the backyard climbing the hill and called his name. He turned and cut his throat. His shirt turned red, she told friends. She tried to stop the bleeding, but he told her to let him go. He also reportedly resisted recovery efforts by his sister-in-law, who was also staying at the house.

An ambulance was summoned at 9:30 a.m. by the Sonoma County sheriff's dispatcher. Welnick was still alive when it arrived. An hour later, he was pronounced dead at the emergency room of Santa Rosa Memorial Hospital, according to the Sonoma County coroner's office.

Friends say Lori Welnick initially directed her rage at the Grateful Dead. Weir brought his family to visit. "When I was with her, it was different," he said. "Someone in that state of grief can be reaching for reasons that may or may not exist. She was in that kind of pain."

Weir spoke about Welnick with the shell-shocked tone of someone still trying to make sense of something that ultimately will never add up.

"I wish I could have helped," Weir said. "I tried, but I failed. The people closest to him wish they tried, but they failed. He tried himself and failed. That's the story and it's a sad one."

San Francisco Chronicle | Friday, June 30, 2006

CHAPTER 3

Fillmore Sunset

Jefferson Airplane

Spencer Dryden

Bill Graham

Long Strange Trip

Texans in San Francisco

Still a Bumpy Ride

Jefferson Airplane members not overjoyed about induction into Rock Hall of Fame

When I saw that the Hall was going to induct the Airplane, I called one of our mutual associates and raved. "I want to be there for the first rehearsal, I want to be there for the first dinner," I said. "I want to be there for the first fight." "Oh, you've already missed that," she said.

NEW YORK – JOEL GALLEN, PRODUCER OF THE ROCK AND ROLL HALL of Fame induction ceremony, had a brilliant idea for the Jefferson Airplane. Or so he thought.

On the eve of the 1996 induction gala last month, star vocalist Grace Slick was missing in action, and Gallen moved to close that gap. He called the band members together, those he could locate anyway, and floated a suggestion.

How about asking Joan Osborne, a newcomer with a hit record, to sing "Somebody To Love" with the group?

Gallen obviously thought he was talking to show business professionals, troupers or something. Wrong. He was talking to the Jefferson Airplane.

"I think I speak for the rest of band," guitarist Paul Kantner piped up, "when I say that we are disinclined to replace Grace. So I say 60 percent no and 40 percent . . . no."

But when Airplane manager Bill Thompson posed the idea a few minutes later to vocalist Marty Balin, a completely different take on Osborne emerged.

"She's kinda hot right now," Balin said. "Maybe we should do her songs."

Eventually the hapless producer got a reluctant go-ahead to explore the idea with Osborne.

The Jefferson Airplane, the band that launched the San Francisco rock scene, never specialized in cooperation. A fractious, contentious group of strong personalities, the band nonetheless ruled over the Summer of Love. As "White Rabbit" and "Somebody To Love" poured out of radios across the country, the band headlined the Monterey Pop Festival, appeared on the cover of Life magazine and ushered in a new era of rock around the world.

Jefferson Airplane

They were a difficult lot who did things their own way and fought with each other as much as they battled record companies, managers and concert promoters.

Last week, everyone from the most famous edition of the group, except Slick, gathered in New York to be inducted into the Rock and Roll Hall of Fame. The trip to New York was a reunion of sorts. With residences across the country – only Kantner still lives in San Francisco – and engaged in separate endeavors, these veterans of Woodstock and Altamont rarely see each other anymore.

"Why would we?" said lead guitarist Jorma Kaukonen, gold tooth glinting in his smile. The band members may have been nonchalant about the event, but Thompson had been campaigning behind the scenes for them for several years, practically hounding his old friend Jann Wenner, publisher of Rolling Stone magazine and vice-chairman of the Hall. But there was considerable resistance from the nominating committee.

"Now we come to an interesting time," said one member, "when we get to groups that were popular but not very good."

Today, the special gifts of the Jefferson Airplane are not well remembered, the band's luster tarnished by the Kantner/Slick-led Jefferson Starship, which produced a string of witless middle-of-the- road '70s radio hits such as "Jane," "Find Your Way Back" and "We Built This City."

The Jefferson Airplane's illustrious chapter in rock history sputtered to a close following the departure of founder Marty Balin, who left during a Winterland engagement in October 1970, the night after Janis Joplin died. A 1989 Airplane reunion album and tour was a debacle. A big-time Hollywood management firm handled the fiasco and Hollywood session musicians added the psychedelic overdubs, leaving the brilliant Kaukonen to play straightforward solos on the unsuccessful record.

"It was a wasted five months that cost me $70,000," Kaukonen said.

A boxed-set retrospective, "Jefferson Airplane Loves You," sold a modest 50,000 copies on release three years ago. The Hall of Fame nominating committee didn't even get around to adding the band's name to the ballot until last year, three years after the Airplane first qualified, and it took a second year of voting before the Airplane was admitted to the Hall.

That didn't mean everything would suddenly become easy. Just getting the members to attend the event in New York proved to be almost impossible. At one point bassist Jack Casady told Kaukonen on the phone he thought that it would only be the two of them on that podium accepting the award.

"You wish," said Kaukonen.

Slick, whose soaring voice guided Airplane hits such as "White Rabbit" and "Somebody To Love," never made the trip. Stricken by a medical condition that left her with swollen feet and an infected eye, Slick, 56, decided there was no way she would appear on the stage of the Waldorf- Astoria barefoot and without makeup. Kantner grumbled about his hotel accommodations, but that was nothing new. Old road managers used to routinely present Kantner with five room keys so the finicky traveler could take his pick. He caved in and came, but not before Thompson called the Waldorf and warned hotel management that Kantner could be more difficult than the Sultan of Brunei.

As for Balin, he still has a home in Mill Valley but spends most of his time in Florida, where he lives with his wife, Karen, and their 1-year-old daughter. Balin plays in Kantner's current edition of the Jefferson Starship, along with fellow Airplane alumnus Casady.

Drummer Spencer Dryden, who had not played with the other members in more than 25 years and hasn't touched the drums in more than a year, posed another concern. The Airplane resolved that by bringing along Prairie Prince, the talented drummer who plays in Kantner's current version of the Jefferson Starship. The Airplane ended up using both drummers.

Kaukonen, by contrast, remains a very active musician, touring incessantly. He still plays in Hot Tuna with his childhood friend Casady, he fronts a rock band called Land of Heroes, and he does solo acoustic performances. Paul Simon recently used Kaukonen on some demo sessions for a Broadway musical Simon is developing.

Casady, too, keeps a busy schedule, not only playing with Kaukonen in Hot Tuna but touring with Kantner and Balin in the ongoing edition of the Starship.

Finally, these old colleagues, whose destinies in and out of the Airplane have been bound for more than 30 years, arrived in New York two days before the ceremonies, along with wives, girlfriends and a handful of old friends. But not before ex-member Joey Covington raised a stink when he discovered he would be excluded. Covington, the band's fourth drummer, who played with the Airplane during its final year and a half, besieged the Hall of Fame office with phone calls and finally took his case to the public, trumpeting to the New York press that he intended to sue the Hall over "historical inaccuracies."

The day before the ceremony, band members showed up at the Grand Ballroom of the Waldorf-Astoria to rehearse their brief performance at the induction ceremony. The musicians discovered Slick would not be attending only when she didn't make her flight, and they hadn't even begun to figure out what they will do without her.

"It's only a couple of songs – it shouldn't be too hard," Casady said. "Of course, Kantner's not here yet." Balin was wandering around the ballroom with a video camera in hand, filming everything in sight. He had spent the morning shopping for clothes in the Upper East Side and looked like a tourist. Although he appeared to be enjoying his trip to New York, the fact that he was being recognized for past accomplishments was lost on him.

"It doesn't mean much to me," he said. "I'm still trying to get people to listen to my new songs."

That night, there was an expensive dinner with top executives from the Airplane's old label, RCA Victor, but no wives were allowed – corporate generosity extends only so far. The day of the induction, band members were left to their own devices.

Kantner and his 14-year-old son, Alexander, went record shopping in Greenwich Village, where Kantner picked up a few bootleg Jefferson Airplane tapes and Alexander bought a huge pile of foreign Metallica rarities.

That night, Kantner nibbled a room service meal in his suite before the awards dinner.

"I don't take this seriously," he said before the ceremony. But he wasn't dissing it, either. "It's not mockable. Free food. Free drinks. What's wrong with that?"

Glad-handers in formal wear crowded the cocktail party that preceded the show. Kantner sought out Harold Leventhal, lifelong manager of his idol, Pete Seeger, who would be accepting an award that night. Kaukonen, in a suit he bought especially for the occasion, admitted that he had never attended any previous industry function. No Grammys. No nothing. Tonight's event would be his first and most likely his last.

All of the band members seemed more puzzled than intimidated by sharing a program with Stevie Wonder, the Velvet Underground and Pink Floyd in front of a roomful of industry fat cats. Kantner did manage to lose his floppy felt hat before going onstage and rushed around looking under tables fruitlessly, which added a small element of panic to the proceedings. Backstage, producers insisted the band play only two songs. No problem, they were told.

Sure. The Airplane played three songs, "Crown Of Creation," followed by Kaukonen's incandescent instrumental, "Embryonic Journey." Flanked by shelves of lava lamps stacked toward the ceiling, a psychedelic light show pulsing on the wall behind them, Balin exploded all over a rousing "Volunteers," punctuating his vocals with raised fist. By the end, the band owned the room, and gets the only standing ovation of the night.

Old friends Mickey Hart and Phil Lesh of the Grateful Dead presented the Airplane's awards, but Kantner dismissed Hart's description of the band as "the best in the world on many a night."

"People didn't come to the Fillmore to see the bands," Kantner said. "We were just some of the louder people on the scene. Grace always said she liked being in the band because it was the least crowded place at the party."

Afterward, they bantered with the press backstage. But even this togetherness was short-lived. Balin headed back to his hotel room while Casady, Kaukonen and Kantner gleefully joined the gala jam session led by Arlo Guthrie and Pete Seeger.

As the septuagenarian folksinger plucked away at a banjo, an assembled chorus including Stevie Wonder, David Byrne and David Gilmour of Pink Floyd sang "Goodnight Irene." Spencer Dryden and his 18-year-old son Jackson watched from the Airplane's table.

As for Joan Osborne, she sang "Signed, Sealed, Delivered" with Wonder.

The next morning, Dryden called Thompson to find out about transportation to the airport. Turns out the Hall of Fame picks up band members on their way into New York, but makes no arrangements for their departures.

"That's the way it is," Dryden told his former manager. "You come in by limousine and go out by bus."

Sunday Datebook | Sunday, February 11, 1996

Former Airplane drummer struggles with hard times

Hard times were not over for Spencer Dryden.
He died less than a year later from cancer.

SPENCER DRYDEN DIDN'T FEEL THE HEAT, but he heard what he thought sounded like kids shooting BBs at the house. Cooking a late lunch in his kitchen in September, he turned and looked down the hallway of his Petaluma home and saw the fire.

"The bedroom door from floor to ceiling was solid orange," he said. "I knew this was no wastebasket fire. This sucker was going up. That was it."

The BBs he thought he heard turned out to be his ammunition going off. Wrapped in a blanket on the tilted kitchen floor of the funky Sonoma County cottage where he now lives are the remains of two charred, cherished rifles, the barrels clotted and scorched, the stocks all but burned off.

"God knows what can be done with those," he said. "I imagine they're a total waste."

The onetime drummer for the Jefferson Airplane lost virtually everything he owned – his gold albums, his Rock and Roll Hall of Fame award, all the posters he saved, his extensive photo and film archive including all the Super 8 home movies he took during the early days of the Airplane, his audio and video equipment, five computers, and all kinds of one-of-a-kind items like the huge painting done by Airplane vocalist Marty Balin that was a gift to Dryden from the band's original drummer, the late Skip Spence, or the Jefferson Airplane metal sculpture that used to hang above the entrance to the Fillmore Auditorium. There was no insurance. The Red Cross found him a hotel room.

"I'm not one of those boo-hoo kinds of people," said Dryden. "But you do realize, when all is said and done and you're sitting in a hotel room with nothing to do, you realize, well, I don't have much anymore."

Dryden, 66, also is dealing with some serious health problems. He underwent one hip replacement surgery and is awaiting a second. He hobbles around slowly with the aid of a cane. Hearing loss has left him nearly deaf. Doctors recently put Dryden in the hospital for heart trouble (a valve was discovered to be pumping backward) and he needs to have an operation for that, too. "The heart surgery is what scares me," he said.

He gets by on Social Security, disability payments and an occasional feeble royalty check. He hasn't really worked since he officially retired in 1995, although, truth be told, he wasn't working that much before then either.

"I'm gone," he said. "I'm out of it. I've left the building."

His friends have organized a benefit for Dryden on Saturday at Slim's. They're calling it a Barn Raiser, and it will include Bob Weir of the Grateful Dead; Warren Haynes of Gov't Mule, appearing with the Flying Other Brothers; Nick Gravenites

Spencer Dryden

and Friends; and David Nelson and Friends (Nelson used to play with Dryden in the New Riders of the Purple Sage after the drummer left the Airplane in 1970). A number of other associates – including his bandmates from the Airplane – have donated material for an EBay auction.

Dryden was playing rim shots behind comics and strippers at the Pink Pussycat on the Sunset Strip in 1966 when he received a call from the Jefferson Airplane's manager inviting him to audition. He joined the band in time to back the group's new vocalist, Grace Slick, on the Airplane's second album, "Surrealistic Pillow," which produced two Top 10 hits – "White Rabbit" and "Somebody to Love" – that vaulted the Airplane into the front ranks of the new rock bands of the day. The bolero beat he played underneath "White Rabbit" was novel for rock music. As a member of the Airplane, Dryden played the Monterey Pop Festival, Woodstock and Altamont, where he dropped LSD, got lost looking for the band after performing and ended up hitching a ride home from some concertgoers.

Sitting at his kitchen table covered with notepads, laptop and cell phones, he freshened his cranberry juice from a pint of vodka in the freezer without rising from his chair, and lit another cigarette. His eyes brimmed with tears as he talked about the benefit.

"I'm trying to think of what I'm going to say. I'll probably just be my sarcastic self. The last thing I want to do is turn all sentimental. But I've got to steel myself. I mean, my ex is coming out from Texas. Warren Haynes, Harvey Mandel and Bobby Weir – I haven't talked to Bobby in 15 years – I'm just blown away."

San Francisco Chronicle | *Thursday, May 20, 2004*

20 Years of Rock

Bill Graham recalls two decades of rock

I showed up for the interview and Bill answered the door. We stood at the doorway for five minutes exchanging pleasantries before I got tired of waiting for him to invite me inside. He was a little low on social skills.

BILL GRAHAM RUBBED HIS EYES AND CHOKED BACK TEARS. He had flown halfway around the world and driven straight to the charred hulk of his South of Market office to view the carnage first-hand. Emerging from walking through the ashes and rubble that had been his office, he looked beaten, shaken and lost.

He had been in Europe last May when he checked with his answering service and got the news that a firebomb had gutted his headquarters and destroyed a great deal of his lifetime collection of personal memorabilia. But how could a few old letters and photos have such a devastating impact on such a strong personality?

"I don't write," said Graham. "I don't paint. I don't sing. I don't perform. I finally thought one day about why I felt so angry. That was our gallery. That was our statement. That was our company's work, our art."

For the past two decades, Graham has ruled the rock concert world from his San Francisco headquarters, beginning with a benefit for the San Francisco Mime Troupe 20 years ago this week. He built the Fillmore Auditorium into the premiere showplace of rock's history, presenting the best bands of the '60s.

In those early days, Graham liked to book jazz, soul and blues greats alongside the rock groups and some of those double-billings were once-in-a-lifetime pairings; Lenny Bruce and the Mothers of Invention, the Who and Woody Herman and His Thundering Herd, the Byrds and B.B. King.

He moved operations to the Fillmore West at the corner of Market and Van Ness and opened a New York branch, the Fillmore East. But Graham closed Fillmore East in June 1971 and Fillmore West less than a month later to concentrate on throwing shows on a less regular basis in the Bay Area only.

But wherever there has been a challenge, he has picked up the gauntlet. He led nationwide tours by former Beatle George Harrison, Bob Dylan, the Rolling

Stones. He produced the giant SNACK benefit to raise money for S.F. school athletic programs, featuring Dylan and Marlon Brando among others. He produced the first US Festival, last year's ARMS tour and last summer, trekked across Europe with Dylan and Santana.

In addition to presenting concerts, Graham has maintained a long and successful management relationship with Santana. His firm also handles Eddie Money and other more recently signed acts such as the Neville Brothers and a new band from Sacramento, Bourgeois Tagg. The firm he founded to sell rock 'n' roll T-shirts, Winterland Productions, turned into one of his biggest money-makers and he sold half-interest in the company last year to CBS Inc.

But, despite a career none can match in the rock field, Graham said he looks at life differently these days, chiefly because of the blaze that swept his office.

Two months after the fire, Graham presided over the daylong Live Aid concert in Philadelphia, certainly the crowning achievement of his career. But it was not the old Bill Graham, tense and imperial. Instead, he was practically euphoric, his moods ranging from good to better. No temper tantrums. No yelling matches. Bill Graham, 54, celebrates 20 years in show business this week. In his mid-30s, after a meandering professional course, he held a comfortable job as an office manager. At that point, he made an uncertain, risky career gamble, and it paid off handsomely. He is rich and famous. But these days Graham is more concerned with his struggle for happiness.

THE impresario lives on the top of a mountain above Mill Valley on an estate built by the late flamboyant attorney Jake Ehrlich. Graham calls it Masada. At night, the road beyond the electronic wrought-iron gates passes a giant floodlit skull and giant globe, both props from old New Year's Eve shows by the Grateful Dead, Graham's favorite band. The handsome hilltop bachelor mansion with its marble floors and beamed ceilings has been transformed into a museum, even more than his old office: Janis Joplin's tambourine on one wall, Keith Richards' boots in the crowded trophy case, the wreaths Graham has worn each year portraying Father Time at New Year's Eve shows, the barrel he used to hand out free apples from at the old Fillmore Auditorium. Huge scrapbooks sit piled up on his dining room table, saved from the fire because they were stored elsewhere.

The house does not have the stray, offhand lived-in touches found in most people's homes. Two unattended fires sputter out in different rooms. Somebody else apparently set them since Graham never so much as stirs the ashes. A note on his spotless kitchen counter from his major domo, gone home for the night, tells

Graham his supper is in the oven. He seems like a weary prince alone in his castle.

Tonight Graham is in a reflective mood. Something is gnawing at him and the occasion of an interview, looking back at his 20-year career, becomes an opportunity to delve delicately into wounds just beginning to heal. Tonight he will not engage in his typical charming, nostalgic banter, so informed by his colorful character and jocular skills as a raconteur. Tonight Graham is serious, searching and sober.

He leaned back into a sofa and considered the significance of his 20th anniversary in rock, starting a slow, rambling dialogue.

Bill Graham

"The meaning has been affected," he began, "by this year, which has been the hardest year, by far. I think I feel different because I'm not more than a year older than last year, but I'm much older in having experienced the fire. The fire had an awesome effect on me in that, for months afterwards, it was hard for me to explain. I couldn't find the words to express what the loss meant to me.

"We put so much value in our society on material things. I do, too. Nice car. Nice home. They were things I had saved over the years, letters and photos.

"I always felt like I did the reverse. Most of the things that were particularly meaningful to me, I didn't keep in a vault. It was there for you to see. The fact that someone just hit it like a gnat . . ." He shook his head, his voice trailed off. "What is it to that person?

"Whatever their reason was - not to accuse - but it's hard to believe that one day after Bitburg would be the one day some rock 'n' roller decided to get even."

President Reagan's visit to the Nazi cemetery in West Germany had particular meaning for Graham. Born Wolfgang Grajonca in Berlin on January 8, 1931, Graham came to the United States as a refugee orphan at the age of 10, he and his family victims of the Third Reich. His mother and a sister died in concentration camps. "My childhood didn't happen," he said crisply. As a private in the U.S. Army, he fought in Korea, winning a Bronze Star for bravery and a Purple Heart for wounds. Nobody ever said Graham backed down from a fight, and it was in character for him to lead a public denunciation of Reagan's visit to the Nazi cemetery. The day after Reagan laid wreaths on the graves of former enemies, someone threw a firebomb through Graham's office window in the dark of the morning hours.

Now the old warrior seemed tired of doing battle. "Over the years, it's gotten to the point where, if I expect more from others, they expect more from me," he said. "I don't know if it's come from work or age, but it has to do with wanting to be a gladiator less. I don't think the word is wisdom. It comes somewhere between wisdom and aging. What I do know is as time goes by, you control your emotions better, then common sense will emerge victorious."

The two-decade mark also brings mortality to his mind. "Twenty years is also a sign of time," he said. "It's a large chunk of time and part of prime-life time, is it not? These are the productive years of a person's life, between 20 and 60. That doesn't mean you can't be productive after, but that's half of those 40 years.

"Twenty years also marks the reality of being a duelist every day," he continued, "being a gladiator of sorts out in the arena every day. There are fair players, and there are people . . . that are truly morally intolerable.

"But the price is high because we're in a high-roller business. Being in that arena has had its great, truly amazing moments. I've had the opportunity to bask in the glory and then turn around and see the X-ray up close." It has not always been a pretty picture. When Graham began throwing concerts 20 years ago, rock was still in infancy. He single-handedly proscribed the dictums of modern-day rock concerts, blazing trails where none existed. "That first six, seven years, " he said, "I was Sabu, jungle warrior, strange territory, in quicksand half the time."

But, 20 years later, Graham frequently finds himself in a business he helped create, but can no longer completely approve. The X-rays of Live Aid, for instance, apparently didn't look too good to Graham. "I would never talk about Live Aid in detail, even when I get to heaven," he said, "because nobody would believe me."

Since the fire more than five months ago, Graham said he occasionally takes a weekday off. He said he envied the man who drives a bus for a living. "I want to do some of the things he does on the weekends, " Graham said. His employees call their outfit the Graham Family, a term not without irony. Graham said his devotion to business in the early days of the Fillmore cost him his wife and family. "It did become my mistress for many years. Thank God the relationship today with my children is wonderful. It's good. But the price of making that the organization the family was one that was paid," he said.

"I'm not married to the business anymore," he added, "but we're still lovers."

Over the past several years, Graham has come to trust the judgment of his hired hands to a greater degree. He pictures his role as head of the family more like a football coach than a godfather.

"At midfield, you can call the plays, " he said. "But sometimes, at second and goal with a few seconds left, you want to come to the bench. I'll give you the play. I'll even come in and play it with you. But I depend so much on the players. I'm not removed from it, although I'd be lying to you if I didn't admit in the past five, six years, I've relied a great deal on other people in the company on the musical end, the aquisition of talent. I rely on their ears to sift through and let me know about the better stuff.

"In the early days, the creative ideas of the company started out as 100 percent my ideas," he said, "the posters, the light shows, whatever it might be. Now, maybe 20 percent of the creative ideas are mine. I just approve 100 percent.

"The way I feel had something to do with the loss of the gallery," he said. "Something died or somebody took something away. Even though it's hard not to, I don't want to guess and I'm not trying to find out why. I haven't gone to a doctor to find out why. But there are devastating changes in the way I think about things and those have all taken place this year."

He kept returning to a conflict between his desire to live life the way he wants and the demands of being the top rock promoter. "I'm far, far from being at peace with life because the industry I'm in will not allow it," he said. "But in other ways, I've been able to get closer to a realistic relationship with more people as time goes by.

"I've always felt I had to joust too much out in the field. If I didn't, I think there could have been many things I could have contributed to society.

"The most awesome change I always see in life is what happens to you when you make it, who you become. The greatest challenge to a character is what happens to you, how do you treat someone who takes orders from you after you've been taking orders. What happens to you as a person. A black person in a white neighbordhood, a white person in a black neighborhood, a Jew in a gentile neighborhood . . . what happened to you?

"Who did you become when you got to where you wanted to get? When you became that, did you remain in touch with your society? As time goes by, I have great affection for those who stayed in touch.

"I've never left," he said matter-of-factly. "It's not a compliment. I don't live any differently. That's the amazing part. I wish I had it in me to take off two weeks and go sailing or go mountain climbing. I don't mean loaf.

"I don't live any differently today. I still go to work every day. I sometimes wish I could acquire the taste for, maybe, fine clothes. The only good thing about that is I don't hassle about the price. Nothing's changed. It changed early on when I was able to eat anywhere.

"I have had the same two cars since 1969. I live here because somebody suggested it was a deal. But as far as my lifestyle, my workstyle, who my friends are, how I relate to my family, in some ways, I wish it were different.

"But in the way I'm pleased, I don't think I'm any different," he said. "Do you want something from me? Do you really need it? Are you a trustworthy human being? Here's my arm."

Sunday Datebook | 11/10/1985

The long strange trip

Powered by a new cocktail of music and chemicals, psychedelia blossomed in San Francisco at an astonishing pace. Then, by the time the world cottoned on, it was all over.

This is like a Reader's Digest condensed version of my book, "Summer Of Love," written for a special edition of Mojo on psychedelic rock.

RALPH J. GLEASON WATCHED FROM THE BALCONY of the Longshoreman's Hall while the San Francisco scene was born. He looked across the cavernous concrete bunker and saw a thousand long-haired freaks wearing Salvation Army castoffs and dancing like nobody was looking. The tweedy music critic for the San Francisco Chronicle, who dropped out of Columbia University in 1939 to start the first magazine in the world about jazz, had seen it all. But this was something altogether new.

It was called "A Tribute to Dr. Strange," a reference to an obscure comic strip character, and was presented by a four intrepid souls who called themselves the Family Dog. They inveigled late-night Top 40 disc jockey Russ (The Moose) Syracuse to act as emcee. He wore so much pancake makeup that Richie Olsen of the Charlatans, under the influence of the burgeoningly popular psychedelic drug LSD, thought he saw it moving around on Syracuse's face.

John Cipollina, who grew up across the Golden Gate Bridge in Marin County's Mill Valley and was currently living in a '54 Plymouth parked on Mount Tam, climbed up on the stage to look out over the crowd. He couldn't believe what he saw – a thousand like-minded weirdos and reprobates who had been holed up growing their hair good and long, getting strange, who were clearly familiar with this new drug rapidly spreading through the underground these past few months. He knew they were kindred spirits, but he couldn't believe how many of them there were.

"I don't think any of us were ready for that many people," the late Cipollina said in a 1976 interview. "'Wow, I didn't know there were that many people doing what we were doing.' We all thought we were original. Look at these people, they're just lying around. They've let their hair grow and they're just being freaky and having a good time. I knew I went there just to have a good time, but I didn't know everybody would go there just to have a good time. And after that, I said, okay, this can work."

Chet Helms, a Texas transplant who had been throwing Wednesday night jam session in the basement ballroom of a Victorian rooming house at 1090 Page Street in the Haight-Ashbury district, experienced the identical gestalt. He dashed out to the Tape Music Center, an experimental dance workshop, borrowed a strobe light and rushed back to splash lights on the dancers.

"This was the first time all these people were assembled in one place," said Helms. "There was a sense of sanctuary. They couldn't bust us all. Suddenly, you're not alone. So there was the music, the dress and mainly there was the sense of all of us being together. I think that was the most important thing – that and the sanctuary."

The colorfully garbed crowd dressed in Victoriana, old military jackets or cowboy outfits was moving and grooving to the old-timey sounds of the Charlatans, dressed in Edwardian finery with a Wild West flair, a kind of loose-knit, rinky-tink relative of the Lovin' Spoonful who had been playing all summer at a restored dancehall in the silver rush ghost town of the Sierra Nevadas called Virginia City. One of the other bands, enchantingly named Jefferson Airplane, had recently started playing at an old Marina district pizza parlor the band had overhauled into a psychedelic nightclub they called the Matrix.

"The bar did no business and the Coke machine ran out," wrote Gleason the following Monday in the Chronicle. "That's where it was at. Long lines of dancers snaked through the crowd for hours, holding hands. Free form improvisation ("self expression") was everywhere. The clothes were a blast. Like a giant costume party."

Chris Brooks, a mother hen to a lot of young musicians on the scene, introduced Cippolina that night to a pair of refugees from California's Central Valley, where guitarist Gary Duncan and drummer Greg Elmore belonged to a frat rock group called the Brogues. The next Wedenesday, the three of them jammed together at Helms' basement salon in the Haight playing a long, extended version of the old Bo Diddley song, "Mona," a song they would play a hundred times as the Quicksilver Messenger Service.

San Francisco in 1965 was a burbling cauldron of social unrest and experimentation. North Beach housed the remains of the beatnik poets and jazzmen of Jack Kerouac's "On the Road." In Berkeley, the Free Speech Movement had ground the wheels to a sudden halt of the country's largest university the previous fall and transformed virtually the entire student body into a raging political beast. San Francisco State students found plentiful cheap housing in the enormous Victorian rooming houses built originally for immigrant Irish workers in the Haight-Ashbury, a short bus ride away from campus. In May 1965, the Rolling Stones played an enthusiastically received concert at the S.F. Civic Auditorium and a dozen rock bands formed the next day. Under the cheeky spell of the Beatles in "A Hard Day's Night," folk musicians all over town were plugging in and twanging away. By the time the Family Dog convened the converted in October, there was already something clearly in the air.

LSD played a central role. The mind-altering substance trickled out into the underground. Author Ken Kesey discovered the drug as a test subject for psychiatric research in the Stanford Medical Center in nearby Palo Alto. Before long, he was living in the hills of La Honda with a group of similarly willfully deranged individuals who called themselves the Merry Pranksters. Kesey and company took to spreading the word of this psychedelic panacea with evangelistic zeal. In December, they presented the first public Acid Test at the private home of someone called Big Nig and selected as the house band for this dawning of the psychedelic apocalypse a former folkie jug band, turned electric rock group, from around the neighborhood that only recently changed its name to the Grateful Dead.

Rebellion and public protest were the order of the day. In Berkeley, another one of these new rock bands sprouting up everywhere around town at the moment, Country Joe and the Fish, introduced their sarcastic "Feel Like I'm Fixin' To Die Rag" from a platform truck during a giant student protest called the Vietnam Teach-In the same weekend as "A Tribute to Dr. Strange" was held across the bay in San Francisco. When the Parks and Recreation department banned the S.F. Mime Troupe for performing for free in the parks, the troupe responded by presenting a 15th century Italian farce in direct defiance of the ban. The police arrested the first actor to appear onstage and the court battle required funds the perennially strapped guerilla theater troupe lacked. Mime Troupe business manager Bill Graham, a failed actor who left New York and Hollywood to work as an office manager in San Francisco, decided to throw a fundraiser for their legal defense fund in November at the troupe's Howard Street office. When the line to gain admission to the tiny loft stretched around the block all night long, and Graham could only get the handfuls of dollar bills upstairs through the jammed staircase and hallway by hoisting a basket out of the window, he decided a second benefit somewhere larger might be a good idea. In December, he rented the Fillmore Auditorium, an old upstairs ballroom in the black ghetto, and put together a program of these local rock bands, although he was suspicious enough of the Grateful Dead's recent name change he put "formerly the Warlocks" prominently on the poster advertising the event. Oddly enough, he managed to get one of the posters under the nose of Bob Dylan, as the young heavyweight champion of folk-rock gave a rare public press conference at the KQED television studios, something the Chronicle's Gleason cooked up with Dylan and the public TV station. "I would like to go, if I could," said Dylan, holding the poster up for the cameras. "Unfortunately I won't be here, but if I was here, I certainly would be there."

Graham's production skills were immediately obvious. The Pranksters sought him out when the madcaps brought the Trips Festival to Longshoreman's Hall in San Francisco in January. With a jungle gym clutter of scaffolding, projectors and colored lights in the center of the room, the Grateful Dead and Big Brother and the Holding Company were scheduled to perform. The Monday before, Kesey was sentenced to six months in jail on a pot bust. Two nights later, he was arrested for possession of marijuana again, after cops found him and his girlfriend Mountain Girl throwing gravel off a North beach rooftop. He pleaded not guilty in court Friday morning and joined the rest of the Pranksters at noon downtown in Union

Jerry Garcia,
Jorma Kaukonen,
Mickey Hart,
Country Joe McDona
Jack Casady

Square banging and walloping the bizarre metal device they called the Thunder Machine to build interest in their Trips Festival.

At Longshoreman's, Graham spent a lot of time running around, a clipboard under his arm, stopping various Pranksters from letting their friends in for free through side doors. At one point, he spied someone dressed in a silver space man's suit opening a door so some members of the Hells Angels motorcycle club could come in for free and he ran up to the man screaming. "What are you doing?" Graham demanded. The man turned on his heels, looked at Graham, nodded his head, closed his spaceman's helmet with a plop and walked off. It was the only time the entire weekend Graham laid eyes on Kesey.

Sam Andrew of Big Brother, high on acid, got into a shouting match with Graham early in the evening and spent the entire night whipping back and forth between terror-stricken stage fright and intense joy. Big Brother bassist Peter Albin, straight-laced, married with children, went home early. The Dead's guitarist Jerry Garcia, also flying high, saw the sign flashing on the screen – "Jerry Garcia Plug In" – and meandered to the stage, dragging his broken, useless guitar. The pickup, freed from its moorings, hung loose and Garcia helplessly held out the broken instrument. Graham dropped to his knees, tucking his clipboard under his arm, and frantically tried to perform some emergency repairs. The Dead never did play that night.

After three benefits for the Mime Troupe, Graham decided to go into business for himself throwing shows. But since he knew nothing about the scene, he recruited an enthusiastic Chet Helms to serve as his partner and alternate weekends at the Fillmore, which he rented from black businessman and shady character Charles Sullivan for an altogether reasonable $60 a night. The place held more than a thousand and he charged three dollars for admission. Graham quickly began booking the hall by himself, as Helms, nursing his wounds, sought other places to put on these dance/concerts. Helms, who was also managing a group that coalesced during his 1090 Page jams named Big Brother and the Holding Company, soon found the Avalon Ballroom, another old San Francisco Edwardian dancehall. Big Brother often served as the resident attraction, although Helms also hired the other bands around town such as the Grateful Dead and Quicksilver Messenger Service, the band that Cipollina, Duncan and Elmore started after that fateful meeting at Longshoreman's Hall. The strobes lights that Helms flashed on dancers that night had grown into enormous tapestries of lights and visual images covering the entire expanse of the walls opposite the balconies. There were no spotlights. The small stages at the Fillmore and Avalon were barely off the dance floors. Dancers and musicians alike were drenched in a tureen of swimming, throbbing colored lights. Almost everyone in the audience was high on LSD. Most of the bands were, too. Jerry Garcia remembered the light show flickering off the body of his guitar and enjoyed the comfort of playing in the semi-darkness. "We were more or less shadows on the stage," he said.

The Jefferson Airplane surged to the forefront of the scene, thanks partly to the efforts of an ambitious manager, Matthew Katz, a Jesuit-trained intellectual, an erudite hipster with a little larceny in his heart. Gleason had written a review of the band's first engagement at their little nightclub for the Chronicle and the press brought the new band to the attention of the record industry. Phil Spector investigated the prospect. But Katz soon settled on signing a contract with RCA Victor and set about recording the band's first album in Los Angeles with an RCA staff producer. But the Airplane was the only band with anything like a career happening. Vocalist Marty Balin started the band. He was sullen and quiet, an unlikely leader, but experienced in the world of show business. He played "West Side Story." He cut a rock and roll single as a teenager and he had most recently belonged to a Kingston Trio-style folk group called the Town Criers. He met Paul Kantner, another bored folksinger, at a popular folk-singing establishment in San Francisco and the two began sharing plans for an electric folk-rock group.

"It was sort of this like a Union Street bar that, for some reason, had folk music," said Kantner. "It was like a beer bar, and I went in with all my esoteric folk music and played about three or four songs. But it was a drinking crowd and nobody gave a shit. So I said enough of this and, as I walked off stage, Marty came up to me and said 'Hey, do you want to start a band?'"

They found their girl singer, Signe Tole Anderson, at the same club where they met. They put together a rhythm section and found a guitarist who Kantner knew from playing blues at San Jose folk clubs when he called himself Jerry Kaukonen. They found some partners and signed a deal to play exclusively at this small club the band members themselves started remodeling an old pizza parlor they called the Matrix. The Airplane's repertoire, at this point, drew heavily from their folk music backgrounds – Fred Neil's "Other Side of This Life," Billy Ed Wheeler's "High Flyin' Bird" – although they also included current soul songs like Wilson Pickett's "In the Midnight Hour" and Lou Rawls' "Tobacco Road."

The rhythm section came and went. Balin spotted a young guitarist auditioning one afternoon at the Matrix for a band that would become Quicksilver

Messenger Service and declared him the new Jefferson Airplane drummer, even though Skip Spence never played drums before. Kaukonen contacted an old friend from the Washington D.C./Baltimore area, a young bassist under the spell of progressive jazz and rhythm and blues named Jack Casady and he came out to join the band in early 1966. They met Matthew Katz when someone told Balin that Katz had access to unreleased Dylan songs. Katz saw the band as avatars as a whole new brand of music – an amalgam of folk and jazz that he called "fojazz," a term he had emblazoned on the Matrix business cards, "San Francisco's Fojazz Night Club."

The Dead followed Kesey and the Pranksters to Los Angeles in early 1966, where they held a few Acid Tests before Kesey escaped to Mexico, a fugitive from justice, leaving behind his pregnant girlfriend, Mountain Girl. The band stayed in Los Angeles after the remaining Pranksters returned north. Living under the sponsorship of Augustus Stanley Owsley, the kingpin LSD manufacturer who had become the band's de facto soundman and patron of the arts, the members of the Dead had to endure some of Owsley's bizarre dietary notions – he lived largely on red meat and often simply fed the band hunks of steak straight out of the frying pan. By April, the band was back in San Francisco, settling into the rooming house at 710 Ashbury, Managing the rooming house was S.F. State student Dan Rifkin. He and his pal and fellow student Rock Scully had been following the band since the first Acid Tests and began to act as the Dead's official representatives.

The band revolved around the prodigious skills of guitarist Jerry Garcia, a bluegrass banjo player who led the former Mother Macree's Uptown Jug Stompers, a group that worked the Palo Alto folk scene on the peripheries of Stanford University, into an electric rock band that blended old folk blues like "Goin' Down the Road Feelin' Bad" or "Sittin' On Top of the World" with more modern urban blues like Jimmy Reed a la the Rolling Stones. Harmonica player and bluesman supreme Ron (Pig Pen) McKernan lent a certain authority to the band's early performances none of the other young musicians could muster, although Garcia's extemporaneous skills as lead guitarist were strongly evident from the start.

"We truly had a friend thing going," said Dead guitarist Garcia in a 1992 interview. "We were friends with each other. You didn't form a band for any reason other than to get crazy, and we did some serious bonding together with those drugs. I m,ean, you start talking about the limits of consciousness and beyond. And when the smoke cleared away, there we were. I don't know. Chemistry is one of those things, you either get lucky with it or you don't, and we were just lucky with it. I don't think we could have ever predicted it. And although I had been in-

Jerry Garcia

volved with everybody in the band to some extent or another before the band got started, there's no way for me to have known what kind of a person (drummer Bill) Kreutzmann was going to turn out to be. Or (guitarist Bobby) Weir."

The scene was flourishing. Both the Avalon and Fillmore presented full programs two or three nights every weekend. Graham and Helms booked bluesmen like Muddy Waters and Bo Diddley to fill out the bills with the colorful new local bands. Brilliant hand-lettered posters by artists such as Stanley Mouse and Alton Kelley, Rick Griffin or Victor Moscoso were produced for each weekly show and festooned shop windows up and down Haight Street, Grant Avenue in North Beach and Telegraph Avenue in Berkeley. Occasionally like-minded bands from elsewhere – such as the Sparrow (later Steppenwolf) and Buffalo Springfield from Los Angeles or the Sir Douglas Quintet and 13th Floor Elevators from Texas – would appear at the psychedelic dancehalls. But, through most of 1966, the phenomenon was concentrated among a relative handful of people living in only a few neighborhoods. But the community was developing certain definite characteristics and Chronicle columnist Herb Caen, who coined the term "beatnik," found a name for these characters, too – "hippies." The bands had broken the three-minute barrier in music. Instead of churning out crafted songs with short instrumental breaks, the new psychedelic bands used the songs as jumping off points for further exploration, bringing the improvisational excursions of the world of jazz into the realm of rock. Under the influence of LSD, these musicians would take off on endless choruses, riding the ebb and flowing rhythms like Indian ragas. And if the Grateful Dead wanted to play "Dancin' In the Street" for a half-hour, the hippies at the Avalon would dance along merrily without missing a beat. "I always tried to create the atmosphere that this is a place where someone could give you something," said Helms of the Avalon.

"It was great to play on acid," said Dead guitarist Garcia. "It was fun. The best thing about it was that the audience all danced. Being there was part of the experience. You didn't feel that performer-audience pull. The stage at the Avalon was low. You could kick people in the face easily, if you wanted to. And a lot of times, you could talk to people. We were part of that world. We were not performers. We were playing for our family, in a sense. It kind of had that feel, that kind of informality."

"There were weeks when we would take LSD every day," said Quicksilver's Gary Duncan, "so much that you just never came down. I learned to exist in that condition and to relate to things while stoned. Which was wonderful. It was all about higher levels of consciousness."

In June, Chet Helms summoned from Texas an old friend of his from the Austin folk music scene. Big Brother and the Holding Company, the band he managed, had become virtually the house band at the Avalon Ballroom, but lacked a distinctive lead vocalist. In lead guitarist James Gurley, the band boasted a truly fiery instrumentalist. Gurley, whose demolition derby driver father used to strap his young son to the hood of his car and drive through hoops of fire, wanted to harness the fury of John Coltrane and the fluid blues of Lightnin' Hopkins. When he first arrived in San Francisco, he used to practice guitar in a closet, listening through a stethoscope he attached to the guitar body. Bassist Peter Albin and rhythm guitarist Sam Andrew shared the vocals in the band, but neither qualified as a dynamic lead vocalist.

"Mostly it was improvised, spontaneous," said Big Brother guitarist Gurley. "We'd get up there with no idea of what we were going to play and play for an hour, an hour and a half. Totally spontaneous. We were on the psychedelic thing, just pouring out. And a lot of people didn't like it when we brought Janis in. They didn't like her. They wanted us to get back to the hard-core thing."

The band flirted with idea of adding a female vocalist and even tried out Lynne Hughes, a waitress at Virginia City's Red Dog Saloon where the Charlatans had been the house band, and Mary Ellen Simpson of the all-girl band Ace of Cups. Helms turned to someone he knew from his days in the early '60s at the University of Texas in Austin, who could electrify the hometown crowd at Thread-gill's in those days with nothing more than an acoustic guitar and some old Bessie Smith numbers.

Janis Joplin had been to San Francisco several years before, but went home with her tail between her legs after getting arrested for shop-lifting some jars of mustard from a grocery store in Berkeley. She came to a Big Brother and the Holding Company rehearsal at the old firehouse that served as the studio for psychedelic poster artists Stanley Mouse and Alton Kelley and played her first date with the band that weekend at the Avalon Ballroom. She switched off lead vocals with the two other male vocalists in the group and took a microphone at the side of the stage. Before long, she would become the first pin-up queen of the scene with a Bob Seideman photograph with her breast discreetly peaking out from behind a neckful of beads. The

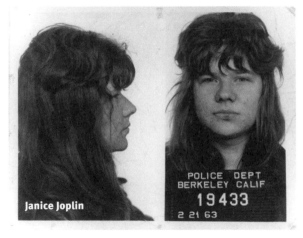

Janice Joplin

POLICE DEPT
BERKELEY CALIF
19433
2 21 63

photo turned into a popular poster around local bookstores. Within two months, Elektra Records producer Paul Rothchild (Paul Butterfield Blues Band, The Doors) would be the first music business professional to try and pry her loose from the group.

Quicksilver Messenger Service, the other headline band on the circuit, came by the band's name through an unusual astrological convergence – four Virgos in the band shared two birthdays and the fifth was a Gemini, which is ruled by Mercury. Their original manager was an astrologer who put great faith in such matters. Like the Airplane and the Dead, Quicksilver drew its repertoire from the folk roots of members such as bassist David Freiberg, who sang Buffy Ste. Marie's

"Codine" and Hamilton Camp's "Pride Of Man." Cipollina, with his long black hair and wan, frail looks, was a favorite of the young hippie chicks, but he was not much of an improviser. He tended to work out his solos in advance and play to perfect them. The band's other lead guitarist, Gary Duncan, had tuned into something of a high-dove artist, ready to charge off into the great unknown. On any given night, the band could match the sweep and vision of the Dead and they were much better looking. They were also fully psychedelic; bassist Freiberg doesn't even remember writing his epic hippie screed, "The Fool." "I took acid one night," he said, "and woke up the next day and found the words in the typewriter."

The band spent the winter living in shacks on Marin mudflats, sometimes burning pieces of the walkway that led to their doors to keep warm. But they soon moved to an abandoned dairy farm in western Marin, which they rented for a modest $60 a month. They would drive into San Francisco and perform over the weekends – Bill Graham or Chet Helms would pay them $1000 – and they had all the dope and women they needed for free. Life was good. Cipollina only slightly alarmed his rancher neighbors by keeping a pet wolf. One night, the Dead, spending the summer living at nearby Rancho Olompali, staged an Indian raid on the Quicksilver outpost dressed in feathers and war paint. They set off firecrackers and smoke bombs, catching the band entirely off-guard and unaware, but ended up smoking the peace pipe together.

(When Quicksilver planned to "raid" the Dead's show at the Fillmore in return, the band showed up dressed as cowboys, ready to lasso the Dead onstage and sing "Kaw-Liga," but the show was running late. Forced to wait outside in the ghetto neighborhood parked in the '50 Dodge panel truck, the Quicksilver fellows in their cowboy outfits quickly attracted the attention of the police and the entire band went to jail on a variety of drug and weapons charges.)

With Big Brother holed up down the road at Teddy Roosevelt's old hunting lodge in Lagunitas, the summer at Olompali allowed everybody to continue to live out their Wild West fantasies, complete with sidearms and antique rifles. The Dead would setup their gear on the rolling lawn in front of the ranch house and bands would play all day, while people danced, swam in the pool, sunbathed or made love in the tall grass. One afternoon, George Hunter of the Charlatans, high on LSD, squeezed off a few rounds into the hills from his vintage Winchester rifle and was astonished to see a naked couple jump up and run away terrified.

In February, former classical music deejay from Detroit, Larry Miller, rented the post-midnight block of time on foreign language station KMPX-FM (the Turkish hour came on just before Miller) and began broadcasting an eclectic assortment of folk, blues and what few records by the new rock bands that were around. By April, Miller had been joined by former KYA Top 40 kingpin Tom (Big Daddy) Donahue, who presented the final Beatles concert, ran a radio tipsheet, owned a record label, a nightclub and a couple of racehorses. Donahue saw in a flash a vision of the future and moved immediately to establish fulltime underground radio on the small station. Before long, everyone in town was abandoning the AM dial for the new FM radio station. Folksinger Dave Van Ronk experienced an altogether unpredictable boomlet when his old acoustic blues, "Cocaine," suddenly became the most requested tune on the new station. Country Joe and the Fish sold out of boxes of the group's self-produced EP, only available at Moe's Books in Berkeley, after the station started playing the wildly psychedelic instrumental "Section 43."

Grace Slick

"By fall there were four or five bands working regularly and Country Joe and the Fish joined them," said Fish guitarist Barry Melton. "We began working all the time at these high school dances. We were getting all the gigs. Good money, too $500 a night."

The debut Jefferson Airplane album, "Jefferson Airplane Takes Off," hardly stormed the charts on release that fall. The record never made the Billboard Top 100 and the band already ran into censorship issues with RCA Victor who objected to the use of the words "trips" on Marty Balin's "Runnin' Round This World" on the band's first single. Nevertheless, Warner Brothers' Joe Smith was introduced to the Grateful Dead by Tom Donahue and he signed the band, granting unprecedented artistic control and other concessions to a band the square label chief realized he didn't entirely understand. Other labels were sniffing around. Musicians and bands were relocating from across the country. But the phenomenon had hardly spread.

In September, Big Brother and the Holding Company came to Chicago to follow the Jefferson Airplane in an engagement at a nightclub called Mothers. The band crashed at the home of Peter Albin's straight uncle and aunt, devout Christians who were appalled at the hippies but couldn't refuse the needy. The nightclub engagement was a disaster. Nobody came and the club management refused to pay the band. Broke and unable to get back home, the band made a quick deal for cash with cunning independent record producer Bobby Shad, who cut half an album with the band before dispatching Big Brother and company back to the West Coast, where they quickly finished the band's cheap, quick debut album in Hollywood.

In San Francisco, the Paul Butterfield Blues Band made its triumphant return, playing several weekends in a row, Graham moving the shows into the larger Winterland Arena down the street for the occasions, a triumphant coronation for this band of giants who loomed over the San Francisco music scene at that moment. The San Francisco bands all aspired to the kind of excellence, imagination and instrumental prowess displayed on the Butterfield band's second album, "East West," especially the incendiary guitar playing from Mike Bloomfield and Elvin Bishop on the thirteen-minute title track. The Airplane was second-billed. It would be the final shows for vocalist Signe Tole Anderson, who wanted to leave the band and raise a family. The band, on their part, were happy to be free of Anderson and her boisterous husband. She would be replaced with the lead vocalist from another San Francisco band, the Great Society, who had appeared further down the bill at "A Tribute to Dr. Strange" at Longshoreman's Hall in what was only the band's second public performance the year before.

Grace Slick was a former fashion model who grew up in the privileged enclave of Palo Alto, where she married her boyfriend-next-door Jerry Slick and the pair ran away to film school at S.F. State. With his brother Darby Slick, they formed a psychedelic band that was one of the last bands to try to record for Tom Donahue's Autumn Records. The label's house producer, a young r&b disc jockey who called him Sly Stone, had produced authentic folk-rock hits for the label with the Beau Brummels and the Vejtables. But something about the untested musicianship of the band and the screechy lead vocalist puzzled the more experienced producer, who wrote and produced the 1964 Top 10 hit, "C'mon and Swim" for Bobby Freeman on Autumn when he was 19 years old. He took Grace Slick and the band through more than two hundred takes of Darby Slick's song, "Somebody To Love," without ever finding a satisfying version.

The Airplane and the Great Society shared many bills in the preceding year and when Signe Anderson announced she was leaving, the idea of offering the post to Grace Slick came up quickly. "Everybody in town was in love with Grace Slick," said Paul Kantner. Jack Casady offered her the job as the band packed up from an Avalon Ballroom show and the Great Society never played together again. The sendoff Winterland performances were to be a sentimental, loving departure. The band gave Signe flowers onstage, as Slick watched from the wings. But Signe never showed up for the second night, so Grace Slick made her hurried debut as the Airplane vocalist that night.

Backstage, a friend of Paul Butterfield's from Chicago watched in amazement. He drove his VW bus out to San Francisco from Dallas, after spending more than three years working in the Chicago blues scene after college, and had five dollars left in his pocket. Swept up by what he saw that night, when Steve Miller came out to jam with his old Chicago pals in the Butterfield Band, he drew a standing ovation by announcing to the sold out audience that he'd just decided to move to San Francisco and start a band. He pulled some musicians together for a rehearsal in an empty basement of a school building on the UC Berkeley campus during the Thanksgiving weekend and by the next month, he was playing the Avalon Ballroom.

In January 14, 1967, fourteen months after "A Tribute to Dr. Strange," more than ten thousand people showed up for the Human Be-In, A Gathering of the Tribes, held in the Polo Fields of Golden Gate Park. Unlike any other public gathering of similar size, there were no incidents, no drunken fisticuffs, no muggings and robberies. The Hells Angels stood guard over the electrical cables and helped lost children find their parents. The police were dumbfounded. LSD was handed out in the crowd like candy. People danced barefoot in the unseasonably sunny weather. LSD guru Tim Leary spoke to the crowd – "tune in, turn on, drop out" he told them. Beat poet Allen Ginsberg recited his Buddhist mantras. A parachutist dropped down on the crowd during the set by the Grateful Dead, who were joined by jazz flautist Charles Lloyd for the Pig Pen blues specialty, "Good Morning Little Schoolgirl." As fingers of fog trickled in from the nearby Pacific Ocean at the end of the afternoon, the crowd picked up all their trash and made their way peacefully home.

The Utopian lure of the Haight-Ashbury was spreading. Not only had the audiences in San Francisco increased tenfold in the intervening months, but delicious reports of the burgeoning hippie underground were beginning to echo as far away as New York and London. The psychedelic movement rippled through all the arts, without the San Francisco rock bands even traveling much outside of

Quicksilver Messenger Service

their native environs. The stage was set for the release of the second album by the Jefferson Airplane, "Surrealistic Pillow," in Februrary 1967.

With manager Matthew Katz jettisoned – his lawsuit against the band would freeze royalties from the first album for more than twenty years – the band returned to Hollywood to record with "spiritual advisor" Jerry Garcia of the Grateful Dead, who supplied the album's title with an offhand quip, as well as playing on several key tracks. RCA celebrated the release with an lavish launch party at Webster Hall in New York, where the band brought the San Francisco experience to Manhattan; full psychedelic light show, onstage jam with some of the Butterfield band. When the album's first single was released, "Somebody To Love," one of the few songs Grace Slick brought with her from the Great Society, the Airplane was suddenly the hottest new rock group in the country. And San Francisco was the place.

The first weekend in March brought more rock shows than ever before. Both the Fillmore (Otis Rush, the Mothers, Morning Glory) and the Avalon (The Doors, the Sparrow, Country Joe and the Fish) present full programs. The Avalon show was commemorated by a landmark Victor Moscoso poster, "Break On Through," that was intended to change colors under the light show in the ballroom. The Matrix featured the Sopwith Camel that weekend. The Charlatans played a hall in the Haight. Big Brother and the Holding Company and the Steve Miller Blues Band appeared in a medical school auditorium up the hill from the Haight. The Grateful Dead, Love and Moby Grape performed at Winterland.

New bands turned up every week. Sopwith Camel actually scored the first Top 40 hit of the new San Francisco bands with the campy, old-timey hit, "Hello Hello," produced by Erik Jacobsen of the Lovin' Spoonful, who also ran some hapless sessions with the Charlatans that never came to anything. The Camel was led by a young beatnik named Peter Kraemer, who grew up Bohemian in Virginia City, his mother best friends with Carisse Crosby, the literary lioness of '20s Paris. Some of the other San Francisco bands saw the band as lightweight and looked down on the Camel for signging with a New York music business management firm and making a commercial hit. The Dead, in the band's peculiar non-confrontational manner, even sabotaged one of the Camel's big moments, a rare headline appearance at an anti-war rally at Longshoreman's Hall, at which the Dead were to precede the fellows with the tacky little hit on the radio.

"There were people who had always been fairly critical of me," said Peter Kraemer, "that said I couldn't sing, that the band didn't have any balls. We were fairly sure we could show them something. But the hall had a 1 a.m. shutdown and the Dead hogged the stage until, like, 12:45. They had fifty of their fans in front screaming for encores and they kept playing. The Camel gets in the middle of our first number and they pulled the power. We broke up shortly after that>'

Moby Grape was a band former Airplane manager Matthew Katz built around Skip Spence, the Airplane drummer who left the band after the first album to pursue his singing and songwriting. Katz pieced together a band with some redneck rockers from the Pacific Northwest and '40s movie star Loretta Young's privileged son, tied up the young musicians in contracts they would spend most of their adult lives trying to reconcile and signed the band to Columbia Records after a spirited bidding war among labels. When the flashy, powerful debut album was ready for release, Columbia decided to simultaneously release eight singles off the album. None were successful and band members spoiled the fabulous record release party at the Avalon by getting arrested later that night in the Marin hills on charges of drug possession and contributing to the delinquency of minors. It was not an auspicious start.

"Matthew did certain things that seemed real good at first," said guitarist Jerry Miller of Moby Grape, "and then later it seemed as though he made it real rough when we were trying to go with Columbia and different labels and stuff, trying to get something going. It seemed we had already signed some kind of paper, that we had signed the name 'Moby Grape' over for some reason, and an atrocious publishing deal. So we found our hands tied and it really started messing us up. But we were still able to record the first album real nice. We were all together on that."

When manager Lou Adler and John Phillips of the Mamas and Papas decided to take over the Monterey Pop Festival planned for the same fairgrounds where the Monterey Jazz Festival took place every year since 1958, they came to San Francisco. The first place they went was to the Berkeley home of Ralph Gleason, whose Chronicle column had turned into the billboard of the scene and whose passionate endorsement of the thriving San Francisco rock bands earned him great credibility with the musicians. Without his approval, Adler and Phillips knew they had no chance of convincing the San Francisco bands to come to the party. Without the San Francisco bands, they didn't have a party. These two Hollywood hippies were exactly the sort of promoters and entrepreneurs more authentic San Francisco hippies such as the Grateful Dead would have never trusted. Their smooth, studio-produced music had little in common with the handmade, rough-hewn music the San Francisco bands were making in their ballrooms. But Gleason, who played a crucial role in starting the Monterey Jazz Festival, played it cool. "Let me know your plans," he said.

They met with some of the San Francisco band managers in their plush Fairmont Hotel suite, with decidedly mixed results. Some of the manager knew more about outdoor rock shows than Adler and Phillips and voiced considerable objections. They wondered about camping facilities and didn't exactly approve of the idea of playing to raise money for some as-yet unnamed charity.

Newspapers predicted as many as a hundred thousand young people would descend on San Francisco that summer. They were already calling it the "Summer Of Love." No less a figure than Paul McCartney secretly swooped down on the city that spring. Borrowing a private jet that belonged to Frank Sinatra, McCartney showed up unannounced at a Jefferson Airplane rehearsal in the empty synagogue next to the Fillmore, carrying an acetate of the album the Beatles just finished recording, "Sergeant Pepper's Lonely Hearts Club Band," more than three months before his bandmate George Harrison made his celebrated stroll down Haight Street in those heart-shaped sunglasses.

While Adler's acts such as the Mamas and Papas and Johnny Rivers still had some currency at the box office, they depended on San Francisco and London to provide the excitement for the festival. Jimi Hendrix and the Who would represent the British wing of the new rock movement. From San Francisco, the contribution was staggering. The Jefferson Airplane, whose second single off the new album, "White Rabbit," was storming radio stations across the nation from the first week of release in June, would close the Saturday night show. Moby Grape would open. The Saturday afternoon show would feature Big Brother and the Holding Company, Quicksilver Messenger Service, Country Joe and the Fish, the Steve Miller Blues Band and the debut of the new group put together in Marin County by Paul Butterfield Blues Band guitarist Mike Bloomfield, Electric Flag. The Grateful Dead were booked on Sunday night.

None of the San Francisco bands had even appeared much outside the Bay Area. Monterey shaped up like a cultural summit meeting taking place on an unprecedented convergence of factors. Phillips tried to capture the pilgrim spirit with a typically sappy folk-rock composition he wrote in a pre-festival flush. He and Adler rushed into the studio with a longtime musical associate of Phillips, vocalist Scott McKenzie, and recorded "San Francisco (Be Sure and Wear Some Flowers In Your Hair)." While the record, released on Adler's own label, soared up the charts, the treacly anthem summed up the fanciful vision of barefoot hippies dancing in the park summoned up by the nation's wide-eyed news media. It also did little to convince the San Francisco musicians that these Hollywood hipsters had any idea where it was really at.

"Nobody had any idea it was going to be so significant," said drummer David Getz of Big Brother and the Holding Company. "Once it got started, though, you definitely got the sense that you were in the middle of something historic. It's just a feeling that what's going on around you is different, important. You couldn't miss the fact that the Stones sent Brian Jones. Ravi Shankar was playing. And everyone sensed that."

After a decidedly uneven opening night – featuring a rollicking new Fillmore-style Animals from Eric Burdon, choirboy pop from Simon and Garfunkel, and schlocky Los Angeles pop from Johnny Rivers and the Association – the San Francisco bands took the stage for the Saturday afternoon show. Backstage, Big Brother and the Holding Company manager, openly hostile to the organizers' plan to film the concert to underwrite expenses and raise money for some nebulous charity, refused to let the cameras film his band. After the band went out and blew a fireball through the whole crowd by the name of Janis Joplin, a backstage drama began to boil. Dylan's manager Albert Grossman made some private remarks to Joplin and the festival producers expressed their disappointment that she wouldn't be included in the film (planned at the time as an ABC-TV special). Joplin exploded on her manager – screaming, yelling, crying. She had been the festival's first hit and she wasn't going to miss this opportunity. The band was hastily booked for a second set on the following evening's program and this time the cameras would capture Joplin's scorching version of "Ball and Chain."

The Dead was sandwiched between the Who and Jimi Hendrix, colorful incendiary acts with flashpots and smashed guitars. The Dead started the band's abbreviated set with an old folk blues to warm up. But before the band could start a second number, Peter Tork of the Monkees emerged from the backstage to interrupt the band's performance with an importantr announcement. He wanted to tell the few thousand people crowded around the end of the arena, watching

from outside, that they needed to calm down and back off. Tork also wanted to deny the rumors that the Beatles were coming.

It was all Dead bassist Phil Lesh could stand, this phony Hollywood TV Beatle acting as a stooge for Adler and company's crowd control policy. "This is the last concert – why not let them in?" Lesh asked the hapless Monkee.

"If the Beatles were here, they'd probably want you to come in," Lesh said. The crowd poured through the gates past the ushers in their armbands and filled the aisles. The cheers were for Lesh.

That weekend was the end of the golden era of San Francisco psychedelic rock. Record company executives like Clive Davis of Co-

Moby Grape

lumbia Records and Mo Ostin of Warner Brothers were sitting in the Monterey audience. Davis immediately determined to sign Janis Joplin and little more than a year later, the band was at the top of the nation's best-selling charts. The Airplane was launched. The band would be photographed on the cover of Life magazine the following year, symbolizing "The New Rock," recognition unmatched in American journalism of the day. The storied career of the Dead, whose first album was barely a month old when the band played Monterey, lay ahead. Joplin convinced the band to fire their manager shortly thereafter. Before long, Big Brother and the Holding Company was being handled by big shot New York talent manager Albert Grossman, who first whispered in Joplin's ear backstage at Monterey.

For the other bands – Quicksilver, Steve Miller, Country Joe – record deals, national tours, even hit records were in the future. Everything changed that weekend. San Francisco's secret was out. After fame and success reared their ugly heads, things would never be the same.

Owsley Stanley made several batches of psychedelics specifically for the Monterey Pop weekend. He introduced a new formula that proved much stronger than conventional LSD that he called STP. David Crosby of the Byrds plastered his guitar with one of the well-known insignias of the automotive additive STP. Jack Casady of the Airplane and Country Joe McDonald were only two of the Monterey musicians whacked out of their wits for days on this strange brew. Casady ended up in jail. McDonald went to his seat in the arena for the festival's final act, Mamas and Papas, in a state of child-like transfixion more than twenty-four hours after he took the drug. He watched in this dream state as these strange looking singers, dressed in "Arabian Nights" costumes, brought out this other fellow to bring the whole festival to a climax by singing his horrifying hit single, "San Francisco (Be Sure And Wear Some Flowers In Your Hair)."

"We've been had," he thought. The entire festival, three days of love and flowers, had been a buildup to this lousy record promotion. Phillips had snookered the entire San Francisco scene – all the bands, all the managers, even the music itself. All of it had been commandeered in the service of the mundane, the clueless fools were were even then hitch-hiking on highway across the country, San Francisco bound. He wandered off dazed.

Somehow in the euphoria and confusion that surrounded the tearing down of such an ambitious festival, certain pieces of equipment that Adler and Phillips borrowed from a Hollywood music store for the weekend disappeared. The next week, that same equipment turned up at a free concert in Golden Gate Park and was being stored in the back of the Free Store on Haight Street. Festival organizers – for some reason – contacted the Grateful Dead about arranging the return of the equipment. The festival organizers were informed by return letter where the missing gear could be picked up the following weekend. "When you come," the letter advised, "be sure and wear some flowers in your hair."

Q Special Edition | February 2005

The Psychedelic Super Highway

How *Janis Joplin, Doug Sahm, Steve Miller* and a host of other Texans made tracks for San Francisco during the Summer of Love

Texas Music editor Richard Skanse thought up this story and decided I was the man for the job. Doug Sahm may be the most under-rated figure in the history of rock.

Mother & Dad ...   *June 6, 1966*

With a great deal of trepidation, I bring the news. I'm in San Francisco. Now let me explain – when I got to Austin, I talked to Travis Rivers, who gave me a spiel about my singing w/a band out here. Seems Chet Helms, old friend, is now Mr. Big in S.F. Owns 3 big working rock & roll bands with bizarre names like Captain Beefheart and his Magic Band, Big Brother and the Holding Co. et cetera. Well, Big Brother et al needs a vocalist. So I called Chet to talk to him about it ...

JANIS JOPLIN WASN'T THE ONLY TEXAS GIRL TO RUN AWAY to San Francisco, just maybe the most famous. San Francisco has always held a mysterious allure for Texans. Perhaps it is their common history in the Ol' West, former nation states brought into the Union by armed forces. San Francisco was a mining town, always glad to see a cowboy after payday. But Janis Joplin traveled a specific road, a bohemian trail well-worn before she set foot on it.

There was a hipster highway in those days that connected renegade outposts all across the country, and the road ran straight from Austin, Texas, to the Haight-Ashbury. Along this highway traveled writers, smugglers, musicians, poets, beatniks and visionaries – nutcases of all sorts. In the early days of psychedelia, hardy pioneers carried Mexican marijuana from over the river and still-legal Texas peyote. A number of prominent music careers started with that trip. At one point, it seemed like there was an entire community of Texan longhairs living in San Francisco. They all seemed to know each other, even if they only met after they landed in San Francisco, and they shared some terrible secret they manfully hid from the natives with a wry smile. They all took the same route. "The underground railroad," says scene pioneer Chet Helms, whom Janis called "Mr. Big" in her letter to her parents.

Texans strode the streets of San Francisco during the Summer of Love wearing cowboy hats and big, stupid grins. It wasn't just that they were in San Francisco – they also weren't in Texas.

In San Francisco, there was tons of dope, lots of work for musicians and plenty of free love. "When you heard about San Francisco, people told these fantastic stories," says Texas music business entrepreneur and horse-racing enthusiast Henry Carr. "This was before birth control pills. None of us got laid unless we had the seven bucks and were in Mexico. As soon as everybody heard you could get laid, they'd throw five pounds [of marijuana] in their trunk and head off. Get it on credit and, at nine bucks a lid, you could pay for the trip."

But it was more than the free love, high times and easy living that made California the Promised Land. While Austin collected every unorthodox, artsy-fartsy-left-winger who grew up in that region, San Francisco was extracting the cream of the crop from across the country. It was the Wild West all over again, and what would the Wild West be without Texans?

For three years, the streets of San Francisco were lousy with free-thinking seekers and miscreants looking for a better way. It was a grand plan to change the world and, while it might have fallen somewhat short of that lofty goal, it certainly changed San Francisco for a while. And there was a breed of Texan who showed up in this mess and couldn't believe their eyes and ears.

Bye Bye Baby: Janis & Mr. Big

Chet Helms certainly must have seemed like Mr. Big to 25-year-old Joplin, who was coming back to San Francisco a second time at his invitation. Helms, who grew up in the Ozarks and Fort Worth, took that California trip many times. By 1966, he was thoroughly established in San Francisco, a major player in the city's burgeoning hip music scene. Joplin's previous trip had not been all that pleasant – she first arrived in San Francisco with Helms after a mad 55-hour hitchhiking spree in January 1963 and went home to Texas with her whipped-puppy, speed-freak tail between her legs little more than two years later. But she had bottomed out on sitting around her middle-class parents' Port Arthur home in pleated skirts, her hair in a bun, and returned to Austin, where she first thrived as the folk-singing beatnik University of Texas student Helms knew when they were in college together.

A modest electric rock scene had emerged in Austin in early 1966. On the primarily black, East side of town, a new crowd gathered at the I.L. Club for St. John the Conqueroo, soon shortened to Conqueroo, the town's first psychedelic band. Songwriter Powell St. John had been a regular in the folk-singing cast of Threadgill's, the long-standing Austin music institution. He lasted with the band until he took off for San Francisco. The mainstays of the pioneering rock band were Bob Brown, a teenage songwriting phenom who teamed with Ed Guinn, a young black man who came from Fort Worth. Having moved back from living with her parents in Port Arthur, Joplin was polishing her Bessie Smith impression that spring in regular dates across town at the 11th Door.

Meanwhile, the New Orleans Room expanded its booking policy beyond Dixieland to include local rock bands like the Wigs, a group that featured guitarists John (Toad) Andrews and Boz Scaggs, and the 13th Floor Elevators. UT student Tommy Hall formed the Elevators to expound on his philosophies about mind-altering chemicals. Not being a musician himself, he surrounded himself with more capable players while he played "electric jug." When Hall heard the local hit by the Spades, "You're Gonna Miss Me," he invited the song's writer and singer, 17-year-old prodigy Roger Kynard (Roky) Erickson, to join his band. Joplin apparently gave some serious thought to joining the Elevators that spring. Hall didn't like the idea. The Elevators already had a first-rate screamer in Erickson, and the band didn't really play the blues.

Around this time, with Joplin singing old blues and playing guitar in business suits at folk clubs while thinking about hooking up with the Elevators, Travis Rivers pulled into Austin on a mission from Helms to retrieve her. Rivers was a fifth-generation Austin native who decided to hang his hat in Frisco, and an old acquaintance of Joplin's from UT. They fell into bed together and headed out of town to San Francisco. Janis was not without apprehension. Before she would leave, she extracted a promise from Helms over the phone that he would give her bus fare home if things did not work out. She went to say goodbye to Powell St. John and took off with a song he'd just written that suited her mood, "Bye, Bye Baby." Rivers stayed in the car outside while Joplin stopped at her parents' home in Port Arthur. She left without telling them she was moving to California. By the time they got to San Francisco on June 4, 1966, Travis and Janis were in love. Helms found an apartment for them on Pine Street, where he had connections with an apartment building manager. Many of his associates in his Family Dog company/commune lived nearby. It might not have been much more than a sink and a bed, but high-rolling Helms – "Mr. Big" – was picking up the tab. In addition to managing Big Brother, Helms was running three or more shows every week at the Avalon Ballroom featuring bands with names like Captain Beefheart and his Magic Band, Daily Flash, Grateful Dead, Oxford Circle, Quicksilver Messenger Service and Big Brother and the Holding Company. Wacky poster artists Stanley Mouse and Alton Kelley produced one masterpiece after another each week to advertise Helms' presentations. The shows were jammed with the colorfully garbed, willfully deranged, psychedelically challenged community that was expanding every day exponentially. San Francisco in the summer of 1966 was a carnival. Freaks were everywhere. And Chet Helms was one of the ringmasters.

The Haight-Ashbury was an old-fashioned neighborhood by Golden Gate Park, bathed in Mediterranean sunlight during the day and cooled by slivers of fog that eased in from the Pacific Ocean in the late afternoon. Large rooming houses, once home to Irish workers, offered cheap housing, and S.F. State students started to rent the rooms. Danny Rifkin was a State student who managed a large Victorian home at 710 Ashbury. One by one, he rented rooms to friends who belonged to a rock band from down the peninsula called the Warlocks, who were about to change their name to the Grateful Dead. Chet Helms, who was making a meager living salvaging antiques from dumpsters outside remodeling jobs and selling a little weed on the side, started organizing weekly parties in the basement of one of the larger old rooming houses.

In fall 1965, a group of transplanted hipsters living in a commune on Pine Street decided to throw a dance. They called themselves the Family Dog and rented Longshoreman's Hall down by Fisherman's Wharf and hired a few of the fledgling rock bands that started appearing around town, including the Charlatans and the Jefferson Airplane. A thousand longhairs showed up out of nowhere at the event, titled "A Tribute To Dr. Strange." The Family Dog threw three more concerts before the partnership dissolved when two of the four founders ran off to Mexico.

Helms took over the name. He had the missionary zeal and, from the start, wanted to play a role in this new community that was developing. He did a couple of concerts at the Fillmore Auditorium with Bill Graham, an office manager for a politically active, financially beleaguered guerilla theater group called the S.F. Mime Troupe. Graham discovered the new community almost accidentally, staging a legal defense fundraiser at the Mime Troupe's loft rehearsal hall that was jammed with people until dawn. He staged a couple more benefits and then went into business with Helms a partnership that lasted only a few weeks before Graham decided he could do fine on his own.

Helms found another hall. The Avalon Ballroom was an upstairs dance hall at the corner of Van Ness and Sutter, near downtown. It was an L-shaped room with a balcony, mirrors along the wall and a sprung dance floor. Light show artists set up shop in the balcony, blanketing the room with swirls of colored, pulsing lights, film loops and splashing liquid projections that moved in time to the music. Tickets cost three bucks. Business was good. The bands were often under the influence of LSD, but then so was most of the audience. Musicians who were high on acid stretched songs well past the three-minute mark, embarking on ensemble improvisations that could last forever. And the audience, also high, danced for hours.

Helms had big plans. In addition to running the Avalon, he managed Big Brother and the Holding Company, a rock band he named after himself. Big Brother had come together over a period of months the previous year at the informal jam sessions Helms organized in the basement ballroom of a Haight-Ashbury rooming house at 1090 Page Street. He dispatched his old Texas buddy Travis Rivers to go back to Texas and bring Janis Joplin out to sing with the band.

Joplin showed up for her audition with Big Brother demure in a sleeveless blouse, her hair pinned up. Big Brother rehearsed at a converted Victorian firehouse on Henry Street that served as the art studio for poster artists Mouse and Kelley. Both guitarist James Gurley and bassist Peter Albin remembered Joplin from her earlier days on the San Francisco scene. Gurley's father was a daredevil car driver who used to strap his teenage son to the hood of his car and drive through hoops of fire. James was still missing his front teeth. Albin was a former folknik whose brother managed the 1090 Page rooming house. Guitarist Sam Andrew had been a roomer, too, and they found drummer Dave Getz playing Dixieland at the S.F. Art Institute. They were not entirely convinced they needed a vocalist.

At the Avalon that weekend, the band did a few of the demolition derby/John Coltrane-meets-Lightnin' Hopkins sonic assaults in which Big Brother specialized. Without great fanfare, they introduced Janis Joplin, who took a microphone at the side of the stage and sang the few songs she and the band had rehearsed. There was some discussion amongst the band members about whether to keep her or not. They kept her.

Lawd, I'm Just a Country Boy in This Great Big Freaky City

With Chet Helms at the other end of a direct pipeline from Austin, the two scenes established a direct link. He could pay bands money they would never see in Austin, but it was more than the money. San Francisco had become the secret center of the world. Any psychedelic rock band like the 13th Floor Elevators in Austin knew about San Francisco. Helms first brought the Elevators to play the Avalon in September 1966. The band had re-recorded Erickson's "You're Gonna Miss Me," and, lo and behold, found themselves the proud beneficiaries of a modest hit record. San Francisco's top teen station, KYA, was banging the hell out of the song and there was the promise of much work. Helms booked the band for several weekends at the Avalon. At first, the band crashed at one of his apartments on Pine Street. But when the Elevators gravitated out of his orbit, they eventually landed in a seedy residential hotel in the Tenderloin, the dark underbelly of downtown San Francisco, far removed from the peace and love.

The Elevators didn't just talk the talk. They consumed enormous quantities of LSD, particularly Hall and Erickson. At one of the nights at the Avalon, Erickson turned his back on the audience, walked toward his amplifier and started fooling around with feedback. He became so absorbed, he never returned to his lead vocal duties for the duration of the set, just stayed by his amplifier making his guitar feedback. They began to develop a reputation as a band that failed to even show up for engagements. The chaos soon infected the other band members, and the Elevators went back to Texas in time for the holidays.

While the Elevators' San Francisco stay was short and unpleasant, the city served as the headquarters for the next five years to the quintessential Texas maverick, Doug Sahm. Sahm was a master at sniffing out scenes, and it didn't take him long to smell San Francisco. His band, the Sir Douglas Quintet, first played the Avalon in July 1966.

Sahm had been a child prodigy, showered with cash as a youngster at the Texas honky-tonks his parents dragged him to, and had made his first records before he was a teenager. Growing up in San Antonio, he learned country music at the feet of formidable cats like Charlie Walker and rhythm and blues from Houston acts like Bobby "Blue" Bland and Junior Parker. He was equally at home in both worlds and had more than a passing familiarity with the Tejano music of San Antone's West side. Sahm eventually hooked up with Houston record producer Huey Meaux, who had been hot as a cheap pistol until the Beatles fell on top of him.

Meaux made Sahm add an organ to his band to get that British sound – organist Augie Meyers on Vox – and gave them the British-sounding name. They cut "She's About a Mover" in January 1965 and by April, it was streaking up the charts into the Top 10. The band hit the road on bills with the Rolling Stones, James Brown and Little Richard. There were dates in New York, where Sahm saw Greenwich Village and first met Bob Dylan. "I think he was a huge influence on Dylan," says Helms. "He was the real deal that Dylan wanted to be."

After the band was arrested in the Corpus Christi airport with some ridiculously small amount of pot, Sahm fled the tough Texas laws and the cops who were ready to shake down any longhair they saw. ("It didn't slow him down," says drummer George Rains. "He was still the poster boy for smoking joints.") Within weeks, he had moved his wife, five children and mother-in-law to a rambling home in Prunedale, about 60 miles south of San Francisco, in the Salinas Valley of Steinbeck novels. Sahm himself never really lived anywhere. He was always passing through, talking a million miles-per-hour, on his way somewhere else. He had girlfriends with apartments of their own in San Francisco. He moved his band members to Marin County.

The Sir Douglas Quintet made its California debut June 25, 1966, at the "Summer Spectacular" at the Hollywood Bowl, headlined by the Beach Boys and the Byrds. The band started making regular appearances at the Avalon for Helms, alongside Big Brother and the Holding Company. Attorney Brian Rohan, who represented the Grateful Dead, cut a record deal for Sahm with Mercury Records, who were interested in establishing a beachhead on the San Francisco scene. By this time, the original Quintet was falling apart. Meyers returned to Texas, while bassist Jack Barber never made the trip West in the first place. A cobbled-together version of the Quintet was playing the Whiskey a Go Go in Hollywood when Sahm ran across drummer George Rains, a friend from Fort Worth. He invited Rains to come to San Francisco and help him put together a blues band. The record company put the musicians on salary, and everybody bought sports cars, except Sahm. He rode around town in a Cadillac. This was definitely better than Texas.

Supporting a nine-piece rhythm and blues band that didn't play "She's About a Mover" proved challenging. Sahm and his new group recorded an album, *Honkey Blues*, credited to the Sir Douglas Quintet Plus Two ("He didn't know how to count," says saxophonist Martin Fierro). Playing the circuit of Northern California clubs like Frenchy's in Hayward, where the guys still wore Brylcreem in their hair and had fistfights in the parking lots, Sahm and company put on a sleek rhythm and blues show, featuring lots of Otis Redding material. "It was seriously drug-induced R&B," says Rains. "Psychedelic Wilson Pickett, Otis on acid."

But when Augie Meyers came back to San Francisco in late 1968, Sahm dumped the unwieldy R&B band and reformed the "original" Quintet (with a few additional players from the *Honkey Blues* band). The band cut another big hit single, "Mendocino." But the album of the same name was peppered with Sahm's songs about being an out-of-place Texan in California ("Lawd I'm Just a Country Boy In This Great Big Freaky City," "Texas Me" and "At the Crossroads," with the immortal line, "you just can't live in Texas if you don't have a lot of soul.") The last line to "Lawd I'm Just a Country Boy..." said it all: "When the whole scene goes down / I'll go back to the local bar in my hometown." Sahm wasn't long for San Francisco. The songs were clearly written by a man who was homesick for Lone Star beer and good Mexican food. "He always wanted to be somewhere else, always had another place he had to be," recalls saxophonist Fierro. "He couldn't sit still." By Christmas 1970, Sahm was back in Texas.

Living With the Animals: The Rise of Mother Earth

The summer of 1967 brought a tidal wave of youth descending on San Francisco. It was the Summer of Love. Scott McKenzie was singing the loathsome "San Francisco (Be Sure and Wear Some Flowers In Your Hair)" on the radio, and the Monterey Pop Festival that June was like a coming out party for underground rock from London and San Francisco. San Francisco bands like Big Brother, Grateful Dead, Quicksilver Messenger Service, Moby Grape and Country Joe and the Fish had rarely appeared outside the San Francisco Bay area before. Joplin was one of the new stars anointed that sunny weekend.

Travis Rivers, meanwhile, who found himself cut out of the whole Janis Joplin deal soon after bringing her to San Francisco, was married to someone else and still looking for his score. (Chet Holms, too, was cut loose by Big Brother before the band signed with big time New York music business broker Albert Grossman, who first saw the band at Monterey and landed them a record deal with Columbia.) Rivers was pissed off at Sahm for running off with his wife. Without revealing his personal agenda, he talked drummer Rains and Sahm's bass player into jumping ship. He was putting together a band called Mother Earth (after a Memphis Slim blues song) around another couple of ex-Austin players who had split for San Francisco – songwriter Powell St. John, who gave Joplin his "Bye, Bye Baby" on her way out to the coast, and guitarist John (Toad) Andrews, who belonged to one of Austin's first rock bands, the Wigs. Rivers was operating out of the former firehouse on Henry St., the Mouse/Kelley studios, where Joplin first auditioned for Big Brother the year before. But if Mother Earth was going to be his Big Brother, he would need to find his own Janis

Enter Tracy Nelson. As a University of Wisconsin student in Madison, she played in rock 'n' roll bands and played folk music. Discovered by blues producer Sam Charters, she cut a folk blues album for the Prestige label in 1965. She was a great singer and had a deep feeling for the blues. She won a talent contest that brought her as close to San Francisco as Los Angeles. She hitchhiked the rest of the way. Rivers arranged for her to audition with Mother Earth, and she came to meet the band in the same room in which Janis met Big Brother. As she started singing, Rivers wept. "I couldn't believe I was this lucky a second time," he says. And, again, he fell in love with the singer.

The band took over a large house on Oregon Street in Berkeley rented by KPFA disc jockey Michael Sunday. Rivers inveigled horn players Martin Fierro and Frank Morin out of Sahm's band and, along with Luis Gasca, they gave the band a distinctly Texas touch – the Latino horn section. Pianist Mark Naftalin of The Paul Butterfield Blues Band, recently relocated to Marin County, also joined the band. (A lot of Chicago musicians had been turning up in San Francisco – Mike Bloomfield, Nick Graventies, Elvin Bishop, Barry Goldberg.) All but unknown at the Fillmore and Avalon, newcomers Mother Earth landed a couple of tracks on a soundtrack to a movie called *Revolution*, which in short order led to a contract with Mercury. Bloomfield and Goldberg helped out on the sprawling but appealing first album, *Living With the Animals*, where Tracy Nelson's gut-wrenching "Down So Low" immediately established the band and brought inevitable comparisons with Joplin. The cover photos were taken on the front stairs at Oregon Street and show the huge, extended family, including many dogs, that the band had become. When a young Texan guitarslinger who had known Rivers from Austin and Tracy from Wisconsin pulled into town, it was only natural that he would crash at Oregon Street. His name was Steve Miller.

The Coming of the Space Cowboy

Steve Miller's father was a pathologist whose hobby was tape recording musicians. Dr. Miller owned one of the first tape recorders guitarist Les Paul ever saw. There is a tape of Dr. Miller's 5-year-old son, Steve, playing guitar for Les Paul, who tells the young lad, "You keep that up and you'll be famous one day." When the family moved from Milwaukee to Dallas, Dr. Miller held sessions in his living room with musicians such as T-Bone Walker, Charlie Mingus and Red Norvo. Young Steve was leading his own band before he was a teenager, playing R&B behind visiting bluesmen such as Jimmy Reed at local clubs.

Attending the exclusive boys' school, St. Marks, Miller put together a band called the Marksmen. He taught the fundamentals of singing and guitar to his best friend, Boz Scaggs, who joined the band. When Miller left to go to college at the University of Wisconsin, Scaggs followed a year later, the day after he graduated high school, and joined the band Miller had going up there, the Ardells. When Miller left to spend his senior year studying in Denmark in 1964, Scaggs went back to Texas, where he started playing frat parties and occasional nightclub dates with the Wigs.

Miller moved to Chicago the following year after his return from Europe and dove into the city's vibrant blues scene. Miller and keyboardist Barry Goldberg signed to make an album with Epic Records, and the Goldberg-Miller Band actually released a single, "The Mother Song," appeared on *Hullabaloo* and took over residency at an uptown Manhattan disco before disintegrating.

Miller came back to Texas, intending to study music at UT. He rented a small farm outside Austin for $125 a month. He had become interested in experimental, avant-garde music, but was seriously put off when he realized his professor didn't even know how to set up his equipment. "They wouldn't teach me any of that," he says. Three weeks later, he sold his textbooks, slapped a new set of tires on his VW bus and headed for San Francisco. "I heard about it in Chicago, and Butterfield came out [there] to play. Who wouldn't rather do gigs in front of 1,500 people than 200 drunks?"

He pulled into San Francisco on October 7, 1966 – the same night Grace Slick made her first appearance with the Jefferson Airplane at Winterland. Miller got up that night and jammed with the Paul Butterfield Blues Band. Swept away by enthusiasm, he announced to the crowd his decision to move to San Francisco. They cheered. He had five dollars in his pocket.

Over the Thanksgiving holidays, Miller used the basement of a vacant building on the University of California campus to rehearse a band. He was sleeping in the attic at Mother Earth's place on Oregon Street, keeping his things in the van. He had to sell his tape recorder. By the end of the year, the Steve Miller Blues Band was playing the Avalon Ballroom and Miller rented an apartment and took the band out to dinner and a movie with the $500 Helms paid him. So rapid was the band's rise through the ranks on the S.F. scene, the promoters of the Monterey Pop Festival added the group to the historic lineup in June 1967, a mere six months later.

Scaggs showed up that fall. He went to college in Sweden for a year, traveled around the world to Nepal and back and found himself lauded on the Scandinavian music scene as "the Bob Dylan of Sweden." But a postcard from Miller ended all that. When he heard from his old band mate that there was a spot in a band with a record contract waiting for him in San Francisco, he made tracks.

You're Gonna Miss Me: The End of an Era

By the summer of 1968, the Musicians' Switchboard, a non-profit community service, listed some 2,000 musicians and more than 500 bands in San Francisco. What had been a paradise two years earlier, a good situation a year before, was turning into a teeming turmoil. Good musicians were all over town. Bands worked every night. But with success, the values shifted. The drug scene changed. Speed became popular. There were killings. The Grateful Dead moved out of the Haight. The first wave of people coming to San Francisco was different than the flotsam and jetsam that drifted into town after the Summer of Love in 1967. The community still struggled with its promise, but increasingly it was more difficult for outsiders to crash the party that was already in progress.

Eventually even that unfailing barometer of hipness, *Rolling Stone* magazine, finally noticed that there were an awful lot of Texans running around San Francisco in music circles. The December 7, 1968, cover featured a picture of Doug Sahm. "Texas," the article by Larry Sepulvado and John Burks began, "is a drag – nearly every musician who comes from there agrees it's a drag – but the fact is that some of the heaviest, funkiest rock available today is Texas music: Janis Joplin, Steve Miller, Mother Earth and Sir Douglas Quintet – the list of fine Texas rock and roll musicians goes on and on."

The article went on to mention the most recent imports from Texas to San Francisco – Conqueroo from the I.L. Club, with Ed Guinn now billed as "Super Spade" – and the most significant talent remaining undiscovered back home in Texas, a 23-year-old cross-eyed albino blues guitarist named Johnny Winter.

"I'd forgotten about that boy," says Henry Carr, who was co-managing Mother Earth with Travis Rivers. He knew Winter and his brother Edgar from Beaumont and their band, Black Plague. Carr wasted no time in getting Winter out to San Francisco to sleep on his couch. Winter cruised the clubs and checked out the San Francisco scene. He jammed with Elvin Bishop and Texas bluesman Albert Collins at the Matrix. But he ended up in New York, signing with club owner Steve Paul for management, who parlayed the two-paragraph *Rolling Stone* mention into an extraordinary six-figure record deal with Columbia Records.

For Conqueroo, the band's pilgrimage to San Francisco was the end of a long road of aspiration and frustration. After deciding they had gone as far as possible in Texas, Conqueroo took the plunge. But it was too little, too late. The drummer freaked out and split for home. The others weren't sure they liked what they saw. "San Francisco started dying about six months before we got there," Bob Brown told author Jan Reid in his book, *The Rise of Redneck Rock* (1974). "The scene was really starting to degenerate. Haight Street smelled like piss, and a lot of little stores were closing down. All the people we thought were running around with flowers in their hair were now lying around with needles stuck in their necks." The band could never crack the scene. Broke and disgusted, they split up. Ed Guinn became a long-haul truck driver and Brown went back to Texas to open an antique store, bitter and angry at age 23.

By the time *Rolling Stone* did the Texas story, it was already over in San Francisco.

Postscript

JANIS JOPLIN

Almost simultaneously with the band's major label debut, *Cheap Thrills*, hitting the top of the charts in fall 1968, Janis Joplin announced her intention to leave Big Brother and the Holding Company. Her solo career soon sputtered and stalled, but was showing signs of finally lofting with the album she was recording, posthumously titled *Pearl*, when she died of a heroin overdose in a Hollywood motel on Oct. 4, 1970.

CHET HELMS

"Mr. Big" was making more money selling concert posters than concert tickets when his empire started to slide. By the end of 1968, he was out of the Avalon Ballroom. By mid-1970, he was out of the music business almost entirely. With the proceeds of the six-figure sale by auction in the '80s of a valuable painting he owned, Helms opened an art gallery, Atelier Dore, in downtown San Francisco.

ROKY ERICKSON

Busted in Texas for possession of marijuana in 1968 with a couple of joints in his pocket, Erickson thought he could skip jail time by pleading not guilty by reason of insanity. He was sentenced to Rusk State Hospital, where electroshock therapy and other treatment permanently garbled his transmission. His first post-asylum recording, "Two-Headed Dog," was produced by Doug Sahm, and Erickson remains a cult figure much beloved for his B-movie, science fiction rock 'n' roll.

DOUG SAHM

Sir Doug returned to Texas in time to catch the rise of outlaw country music. He came to represent Texas music – at home and abroad – in virtually everything he did; from various Quintet reunions through the years to creating the Lone Star all-stars, the Texas Tornados. On Nov. 18, 1999, he died of a heart attack in a New Mexico motel room, on his way to somewhere else.

MOTHER EARTH / BOZ SCAGGS

Tracy Nelson, Travis Rivers and most of the band left Berkeley for a farm outside Nashville, where they continued to make records through the '70s. Boz Scaggs showed up to help out on the band's 1969 sophomore album, *Make a Joyful Noise*, while he was living in Macon, Ga., after recording his first solo album in Muscle Shoals, Ala. He grabbed drummer George Rains and went back to San Francisco to start his own band and never left. Scaggs made one of the most popular make-out albums of the '70s (*Silk Degrees*) and has become a solid citizen in San Francisco, where he often appears at symphony galas, as well as sitting in at his own club, Slim's.

STEVE MILLER

Miller and his longtime associate Boz Scaggs parted ways after the Steve Miller Band's second album, *Sailor*, and Miller soldiered on with his band for several years before finally hitting the Top 40 with "The Joker" in 1973. It was the beginning of a string of smash hits that lasted through the '70s. His *Greatest Hits 1974-78* album has sold more than 10 million copies.

Essential albums

JANIS JOPLIN/BIG BROTHER AND THE HOLDING COMPANY
Big Brother and the Holding Company
Cheap Thrills
The first Big Brother album (self-titled) was a hastily recorded, warts-and-all document of the band's early Avalon repertoire. Joplin almost overpowered numbers like "Women is Losers," "Bye, Bye Baby," "Down On Me" and serves notice. *Cheap Thrills* delivers on that promise. Again, the album is based on well-practiced pieces from the band's ballroom songbook and Joplin's performances on "Summertime," "Piece Of My Heart" and "Ball and Chain" stand as landmarks.

SIR DOUGLAS QUINTET
Honkey Blues
Mendocino
Throughout his career, Doug Sahm would record blues records, but *Honkey Blues* remains in a class by itself. Sahm injects blues, jazz, country and anything else he can think of into a bright, snappy R&B sound. A horn riff from Junior Parker gives way to a Cajun fiddle solo. A vamp lifted from James Brown leads to some Horace Silver piano. Sahm's true heart steers the music through these potentially rocky shoals. *Mendocino*, on the other hand, is pure Texas cantina rock 'n' roll, featuring Augie Meyers' trademark Vox punched up by tight, tasty horn parts and Sahm singing everything like his life depended on it, including a saucy remake of "She's About a Mover." A neglected rock 'n' roll classic.

THE 13TH FLOOR ELEVATORS
The Psychedelic Sounds of the 13th Floor Elevators
"Recently," read the liner notes to the collector's item, classic first album by the 13th Floor Elevators, "it has become possible for man to chemically alter his mental state. He can then restructure his thinking and change his language so that his thoughts bear more relation to his life and his problems, therefore approaching them more sanely. It is this quest for sanity that forms the basis for the songs on this album."

MOTHER EARTH

Living With the Animals

Mother Earth's debut album, which features their version of the Memphis Slim song that gave them their name, boasts Chicago blues pros Mike Bloomfield, Barry Goldberg and Mark Naftalin. But it's Tracy Nelson's show all the way. Her "Down So Low" ranks with the greatest female rock vocal performances of the era.

STEVE MILLER BAND

Children of the Future

Sailor

The Steve Miller Blues Band of the Fillmore and Avalon ballrooms evolved into just the Steve Miller Band, a Beatles-influence pop-rock band with a blues undercurrent, on their debut album, *Children of the Future*. By the time the original five-member band finished their second album, *Sailor*, the only trace left of the raucous blues sound was the modest hit single, "Living In the U.S.A."

Texas Music | Summer 2002

CHAPTER 4

The Dead

Garcia Returns To a First Love

This was a difficult time for me. My boss at the Chronicle, John L. Wasserman, had died in a car crash a couple of weeks before and I stepped into the column. This was the kind of conversational coverage I envisioned, but the brass didn't see it. I was back down below the fold beside the adult theater ads again so fast my head swam. Jerry was always game to talk to the press, bless his heart.

JERRY GARCIA HAD FINISHED AN HOUR AND A HALF SET, but he wasn't through playing, just as he never finishes learning or experimenting. Sitting backstage, his eyes gleamed as he tried out a flathead banjo, plucking the complicated bluegrass runs as casually as just talking.

"I'm not real heavy," he said seriously. "I can't hardly play. At this point, I'm like super primitive."

But for the past few months, the Grateful Dead guitarist has worked out on the five-stringed instrument at least two or three hours a day. Bluegrass was his first musical love, and he's at it again.

Garcia constantly searches for new ways to express himself, be it playing pedal steel guitar with the New Riders of the Purple Sage, a country band, or jamming hard rock with the Merl Saunders group.

Joining up with David Diadem, Peter Rowan and John Kahn, they formed "Old and In The Way," an all-acoustic bluegrass band that made its debut at San Anselmo's Lion's Share two weeks ago and appeared last night and Monday at Keystone Berkeley.

"This is the group I wanted to play with when I was first real deep into bluegrass, but they weren't around then.

"These guys are really much more accomplished than I am," he said. "David is world famous – at least in the bluegrass world – as a mandolin player and Peter played with Bill Monroe for two years."

On stage, Peter Rowan led the group (formerly with rock group Seatrain) playing guitar and handling most of the lead vocals. Rowan also provides original material that forms approximately a third of their performance. The remainder of the tunes are traditional.

Jerry Garcia

Diadem plies his mandolin wildly, unleashing notes at the furious speed for which bluegrass is known. Garcia contents himself with a slightly more moderate tempo, allowing his banjo to speak with clear authority.

The delicate music cannot be played loud and, indeed, the three instruments in the front line shared only two microphones – one for the particular soloist of the moment and one for vocals. But the soft, rich music spun its web and it didn't take long for the rowdy Keystone crowd to quiet down.

"There's a high-level of virtuosity in straight bluegrass," Garcia noted. Compared to guitar, he characterized banjo playing as "complicated" and "hard."

"It's an acoustic instrument, so if you want to be heard," he said, "you have to play hard. Bluegrass is a real good trip . . . lots of fun."

There are no real plans for "Old and In The Way," except to add a fiddler. The group will perform around the Bay Area, in between Dead engagements, and Garcia is looking forward to improving.

Rod McKernan, called Pig Pen, died late last week apparently of liver failure. He was an integral part of the Grateful Dead experience. The son of an R&B disc jockey, McKernan brought his rhythm and blues background to Mother Macree's Uptown Jug Stompers and the rest is history.

His R&B specialties, like "Turn on Your Lovelight" or "It's a Man's World," became an essential highlight of any Dead concert. Furthermore, his post-Kesey-Hells Angel image was key to the image of the whole band.

"He was shy," Garcia said Monday night. "And a juicer. The kind of juicer who turned inward and became introverted. Oh yeah, he was a juicer. That was what did him in."

Garcia said McKernan had not played regularly with the band for well over a year, though he traveled to Europe with them last year against doctor's advice.

"We were all prepared emotionally for it a year ago when he first got sick. He almost died then and it was out of the clear blue sky."

A wake was held Saturday night at guitarist Bob Weir's home. All the Dead family and many of Pig Pen's friends assembled for a high time and sent McKernan off in a style closely akin to his own.

Monday's funeral services were quite different. "It was a bummer," Garcia said. "They had an Irish Catholic priest to say kind words, but it was for the straights."

The Dead left today for a two or three week tour, taking in Boston, Philadelphia, New York and other East Coast high spots. Warner Brothers Records is owed one more album to fulfill contractual obligations. In the future, they want to establish their own mail order record company, modeled after Rod McKuen's immensely successful enterprise. The next local Dead appearance is scheduled for spring in an outdoor facility.

San Francisco Chronicle | *March 14, 1973*

The Grateful Dead Decides to Try a Guiding Hand

Before going to the studio to play the orchestrations producer Keith Olsen overdubbed in London to the Grateful Dead, we listened to the tapes at his house. When I asked him how close to a final mix it was, he held his thumb and forefinger right next to one another. At the studio, when the Dead started giving him static about the rich, ornate decorations smothering their little rock band, Olsen turned down the volume. "Don't worry," he said. "This is just an orchestration mix with the strings and horns turned up way loud."

Keith Olsen

VAN NUYS – THE MYSTERIOUS, AMBIGUOUS ROLE PLAYED by record producers is often difficult to understand, although producers clearly exert much influence on the final product. The results sometimes even surprise the artists involved, as the Grateful Dead recently discovered.

After more than a dozen years of recording, and releasing 15 albums – all produced by the band itself – the Dead decided to bring in the guiding hand of a producer to oversee its first album for Arista Records, "Terrapin Station," due out this week.

A producer can supply musical, technical or philosophical direction behind the scenes. As the Dead learned, it is strictly a matter of personal style and the specific requirements of the producer's client.

Naturally, working with a major rock act like the Grateful Dead is a collaboration between the group and producer, although the producer still retains ultimate creative judgment – a tricky matter with any group, but especially with one as talented, experienced and strong-willed as the Dead.

Despite the band's international fame, the Dead never achieved spectacular success on record. The group sought a producer who would create an album with far broader appeal than any of its predecessors, at the same time retaining the trademark Grateful Dead sound.

At first, the band considered Bill Szymczyk (who does the Eagles and Geils) and Peter Asher (producer of James Taylor and Linda Ronstadt), before approaching Keith Olsen, who has been a recording engineer and producer for more than ten years in Los Angeles.

He came to sudden prominence two years ago with his production of the Fleetwood Mac album that turned the modestly popular group into superstars.

The Olsen-Dead relationship has worked out so well that, when "Terrapin Station" was done, Olsen began work on a solo album by Dead guitarist Bob Weir.

For most of the past five months, Olsen would arrive early in the evening at the Cabrito Industrial Center, which houses Sound City Studios, to work on the Dead album. He stayed usually until the middle of the next morning.

"When the band first called," he remembered, "I was scratching my head thinking, 'the Grateful Dead, they haven't done an album I liked in years.'"

Intrigued by the possibilities, he flew north to meet with the band and spent six hours the first night talking with members, returning at noon the next day for a second meeting at Weir's house. "Bob and I talked for seven hours while we waited for the others to show," he laughed. "Garcia never made it."

The producer finally met the Dead's lead guitarist, Jerry Garcia, the following week at Burbank studios, where Garcia was busy working on the recently released Grateful Dead movie. "When I saw his energy – working on the movie – that excited me," Olsen said.

Recording the Dead, however, required more than energy. "The band had to break a lot of habits," Olsen said, "and they also had to learn that, in recording, less is more."

That same quality that makes the Dead special in concert makes them difficult as recording artists. Onstage, the band has always specialized in long, involved improvisations. In the studio, where musicians are called on to perform endless repetitions with flawless precision, the band loses its edge.

"The Dead are good musicians," Olsen said, "who have never been exposed on record as such – especially Weir. He had never been able to play a rhythm guitar partly because he had to cover the chord for Phil Lesh, whose bass parts did tend to get a little esoteric at times. Phil is very inventive. His only problem is, at times, that he utilizes more than a three-octave range, and that takes his bass up into the guitar space."

The first two weeks were spent rehearsing in Marin. "There were two drummers playing exactly the same part," he said, "and never once did those two drums hit like this (he slapped his hands together). Two bass drums actually weaken it. 'Oh my God,' I thought, 'how are we going to record with two drums?'

"Working on it in rehearsal, we started them on orchestrating their drum parts; Mickey, you be the pulse, Billy, you be the color, because those are your personalities, and that's the way it's going to work best. It was several weeks before they really got the idea."

To help the rhythm section learn this new approach, Olsen held section rehearsals – the first in the history of the band.

"The next situation or problem, so to speak, was getting material structured down to something that's viable on radio – that wonderful medium for selling albums."

Vocals, never a Grateful Dead long suit, played an important role in the new album, too. "Garcia has amazing color in his voice," Olsen said, "if you place it just right, bridging the gap between Donna (Godchaux) and Bob. He has a George Harrison quality to his voice that makes an incredible blend if you voice the parts correctly."

Probably most important, the Dead had to learn patience in the studio. "At first, it was difficult to get six musicians to put out a good performance at any one time," he said, "a performance that I would accept, 'cause I'm a critical son of a bitch. So I'd have them come in to listen and give them not-very-flattering playbacks.

"Half of this gig is being a psychologist," he smiled.

The Dead spent six weeks recording the basic instrumental tracks to the album, an extraordinarily long time for Olsen. Accustomed to working with seasoned studio veterans, Olsen usually records basics in ten days, he said.

He joined the band later on tour in New York to record some additional overdubs, before flying to London to compose and record the orchestrations.

Paul Buckmaster, who wrote the 58-page score to "Terrapin Station" with Olsen, has worked with the biggest names in rock, including the Rolling Stones and Elton John. "I have calloused knees," Olsen said, "From crawling around on all fours for two weeks. He doesn't have a table, so he spreads all his papers over the floor. He's amazing...I love the man. But he's hard on the knees."

The Martyn Ford Orchestra recorded the sumptuous orchestrations at Abbey Road Studios in London. As many as 90 musicians and singers were involved.

The producer returned to Van Nuys to add some finishing touches, before the band came back from tour to hear the final product.

A few weeks ago, members of the Dead assembled at Sound City Studios to hear completed versions of songs they had left unfinished before going on the road.

They listened to Bob Weir's "Estimated Profit," with a saxophone part added by Tom Scott, ace Hollywood hired hand. "Well," said guitarist Garcia, breaking the silence that followed the end of the playback, "it's an unfortunately bizarre choice of notes. It's all right, I guess."

Olsen continued the playback. "I didn't want you to think I didn't like the last one," Garcia added gently.

Next up was "Terrapin Station," a 17-minute, five-part suite that takes up half the album and is covered with the Buckmaster orchestrations.

The staggering collection of horns, string and choruses is a dramatic departure from any past Grateful Dead recording.

"A couple of things bother me," Garcia started in, and a reserved, almost academic critique followed ("the counterpoint is too busy for my taste...the horns are a little too bright here...").

"As far as I'm concerned," Garcia concluded, "it's just a matter of taste, and that's really up to you."

"Basically we all agree," said Weir, "that you've got to feature the bank over the orchestrations."

Weir left a few minutes later. "It's a whole lot to choke down at once," he admitted in the hallway, "because that's a whole lot grander than we've ever sounded.

"Maybe a little too fabulous right now, but we'll hammer out an agreement," he continued. "The one thing we've never done with our music is dress it up, and why not? It sounds great."

Back inside the studio, however, producer Olsen had the last word.

"Well, you better love it," he said amiably, "because there it is."

San Francisco Chronicle | July 28, 1977

Liner Notes From "Grateful Dead From the Mars Hotel"

WHEN THE GRATEFUL DEAD WENT INTO CBS STUDIOS on March 25, 1974 to record the band's next album, the group was careening nearly out of control, although they didn't know it at the time. Only two days earlier, the band had staged a public "Sound Test" of the epic Wall of Sound sound system the band spent years and more than $350,000 building. It weighed more than fifty tons and contained more than 600 individual speakers. And it was not only the highest quality sound system any rock band had yet devised, it was an expensive monster on their backs that required even larger gigs to pay for it.

In the two years since leaving Warner Brothers Records and starting their own label, Grateful Dead Records, the band had watched as their operations mushroomed, their payroll exploded and their expenses went through the ceiling. They supported something like three hundred people, many of them developing expensive habits. The label's first album, "Wake Of the Flood," ran into unexpected pitfalls when a Mafia counterfeit operation slammed them, producing counterfeits so good distributors were taking them back as returns and charging them to the Dead's label. There was no telling how much this cost the band, but the record business was clearly going to be more complicated than they originally envisioned.

In January, Garcia slapped together his second solo album, barely involved in the process, to give the label some product. In February, the band roused itself from the traditional post-New Year's stupor to play three nights at Winterland to raise funds for Keith and Donna Godchaux to buy a house, Phil Lesh to get a computer he needed for musical experiments he was running with Ned Lagin, and to make a donation to an old friend's public school program. The band's next gig was the "Sound Test" at the Cow Palace, two days before starting the sessions for "From the Mars Hotel" at the studios on the seedy edge of downtown San Francisco.

Garcia did some sessions for his solo album in Studio A, far away the most modern recording facility in the Bay Area at the time. Columbia Records outfitted the building when the label decided to open an artist and repertoire wing to capitalize on the booming San Francisco music scene in 1970, installing to run the operation the company's most prestigious producer, Roy Halee, and another veteran CBS engineer, Roy Segal, who began his career doing audio at the United Nations. Neither of these guys could get over not wearing a tie to work, and they brought a taste of the corporate recording world of New York to this barbarian outpost.

Studio A was a large cinderblock room built for Halee to record Simon and Garfunkel (they spoiled that plan by breaking up, but they both recorded their first solo albums, at least parts, in this room). With Segal engineering, the Dead synched up two sixteen-track machines and, after cutting the basic tracks live, began to doodle over the back sixteen. Steel guitarist John McFee of Marin County rock band Clover put some licks on Lesh's country song, "Pride Of Cucamonga." Ned Lagin supplied some synthesizer material for Lesh's "Unbroken Chain," although the heart of the album was the Garcia-Hunter compositions such as "Scarlet Begonias," "Ship of Fools" and "U.S. Blues," songs the band had introduced during the February run at Winterland.

To suggest that the Dead ever did anything to compromise their music just to sell records would do the band an injustice. But with the weight of fiscal responsibility bearing down on the fellows at the approximate rate of $100,000 a month, a hit record on their own label would not have been a bad thing. And one of these new Hunter-Garcia compositions, "U.S. Blues," had a certain friendly, accessible ring that seemed like it might be just right for the times. With the two-year drama of Watergate reaching an operatic crescendo, Nixon's presidency rapidly crumbling, Hunter's smart-alecky lyric contained an appealing balance of cheeky good humor and defiant pride. When Warner Brothers asked the band to think about making a single radio could play, they laughed scornfully. But when fellow pirate and co-conspirator Ron Rakow of their own label gave them the same suggestion, a nifty little 3:12 edit of "U.S. Blues" was promptly made.

The album was named for a transient hotel a couple of blocks from the studio and the band dutifully trooped over to another fleabag in the Tenderloin to pose for the back cover photo. They were joking about naming the album "Ugly Roomers," but opted for "Ugly Rumors," lest the pun be construed as insulting to the hotel's actual residents. Album cover artists Stanley Mouse and Alton Kelley rendered the phrase in pseudo-Aztec psychedelic script, hard enough to read as originally drawn, but when it was plopped on the cover upside down and backwards, it looked truly like a message from Mars.

The single to "U.S. Blues" never charted and, after the album was released on June 10, it had sold a fairly unspectacular 258,000 by mid-August, a little more than half what "Wake Of the Flood" sold, counterfeiters and all. The band started touring in May, carting the enormous Wall of Sound around the country, the crew spending an entire day setting it up before each show, playing bigger and bigger halls to support the expense. Band and crew alike were buried in a blizzard of cocaine. By the time the Dead headed for a grueling European tour in September, everybody was running out of gas and they were already talking openly about breaking up.

When the band returned home, the first order of business was to scrub a planned October tour. Garcia was having more fun playing in dumps like Keystone Berkeley with Merl Saunders. No matter how hard they worked or how big the crowds were, nobody had any money. In October, the band booked five nights and Winterland and announced that the band would be taking a hiatus from any further live performances for the next year and a half. Although the truth was nobody really had any idea what was coming next, the first great era of the Grateful Dead had come to a close.

Beyond Description (1973-1989) April 2004

Closing Down Winterland

It was 1978, the night they closed old Winterland down – and the Grateful Dead's all-night show lives on in memories, flashbacks – and now a DVD

Do you think if we knew that it was a golden era, we would have paid any more attention at the time? Me, neither.

BILL GRAHAM PUT A BILLBOARD ON THE SIDE OF WINTERLAND for New Year's Eve 1978, the night the Grateful Dead closed the dilapidated old hall, which had an appointment with the wrecker's ball. "They're not the best at what they do, " it read, "they're the only ones that do what they do." On the sidewalk under the sign, a Deadhead waiting days in advance of the show held a sign of his own: "1535 Days Since Last S.F. 'Dark Star.' "

In a news conference two weeks before the event, producer Graham speculated he could have sold 500,000 tickets. Radio advertising executive Jeff Nemerovski, sensing an opportunity, was able to persuade KQED-TV to broadcast the proceedings live, while KSAN-FM would simulcast a stereo soundtrack.

Frank Zamacona was a young floor director on the broadcast that night. It was an evening he never forgot, and when he found himself working on another video project with the band eight years ago, he started digging out the videotapes from that New Year's Eve broadcast. "I'm not a Deadhead," Zamacona said. "I've been trying to put it out there so people will understand what it was like."

KQED-TV will air an 80-minute selection Zamacona edited from those tapes at 9 p.m. Saturday, the first time these performances have been seen since they were originally broadcast, a pledge drive sneak preview of the nationwide PBS broadcast in November to coincide with the release of a two-DVD set that contains the complete, unedited version of the epic four-hour performance.

"We played all night, till dawn," said drummer Mickey Hart.

"We were pretty on our game," said guitarist Bob Weir. "As the night wore on, I'm not sure we got a whole lot tighter."

A huge banner of the Dead's skull and roses emblem always hung from the rafters of Winterland like the home team's pennant. The Dead played the old ice rink at Post and Steiner 59 times beginning in 1968, including four New Year's Eves. The night Janis Joplin died in a seedy Los Angeles motel room, the Dead worked Winterland with the Jefferson Airplane and Quicksilver Messenger Service (another evening, coincidentally, broadcast on KQED). That was also the last night that founding members Marty Balin of the Airplane and John Cipollina of Quicksilver played with their respective groups.

The Dead, who recorded some of their 1971 live album at the hall, took over the place for five nights in 1974 to film "The Grateful Dead Movie." Another five-night run in 1978 celebrated the band's return from Egypt.

Winterland itself was built in 1928 for what was then an astronomical cost of $1 million on the site where a temporary theater had once been erected after the 1906 earthquake and young unknown Al Jolson gave one of his first important performances. The 5,400-capacity room played host to opera and boxing, and was home to Shipstad and Johnson's Ice Follies.

When Graham began operating the nearby Fillmore Auditorium in 1966, he would occasionally rent the bigger hall for larger shows, starting with the September 1966 double bill of Jefferson Airplane and the Paul Butterfield Blues Band. Jimi Hendrix played one of his great shows at Winterland. Cream recorded portions of "Wheels of Fire" there, and the Dead's Jerry Garcia and Mickey Hart caught the show. Hart thought the three-man group featuring Eric Clapton on guitar must have been the greatest group in the world.

"No," corrected his bandmate Garcia. "Tonight they're the greatest group in the world."

After Graham closed the Fillmore West in 1971, he ran shows at Winterland almost every weekend. The Rolling Stones gave four memorable shows at the rickety old hall in 1972. Peter Frampton recorded his blockbuster double album "Frampton Comes Alive" there. The Band filmed "The Last Waltz" and the Sex Pistols closed the band's U.S. tour at Winterland. But pieces of plaster were raining on the heads of concertgoers at almost every show, and Graham estimated the cost of repair at more than $350,000, which his landlords refused to deduct from his rent.

He made an emotional appeal to the Grateful Dead to play New Year's Eve and close the hall for him. He wrote a letter asking the band to rehearse for the concert and to play some old favorites that had been dropped from the repertoire. As a supporting act, he booked the great party band of the moment - - the Blues Brothers with Dan Ackroyd and John Belushi, at the height of "Saturday Night Live" mania. The evening promised a rich emotional subtext, even for the rela-

Grateful Dead

tively unsentimental Dead.

"This was home base," said drummer Hart, "Dead Central, longtime center for the San Francisco Dead universe."

Instead of a touching farewell, however, the evening descended into a deranged bacchanalia. The place was a cocaine speakeasy – even the janitor was holding. "There was a bit of blow going around," said Weir. "The Blues Brothers brought mounds of it. I think they had it for breakfast."

The "Saturday Night" crowd – Bill Murray, Father Guido Sarducci, Al Franken, Paul Shaffer (playing in the Blues Brothers band) – mingled backstage with psychedelic bull goose loony Ken Kesey, NBA all-star Bill Walton, Chet Helms of the Family Dog and members of the Jefferson Airplane. After their set, the Blues Brothers moved their scene to an after-hours party at the Airplane mansion on

Fulton Street that lasted through the night.

Backstage, the Hells Angels motorcycle gang swarmed over the party en masse, which sent Graham overboard with anger.

"They started pouring in the place," said Dead road manager Steve Parish. "They literally took the backstage over. There were hundreds of them. We gave everyone onstage a dose of acid. That was our way of dealing with it."

After Bill Graham made his annual appearance as Father Time, riding to the stage above the crowd from across the hall on a giant marijuana cigarette, the Dead kicked off the New Year at midnight with "Sugar Magnolia" under an avalanche of balloons. Weir started the second set with the never-more- appropriate "Samson and Delilah" ("If I had my way I would tear this old building down . . ."). Lee Oskar of War and Gregg Errico of Sly and the Family Stone joined the onstage throng during the drum solo. Ken Babbs of the Merry Pranksters rolled out the Thunder Machine, with Kesey banging away from inside, and then set off a small bomb, while wild-eyed Hart attacked the percussion contraption from the outside. Cipollina joined the band for the last two songs of the set.

The band played until morning. Graham served champagne, ham and eggs to the entire crowd. With the house lights up full, the band members threw their arms around one another's shoulders and took their final Winterland bow after "We Bid You Goodnight."

The band would soon graduate to hockey rinks and baseball parks. But on this last New Year's Eve at Winterland, the Dead was still part of a small community in which band members could actually read the signs in the crowd.

At the start of the third set, deep into the post-midnight hours, Jerry Garcia tickled opening notes out of his electric guitar and a shudder of recognition swept through the crowd. As the band lurched into "Dark Star," the "1535 Days" sign came flying out of the balcony and fluttered to the floor below.

San Francisco Chronicle | *Thursday, October 23, 2003*

Strings of gold

There was something special about Doug Irwin's guitars, and Jerry Garcia knew what it was

Steve Parish, Garcia's trusty roadie, was the key to this story. The lawyers didn't know where the first Irwin guitar was, but Parish's long-suffering associate, the one and only Ramrod, knew. He had it. Garcia gave it to him years ago. Did he care if I mentioned that in the paper, I asked. He didn't care. How come he didn't tell the band's lawyers? They never asked.

JERRY GARCIA PLAYED VERY FEW GUITARS.

For more than 20 years, he played only one-of-a-kind objets d'art made for him by Doug Irwin, who won back ownership of two of the four guitars he made for Garcia in a lawsuit settlement reached last week. Garcia played Irwin guitars every day until two years before his death in 1995, when a mystery guitar from a fan arrived in the mail.

The lawsuit between the surviving members of the Grateful Dead and Irwin placed the instruments in the spotlight. While the Dead hurried to put the Garcia guitars that are under the band's control on view at Cleveland's Rock and Roll Hall of Fame, others remained tucked away in an East Bay fine arts storage facility. Now Irwin, who is destitute and living with his mother in the Southern California desert while recovering from car-crash head injuries, will be able to put up for sale two guitars he made for Garcia.

Garcia's only bequest to someone outside his immediate family was to Irwin. He wanted all the guitars Irwin made for him to be returned. The Grateful Dead partnership sued to fight the codicil, maintaining that the band members collectively owned all instruments purchased with Dead funds. The group has long had plans to open a museum in San Francisco called Terrapin Station, and Garcia's guitars would be a cornerstone exhibit.

But last Tuesday, on the courthouse steps in San Rafael, lawyers for Irwin and the Dead came to terms: Irwin would get two guitars and the Dead would keep two. The rest of Garcia's surprisingly small collection of instruments belongs to his estate.

Over more than 20 years, Irwin built four guitars for Garcia so special that each had a name – Wolf, Tiger, Headless and Rosebud. Under the terms of the agreement, Irwin takes Tiger and Wolf; the Dead keep Rosebud and Headless, which has a unique design with no tuning pegs. Garcia never played it.

"We slept with these instruments," said equipment manager Steve Parish, who handled Garcia's guitars for more than 25 years. "You could lose amps. You could break things, and sometimes we did. But I could never look Jerry in the eye and say, 'I don't have your guitar.'"

Garcia began playing electric guitar with the Warlocks, before the band changed its name to the Grateful Dead. He used an inexpensive cherry-red Guild Starfire. He played that instrument for several years and used it on the band's early recordings.

But as early as 1971, Garcia expressed dissatisfaction with factory-made guitars, even though he played models favored by other rock guitarists – the Gibson Les Paul and the Gibson SG. Until he walked into Irwin's Sonoma studio in early 1972, he had been playing a vintage '57 Fender Stratocaster, a classic rock 'n' roll guitar given to him by Graham Nash, with an alligator decal on the body that gave the guitar its name, Alligator.

Garcia bought the first guitar Irwin ever made for $850 (known as 001) and ordered another one custom-made. Irwin delivered Wolf, named after its distinctive inlay of a wolf, in May 1973 for $1,500. (Garcia gave Irwin's 001 to original Dead road crew member Ramrod. Garcia gave away a lot of guitars.)

After a brief dalliance with an aluminum guitar designed by Southern California maverick Travis Bean, Garcia replaced Wolf with Tiger in 1979. The guitarmaker spent more than six years working on it, and Garcia played the heavy 14-pound guitar for 11 years.

Irwin mixed exquisitely detailed, intricate brass work with dense, exotic hardwoods in his designs. He also incorporated a lot of special features Garcia himself devised, like a loop that ran the signal back through the guitar so he could control his special effects with knobs on the body of the guitar or a built-in pre-amp hidden beneath Irwin's inlays. "Jerry knew more about his guitars and equipment than anyone," said Parish.

Wolf briefly came out of retirement in 1988 as a guinea pig for MIDI synthesizer experiments. After a Roland synthesizer was successfully attached to Wolf, Tiger went back to the shop for retrofitting. Garcia used the synthesizer attachment to make his guitar sound like a trumpet or other instruments.

In 1989, Irwin delivered his $11,000 masterpiece, Rosebud, with MIDI controls built in. "Everything he had learned about guitars went into Rosebud," said Parish.

Garcia's next guitar arrived in the mail at the Grateful Dead office in 1993. Stephen Cripe, a 39-year-old Florida woodworker who spent years building custom interiors for Caribbean yachts, decided to try his hand at making a guitar. Using a few photos and a Dead video, he knocked off Irwin's design of Tiger with a few flourishes of his own, like carving the body out of a piece of East Indian rosewood recycled from a 19th century Asian opium bed.

Garcia was floored. He gave the piece to San Francisco repairman Gary Brawer to fix the electronic guts, but it was a miracle guitar.

"Garcia was amazed when it came around," said band mate Bob Weir, "at the guesswork he had to make – and got right – to give that guitar Irwin's look and feel. It was astounding."

He pronounced the piece "the guitar I've always been waiting for" and began playing the instrument exclusively. It came to be called Lightning Bolt. Garcia met with Cripe briefly backstage at a Florida concert and commissioned a second guitar for $6,500, known as Top Hat, although Garcia almost never played it. Cripe, whose hobby was making fireworks, died in May 1996 when his work shed blew up. He used an exploding firecracker as the insignia on his guitars' headstocks.

Lightning Bolt was in the shop on the last tour. In his final show at Soldier Field in Chicago on July 9, 1995, Garcia started out playing Rosebud, but midway through the show, the guitar developed problems. Garcia strapped on the tour's spare guitar – Tiger, out of mothballs for the occasion – and finished his final concert on his old trusty ax.

Guitars may bring six figures at auction

How much are Jerry Garcia's guitars worth?

Under the terms of the settlement, the Dead keep Rosebud and Headless, a strange-looking Doug Irwin design with no tuning pegs that Garcia never played.

Guitarmaker Irwin gets Wolf and Tiger, the latter the guitar both sides considered the prize because Garcia spent so many years playing it. The Dead retain the right to match the best offer and buy the guitars back. Irwin has already said he will auction the guitars.

"The question is 'What will someone pay for it?'" said Steve Routhier, the buyer who assembled the Hard Rock Cafe's collection. Routhier has bought hundreds of rock-star guitars at auction, including models previously owned by greats like Jimi Hendrix, Eric Clapton and John Lennon.

He believes the auction gallery would set an estimate of $80,000 to $100,000, a low figure designed to entice bidders. He estimated the value of the guitars at $200,000 to $300,000 each. But these one-of-a-kind pieces could attract the sort of crazy, spend-anything buyers that make auctions so unpredictable.

An acoustic guitar that belonged to Buddy Holly, originally estimated by Sotheby's at $20,000, was sold for more than 10 times that

Wolf

in 1990 to actor Gary Busey, who played Holly in the movie "The Buddy Holly Story."

The same year, the white Stratocaster that Hendrix played at Woodstock sold for $325,000 to an Italian collector (the guitar is now owned by Microsoft billionaire Paul Allen and displayed in his Seattle rock museum).

The highest price ever paid for a rock guitar was $450,000 in August 1999 for Eric Clapton's "Brownie," the tobacco-burst Stratocaster he recorded "Layla" with during his Derek and the Dominoes days. That guitar, too, is part of the permanent collection in Allen's Experience Music Project in Seattle.

Jerry's guitars

WOLF

Years played: 1973-1978

The first guitar Doug Irwin made for Garcia featured hallmark detail work such as the brass inlays on the neck and almost handmade brass hardware. Goes to Irwin in the settlement.

Played: At the Great Pyramids, Sept. 14-16, 1978.

Price: $1,500 .

TIGER

Years played: 1979-1990

Irwin spent six years building his second guitar for Garcia, who played the hefty 14-pounder longer than any other guitar in his career. Goes to Irwin in the settlement.

Played: "Touch of Grey," 1987

Price: $5,800 .

ROSEBUD

Years played: 1990-1993

The first Irwin guitar to incorporate built-in MIDI synthesizer controls as a part of the original design, "Rosebud" was the culmination of a nearly 20- year collaboration between the guitarmaker and the guitarist. The Dead keep this one.

Played: Pulled out of retirement for the final Grateful Dead concert, July 9, 1995, at Soldier Field, Chicago.

Price: $11,000 .

LIGHTNING BOLT

Years played: 1993-1995

The so-called "Florida guitar" was made by boatmaker Stephen Cripe out of a 19th century Asian opium bed with a cocobolo wood neck and rosewood fingerboard. He made the guitar, his first, by studying photos and a Dead video and mailed it to Garcia as a gift. Belongs to the band.

Played: "Dear Mr. Fantasy" with Traffic, opening for the Dead Aug. 3-4, 1994, at Giants Stadium in New Jersey.

Price: gift

San Francisco Chronicle | Tuesday, November 6, 2001

Dead man talking

Sammy Hagar asked me when Bob and I first met. I looked
at Weir and said "It was 1970, but probably three more years
before he noticed me." "More like five," said Weir.

BOB WEIR SHOWED UP AT REHEARSAL WITH HIS SIDELINE BAND RatDog to discover the other musicians already working up a version of "Black Peter" – the old Grateful Dead song that had always been sung by Jerry Garcia.

"They had this up and running," bandleader Weir said, "so I thought we'd give it a try."

Reading the lyrics from a music stand, Weir bobbled his way through the singing. But the guitar playing he knew. He laughed when his guitar part banged up against what RatDog lead guitarist Mark Karan was playing in the new arrangement. "After 30 years," Weir said, "I don't know what else I would play."

Weir served as one of the Dead's main vocalists and front men alongside Garcia, the charismatic lead guitarist, for much of the band's 30 years. The Dead thrived from the dawn of the psychedelic apocalypse at Ken Kesey's Acid Tests to the football stadiums full of Deadheads that followed the band until Garcia's death in 1995 and beyond.

No major rock star's solo career has ever received less attention than Weir's. Without much fanfare or grand ambitions, he has been working away in various configurations outside the Grateful Dead pretty much all along.

RatDog has been Weir's other band for almost 10 years, although he has always kept something else going on the side, whether it was the spare two-man approach of his acoustic performances with bassist Rob Wasserman or the fusion rock of Bobby and the Midnites.

A two-CD set titled "Weir Here" will be released this week to shine some light on Weir's long-term (albeit secondary) solo career. The album will not only spotlight his songwriting contributions to the Dead, but also his work outside the band. One CD features studio recordings from his solo albums. The other is a live CD that includes several never-before-released Grateful Dead performances plus a recent RatDog version of Bob Dylan's "Masters of War," a timely selection.

Having belonged to the Grateful Dead since he was a 17-year-old high school

Bob Weir

dropout, Weir, 57, is not like other people.

He doesn't need to be. Nobody is more comfortable in his own skin. He can let other musicians pick out the material he sings. He doesn't care about that. He is the rarest of musical animals – a hands-off bandleader.

As the one good-looking guy in the Dead, baby-faced Weir was always what passed for the band's sex symbol. He didn't care about that, either. In fact, he always seemed to secretly relish subverting that image. With his new bushy beard, he looks like Commander Whitehead, the old bloke in the advertisements who used to sell "Schweppervescence."

Almost invariably dressed in short pants and Birkenstocks, Weir was wearing long khaki trousers this day because of what he called "laundry problems." Somewhat typically, he was late for rehearsal at the small studio the Dead still maintains in Novato. But he'd been running late all weekend.

Weir blew his schedule out two days before to rush down to Santa Cruz at the last minute to play a benefit concert where his presence would ensure an additional $15,000 donation, and he had been scrambling to catch up ever since.

His longtime friend and musical collaborator Matthew Kelly, who attended Weir's 10th birthday party, made the call. And Weir, an enthusiastic and knowledgeable supporter of Amicus Foundation, the fund-raiser's beneficiary, dropped everything and took off to play with Kelly, who started Weir's first solo band, Kingfish, with him more than 30 years ago.

He did the hippie-jam-band thing with Kingfish. His 1972 solo debut, "Ace, " was, ironically, one of the best records the Grateful Dead ever made (the band served as his backup), and the Dead does songs from that album to this day. He tried to make a commercial Hollywood solo album when he recorded "Heaven Help the Fool" in 1978 with producer Keith Olsen (Fleetwood Mac, Foreigner).

It hasn't exactly been a bell-ringing, million-selling solo career, but under-achiever Weir has never gotten his due for some genuine high points and a whole lot of good music under his own brand.

Laboring under the behemoth shadow of the Grateful Dead and its com-manding centerpiece, Garcia, all those years has been a thankless task for many more than Weir. His solo career has been primarily something he does when the Dead isn't working.

Characteristically, Weir left compiling the new anthology to other people. "Actually it was coordinated by somebody I have yet to meet," he said. Outside of having made the actual music some time ago, Weir's big contribution to the pack-age was operating the Photoshop program for psychedelic poster artist Al Kelley when he designed the cover.

But Weir has always been an under-the-hood kind of guy who can repair his own guitar, navigate the Internet, even crank up the sound system at the Dead rehearsal hall. No roadies attended this rehearsal, only the musicians, and Weir himself ran all the equipment, walking around the board to make adjustments while the band played.

"They did ask me about certain songs," he said. "Every so often I'd throw a fit to keep some song off the package I definitely didn't want. But I've been way the hell busy."

With the Dead back in business, Weir will spend this summer on the road with them. He is in the middle of RatDog's spring tour – it passed through the Fillmore Auditorium a couple of weeks ago – and will do another RatDog tour in the fall after he gets home from the Dead road trip.

He has traveled 250,000 miles in the past two years. He could be staying home to watch his two daughters, ages 2 and 6, with his beautiful wife of five years, Na-tascha. The family has just finished a 2 1/2-year remodel of his longtime home in Mill Valley.

But Weir is on the road with RatDog.

"It's what I do," he said. "I love it. The more I do it, the better I get. "

RatDog has been around for almost 10 years, starting the band's first tour just before Garcia's death. Drummer Jay Lane, who came out of the multicultural Berkeley funk band Freaky Executives, joined up with Weir and Wasserman, who had been performing as a duo since 1988. Kelly played harmonica and guitar.

For the first three years of RatDog, Weir, grieving in his own way over Garcia, refused to have a lead guitarist in the band.

For more than a year, the band featured pianist Johnnie Johnson, the man who played on all the original Chuck Berry records, but RatDog's schedule proved too hectic for someone pushing 80. Drummer Lane brought in a couple of Young Turks from the '90s San Francisco acid jazz scene that centered on the Up and Down Club: keyboardist Jeff Chimenti of Alphabet Soup and saxophonist Dave Ellis (since replaced by another Up and Down alumnus, Kenny Brooks). Slowly the band began to develop into a more meaningful musical experience.

Chimenti, who now also plays keyboards with the Dead, still does occasional gigs with his old jazz group at tiny Bruno's in the Mission District when he isn't working with RatDog or the Dead.

Playing with Weir has turned all these hipster jazzbos into Deadheads. Chimenti has been picking out Dead songs for Weir to play. Drummer Lane sounded like an old hand discussing the version of "Black Peter," Grateful Dead lyricist Robert Hunter's doleful song about mortality, on the "Bear's Choice" live album.

"What is Black Peter anyway?" Lane asked. "Tuberculosis?"

"It's a British flag signal," bassist Robin Sylvester said. "It either means send help or help is coming. I forget which."

Weir, who grew up in Atherton, was kicked out of seven schools before dropping out of high school to run off with a rock 'n' roll band. He suffered from dyslexia, a learning disorder that makes it difficult to read. He is still a slow reader. But when he wants to investigate a subject, he does the heavy lifting.

He is extremely well versed in a wide variety of subjects, from technology to environmental issues. He talked in detail about the Amicus operation, the outfit he dashed down to Santa Cruz to support two nights earlier, and praised the foundation's approach of teaming old-age homes and orphanages in Burma. He expressed some skepticism about the role Christian evangelists played in the region and then related his experiences with evangelists when he was visiting with Aborigines on the remote north coast of Australia, researching one of the rain forest children's books he did with his sister.

"He's smarter than you think, and he uses that as a weapon," said drummer Mickey Hart, Weir's band mate in the Dead. "You think he's spaced – and he is –

but meanwhile he's in there the whole time going tick ... tick ... tick."

Life is an inexact science for Bob Weir. Or is it a science of the inexact?

RatDog finished making its way through "Black Peter." "Now I have to learn how to sing it," said Weir, rising from his stool. "Let me try by singing it standing up."

"Is that how it ends?" Lane asked.

"We'll probably just bail out and it'll morph into something else," Weir said.

Instead of playing "Black Peter" again, however, Weir and company started running a new original.

RatDog has made only two CDs, a 2000 studio session called "Evening Moods" and a double-disc live set in 2001. Weir said the Dead, too, is working up some new material and that there are a couple of new songs by Hunter floating around.

He is typically guileless when asked to describe the difference between work he does with his own band and the Dead.

"I think the stuff I do with my own band is a little more adventurous – no, wait, let me think about it," he said, interrupting himself. "If anything," he continued, "and I don't know how to back this up, the stuff I do on my solo records is not as developed. Things are a little more formal with the Grateful Dead. We tend to frame it more carefully. That's the main difference. But I'm not sure anyone would hear it."

Weir has no plans to record with RatDog – or the Dead – although he thinks that he might post some new recordings on the Internet in the near future.

"That's how it's going to be done now," said Weir, an enthusiastic iPod user. In fact, he expects the coming generation of digital recorders to make recording studios somewhat obsolete and dissolve the barriers between rehearsing, recording and performing.

Weir and RatDog launched into his new piece, a solid bluesy composition with a Dylanesque sound. Keyboardist Chimenti moved around some chords. He tried a couple that didn't work. All the musicians conferred, Weir listening intently. The band members are writing this song together, laying out a musical bed as they push and prod their way through the piece. Weir only supplied the raw material. They took the piece as far as it goes and Weir broke it off at the end of a verse.

"We'll have no idea where it goes from here until I get the words," he said. "I can see them, but they're not in the clear yet."

Sunday Datebook | March 21, 2004

Weir finds his birth father and adopts a vintage guitar

This is one of the great guitar stories of all time. Bob Weir told me the tale at dinner, while he were waiting for his father, Jack Parber, to show up. When Jack did finally take his seat, I couldn't help asking "What do you think, Jack – any more out there?"

BOB WEIR WAS ADOPTED AND HAS NEVER KNOWN the circumstances of his birth. His biological mother's name on his birth certificate was a phony – that much he knew.

So when Weir's office received a phone call in the mid- to late '80s from someone claiming to be his mother, who said she could identify herself by the false name she used on his birth certificate, he was reasonably certain she knew what she was talking about.

Bob Weir

His birth mother told him that she and a fellow college student in Tucson, Ariz., had a fling in 1947. When she discovered she was pregnant, she moved to San Francisco, arranged for the baby's adoption, gave birth and went back to Tucson a year later. She never told the child's father. She did tell Weir the man's name.

A private detective informed Weir that a man with the same name was an Air Force colonel running Hamilton Air Force Base in Marin County. Weir let the matter drop. "I'm pathologically anti-authoritarian," he said.

Then in 1996, after some prodding from his wife, Natascha, Weir looked in the phone book and found the now-retired John Parber listed. He called him up.

"I'm Robert Weir of Mill Valley," he told the man. "I've been doing some research and I've run across some information that might be of considerable interest to you."

"The only Robert Weir I know plays guitar for the Grateful Dead," the colonel replied.

Parber and his wife hit it off with his newly discovered grown son and became what Weir called "wonderful doting grandparents" to Weir's two small daughters. The Parbers raised four sons of their own, and the oldest, James Louis Parber, pursued a career as a musician for a number of years. He played with local country-rock outfit Lawrence Hammond and the Whiplash Band, who recorded the 1976 album "Coyote's Dream," and played in the solo band led by Billy C. Farlow, former Commander Cody and His Lost Planet Airmen vocalist, before spinal cancer made it too painful to play. He spent the next 12 years under the care of his parents, dying a slow, agonizing death that finally came in 1991.

James Louis' three brothers split up his guitars, but left one beat-up electric guitar with their parents as a kind of memento.

Every time Weir spent the night in the Parbers' spare bedroom, he practically had to step over the guitar case they left in the room. Inside, he found a battered old Fender Telecaster, the pickup sprung from its moorings, the strings all broken. He finally asked the Parbers if he could take the guitar and have it fixed up. Weir, who was just starting rehearsals with the newly re-formed and rejuvenated Dead, gave the guitar to his roadie. Within 10 minutes, the roadie was back, the pickup screwed down, the guitar strung with Weir's strings.

Weir tried the guitar out with the Dead.

"The Telecaster has a thin, reedy sound," Weir said. "It was instantly perfect. It cleared out a lot of clutter and made the whole band sound jell."

On the back, Weir noticed a five-figure serial number and asked the roadie to inquire with the Fender company. The factory confirmed that the model was a 1956 vintage Fender Telecaster, one of the original models, a true relic. It has become Bob Weir's No. 1 guitar.

James Louis Parber never made the big time. But his guitar did.

Sunday Datebook | March 21, 2004

Mickey Hart Marches on to His Own Beat

Ex-Grateful Dead drummer about to release magnum opus

Mickey Hart is a force of nature. He tackles every project with his full and complete enthusiasm. His intense focus and motivation kept him, more than any of his other bandmates, between the gutters after Garcia died.

FOR FOUR YEARS, WHEN HE WASN'T ON THE ROAD with the Grateful Dead, drummer Mickey Hart walked to work. Down the road from his house in the Sonoma foothills, Hart had built an enormous recording studio, complete with a fireplace in the corner and windows open to the pastoral views on his ranch.

Hart may seem to be an unlikely candidate to emerge from the ashes of the band that dissolved last year after guitarist Jerry Garcia died. His previous sideline projects have included such relatively esoteric endeavors as transferring ancient Woody Guthrie tapes to digital tape, recording New Guinea rain-forest dwellers and making "Planet Drum," a multicultural all-percussion album that became the best-selling world-beat record ever.

But Hart has spent thousands of hours in his studio during the past four years fashioning a sleek, contemporary soul album, "Mickey Hart's Mystery Box," that will be released next month by Rykodisc. Using vocals by a British a cappella group called the Mint Juleps and lyrics by Dead stalwart Rob ert Hunter, Hart supplied almost all the instrumental sounds himself by feeding his drums through computers, with only a few guest appearances by musicians such as Bob Weir and Bruce Hornsby.

Cadre of percussionists

For the past couple of weeks, Hart has convened the Juleps and a select cadre of other percussionists at the 50-acre ranch he calls YOLO (You Only Live Once) to assemble the live version of "The Mystery Box," which he will unveil this afternoon at Laguna Seca Raceway in Monterey. He'll lead the band on the road through the summer as part of "The Furthur Festival," which he will co-headline with Bob Weir's solo band, Ratdog (see Page 31). He also has written a piece that 100 percus-

Mickey Hart

sionists will perform at the opening ceremonies for the summer Olympic Games. More than 3.5 billion people are expected to tune in to the July 19 event.

Wearing a personalized tie-dyed basketball jersey from the Lithuanian basketball team the Dead sponsored in the 1992 Olympics, the intense, wiry drummer leaned back in an easy chair in the office above his studio, where a large pond and a llama pen across the road were visible through a win dow, and talked about life after the Dead.

"People want to know if it's going to be a Grateful Dead concert," he said. "The audience is the Grateful Dead now. They've got the power to make it a Grateful Dead concert once the groove starts and the lights go down.

"The musicians bring some of their past with them, but the audience does, too. They have the power to make this happen without Jerry (Garcia)."

Downstairs in the center of the large room that houses most of the studio stands a remarkable creation Hart dubbed RAMU, for Random Access Music Universe. Arrayed across chrome pipes is an assortment of drums, drum pads that trigger computers, bells, gongs, twangy things and a tall set of steel cables that go thwump when struck. From this unique contraption, Hart will oversee the live performances.

The centerpiece of the album is undoubtedly "Down the Road," a brilliant Hunter talking blues delivered by Hart, his half-spoken vocals cushioned by a pillowy bed provided by the six Juleps. In Hunter's original narrative, he portrays

Hart encountering a set of fallen heroes – Joe Hill, John F. Kennedy, John Lennon and Martin Luther King Jr. But the King verse never quite worked out and, after the death of Garcia, Hunter was commissioned to come up with a new one.

When Hunter brought his sheet of paper into the studio, he refused to let anyone see it, insisting instead on laying down a rough vocal himself. When he returned to the control room, the faces on the other side of the glass were streaked with tears. "He laid me right out," Hart said.

"When the smoke and thunder cleared, enough to look around/ I heard a sweet guitar lick, an old familiar sound/ I heard a laugh I recognized come rolling from the earth/ I saw it rise into the skies like lightning giving birth/ It sounded like Garcia, but I couldn't see the face/ Just the beard and glasses and a smile on empty space."

Rehearsing night and day

It was Garcia, in fact, who directed Hart's attention to the Mint Juleps, a group of four Jamaican sisters and two friends, after seeing them sing on a Spike Lee-directed PBS special. Hart brought them to his ranch and kept them singing, night and day, for a month. They sang some songs more than a hundred times, and each performance was saved, ultimately to be edited into a shimmering composite.

It was Hornsby, who added an accordion part to "Down the Road," who noticed the similarity with the work of British soul chanteuse Sade and suggested finding her producer to help finish the record. Hart contacted Robin Millar, who steered the ship into port, painstakingly assembling the thousands of vocal and instrumental parts on the more than 250 tape reels. "Some people would call it insane," Hart said. "Some people would call it a masterstroke. It sounds great, doesn't it?"

He spent more than three years recording the album, which he originally envisioned as an extension of "Planet Drum," working up the initial recordings with "Planet Drum" colleagues Zakir Hussain, Giovanni Hidalgo and Sikiru Adepoju.

"First, I got Hunter's attention," he said. "You've got the mother lode if you've got Hunter on the case. Then you have to do justice to Hunter's songs. He's given me 10 gems."

The brilliant Dead lyricist, who wrote the original version of the Dead staple "Fire on the Mountain" for an unreleased Hart solo album 25 years ago, composed the songs from skeletal drum tracks, and Hart began to build the record from there. As Hart grew obsessed with the project, the budget went through the roof.

"I just wanted to make a great work," he said. "I had nobody pulling my chain telling me to stop, and that's a dangerous situation. I didn't skimp."

As recording entered the final stages, Garcia died and Hart's world went into a tailspin. Within months, the Grateful Dead decided to disband. "When Jerry went down," he said, "my life turned upside down. I (had gone) into the music deep. As soon as the music stopped, it started to get weird. So I just kept the music going. I finished it in a cathartic state, a passionate burst of energy."

The onetime Air Force corpsman and member of the president's drum and bugle corps came to San Francisco shortly after he mustered out and was running a drum store in San Carlos with his father when he fell in with the Dead. He sat in with the group one night at the Straight Theater on Haight Street and never left.

But Hart is a different man than he was. He has started a new family. He and his wife, Caryl Ohrbach, have been married six years and have a 2-year-old daughter, Reya, whose toys litter the giant sandbox in the front yard. Every morning Hart does yoga on a platform in the middle of an exquisitely landscaped Japanese garden surrounding his house. The new album is more than just a solo record; it is Hart coming into his own. "I don't have to be Mickey Hart of the Grateful Dead," he said. "This is a breakout, new energy, a new horizon. It's new growth, new life. It's not a retread. I'm not trying to play songs like the Grateful Dead. In fact, I went out of my way not to sound like the Grateful Dead. I want to keep the spirit, but I want it to be me. No guitars – just drums and voice.

"I'm in love with sound. I've got to be around sound. I love the creative moment, the creative spirit. It's about life and that's what I'm after – the good in life. I try to move to the good now and this makes me feel good. Making music is like sex or looking at your baby. It makes your heart jump."

But Hart is hardly some pop-savvy hustler trying to contrive his way onto the charts. He recently struck up a friendship with Van Halen vocalist Sammy Hagar, but didn't even know who Hagar was when they met. Hart thought Hagar was some Deadhead trying to be friendly. He has spent his entire adult life in the Grateful Dead, a bubble carefully protected from the vagaries of pop life.

"I never played in a pop band," he said, "but I love pop music – the Beatles, the Supremes, vocal stylings from the '50s and '60s, `Duke of Earl.' Pop music just means that a lot of people will enjoy it.

"What do I know about pop music?" he said. "We're going to find out. I'm not trying to copy any particular style. It's an experiment. If this becomes popular, then it will be pop music. If not, then it will be another one of my enthusiasms." \

Sunday Datebook | *May 26, 1996*

The Other Ones Take It Furthur

Lesh is out but Kreutzmann is back in *post - Grateful Dead* lineup

Chronicling the absurd soap opera that surrounded the members of the Grateful Dead after Jerry Garcia died became something of an obsession of mine. It was a never-ending fount of newspaper articles. Following the tides of intra-band politics and economics was great sport, especially after Phil Lesh started to take it all personally.

Mickey Hart was plucking an electric kalimba, a handheld African thumb piano, while wandering across a room littered with cables and sound equipment. The plink-plunk of the little instrument surfed a mighty wave of sound from the rest of the Other Ones, who were rehearsing for the band's tour in the cavernous sound-stage at the Novato headquarters for what remains of the Grateful Dead.

As the rest of the band played on, Hart put down the kalimba and climbed behind the second set of drums next to the man he played beside for almost 30 years, Bill Kreutzmann. As Hart slammed his sticks into the giant drum set, familiar sheets of thunder crackled and exploded. The two sounded for all the world like the Grateful Dead.

The Other Ones is the living Dead. With its second tour starting tomorrow (the band comes to Shoreline Amphitheatre on Friday as headliners of the Furthur tour), this seven-man band built around three surviving members of the Grateful Dead spent last week working in two new members — one entirely new and one only sort of new – and refreshing everybody's recollection of a repertoire untouched since the end of the band's first tour in 1998.

Kreutzmann has not played with the other members of the Dead since the death of guitarist Jerry Garcia five years ago. His return to the fold comes amid a fractious split in the band's ranks. Bassist Phil Lesh took the other Other Ones' drummer, John Molo, and went on the road this summer as Phil Lesh and Friends.

The apparent cause of the rift was the band's proposed plans to put the Dead's

vault of live recordings on the Internet, but the differences seem to run deeper. Both Hart and guitarist Bob Weir strongly implied that Lesh's split followed a failed bid to take over the leadership of the famously rudderless ship that is the Grateful Dead.

"You can't just summarily dismiss your old friends, all of them," said Weir, sounding a conciliatory note. "He's going to be doing some rethinking."

After not touring last summer, while the band reportedly waited for Lesh to decide whether he wanted to tour after his liver transplant, the Other Ones will tour without Lesh, but with Kreutzmann. Playing bass is Alphonso Johnson, a highly regarded hired gun who has worked for Weather Report and Santana.

Last week, the musicians were working hard to learn a daunting list of 59 songs. Three blackboards covered with lists of songs stared back at the band as the musicians raced through a briskly disciplined rehearsal, already a stark contrast to the Dead. There were long periods when the Grateful Dead didn't rehearse at all.

Replacing Garcia was too much of a hot seat for any one guitarist, although

The Other Ones

that, too, was apparently a point of dispute with Lesh. Returning are the two players from the 1998 Other Ones tour, Steve Kimmock and Mark Karan. Kimmock is well-known to Deadheads as a Garcia disciple who used to lead the band Zero. Karan, not so well- known, was a journeyman in the Marin County music scene for years before moving to Los Angeles, where he was living when he landed the job with the Other Ones.

Conjuring Garcia

Kimmock can evoke Garcia flawlessly, squeezing off his skipping, spinning, silvery lines. He also played briefly on the Phil Lesh and Friends tour this year, but left midway ("I don't want to work on Maggie's farm," he said at the time). Karan has been playing in Weir's sideline band, Ratdog, for two years and worked in Hart's solo band for a while. Nevertheless, they are still outsiders. They have studied tapes of the band and know the Dead's music as fans and students. "This is a startlingly original idea I stole from you," Kimmock said to Weir at rehearsal.

The Other Ones' pianist, Bruce Hornsby, is another fan who joined the band. Hornsby toured as a temporary member of the Dead for almost two years after keyboardist Brent Mydland died in 1990, while the band looked for a permanent replacement. Hornsby has pursued a highly successful, adventurous career as an artist himself both before and after his stint with the Dead. But he is no longer "the new guy" – a position poor Mydland held for more than 10 years.

The Other Ones is a strange combination of new and semi-new pieces grafted on to the remaining parts of the Grateful Dead. Weir, Hart and Kreutzmann made music together for more than 30 years, but this band has performed only a few times. Bassist Johnson and Kreutzmann, new to the lineup for this tour, actually showed up a couple of days early to practice alone together. Kreutzmann needed to learn a few new songs that Weir and Hart brought to the repertoire.

"It's fresh," said the drummer, who retreated to the north shore of Kauai shortly after Garcia died. "It's basically a new band, but I have the benefit of knowing the songs"

Sounds like the dead

With Hart and Kreutzmann back together, this unruly mess forming itself into a rock band sounds like the Grateful Dead in ways it couldn't any other way. With Kreutzmann keeping a tidy rhythm figure going, Hart decorates the beat. They are brothers in rhythm. While Kimmock lays the Garcia- brand solos on top, the two other guitarists drive the interior sound with punchy contrapuntal accents. It is a deep, resonant and satisfying evocation of the Grateful Dead, not so much a re-creation as a calling forth of the spirit.

But with Hornsby finally joining for full band rehearsals only three days earlier, and the week's schedule cut short by Hart leaving to appear at the Democratic National Convention with his pal Al Gore, there was a lot of work to be done in a short time at rehearsal. And the debate over how much rehearsal is actually good for a band that depends on improvisation is always a topic of conversation with the Dead.

Hornsby overheard Hart saying he didn't care about fine-tuning the songs, a typical Grateful Dead attitude. "No," Hornsby interjected, "we want to get them as tight as possible and take off from there."

"I just don't want all those guitar players tripping over each other," said Hart.

"101 Strings," said Hornsby, laughing.

"My worst nightmare," said Hart. "At least there's no saxophone." ..

San Francisco Chronicle | Tuesday, August 22, 2000

Other Ones reunite

Former *Grateful Dead* mates patch things up

Not only did Phil Lesh refuse to give me an interview for this piece, he insisted that Bobby Weir and Mickey Hart not talk to me either. Both of them owned up to me privately, but they weren't going to cross Phil. There was too much money at stake.

PHIL LESH BROUGHT MICKEY HART OUT ONSTAGE as 18,000 fans showered applause on them in July at Jones Beach in New York. The two former band mates from the Grateful Dead smiled at each other, and Lesh leaned over and planted a kiss on Hart's forehead.

"The good times are back," he told Hart.

Only months before, the two weren't speaking. Their battles spilled over into public view, regardless of the long standing band policy of keeping family disputes private, culminating with an injudicious remark an angry Hart let slip to a reporter: "Phil might have gotten the liver of a jerk," Hart said about Lesh, recipient of a liver transplant in 1998.

Hart quickly offered a public apology, but his colorful comment was a high point in a rancorous fracture that band members quietly healed earlier this year. For the first time since guitarist Jerry Garcia died in August 1995, all four surviving principal members of the Grateful Dead – Hart, Lesh, Bob Weir and Billy Kreutzmann – are touring together as the Other Ones, the post-Dead umbrella under which three of the four have toured twice previously. Lesh was onboard for the first tour in 1998, but was no longer speaking with his old mates when drummer Kreutzmann returned from Hawaii to join the summer 2000 Other Ones tour.

The first public sign that the feud was mending came in spring 2001, when Weir's Ratdog opened some shows for Phil Lesh and Friends. All three other members made a surprise appearance at Lesh's show last New Year's Eve, only the second time all four had performed together since the death of Garcia. Both Weir and Hart played dates this summer with their bands opening shows for Lesh.

But a two-day festival performance by the renewed Other Ones in July at Alpine Valley in East Troy, Wis., went so well the band members decided to do a fall tour, including sold-out shows next weekend at Henry J. Kaiser Auditorium in Oakland and a New Year's Eve show at the Oakland Arena, although there are no further plans.

In fact, in the giddy joy immediately after Alpine Valley, they briefly considered readopting the name Grateful Dead. That happy thought lasted until it occurred to them that such a move would bring the Garcia estate back into the picture, while as the Other Ones they would remain a separate entity. The great dysfunctional family that is the Grateful Dead has not suddenly turned into Ozzie and Harriet. Band members could not even agree about being interviewed for this article.

When the legendary band ceased to exist with Garcia's death, the living Dead went their separate ways. Lesh announced his intention to retire from performing. Kreutzmann went tropical in Hawaii. Weir and Hart took their solo bands on the road with a repertory company of like-minded musicians called the Furthur Festival the next summer, followed by a second Furthur tour in 1997.

Meanwhile, the band's main source of revenue, nearly $50 million a year, according to a band spokesperson, turned out to be mail-order marketing of merchandise such as the popular "Dick's Picks" series of CDs drawn from the Dead's vast tape vault of past performances. Many of these CDs, manufactured and marketed by Grateful Dead Productions, have sold more than 100,000 copies. Among other projects the post-Garcia band was pursuing was a high-tech museum to be called Terrapin Station, for which the band was considering San Francisco waterfront real estate parcels and meeting with developers.

Researching ways to finance the museum, the band talked with Silicon Valley high-tech investment experts, who began to develop a business plan for an Internet operation that would use the Dead's huge tape library in new ways online, right about the same time Napster was starting and dot-com revolution was in the air.

Bassist Lesh, meanwhile, came out of retirement. He returned to the stage as Phil Lesh and Friends in early 1998 with a rotating cast of musicians in appearances around the Bay Area. He also joined Hart, Weir and their sometime associate Bruce Hornsby on a summer tour as the Other Ones, taking the name from an old Dead song. Guitarists Steve Kimock and Mark Karan took the Garcia chair. A month after the tour ended, Lesh underwent an emergency liver transplant, a result of previously diagnosed hepatitis C.

Lesh recovered to hit the boards in April 1999 with two-thirds of Phish in his band. There was no Furthur tour that summer, while Weir and Hart reportedly waited too long for Lesh to decide whether he wanted to tour after his surgery.

The Other Ones

He spent the summer, instead, woodshedding his new band in a series of Warfield shows, and, when Phil Lesh and Friends went out that fall on a bill with Bob Dylan, his band was an immediate hit with jam-starved Dead fans.

But he was growing estranged from his band mates, vocally opposing their plans to put the tape vault on the Internet. He stopped attending Grateful Dead Productions board meetings, according to a source close to the band.

With Alphonso Johnson of Weather Report replacing Lesh on bass, and Dead drummer Kreutzmann back from Hawaii, the Other Ones went out the next summer, while Lesh toured again with Dylan, topping the bill this time. At the end of 2000 the Other Ones played New Year's Eve at the Arena in Oakland, while Phil Lesh and Friends camped out down the freeway at the Henry J. Kaiser Auditorium in competing concerts.

At the New Year's Eve show 2001, in which all four played together, however, a Harry Potter-themed float appeared near midnight bearing three wizards – Weir, Hart and Kreutzmann in costume. "Unity is possible," Lesh told the crowd.

Lesh was in a position to dictate the terms of his return to the fold. He had sidestepped Grateful Dead Productions by signing a big-money record deal with Columbia Records (the first Phil Lesh and Friends album, "There and Back Again," released last May, sold a modest 40,000 copies). And he was touring – prosperously – without his old band mates.

"When he came back," said ex-Other Ones guitarist Mark Karan, "he said, 'OK, but do it my way.' "

Karan and Kimock (who quit Phil Lesh and Friends in the middle of the band's first tour) were out of the new Other Ones, and guitarist Jimmy Herring and keyboardist Rob Barraco from the current Lesh band were in. Keyboardist Jeff Chimenti from Weir's Ratdog also got the nod (Karan continues to play with Ratdog).

Also out was Grateful Dead Productions President Peter McQuade; former Grateful Dead manager Cameron Sears was brought back. John Scher, the New York promoter who did the Furthur tours, signed on as co-manager. Lesh's wife, Jill, serves as his personal manager. The band's lawyer for the past eight years, who led the group through a variety of byzantine court cases, including a much-publicized suit with Garcia's guitarmaker over possession of his guitars, quit.

"The Leshes and I don't get along," attorney Eric Donay said.

The idea for an Internet deal came and went. The museum plans are gathering dust. But in the past year Grateful Dead Productions has released a 12-CD box set, two more "Dick's Picks" (Vols. 25 and 26), three additional Dead CD collections and a video, "View From the Vault III."

Meanwhile, the new band is on the road, making music that fans and the musicians are loving. The band drafted blues singer Susan Tedeschi to add harmonies, and she joined the tour in progress. Partying backstage at the Other Ones show in Washington, D.C., was Sen. Barbara Boxer.

"When they get together to play, when the music is happening," said ex-Other Ones keyboardist Hornsby, "all that other stuff is rendered so unimportant. Getting those chills onstage – that's something you always covet. I guess they're having 'em again."

The Grateful Dead is no more. But because these four men, whose compatibility means so much to so many, have rediscovered their common bliss, the Other Ones are as close to the Dead as anyone's going to get.

Sunday Datebook | December 1, 2002

For the unrepentant patriarch of LSD, long, strange trip winds back to Bay Area

The name Owsley became a noun that appears in the Oxford dictionary as English street slang for good acid.

Owsley

Bear did this as a favor for John Meyer, the great acoustic technician and speaker manufacturer. Meyer knew Bear owed him a solid, but couldn't think of anything he wanted from him. He suggested the interview, in part, just because he knew he could make Bear do it. Bear, of course, did make it difficult, but when he finally sat down to do it, there was no stopping him. He called again the next day, stopped by the house at odd hours, gave me CDs of his old tapes he wanted me to hear. The only question he didn't answer was when I asked him if he still took LSD. He looked straight into my eyes, widened his eyes at me like I was an idiot, and then glanced down at the tape recorder. No fool he.

THE SMALL, BAREFOOT MAN IN BLACK T-SHIRT AND BLUE JEANS barely rates a second glance from the other Starbucks patrons in downtown San Rafael, although he is one of the men who virtually made the '60s. Because Augustus Owsley Stanley III has spent his life avoiding photographs, few people would know what he looks like.

The name Owsley became a noun that appears in the Oxford dictionary as English street slang for good acid. It is the most famous brand name in LSD history. Probably the first private individual to manufacture the psychedelic, "Owsley" is a folk hero of the counterculture, celebrated in songs by the Grateful Dead and Steely Dan.

For more than 20 years, Stanley – at 72, still known as the Bear – has been living with his wife, Sheila, off the grid, in the outback of Queensland, Australia, where he makes small gold and enamel sculptures and keeps in touch with the world through the Internet.

As a planned two-week visit to the Bay Area stretched to three, four and then five weeks, Bear agreed to give The Chronicle an interview because a friend asked him. He has rarely consented to speak to the press about his life, his work or his unconventional thinking on matters such as the coming ice age or his all-meat diet.

Sporting a buccaneer's earring he got when he was in jail and a hearing aid on the same ear, he keeps a salty goatee, and the sides of his face look boiled clean from seven weeks of maximum radiation treatment for throat cancer. Having lost one of his vocal cords, he speaks only in a whispered croak these days. At one point, he was reduced to injecting his puree of steak and espresso directly into his stomach.

"I never set out to change the world," he rasps in recalling his early manufacture of LSD. "I only set out to make sure I was taking something (that) I knew what it was. And it's hard to make a little. And my friends all wanted to know what they were taking, too. Of course, my friends expanded very rapidly."

By conservative estimates, Bear Research Group made more than 1.25 million doses of LSD between 1965 and 1967, essentially seeding the entire modern psychedelic movement.

Less well known are Bear's contributions to rock concert sound. As the original sound mixer for the Grateful Dead, he was responsible for fundamental advances in audio technology, things as basic now as monitor speakers that allow vocalists to hear themselves onstage.

Says the Dead's Bob Weir: "He's good for a different point of view at about any given time. He's brilliant. He knows everything."

Bear, whose grandfather was a Kentucky governor and U.S. senator, grew up in Los Angeles and Arlington, Va. He was thrown out of military school in the eighth grade for being drunk and dropped out of school altogether at 18. He managed to get accepted to the University of Virginia, where he spent a year studying engineering. By 1956, he was in the Air Force, specializing in electronics and radar.

Later, Bear studied ballet, acting and Russian, worked in jet propulsion labs as well as radio and television, and then entered UC Berkeley in 1963, but lasted less than a year.

Then he discovered acid.

He found the recipe for making LSD in the Journal of Organic Chemistry at the UC Berkeley library. Soon after, Bear began to cook acid.

The Berkeley police raided his first lab in 1966 and confiscated a substance that they claimed was methedrine. When it turned out to be something else – probably a component of LSD – Bear not only walked free but successfully sued the cops for the return of his lab equipment.

By the time he made a special batch called Monterey Purple for the 1967 Monterey Pop Festival – Owsley Purple was the secret smile on Jimi Hendrix's face that night – "Owsley" was an underground legend.

In December 1967, agents arrested him at his secret lab in Orinda. The "LSD Millionaire" headline in The Chronicle prompted the Dead to write the song "Alice D. Millionaire." In 1970, after a pot bust in Oakland, a judge revoked Bear's bail, and he served two years at Terminal Island near the Los Angeles Harbor.

"If you make some, you've got to move some to get some money to make it," he says now. "But then you had to give a lot away to keep the street price down. So anyway, I'm sort of embedded in this thing that I'm tangled up in. ... Just as soon as it became illegal, I wanted out. Then, of course, I felt an obligation."

Bear, chemist to Ken Kesey and the Merry Pranksters, was involved with the Dead almost from the band's beginnings at Kesey's notorious Acid Tests. Bear was the Dead's first patron and, briefly, their manager. He bought the band sound equipment and began to use the Dead as a laboratory for audio research.

"We'd never thought about high-quality PAs," says the Dead's Weir. "There was no such thing until Bear started making one."

Bear made the first public address system specifically dedicated to music in 1966. If he was the first concert sound engineer in rock music to take his job seriously, his habit of making tape recordings of the shows he mixed also gave the Dead an unprecedented archive of live recordings dating back to the band's first days. Many of Bear's tapes have been turned into albums.

Bear has always lived in a quite particular world. "He can be very anal retentive, on a certain level, on a genius level," says Paul Kantner of Jefferson Airplane. "I've seen him send his eggs back three times at Howard Johnson's."

His all-meat diet is a well-known example. When he was younger, Bear read about the Eskimos eating only fish and meat and became convinced that humans are meant to be exclusively carnivorous. The members of the Grateful Dead remember living with Bear for several months in 1966 in Los Angeles, where the refrigerator contained only bottles of milk and a slab of steak, meat they fried and ate straight out of the pan. His heart attack several years ago had nothing to do with his strict regimen, according to Bear, but more likely the result of some poisonous broccoli his mother made him eat as a youth.

As a sound mixer, Bear holds equally strict viewpoints, insisting that the most effective rock concert systems should have only a single source of sound, his argument quickly veering into the realm of psycho-acoustics.

"The PA can only be in one spot," he says. "All the sounds have to come from a single place because the human brain is carrying around the most sophisticated sound processing of any computer or living creature. It equals the bats that fly by echo. It equals the dolphins. It equals the owls that hunt at night without any daylight at all. It is a superb system for locating and separating one sound from everything else."

Bear left Northern California in the early '80s, convinced that a natural disaster was imminent. He predicted at the time that global warming would lead to a six-week-long ultra-cyclone that could cover the Northern Hemisphere with a new ice age. Determining that the tropical northern side of Australia would be the most likely region to survive, Bear made a beeline for Queensland and says he felt at home the moment he set foot on the new continent.

"I might be right about the ice age thing," he allows. "I might be wrong."

Old friends express shock that Bear would ever even admit to that possibility, but, if not exactly mellowed in his old age, he has found room to accommodate other points of view.

"He's come a long way," says Wavy Gravy, who visited Bear in Australia this year. "He used to be real snappy and grumpy. Now he can be actually sweet."

His four children are grown. He has five grandchildren, and his oldest son, Pete, in Florida, just became a grandfather, making Bear a great-grandfather for the first time. His other son, Starfinder, a veterinarian, hosted a party for him last month at his Oakland home attended by the old Dead crowd, a tortoise and a caged iguana. He has two daughters, Nina and Redbird, and maintains his own Web site (www.thebear.org) where he sells his sculpture and posts various diatribes and essays.

He keeps up with the music scene – he singles out Wolfmother and the Arctic Monkeys as new bands he likes. "Any time the music on the radio starts to sound like rubbish, it's time to take some LSD," he says.

Owsley Stanley (he legally dropped the "Augustus" 40 years ago) has also not joined the ranks of the penitent psychedelicists who look on their experiences as youthful indiscretions.

"I wound up doing time for something I should have been rewarded for," he says. "What I did was a community service, the way I look at it. I was punished for political reasons. Absolutely meaningless. Was I a criminal? No. I was a good member of society. Only my society and the one making the laws are different."

At the hilltop San Anselmo home where Bear had been house-sitting, pretty much all available space was taken over with his belongings. He squatted over the piles, trying to figure out what to ship and what to take with him. Two days before his flight, it looks like he'll need every minute.

This time, he was extending his stay to catch his old friends Jorma Kaukonen and Jack Casady of Hot Tuna play at the Fillmore. But when he left for the airport the next day, he got as far as Sausalito before he discovered that he had left the briefcase with the tickets back in San Anselmo, and the trip home was postponed for another week.

"I even said, 'I wonder what I'm leaving behind this time?' before I left," he says, somewhat sadly.

San Francisco Chronicle | Thursday, July 12, 2007

Lawrence 'Ramrod' Shurtliff: 1945-2006

Mainstay of Grateful Dead crew dies – 'he was our rock'

> This is the piece that made me realize the Grateful Dead had come to the end of its road. Without Garcia, everybody lived in denial for awhile. Without Ramrod, nothing was left. They packed up the vault a few days later and closed the office.

HE WAS A PSYCHEDELIC COWBOY WHO RODE THE BUS with Ken Kesey and took virtually every step of the long, strange trip with the Grateful Dead. Known to one and all solely as Ramrod, he died yesterday of lung cancer at Petaluma Valley Hospital. He was 61.

"He was our rock," said guitarist Bob Weir.

Born Lawrence Shurtliff, he was raised a country boy in eastern Oregon and once won a county fair blue ribbon in cattle judging. He got the name Ramrod from Kesey while he was traveling through Mexico with the author and LSD evangelist, at the time a fugitive from justice.

"I am Ramon Rodriguez Rodriguez, the famous Mexican guide," he boasted, and he was known ever after as Ramrod.

"It fit him," said Steve Parish, his longtime associate on the Dead crew. "He used to keep us in line."

"I remember when he first showed up at 710 Ashbury," said Dead drummer Mickey Hart. "He pulled up on a Harley. He was wearing a chain with a lock around his waist. He said 'Name's Ramrod – Kesey sent me – I hear you need a good man.' I remember it like it was yesterday."

Ramrod joined the Dead in 1967 as truck driver and was held in such high regard by the members of that sprawling, brawling organization that he was named president of the Grateful Dead board of directors when the rock group actually incorporated in the '70s. It was a position he held until the death of guitarist Jerry Garcia in 1995. Like the rest of the band's few remaining staff, he was laid off last year.

He traveled the full length of the Dead's tangled odyssey, joining up with the band when the it first began playing out of town, about a year after the Dead got is start playing gin mills on the Peninsula.

Ramrod went to work setting up and tearing down the band's equipment for every show the Dead played. He puzzled his way through elaborate situations and circumstances: from the myriad psychedelic dungeons the band played through the '60s, to a concert at the base of the Great Pyramids in Egypt in 1977 to the baseball parks the Dead filled on the endless tours of the '80s and '90s up until Garcia's death.

"He was always there," said Hart, "making sure everybody was taken care of."

Hart said that it was Ramrod's practice to say "all right" at the conclusion of every performance as the band filed off the stage. "I looked forward to those 'all rights,' " said Hart. "It was the way he said it. It was the tone that said it all – 'it was all right ... not great.' You couldn't fool old Ramrod. I was playing for him."

Hart also remembered one New Year's Eve when he thought he might be too high to play. Ramrod solved the problem by strapping Hart to his drum stool with gaffer's tape. Hart recalled another show in San Jose with Big Brother and the Holding Company, where the starter's cannon the band used to punctuate the drum solo of "St. Stephen's" went off early.

"I looked back," Hart said. "His face was on fire. He'd lost his eyebrows. You could smell his flesh. And he was hurrying to reload the cannon in time. That was the end of the cannons."

A protege of Neal Cassady of the Merry Pranksters, the intrepid band of inner-space explorers who gathered around Kesey, Ramrod absorbed lessons from Cassady, a Beat era legend and model for the character Dean Moriarty in Jack Kerouac's landmark novel "On the Road." "He knew Neal better than anyone in our scene," said Weir.

He was a quiet, unflappable road warrior. Hart and fellow crew member Rex Jackson once decided to see how long it would take Ramrod to say something on a truck trip across the Midwest. He said nothing through three states before speaking. "Hungry?" he finally said.

"He was never a loudmouth," said Parish. "He was never anything but an honest, hard-working guy with a grip of steel and a hand that felt like leather."

He was first married to Patricia "Patticake" Luft – their son is Strider Shurtliff, 38, of Los Angeles. His wife of the past 38 years, Francis Whalen, is recovering from an anoxic brain injury. Their son is Rudson Shurtliff, 34, of Novato.

A lifelong cigarette smoker, he was diagnosed with lung cancer only a few weeks ago. Typically, he didn't want anybody to know he was dying, although band

and crew members visited him daily.

Guitarist Weir said he could barely remember the Dead before Ramrod. "When he did join up, it was like he had always been there. I won't say he was the missing piece, because I don't think he was missing. He just wasn't there. But then he was there. And he always will be. He was a huge part of what the Grateful Dead was about."

Parish said he and Weir left a recent visit from Ramrod's hospital bed. "Weir said 'They say blood is thicker than water, but what we've got is thicker than blood,'" said Parish.

Funeral arrangements are pending.

San Francisco Chronicle } May 18, 2006

CHAPTER 5

The Boys

For the Beach Boys, fun, fun, fun began in humble Hawthorne

> Until I actually got in my rental car and drove there, I had no idea that the Barbie doll and the Beach Boys came from the same neighborhood.

HAWTHORNE (LOS ANGELES COUNTY) – HAWTHORNE IS A CHARMLESS, flat, blue-collar town where workers from the plants in the South Central industrial belt could buy tiny two-bedroom stucco-front boxes. In 1959, the same year the film "Gidget" first exposed the Southern California beach culture to the outside world, the Mattel Toy Co. in Hawthorne started producing a new doll named Barbie, which outsold even the Mickey Mouse ears the company also made.

Brian Wilson was a senior that year at Hawthorne High School (home of the proud Cougars, whose fight song he cribbed for the middle-eight to his "Be True to Your School"), hanging out on weeknights in the parking lot behind the Fosters Freeze on Hawthorne Boulevard in his two-tone '57 Ford Fairlane 500. On week-ends, the guys would pick up a six-pack and head for the double-bills at Studio Drive-In on Slauson.

It was a long way from Hollywood, a town where things were still possible, but it was close enough to Disneyland that the Wilsons' father took his three boys to the recently opened amusement park at least twice a year.

Few traces remain of songwriter Brian Wilson's Los Angeles. He wrote of a world he knew growing up during the '50s in unremarkable Hawthorne, where he created mythic Southern California in songs such as "Surfer Girl," "Fun Fun Fun," "Little Deuce Coupe," "The Warmth of the Sun" and "California Girls."

If you're going to go looking for Brian Wilson's Southern California, it's not a bad idea to hook up with Beach Boys expert Domenic Priore and have him give you the tour. But first, to supply some context, we met for breakfast at a Hollywood coffeehouse with Wilson's genial and erudite collaborator, Van Dyke Parks, who still has the slightest Southern accent after more than 40 years living in L.A. He is a small, compact man with a salt-and-pepper mustache, gracious manners and an

Hawthorne CA

impish grin. He likes to talk about the band and Brian Wilson in particular.

"His music had an animate quality," said Parks, the co-writer of Wilson's iconic "Smile." "It was vigorous, an athletic kind of music. It looks in all directions. It takes everything in. It's anecdotal – lots of little events. It was a reflection of the real rapture of the feel-good set that grew up in the Eisenhower era."

The Wilson home on 119th Street no longer exists. It was torn down to make way for a freeway 20 years ago, but its site was marked on May 20 with a large brick monument and named an official California State Historical Landmark. A few blocks away, the Fosters Freeze still stands, the hamburger stand where Wilson saw a girl with her daddy's T-Bird. Sometimes Wilson would cruise several miles north to the Wich Stand at Slauson and Overhill, where the parking lot would hold a hundred cars from all over the South Bay, which is what locals call the area between South Central and the bottom half of Santa Monica Bay. He might have immortalized the destination drive-in in a 1964 recording, "The Wich Stand," but the track went unreleased.

With a decorative spire poking through the slanted roof, buttressed by Swiss cheese struts, the Wich Stand looked like Southern California itself – open, airy, offbeat and futuristic. Today the building is painted an unlikely forest green and houses a health food restaurant, Simply Wholesome, that caters to the large African American community in the neighborhood. The spacious parking lot in the rear, once packed with hot rods and surf wagons, stands nearly empty. More than the neighborhood has changed in South Central Los Angeles. over the past 45 years. But signs of the bygone era, the California of young Brian Wilson, are sprinkled all over the South Bay.

Priore knows where to find them. Author of a book about Wilson's long- lost masterpiece, "Smile," as well as another book about the Sunset Strip in the '60s, Priore dresses like the pop scholar he is: Mod burgundy corduroy shirt and chocolate suede Cuban boots. As part of the weekend-long activities surrounding the recent landmark unveiling, which drew fans from all over the world, he led a bus tour of the Beach Boys' old neighborhood. A few days before, he did a test run, checking out some of the locations he'd never visited before, like the boyhood home of Beach Boys rhythm guitarist Al Jardine, a classmate of Brian Wilson's at nearby El Camino Community College who likes to take credit for suggesting Wilson start the group.

"I didn't know Al Jardine lived in an apartment building," Priore said, pulling up to a Hawthorne address of matching duplexes built in that unique Southern California '50s mode of frenzied modernism. Futurism was more than an architecture style in Los Angeles during the '50s – it was a way of life.

Dennis Wilson used to go down to the Redondo Beach breakwater and watch the hotshots ride the big ones. He brought home the tales to his older brother Brian, who rarely set foot on a beach. But those Waimea-style titans don't break at Redondo anymore, not since a 1981 wave wiped out the breakwater and did $13 million worth of damage to the beachfront hotel. City fathers moved the breakwater farther out and knocked the historic South Bay surfing spot off the maps.

Much has changed since the Beach Boys lived in Hawthorne, but time stands still on Manhattan Beach, where Dennis Wilson and Mike Love used to fish from the pier. This white sand jewel sits in the middle of the Strand, the string of South Bay beaches that runs from El Segundo to Palos Verdes.

Surfers catch waves alongside the pier where Dennis Wilson would ride the breakers. Girls in bikinis lie basking in the sand. People still fish from the pier.

Away from the hectic beach scenes farther north at Venice or Santa Monica, Manhattan Beach remains what Priore called "a neighborhood beach." At Manhattan and nearby Hermosa Beach, the first few lonely surf shops opened in the late '50s, as the Hawaiian sport was just starting to take hold on the mainland.

Priore points to a social convergence coming together over the Southern California beaches in those few innocent years – "Gidget," Surfer magazine, Bruce Brown surfing documentary films, the emergence of surf guitar king Dick Dale and the Del-Tones at the Rendezvous Ballroom in Huntington Beach and subsequent surf music instrumental hit singles by South Bay combos such as the Frogmen ("Underwater") and the Belairs ("Mr. Moto"). Into this yawning vortex stepped Brian Wilson, his two younger brothers, their cousin Mike Love and Brian's El Camino classmate Jardine.

Over Labor Day weekend 1961, with the Wilson parents on a Mexican vacation, the group took over the 119th Street house, stocked it with rented equipment and worked up the Brian Wilson composition, "Surfin' " which he cobbled together from information supplied by his younger brother Dennis, the only surfer in the group, and cousin Love, who knew some of the lingo.

Wilson's father, an amateur songwriter, took their homemade Wollensak tape to a music publisher he knew, who arranged the have the boys record the song professionally and get the results released on a small label in early December. It was the label's promotion man who named the group the Beach Boys.

The leading Los Angeles Top 40 radio station, KFWB, already broadcasting daily surf reports and quite aware that something was going on with the region's youth out on the beaches, jumped on the record. A minute later, the Beach Boys were signed to Capitol Records – home to Nat King Cole, Frank Sinatra, Dean Martin, with its instant '50s landmark Hollywood headquarters designed to look like a stack of records, a red beacon on top blinking all night long in Morse code H-O-L-L-Y-W-O-O-D, a long way from Hawthorne.

In a matter of months, the Studio Drive-In was showing nothing but insipid beach party films that were little more than cheap movie-length musicals based on imitation Brian Wilson music (he actually did write the songs for one of the Frankie Avalon-Annette Funicello clinkers, "Muscle Beach Party"). An entire school of pop music emerged in his wake – Jan and Dean, Bruce and Terry, Ronny and the Daytonas, the Hondells and others.

He painted California as the land of youth, tanned surfers with fast cars and blond-haired, beach bunny girlfriends ("some honeys will be coming along"). He threw in local references, details that fixed his songs firmly in the Southern California coastline.

"That's part of his olio," said his collaborator Parks, "his real ability to osmote and to become a part of what he observes, to drink what he loves and let it kill him – the comic and the tragic, the sacred and the profane."

The Wilsons all still lived at home in Hawthorne. Love dropped out of Los Angeles City College after his girlfriend got pregnant and her parents insisted they get married. Love's mother threw his clothes out of the upstairs window of the three-story Love family home in the upscale Baldwin Hills neighborhood. Shortly thereafter, his father experienced severe financial setbacks in his sheet metal business and the family moved to a smaller house directly under the path to the Los Angeles Airport runway. Love and his new wife were living in a tiny studio apartment and he was working at his father's business during the day and pumping gas at night for Standard Oil at the busy intersection of Washington and La Brea.

Given his natural talent – his voice was once famously described in a Beach Boys "joke" album track as "Mickey Mouse with a cold" – only a family member like Brian Wilson would have ever thought of Love as a candidate for lead vocalist of his rock 'n' roll group. His job at the gas station was probably the last position Love was truly qualified to hold.

The station, which still sits like a fort at the hectic crossroads, has been remodeled, expanded and rebuilt a number of times since he worked there. But Love would probably recognize it in a heartbeat.

San Francisco Chronicle | Tuesday, May 31, 2005

An Endless Surfari

By the time the publicists brought the San Francisco Chronicle on the scene, Brian Wilson, who had emerged from the depths of his schizophrenia long enough to semi-supervise a new Beach Boys album at just the right moment in the group's sagging fortunes, had gone back home, leaving the rest of the group to put the finishing touches on the album and conduct the interviews.

SANTA MONICA – DENNIS WILSON LIVES ON THE EDGE of the Pacific Ocean in Malibu, about 25 minutes away from the recording studio he owns with his brother Carl. Every day for the past two years, Denny made the drive in his VW van and spent the day making music in the studio, without really intending to record.

Music, he says, is his hobby.

But early this year, recording began in earnest again when older brother Brian Wilson showed up at Brother Studios and started the first Beach Boys album in four years. It had been even longer since Brian was in charge of the group's work.

Despite a lack of new records, the Beach Boys are currently among the most popular rock groups in the country. Last summer the Beach Boys pulled more than $7 million at the box office on a 12-city U.S. tour.

First two summers ago, and then again last year, re-released Beach Boys albums earned gold LPs for Capitol Records, the group's former record company. Meanwhile, Warner Brothers, with whom the group has been signed since 1970, has released only one album by the group in three years.

This year there had to be a new record; Warner's "15 Big Ones," a title that refers both to the number of cuts on the album and the group's 15th anniversary this year, will be the band's first album in nine years to bear the legend: "Produced by Brian Wilson."

In a sense, it was Dennis Wilson who started it all. Dennis, an avid surfer, convinced his land-locked brother Brian to write a song about the sport. Dennis, always the only surfer in the group, still goes out every day the waves are happening.

But Denny Wilson is more than the Beach Boys' link with the ocean. He is the rebel of the group, the outlaw with a lengthy list of minor skirmishes with the authorities, the outsider who befriended Charles Manson ("I guess he let the drugs get away with him," he said).

A bundle of constant energy, Denny is alert and volatile, not given to reflective statements. He hides compassion behind a tough-guy mask, but is entirely without guile. Asked why it took so long for the Beach Boys to make another album, he didn't even pause before answering.

"Because the group wouldn't be the Beach Boys without Brian Wilson, and he wasn't ready. It's as simple as that."

Why is Brian ready now?

"Because he wants to. That's all. He wants to now. He was a recluse for three years. Every day I'd go over to his house and he'd be lying on his couch with a pillow over his face."

In between the Cottage Thrift Shop on the corner and a parking lot across the street from the Greyhound station, Brother Studios hides behind an anonymous exterior.

Inside, however, gold albums line the walls, all by the Beach Boys. Out back, at the top of the loading dock ramp, the first gold album, for "Surfing USA," is embedded in concrete. The studio is dominated by a huge circular stained glass window at one end. Window boxes of green plants run along another wall.

In the control room, Carl mixed down the final version of Mike Love's song, "Everybody's in Love," in one of the last sessions for the new album. Engineer Steve Moffitt assisted, but Carl actually operated the board.

The mixing process is the crucial selection of values and proportions of recorded sound which, given the capabilities of 24-track recording, present an almost limitless array of choices. In about 90 minutes, Carl had it just about right.

"Time to call in the braintrust," he said. The other Beach Boys came in from various parts of the building. Mike, wearing a hat even inside, hovered over the console, fiddling slightly with the knobs. Al Jardine settled back in the engineer's chair. As the tape began to roll, Dennis popped inside the door and cocked his ear. As the tape ended, he made a quick comment, turned and left.

Love was concerned chiefly with the flute fills between verses (played by jazzman Charles Lloyd) and he took over the flute track on the next mix down. Jardine wanted to hear more harp, but refused to touch the board ("I just listen"), even when Carl offered.

The next time through did it. The mix was committed to the master tape, ready to go to the factory.

"Where's Brian?" someone asked.

"Probably went back to where he came from," said another. Older brother Brian had not been around the studio for the past few days, but no one seemed surprised.

"Brian was finished," Carl explained later. His older brother may be rock's best known eccentric, but Carl and the other Beach Boys long ago accepted Brian – both for his sometimes oddball behavior and his occasional equally baffling musical genius.

Brian Wilson suffered his first nervous breakdown at age 21 on an airplane trip to Houston two days before Christmas, 1964. Shortly after, he retired from touring with the Beach Boys to concentrate on making the group's records.

He formed the band during his senior year at Hawthorne (Calif.) High, with his two brothers; an older cousin, Mike Love; and a classmate, Al Jardine. The Wilsons were a musical family – the mother, Audrey, played organ at home; the father, Murry, never gave up his songwriting aspirations – and the three brothers had been singing together at home since they were small.

The first record ("Surfin'") became a Los Angeles-region hit, earned the group its name, and landed the boys a contract with Capitol Records. The first Capitol release, "Surfin' Safari," was a nation-wide hit.

From the onset, Brian dominated the group. He wrote, arranged, produced, played and sang on all records. He quickly moved from car and surf songs to subjects with broader scope, as his composition and production skills blossomed. The group's records never left the charts through 1963 and 1964. Ironically, Brian has been deaf in one ear since early childhood.

After he quit touring, Brian began to experiment with orchestration, ultimately leading to his 1965 masterpiece, "Pet Sounds," an album far ahead of its time and misunderstood in its day. No pop producer before, not even Phil Spector, had marshaled such lush, ambitious arrangements, and the commercial failure of the LP was a blow from which Brian never recovered.

He immersed himself for the next year recording an album with lyricist Van Dyke Parks that was to be an even more ambitious project. He was locked in some unspoken competition with the Beatles, who had yet to release "Sergeant Pepper," and whispered rumors of the grand scale of the "Smile" album added to its pre-

Beach Boys

release reputation.

In October, 1966, with no sign of "Smile" in sight, the Beach Boys released "Good Vibrations," the group's first million-selling single and Brian's definitive statement. It remains to this day the Beach Boys' biggest single. Without explanation, "Smile" was scrapped. In its place came "Smiley Smile," an album recorded in about two weeks, with "Good Vibrations" on it. "'Smiley Smile' was a bunt," Carl said, "instead of a grand slam." For the first time, the credit on the LP read "Produced by the Beach Boys."

Brian retreated to his Bel-Air mansion, where he set up a recording studio in his living room and recorded the next Beach Boys album, "Wild Honey." "When we did 'Wild Honey,'" Carl said, "Brian asked me to get more involved in the recording end. He wanted a break. He was tired. He had been doing it all too long."

(Tomorrow: The Beach Boys' biggest year)

San Francisco Chronicle | June 16, 1976

Part Two: Beach Boys: It's a Family Affair

> If all goes according to plan, this year will be the biggest in the 15-year history of the Beach Boys. The rock group will start its summer tour July 2 at the Oakland Coliseum Stadium, with concerts to follow in Anaheim and Washington, D.C. that weekend. In three days, the Beach Boys will earn more than a million dollars.

A ONE-HOUR TELEVISION SPECIAL, TO BE PRODUCED by Lorne Michaels of "Saturday Night," will be broadcast in August by NBC TV. There are plans for a joint Carnegie Hall concert with the Joffrey Ballet, which has performed to a suite of Beach Boys songs for several years.

Next week, the first new Beach Boys album in four years, "15 Big Ones," will be released to coincide with the tour. The album also marks the return of Brian Wilson, the musical genius behind all the early classic Beach Boys records.

In a business where no act since Frank Sinatra has made it back up after being there once and slipping, old records rose to the top of the charts, and the Beach Boys became, once again, one of the hottest concert attractions in rock.

How did the group become so popular again? How did the band stay together so long in the first place?

Family is one big answer to the latter question. The Beach Boys started as such – the three Wilson brothers, Brian, Dennis and Carl; a cousin, Mike Love; and a close friend, Al Jardine. Murry Wilson, the brothers' father, managed the group during its early years. Their mother, Audrey, played on their first record.

Today, Carl's brother-in-law, Billy Hinsche, plays in the band. Mike Love's brother, Steve, manages the Beach Boys, and his other brother, Stan, a six-foot-nine former NBA forward, also works for the group. Mike's sister Maureen played harp on the new album.

All Wilson brothers are married (Denny was wed for the third time just last month) and all have children. They all still live in the Los Angeles area, Denny and Carl on the beach. Mike Love resides in Santa Barbara, and Al Jardine lives on a ranch near Big Sur.

The group's climb back to popularity has been slow but steady. In 1970, after seven years with Capitol, the Beach Boys signed with Warner Brothers Records. The release of an outstanding LP, "Sunflower," that year, and subsequent live appearances at Hollywood's Whiskey a Go Go and the Big Sur Folk Festival helped establish the group's credibility with the counterculture.

The late '60s rise of FM "underground" radio, along with bands like the Grateful Dead, pushed the Beach Boys out of the limelight. Always essentially a "singles" band, the group had to withstand a period where hit singles ran against the hip esthetic. Resistance began to wear thin in 1971, when the "Surf's Up" LP was released.

The group spent the entire following year and a small personal fortune recording the last Beach Boys studio album, "Holland," in The Netherlands. After recording facilities there were found inadequate for their needs, the group shipped an entire 24-track studio, piece by piece, from the West Coast. When it was turned on for the first time, smoke poured out of the board.

To make matters worse, when the group first submitted the finished album to Warner Brothers, the company rejected it. A last-minute composition by Brian Wilson, "Sail on Sailor," was recorded in California, and Warners accepted the work.

Over the next three years, the group worked extensively on the road, building its following through literally hundreds of concerts and re-released albums of old records. Now, with Brian back at the helm of the group's recordings, the Beach Boys have returned to full strength, ready to do it again.

Carl Wilson was the lone Beach Boy in the studio, putting final touches to two tracks on which he sang lead. It was the last night; the album was done. A slipped disc put Carl flat on his back for the first three months of the year, during most of the album sessions. "Somehow, I ended up all over the album anyway," he said.

Out of the playback monitors roared the Righteous Brothers oldie, "Just Once in my Life," Carl singing the verses, Brian taking the chorus. The new album will contain half new original material and half other people's oldies. The Phil Spector/ Righteous Brothers song is an appropriate choice, given the prominent Spector influence in Brian's work. Synthesizers and voices, not strings, build Brian's wall of sound, and the lead vocals stand naked against the elaborate, sculptured backdrop. The customary smooth and polished Beach Boys vocal sound has – throughout the album – been altered to something much more raw, vital and urgent. Precision gives way to immediacy.

During the album sessions, the group worked on more than 30 songs, trimming the final selection to 15. Lids of tape boxes lying around the studio listed some of the unused titles, and they are tantalizing: "Sea Cruise," "Come Go With Me," "On Broadway," "Shake, Rattle and Roll," "Mony, Mony."

The oldies on the album are "Rock and Roll Music" (the current single), "Chapel of Love," "Talk to Me," "Palisades Park," "A Casual Look," "Blueberry Hill," "In the Still of the Night" and "Just Once in my Life."

Brian contributed five new songs, which run from the summer-inspired fantasy "Back Home" and the summer credo "It's OK" to an interpretation of rock history, "That Same Song," a love song, "Had to Phone Ya," and the jingle-like "TM Song." Mike Love's "Everybody's in Love" and Al Jardine's "Suzie Cincinnati," a leftover from "Sunflower" days, complete the LP. The average song length is less than 2½ minutes.

An uncompromising artist, Brian has fashioned an album that is certain to provoke controversy. The intentionally crude vocals found critics even among band members. "Brian's leaving in things that were just first or second takes," complained one Beach Boy.

The success of this new album is important enough that the band staged an extravagant press affair in San Francisco two weeks ago, with all members of the group, including reclusive Brian, in attendance.

Wringing his hands and nervously tapping his feet, Brian sat as straight as a pole, obviously uncomfortable, but smiling bravely. A television interviewer asked his first question. Brian blurted out an answer and glanced quickly over his shoulder at younger brother Carl, sitting on the next couch. Carl gently nodded his approval and Brian turned back to the interview.

"I read in the background material," the interviewer continued, "that you don't care much for touring, going on the road, doing interviews like this."

"No. I feel more secure at home," said Brian, "where I can do sketchworks for albums, sketching out songs, calling up Paul McCartney, being on an ego trip. Something where there's some kind of ego involved keeps me going." People were listening intently, taking him seriously, and Brian warmed to his role.

"Elton John was over at my house ... Andy Williams. I get this kinda rush. I think, hey, I like it here." The other Beach Boys began chuckling.

"I like to get that social thing moving," he continued, as the laughter accelerated. "In fact," he declared, "I think it's healthy to meet stars ... Hey! What's so funny?"

After the television crew finished, the press broke into four rooms for individual interviews, as Brian roamed between them. He joined Mike Love and a dozen or so reporters in one room briefly and held court with the same combination of excitement, bluster and nervousness he exhibited before the TV cameras. He fielded a question about how he selected lead singers for specific songs.

"I know their voices and I know which one is right for what song," he said. "There's no politics in the Beach Boys. There's no grappling for leads like there is in other groups, like America. Those guys really grapple for leads. And Three Dog Night, who, as you know, broke up. Danny Hutton is now a solo and the other two are Two Dog Night ... What's so funny? If I brought a comedian in here, you'd probably cry."

Brian lasted a little more than an hour at the interviews, and then headed back to his hotel room to nap. The other Beach Boys continued for four hours.

After hosting a party at the Joffrey Ballet, the entourage repaired to Ernie's for a late-night supper. Again, Brian was on hand for a round of introductions, looking extremely uncomfortable, and split in less than 15 minutes after creating a small scene at his table.

Even so, it was clearly a monumental effort for Brian, who is quite unaccustomed to unfamiliar surroundings, and a painful effort that spoke more eloquently than anything as to just how important the Beach Boys feel this album is.

Carl Wilson understands Brian making people laugh from when they were children. "We all slept in the same room," he said, "and after we went to bed, Brian would sit there trying to make us laugh.

"First, my mother would come in and warn us. If our father came in, then it was curtains. So we'd be trying not to laugh, covering our mouths, hiding under the sheets, and Brian would keep cracking us up."

San Francisco Chronicle | June 17, 1976

Manson and Drugs –
A Beach Boy's Troubled Life

A broadly smiling Dennis Wilson came walking down the hallway at Brother Studios, the Beach Boys' Santa Monica headquarters at the time, away from the little shag rug lined cubicle under the stairway that Mike Love kept as his meditation chamber. "I just jacked off in Mike's room," he said.

DENNIS WILSON, THE BEACH BOY WHO DROWNED A WEEK AGO last Wednesday, never got that many headlines in life. He may have been the most friendly, voluble and open member of America's longest-standing rock band, but he was never one of the group's main composers, vocalists or even instrumental contributors.

Being a Beach Boy didn't make Dennis Wilson happy – far from it. He was the ignored Beach Boy, snubbed by fans and fellow band members. His personal life was full of difficulties. Early this year, his younger brother, Carl, tactfully said Dennis was having "personality problems."

Dennis Wilson was married five times and was in the process of divorcing his fifth wife. In 1976, one of those wives had him arrested, but not charged, for battery, and former Beach Boy associates allegedly assaulted him in 1982 because they said he was providing his other brother, Brian, with drugs.

On Christmas Eve, four days before he drowned while diving off Marina Del Rey, Wilson was admitted into a drug and alcohol treatment clinic at St. John's Hospital in suburban Santa Monica. Dr. Joe Takamine there noted that Wilson had said he was drunk and had taken some cocaine. Nurses reported that the musician complained of problems with his wife, Shawn, 19, who is the daughter of another Beach Boy, Mike Love, and his children. But he left the clinic the next day.

As a drummer, Wilson developed a style of pounding and thrashing uniquely his own, but he was not the sort of marksman timekeeper on which a major league band such as the Beach Boys would depend. For many years, the band always toured with a second drummer in addition to Dennis. In the early '70s, somebody punched Wilson in the throat. The blow damaged his larynx and left him with a gruff growl of a voice that stood out awkwardly amidst the clean, soothing harmonies in which the Beach Boys specialize. As a songwriter, his contributions to the Beach Boys repertoire were few and far between.

But Wilson was the group's heart and soul in other ways. He was the Puck of the Beach Boys, a bad boy who refused to grow up, a benign hooligan, a reprobate with an infectious grin and a naughty gleam in his eye. Among a group of musicians more accustomed to carrying attaché cases than instruments to recording sessions, Dennis Wilson was the rock'n'roller of the band.

He spent his entire adult life as a Beach Boy. He was the surfer who told older, non-surfing brother, Brian, about the beach scene, which Brian plumbed for his '60s rock classics, such as "Surfin' U.S.A." and "Catch a Wave." He participated in the group's musical work like a minority stockholder, lacking the intra-group political clout of his cousin, Love, or businesslike Al Jardine. He was the middle brother of the three Wilson boys, flanked by Brian, the neurotic producer-composer genius behind all the great Beach Boys' records, and younger brother Carl, the Buddha-like baby brother who has always seemed to manage the stormy seas of Beach Boy life with surprising tranquility and equanimity.

Dennis was also responsible for one of the group's darkest secrets: the link between the Beach Boys and the Manson Family, a subject not frequently discussed in public. Some of this came out in personal conversations with this reporter nine years ago, when the Beach Boys were preparing for one of the band's endless comebacks. Brian Wilson had been coaxed back into the studio to oversee his first production of a Beach Boys record since "Good Vibrations." Most of the work was finished – Brian had gone back home and wasn't coming to the studio anymore, while Carl and the others tended to a few last-minute details.

At this 11th hour, Dennis decided he wanted to contribute a song to the album, but things just weren't going well. It was about that point that one of the musicians hanging around produced a meager amount of cocaine and chopped it into a small line for Dennis.

The Beach Boys, at the time, were on a careful drug watch, especially scrupulous to see that Brian didn't get any.

Mike Love, who held big sway in the group's leadership, was strongly anti-drug and deeply into transcendental meditation. To use even this smidgen of drugs brought Dennis to a verge of paranoia that made him extremely uncomfortable. The recording session was changed to another night.

He invited me to spend the night at his home and we piled into his VW van for the 25-minute drive from the Santa Monica recording studio, which he owned with brother Carl, to his Malibu beachside house. It was well past midnight. A few minutes after he showed me the guest room, Dennis Wilson reappeared. His girlfriend, he explained, had thrown him out of their bedroom, insisting he finally decide to get married or she would be moving out the following morning. He sheepishly allowed that he wanted to talk.

He put a videotape of "Deep Throat" on his giant projector and slumped into the living room couch, with ocean waves beating on the beach just outside the French window across the room. The plushly appointed house contained no stereo equipment or any hint that its occupant was a professional musician. He began to talk, slowly at first and picking up momentum, as he sorted through the psychological pieces of this particular puzzle.

He raged about his father, the group's original manager. At age 15, Dennis and the rest of the Beach Boys toured the country under the close scrutiny of their father/manager. Fifteen years later, Dennis still felt the humiliation. "Can you imagine what it was like," he fumed, "to have all these thousands of girls screaming at you during concerts and still be a virgin yourself?"

He openly doubted his ability to maintain a monogamous relationship with any woman. Only that afternoon, he had returned to the studio from a lunch break, boasting he had visited a friend at a massage parlor for some sexual healing.

He turned shaky remembering a homosexual experience, recoiling in some shock at the mere recollection. Then he turned the subject to group sex.

"Me and Charlie," he said, seemingly out of nowhere, "we founded the Family."

The dread unspoken topic had been broached, as far as I know, for the first time with a reporter.

He went on to describe the various delights and joys to be found in love between five, six, seven or more people. Manson, he explained, had a gift for attracting young women into his lair. Ultimately, Wilson said, Manson turned strange.

"I guess he let the drugs get away with him," he said wistfully, as if Manson had let lunacy ruin all their happy fun and games.

Few accounts of the Charles Manson case mention his involvement with the Beach Boys, although occasional references to Wilson's and Manson's sharing a house can be found. Manson once sold a song to the Beach Boys, "Never Learn Not to Love," recorded on the group's "20/20" album with Dennis Wilson credited as author. However, Wilson and Manson parted company well before the notorious August 1969 Sharon Tate-Leon and Rosemary LaBianca killings.

But, on this night, the talk drifted on to other matters, and Wilson continued to replay, over and over, orgy scenes from "Deep Throat" on the huge television screen.

The night sky was giving way to the gentle glow of morning at the beach when we packed it in and hit the hay for, at least, a couple of hours.

The next day, he burst into the studio, fired up with emotion, and suggested a meeting across the street at a coffee shop, away from the other Boys. He revealed he had agreed to marry his girlfriend, Karen Lamm, former wife of the lead vocalist of the rock group Chicago.

That morning, he had conferred with his lawyer, who called him a fool and insisted, at the very least, he get Lamm to sign a prenuptial agreement. Wilson was incensed at the idea. He was voting for love, not distrust, apparently having assuaged his demons through his verbal purge the night before.

It was a happy, decisive moment in a troubled life. He was determined to go through whatever obstacles his friends and family would pose to this marriage and he was inspired to do so. The marriage, of course, ended in divorce.

It was almost a year later when I saw Dennis Wilson again.

Fumbling my way into a third-row center seat at an Oakland Coliseum concert by the Beach Boys, I caught Dennis holding the band back from starting the set's first number, standing behind the drum set trying to get my attention. When he finally did, he delivered a deep, showy bow, sat down and brought his sticks down to start the show.

That is the impish Dennis Wilson, kindly and warm, that I will remember.

Sunday Datebook | January 8, 1984

Brian Wilson

Out of His Shell

Former Beach Boy Brian Wilson emerges for solo tour

I knew his brothers Dennis and Carl better, but Brian Wilson
is the George Gershwin of his generation. We had a number of
brief encounters before this interview at his place in the gated
Mullholland Drive enclave. When I first saw him play with his
new band, it took five songs before I could stop crying. I saw
the event as a radiant triumph over the darkness of mental
illness.

BEVERLY HILLS – BRIAN WILSON SITS IN THE CORNER OF A GIANT L-shaped
couch that takes up most of the large living room off the backyard. The house is
frosted by air conditioning, and he keeps a blanket across his legs. The piano in
the front room is idle, the recording equipment on top little more than a decora-
tion now. The man who wrote all those Beach Boys songs hasn't written a thing in
more than a year.

"I stopped trying," he said. "I'm taking some time off songwriting." Wilson
doesn't need to write any more songs – his stature as one of America's greatest

songwriters is assured. But at this point Wilson, 56, is almost as well known for his tortured personal life as for the sunny songs he wrote for the Beach Boys, a group he threw together with his two younger brothers, their cousin and a neighbor one weekend 38 years ago.

Up in this gated community of prefab palaces off Mulholland Drive overlooking the San Fernando Valley, where he lives with his new wife and their two young adopted daughters, Wilson has finally found a measure of peace. His brothers and his parents are gone. He does not speak to the other Beach Boys. He is free of the controlling influence of the psychologist who ruled his every waking hour for years. He looks trim and healthy, well groomed and handsome in gunfighter black.

With lots of help and anti-depressant medication, he is handling more of a public profile than he has since the 1964 nervous breakdown on a flight to Houston that caused him to stop performing with the Beach Boys.

He is uncomfortable being interviewed. He leans toward brief answers, often no more than a word or two. He will not be drawn out. Every so often, his eyes darken as if some unbidden thought is flashing through his mind.

For the first time in his life, reclusive Wilson is taking his show on the road. He has already played a handful of East Coast dates and has now embarked on a round of West Coast performances (he plays Wednesday at the Warfield). Backed by a 12-piece band with eight backup vocalists, Wilson sings the songs he wrote for the Beach Boys – songs like "Don't Worry Baby," "I Get Around," "California Girls," "Surfin' U.S.A.," "In My Room" – an unlikely undertaking for someone as uncomfortable as Wilson in the presence of strangers.

"I have a little bit of stage fright," he said.

For Wilson, who once spent three years in his bedroom, this qualifies as a major personal triumph. Touring certainly wasn't his idea. He said his wife thought he should. "I was advised that it would be a good idea," he said.

In the past, appearing onstage could send him into chest-heaving, eye-spinning terror. But he is obviously a long way from the terrified, obese, chain-smoking, drug-addled sloppy hulk who was trotted out in 1976 to produce the band's last new album to make the top 10, "15 Big Ones" – the first of many "Brian's Back" publicity campaigns. He appeared occasionally onstage with the Beach Boys and participated in their recording sessions, but Wilson never came all the way back.

"I'm very happy," he says now. He exercises daily and likes to eat dinner out, he said. He and his wife of more than four years, Melinda Ledbetter Wilson, have adopted two young girls, Daria, 3, and Delanie, 1 1/2. A blonde cutie clutching a stuffed animal peaks around the corner until her father sees her, giggles and runs off.

He has patched up his relationship with his grown daughters, Wendy and Carnie, once members of the hit pop group Wilson Phillips. He said hearing music helps him feel good and that he likes to listen to the Los Angeles AM oldies station. He wants to make a record that feels like the early rock and 'n' roll dance records, maybe next year, but admits he has no real plans to make a new album.

His last album, "Imagination," entered the charts at No. 88 last year and then disappeared. He recorded it in St. Charles, Ill., on the distant outskirts of Chicago. Wilson built a studio in the house he rented because it was next door to his latest in a long string of collaborators, co- producer and former professional wrestler Joe Thomas, who is also serving as the musical director on this tour.

But even Wilson can't work up much enthusiasm for "Imagination." He doesn't even like the songs that much. " 'Happy Days' is about the only one I like," he said. "But I'm my own worst critic."

Since his brother Carl's death at age 51 from cancer last year, for the first time in the history of the group, no Wilsons have been connected with the Beach Boys who continue to tour with vocalist Mike Love, Brian's cousin.

"We licensed him the name and we get a percentage. I hear it's really good. We don't talk much, but he sure is an on-the-ball businessman."

Later, Wilson gives a slightly more candid appraisal of his longtime foil in the Beach Boys; "He's a maniac, an egomaniac."

Also out on the road is a group headed by the other living former founding member, Al Jardine, called Beach Boys, Family and Friends ("Al," said Wilson, "he's nuts.").

There's no happy ending for Brian Wilson. He sits on top of the hill, living in plasticine luxury with his new family. Going on tour may be a current enthusiasm – "I'm trying to get something going," he said, "build a following" – but he is not a road dog who is going to spend the rest of his life making one-nighters and late-night bus rides. He may have found some stability in his life and he may have distanced himself from the fractious infighting and family feuding that was always a part of the Beach Boys history. But he is alone with the pain and the memories, and the weight of his terrible burden shows in his face. His crooked smile never seems to fall comfortably on his lips.

"I feel good," he said. "I feel happy." But he didn't smile.

San Francisco Chronicle | Monday, October 18, 1999

Creedence and Beyond

Bayou Country

These two liner notes for yet another reissue of the Creedence catalog won the Deems Taylor/ASCAP Award as sort of the liner notes of the year. Collecting the award at Lincoln Center was hilarious. After a big, pillowy hug from ASCAP president Marilyn Bergman, I looked out at a sold out room full of people in tuxedos and said the first thing that popped into my head. "Gee, I wish my mother was here."

SWEATING OUT HIS NATIONAL GUARD DUTY in summer 1968, living in a tiny El Cerrito apartment with his wife and kids, John Fogerty developed insomnia. The tension was understandable. The band he belonged to with his older brother and two best friends from junior high faced a crossroads. His life and his dreams hung in the balance.

Although the group managed to nearly crack the Top Ten with "Susie Q" from the first Creedence Clearwater Revival album, the second single failed to see the sunny side of the Hot 100. He was afraid the band was going to fall off the face of the earth and he would have to go back to work at the car wash. He still played soldier every month, taking crap from the other weekend grunts as the hippie with the record on the radio. Bobby Kennedy was shot as John watched on late-night TV, and the stations showed the nightmare footage over and over.

He had already discovered the guitar riff during a sound check at the Avalon Ballroom, just pounding the delicious figure endlessly while the band stayed on the E chord. Slowly, in those quiet, lonely, desperate hours before the dawn at his little apartment, he began to untangle "Born on the Bayou," "Proud Mary," and "Keep On Chooglin" from the mists of Mark Twain books he never read in school and grainy black and white B-movies of crocodile hunters in the dark Cajun swamps and Will Rogers playing a steamboat captain.

In his mind's ear, he heard the Mississippi jungle boogie of Bo Diddley and the muddy voice of Howlin' Wolf. He saw James Garner playing the riverboat gambler in *Maverick*. He felt the throbbing vibrato of Pops Staples's guitar and the supple soul of Booker T. & the MGs. He knew Elvis Presley and the yellow Sun Records. He was drinking from the Mississippi River, long a mythic force in America's history.

His discharge from the Army arrived and the pieces all started to fall in place.

"Proud Mary" came together when he combined parts from different songs already underway in his notebook, including one about a washerwoman named Mary. He began to link the songs he was writing to a mythical Deep South, a South this California kid had never seen, but could only imagine.

It was a deceptively simple set of material. In addition to the three major pieces, Fogerty also had a couple of suitable blues and a concert rouser under his belt with "Graveyard Train," "Penthouse Pauper," and "Bootleg." "Good Golly Ms. Molly" was standard Creedence frat party fare and his ripping Little Richard impression was well-practiced.

Recording at the imposing RCA Studios in Hollywood, famous at the time as the place where the Rolling Stones made "Satisfaction," the basic tracks for *Bayou Country*, Creedence Clearwater's second album, were cut by all four musicians playing together live. Fogerty finished the album by himself, over-dubbing a few additional instrumental parts and all the vocals. He toyed with the lyrics to "Proud Mary" right up to just before he recorded them. He laid down a guitar solo he thought sounded as much as he could like Steve Cropper of the MGs.

Later, when you asked any of the other three members when did they know the band had made it, they all said the same thing: "The first time John played us 'Proud Mary.'" Fogerty himself has always said he knew he had written his best song almost as soon as he finished writing it.

Released just before Christmas that year, the single of "Proud Mary" (with "Born on the Bayou" on the B-side) simply exploded. With radio tip sheets noticing the record in the first weeks of the new year, it bolted to the top of playlists across the country by February. It echoed out of every radio station in the country, out of record store windows, passing cars, neighbors' apartments. Bob Dylan declared it his favorite record of the year. *Life* magazine ran a glowing review. Soul man Solomon Burke rushed a cover version into the r&b market. Creedence Clearwater Revival had arrived.

Bayou Country is not only the album that defined the sound of Creedence, it was the band's first masterpiece. In a single, bold stroke, it announced Creedence Clearwater as a bright, vital force in rock and staked a place for what was yet to come.

March 2000

Pendulum

As a cub reporter with an assignment for a long-gone magazine called Earth, I spent several days hanging around while the band rehearsed 'Pendulum.' I didn't know at the time that I would never see anything like it again.

IN APRIL 1970, PAUL McCARTNEY ANNOUNCED HE WAS LEAVING the group and breaking up the Beatles. As Creedence Clearwater prepared to record the band's sixth album, the Beatles loomed large over their shoulders. The boys from El Cerrito had actually outsold the mop tops the previous year and there seemed to be a throne vacant.

No less a palace player than Allen Klein, the hardball accountant whose tough business practices contributed to the split between McCartney and his bandmates, turned up for a meeting at the Factory, the warehouse in industrial Berkeley that served as Creedence's headquarters. Klein had gone so far as to check sales figures of the band's previous album, *Cosmo's Factory*, with the plant that printed the album covers. The record sold more than five million copies.

Not content with merely being the top-selling rock group in the world, coming off seven consecutive Top Ten hits, the members of Creedence chafed under the band's dismissal by the hip underground cognoscenti as nothing more than a Top 40 act. They determined to launch a campaign to take their rightful places in the contemporary rock pantheon. A big-time Hollywood public relations agency was hired. Interviewers dutifully trooped in and out of the Factory daily. It seemed like a strange reaction to success. Why would they want to do this?

John Fogerty didn't have to give the question a moment's thought. He was sitting on a stack of cartons that contained thousands of little plastic games – roll the b.b.'s into the holes on the photo of Creedence Clearwater. The dime store toys were awaiting shipment to the nation's great disc jockeys. He shot back the answer instantly.

"Because I want John, Tom, Stu, and Doug to roll off people's tongues like John, Paul, George, and Ringo."

Behind the scenes, the other three members led a mutiny. They insisted singer-songwriter-producer Fogerty relinquish his complete control of the group's recordings. He reluctantly agreed. *Pendulum* would be the last Creedence album

John Fogerty would produce.

As was the band's custom, rehearsals began daily at noon. The musicians' vans pulled into the warehouse and the band assembled behind a blue velvet curtain in the corner. John Fogerty conducted the rehearsals from the bench behind a Hammond B-3 organ, a stylistic shift he planned for the new album, inspired no doubt by Booker T. & the MGs. The famed Memphis soul instrumentalists had not only been an early influence on Creedence, the band paid big money for Booker and the guys

to appear as special guests on Creedence's triumphant 1969 headline tour. Organist Booker T. Jones and guitarist Steve Cropper were filmed jamming with Creedence at the Factory for a Creedence TV special.

The four musicians spent six weeks practicing the basic instrumental parts to John's songs. The other band members didn't know the titles, the melodies, the lyrics. Every afternoon, they would go over the instrumental tracks with a jeweler's eye for detail. Drummer Doug Clifford taped masking-tape targets on his cymbals. Stu Cook joked about rubbing Vaseline on his amplifier speakers to get that funky bass sound.

After having the basic tracks drilled into them, the four musicians repaired to Wally Heider's Studio in San Francisco, where they laid down the tracks in short order. For once, a couple of new songs bloomed during the sessions. "Pagan Baby" and "Have You Ever Seen the Rain" were actually rehearsed and recorded in the studio. The album took a month to finish, a long time by Creedence standards, while Fogerty fussed with horn parts he was playing, keyboard overdubs, even group choral background vocals on "Sailor's Lament."

With the album set to ship one million copies the day of release in December 1971, Creedence invited the entire rock press from across the country to Berkeley to celebrate the release. Several hundred writers were flown in, wined, dined, and driven around town in buses. They saw the TV special. They ate a catered dinner at the Factory, followed by a short performance by the band. After a few of the songs from the new album, including Creedence's next Top Ten hit, "Hey Tonight," the band offered an encore of the epic "I Heard It Through the Grapevine" from the previous album. "This is for Saul Zaentz," said John Fogerty, "who believed in us when the whole world was a $400 lead guitar amplifier." Most of the articles resulting from the expensive press junket – dubbed "The Night of the Generals" by some members of the band – largely ridiculed the group.

Two months later, Tom Fogerty quit the band. The golden age of Creedence Clearwater was ended.

April 2000

Creedence Clearwater Revival

Big Wheels Stop Turning – End of Line for Creedence

My first scoop – I also did the story for Rolling Stone. Of course, if it had really been important, would they have given me the interview?

THE FINAL NOTES HAVE SOUNDED FOR CREEDENCE CLEARWATER REVIVAL – the great white hope of American rock. The last press release of their illustrious, 24-carat career stated soberly that Creedence "has decided not to record as a unit any more."

In 3½ years, that unit sold approximately 20 million albums and 10 million singles, good for at least $75 million in sales. That just about puts them in league with the Beatles, Elvis and Bing Crosby.

"It was the biggest American thing – at least as far as groups go," bassist Stu Cook said last week at their Berkeley headquarters. "And one of the bigger international things.

"It was right that it ended when it did," he continued. "We all would have quit anyway, even if we hadn't made the decision."

The announcement followed by six months the release of their seventh straight gold album, "Mardi Gras." The first compilation of past glories, "Creedence Gold," is expected imminently from Fantasy Records. Only a live album recorded on this year's European tour remains unissued.

In retrospect, the split was probably inevitable after rhythm guitarist Tom Fogerty left the group in January, 1971, on the heels of album number six, "Pendulum."

"I don't think we were ever given credit for knowing what we were doing," Tom said just last week. "You don't have so many gold records in a row without knowing what you're doing."

The members of Creedence often felt the group was unjustly snubbed by rock critics and the other observers of the scene. This was one major bone of contention within the group prior to Tom's departure.

"When I left the group that was a real big thing for me," Tom said. "Now it doesn't seem so important."

In addition to their failure to become rock music cult figures, the other main factor at the time revolved around songwriter John Fogerty's creative dominance and the desire on the part of the other musicians to contribute equally.

All four resolved to finish "Pendulum" and begin a new regime thereafter. Unreconciled, Tom left anyway.

The remaining three decided to continue as a trio and a single – "Sweet Hitch-hiker," coupled with Stu Cook's first songwriting effort "Door to Door" – was recorded and released. It was the first Creedence single in three years not to make gold.

During the next year there was considerable activity: tours of Europe, Australia as well as two U.S. tours.

The second of those trips – behind the release of "Mardi Gras" – played to a surprising number of half-empty halls, even with John Fogerty's beautiful "Someday Never Comes" off the album riding high on the charts.

At least one observer felt that John's evolving solo career first showed itself – then perhaps only as an unconscious desire – as early as the debut appearance of the trip closing night at Fillmore West, where John traded his customary flannel shirt for a turquoise suit and an Elvis-like hairdo.

His growing isolation from Creedence became obvious, however, when John started recording his first solo album as The Blue Ridge Rangers, playing and singing every part himself.

The album will be devoted entirely to country music roots – no Fogerty originals – and two singles have already been released. The latest (Hank Williams' "Jambalaya" backed with a hundred year-old gospel tune "Working on a Building") has already received considerable airplay.

Creedence drummer Doug Clifford delivered his first solo album to the stores last month. To date, it has received little or no attention. Stu Cook is presently engaged producing demonstration tapes for a Marin county band, Clover.

Tom Fogerty will have his second solo album out in the middle of November. The big news went down without interrupting – or surprising – anyone.

Sunday Datebook | November 5, 1972

John Fogerty on Threshold of Big Comeback

Ex-Creedence Clearwater leader breaks a nine-year drought

This piece landed me smack dab in the middle of the epic Zaentz v. Fogerty lawsuits. They never liked me much at Fantasy Records and, in fact, the day after he won all those Oscars for "Amadeus," the only day The Chronicle managing editor would even recognize his name, Saul Zaentz had delivered to the paper an eight-page letter calling for my dismissal. I always admired his attention to detail.

JOHN FOGERTY COULDN'T FINISH A SONG. The whole world used to sing his tunes when he led Creedence Clearwater Revival, once the world's most popular rock band, but for the past nine years, he suffered a crippling writer's block.

He couldn't sleep more than a few hours a night. He developed an ulcer. He withdrew from friends and associates, turning into a recluse, by his own admission.

Still, every day he would arrive at his small East Bay studio on a quiet residential side street and put in a full eight hours by himself, playing music, recording the results and trying to write a song.

What happened to Fogerty? Had he lost his mind? His talent? Was he doomed, as he himself wondered, like the character in "The Shining," to write the same sentence over and over hundreds of times?

He had been ruined financially, his life savings of more than $4 million lost in the 1977 collapse of a tax haven Bahamian bank, and the people he blamed for this disaster – Berkeley's Fantasy Records – still owned his recording contract. Every time he got started on a song, he would think about buying these people yet another Mercedes with his music and choke up, unable to work, flooded with anger and frustration.

Last year, he finally gained his freedom – at no small cost – and got down

John Fogerty

to writing songs and recording an album. Even after he finished six tracks, he still wasn't sure the songs warranted release. In fact, he was not finally convinced until last month, when he heard his first record in nine years, "The Old Man Is Down the Road," on the radio, where it is currently scorching up playlists across the country.

"This is not just a comeback," he said evenly. "It is a triumph over evil."

The ringing guitar licks that open the record sound familiar but the instant that intensely wrought voice that sold millions of records 15 years ago kicks in, it is suddenly obvious – John Fogerty and the sound of Creedence is back with a vengeance. There is no Creedence anymore, but this album makes it abundantly clear, if it wasn't already, that John Fogerty alone was Creedence Clearwater. The album, "Centerfield," will be released tomorrow, setting the stage for what could well be one of the most amazing comebacks in the history of rock music.

"I was a nine-year question mark," he mused two weeks ago over a cup of coffee at his East Bay studio. "I knew I was not there and had no idea what to do to get there. I knew I had to make a record. That was always on my horizon and I never saw past it. Ideas, creativity, all that stuff that used to happen wasn't happening. But I told all my friends, 'This is only going to end one way.'"

Fogerty can talk about his traumas cheerfully now. The album is done. The single is on its way to the Top 10. "I thought I'd be cocky," he said, "but I really feel grateful." His determination paid off and he speaks from the strength and confidence that comes with victory over adversity. At age 39, Fogerty still boasts youthful good looks – possibly the product of clean living; his biggest vice has always been hard work – and sounds upbeat talking about overcoming his problems and surmounting his painful period of seclusion and unhappiness.

Like some former batting champion confined to the obscurity of minor league baseball who suddenly starts to hit balls out of the park again, Fogerty returns with a home run of an album, a record that at once revives and expands on the sound of Creedence's.

The title track, "Centerfield," Fogerty admitted, is about himself:

Hold the phone, beat the drum

The sun came out today There's a new grass on the field Rounding third, headed for home It's a brown-eyed handsome man Anyone can understand how I feel Put me in coach, I'm ready to play Look at me, I can be centerfield

Fogerty wrote, sang, arranged, produced and played most of the instruments on the million-selling records by Creedence Clearwater, the band he founded in

1959 in a garage with two friends from his El Cerrito junior high school. His older brother joined the band and, after years of working frat parties and pizza parlors under a variety of names, landed a contract with the small East Bay record label, Fantasy Records, a tiny company run out of a cramped West Oakland office that specialized in jazz and comedy albums.

"Suzie Q," off the group's 1969 debut album, squeaked onto the Top 20. With the second album, "Bayou Country," and "Proud Mary," Creedence vaulted immediately into the front ranks of the rock bands of the day. An extraordinary string of smash hits followed – "Born on the Bayou," "Bad Moon Rising," "Lodi," "Fortunate Son," "Who'll Stop the Rain," "Up Around the Bend, " "Hey Tonight" – with Fogerty virtually running the whole show himself, business affairs as well as the music.

His older brother, Tom, left the group in 1971 and, after one more album, Creedence disbanded the following year. The group had sold more than $120 million worth of records in three short years. Fogerty began the painstaking process of making records by himself, releasing an album of country and western standards under the name Blue Ridge Rangers in 1973. He has not recorded with another musician since. Shortly thereafter, Fogerty and Fantasy began fighting.

His current problems all stemmed from a troubled relationship with Fantasy, where he once worked as a stock boy long before his songs put millions of dollars in the company coffers, literally funding the construction of new plush headquarters for the label in industrial Berkeley.

He said his contract called for him to give the company something like 35 masters a year. "I owed them so much product," he said, "I couldn't even brush my teeth. I couldn't focus. The pressure was there all the time. I felt like I was chained in a dungeon."

He met with the company chiefs and asked for some relief. "I told them 'I made you all rich,'" he said. "'I need some relief.'" Somebody made a comment about depression producing art, Fogerty said, and when not a single comment he considered sympathetic was forthcoming, he got up and started for the door – "like a little boy," he said – and decided if he got all the way to the door, he would walk through it and never come back. He did. "They've been as thoroughly compassionate ever since," he said.

A deal was arranged for Fogerty to record for Asylum Records, although Fantasy retained international rights to his work. A solo album was released 10 years ago to modest interest and a second album, "Hoodoo," was finished, although Asylum didn't feel the record was good enough to release.

"The first album wasn't very good," Fogerty said, "and 'Hoodoo' was even worse. The songs aren't finished and the music isn't very good. I couldn't concentrate."

It was also about this time that Fogerty met with his accountants to investigate his financial status. "I asked my accountant how much money I had and he couldn't answer me. I thought it was a pertinent question."

He told the accountant he wanted a "shoe-box meeting," Fogerty said. "I wanted him to take an empty shoe box and put in all the money I ever made, take out all the money I ever spent and tell me what was left." Fogerty wondered about certain minus signs on the ledger and was told they were managerial fees.

"People were in my bank account, taking my money without telling me," he said.

Years before, when Creedence was riding at the top, the group had gone to Fantasy about a royalty increase. Instead, the company arranged to bank money for the group with Castle Bank and Trust Company of Nassau. "They wanted to avoid taxes and said that would be like a raise. It looked great at the time, but it started to get smelly later."

Indeed, when Fogerty asked to withdraw the $4 million he deposited with the bank, it folded. The money was gone. The Internal Revenue Service had been investigating the Caribbean bank under the code name Project Haven. "Miraculously, Fantasy had withdrawn all their money some months before," Fogerty noted dryly.

All this led to a lawsuit, currently under appeal, in which Fogerty won a judgment in 1983 of more than $4 million from his accountants because a jury decided his investors failed to properly protect the group's financial interests. Creedence's lawyers have added Fantasy Records as a defendant in the appeal.

Meantime, Fogerty scraped together what funds he had outside the collapsed bank and gave it to the tax man. "I was pretty well wiped out, " he said. He blamed Fantasy, who still owned the international rights to his recordings.

"I still owed them three albums," he said. "I'd bust my butt making records, and Castle went down and they were part of that. There was no way I could give another record to those jerks in Berkeley. I had to get away from those people 'cause they're evil – no matter what it cost and it cost plenty."

Fogerty negotiated his release from Fantasy by giving up all future artist royalties from his Creedence records, which still sell substantial amounts every year. "I traded my past for my future," he said.

Fantasy Records president Ralph Kaffel would offer no comment on any matters pertaining to Fogerty and Creedence.

Fogerty still couldn't break his mental block. "I tried writing songs, but I was like a blind man in a fog. I had no more idea of how to do it than the man in the moon and not a clue how to get there. I just knew when I got there, I'd know. I recorded an album every day; it's just a question of quality," he laughed.

The breakthrough finally came, like the scene in "Pinocchio," he said, where the boy puppet is drowned and the fairy sprinkles dust over him to bring him back to life. "I woke up and said, 'I'm a real band,'" he said. The first song came.

"I had these lines – 'I know it's true, 'cause I saw it on TV' – and I had an outline of things I wanted to be in the song. I took my notes and got in a boat, went out on the lake and got back at six o'clock in the evening. I had a verse and a half, maybe, and the chorus – enough I knew I had a song. I had gone out to do something and now it was happening."

The song, "I Saw It On TV," is one of the centerpieces of "Centerfield," encapsulating 30 years of history as witnessed through a television screen – a kind of video "American Pie," spindling the American obsession with watching life on a little silver screen.

Last September, he took cassettes of six finished tracks to the president of Warner Brothers Records. "I had my hat in hand, wondering, 'Is it going be good enough to put out?'" he said. The company executives loved the tapes and were so enthusiastic, they initially considered rush-releasing the album before Thanksgiving. "I was so relieved and validated," Fogerty said.

When he got home that night, his wife and three teenaged children were asleep. Fogerty pulled out a piece of scratch paper and scribbled, "The monkey is off my back," drew a chimpanzee dancing on the page and posted it on the refrigerator.

"This is me," he said. "It took me all that time to find me again. It was not a conscious effort on my part to be contemporary. It was not a conscious effort on my part to sound like CCR. But I started to have a signature. Obviously, 'Old Man' sounds like Creedence, but that really sounds like what I like. And this really sounds better than Creedence."

Sunday Datebook | January 6, 1985

The Fortunate Son Returns

After lengthy lawsuits and years on a new album, ex-Creedence Clearwater singer-songwriter 7ogerty goes back to the bayou

As is so often the case, the record wasn't as interesting as the interview, but I can never resist John Fogerty.

BURBANK – THE GHOSTS OF LONG DEAD BLUESMEN called out to John Fogerty.

Before he even began the 4 1/2-year recording ordeal that resulted in "Blue Moon Swamp," the former Creedence Clearwater Revival leader's first album in 11 years, he took a series of journeys to Mississippi, pilgrimages to the spiritual home of "Proud Mary," "Born on the Bayou," "Run Through the Jungle," "Bad Moon Rising" and all his other enduring songs.

Fogerty didn't know what he was seeking. After being embroiled in a 20-year legal battle with his former record company, a kind of rock 'n' roll "Bleak House," he wanted to connect with his music's past. He walked unkept graveyards where the giants of Mississippi delta blues long lay buried. He took photographs of the Riverside Hotel in Clarksdale, Miss., where Ike Turner rehearsed his band before making "Rocket 88," which many call the first rock 'n' roll record.

"I saw all these guys, their life's work," Fogerty said. "I don't know anything about the white guy that ripped them off – and I'm sure there was one. All I know is this great music. And that made me go, 'Wow, forget all that other stuff, just be you. You play your music. You write your songs like you always did.' I thought about Robert Johnson and Muddy Waters. These guys didn't take no s—. Screw that."

He recalled his Southern sojourns sitting in an office at Warner Bros. Records last month, his wife, Julie Kramer, quietly watching from a couch in the corner. Dressed in blue denim shirt and jeans, his brown hair giving off a golden sheen, Fogerty, 51, is a complex person underneath an easygoing exterior, eyes bristling above a ready smile. He has emerged from the shadows that have engulfed his life for most of the past 20 years with a new outlook, a new wife, a new family and a fabulous new album, due May 20, that he thinks stands with his finest work. When he launches a national tour next weekend at the Fillmore Auditorium, Fogerty will be playing his Creedence classics for the first time since the band broke up in 1972.

For years he refused to perform them because Berkeley-based Fantasy Records owned the publishing rights, leading to some of his legal problems. But his Mississippi experiences changed him.

"Nobody talks about who owns Robert Johnson," Fogerty said. " 'Proud Mary' is spiritually mine. I will do myself."

The Fantasy lawsuits may have dwindled to one remaining case, but Fogerty remains the sworn enemy of the chairman of the company, Oscar-winning film producer Saul Zaentz, as well as of his former band mates. The other Creedence members not only failed to join him in battling Fantasy but also enraged him by touring under the name Creedence Clearwater Revisited, with somebody else at the front of the band singing Fogerty's songs. With "Centerfield," his 1984 comeback album, Fogerty took his anger public with a song called "Zanz Kant Dance," where he told the story of a money-thieving, trained pig named Zanz. The song brought a defamation of character suit from the Fantasy chairman. Fogerty also faced a plagiarism suit from Fantasy, which he won, that accused him of stealing the album's No. 1 hit, "Old Man Down the Road," from his earlier "Run Through the Jungle."

Meanwhile, his older brother Tom Fogerty, another Creedence alumnus, sided with Zaentz. The brothers' breach was not healed by the time Tom Fogerty died of a respiratory ailment in 1990. John Fogerty was there only as "the dutiful, polite relative."

In the grip of these conflicts, Fogerty couldn't work and couldn't sleep, tormented by insomnia. But slowly over the past few years his life turned around. He heard the voices of the dead bluesmen and he fell in love with the woman who became his wife. He even felt confident enough to sign with the first real manager of his career, Nick Clainos, co-president of Bill Graham Presents.

"Julie is the main thing," he said. "I can't say enough about her. When you find the love of your life and you're able to sit with another guy and actually say that unashamedly, then you know you've arrived some place."

Fogerty met Kramer, a divorced mother from South Bend, Ind., in 1985, during his only post-Creedence solo tour. They have been married for six years and have two sons, ages 4 and 5. Fogerty has three grown children from his first marriage, and his 3-year-old grandchild plays with his new sons when the families visit. "I'm just a really lucky guy," he said. "About the first time I saw her, I recognized that she would be good for me. We both did this very cautiously. We instinctively knew, 'Let's not mess this up.' The first time we met, I was on tour and we were in the hotel lounge. We talked and had a nice chat. Her sister was there and it was all quite wholesome. Of course, I tried to ruin it all by inviting her back to my hotel room, but she wisely said, 'Uh-uh, ain't going for that.' "

Four-and-a-half years ago, Fogerty began "Blue Moon Swamp." He suffers over his recordings. When he made the Creedence records, he and his then-life-long associates – bass player Stu Cook, drummer Doug Clifford and rhythm guitarist Tom Fogerty – rehearsed every day for weeks before record ing. Once in the studio, the band would lay down basic tracks and Fogerty would overdub any additional instruments, perform the vocals and mix the album within a couple of weeks. His solo records have been more torturous.

Fogerty worked on "Blue Moon Swamp" every day. It took 18 months before he completed one track he deemed usable. The budget reportedly soared past $1 million. When he couldn't find anyone else who could do it to his satisfaction, he spent more then three years teaching himself dobro well enough to play the parts on his record.

"More than anything, getting the musicians right was the thing that eluded me," he said. "What that means when I say that is getting it to really feel like I thought it should feel."

Fogerty used a large number of session musicians on the album, includ ing Linda Ronstadt bassist Bob Glaub and John Mellencamp drummer Kenny Aronoff, who will join the band on tour.

For Fogerty, it has never been enough simply to play the song and capture a mistake-free performance on tape. His compositions, he has always said, appear in his imagination as full-blown productions, as records, and his mission has been to re-create the sounds he hears inside his head as exactly as he can. His perfectionist instincts sent him through more than 25 drummers while cutting "Blue Moon Swamp."

"I was searching for a really rocking record," Fogerty said. "I didn't want it to be some guy's impression of a rock 'n' roll record. It has to be a rock 'n' roll record. The record speaks for itself. You put it in there and, in five seconds, either it is or it ain't. Start with the drums. The drums is the foundation of the house. If it's not right, no matter how much garbage – echo and fuzz and doo-wah doo-wah – on there, if it's not right, well . . . you can be a tricky producer-mixer and maybe cover it up a little. It's so much better when the drums are cool."

Yet for all his obsessive refinements, the finished record sounds anything but labored. On "Blue Moon Swamp," Fogerty aims all his formidable skills at the heart of rock 'n' roll and hits a bull's-eye. More than just a comeback, this album convincingly stakes his claim as one of rock's most forceful, original stylists.

Each of the dozen new songs is stamped with his signature vocals and swampy guitar blends. They range from the trademark twangy guitar of "Blue Boy" to the Rolling Stones-style crunch of "Bring It Down to Jelly Roll," from the country romp "Rambunctious Boy" to the eerie "Walking in a Hurricane," the first single. Fogerty makes no concessions to trends, just the same basic rock 'n' roll music he always did.

"What I used to say all the time – and I still do – is that I'm trying to make records that will be played in 10 years. I used to say that all the time around 1969-70. I wanted to go right to the purity, the center of rock 'n' roll, and not be surrounded with this stuff that was the in-and-out phases of any given time – meaning wah-wah pedals and go-go girls, those things that sort of trap you in a time."

He ponders the fate of an authentic rock 'n' roll record in 1997 ("no one knows"), and mutters something about liking the new Wallflowers record. It's not easy to measure up to his exacting values.

"Nirvana was pretty cool," he said. "I don't know if you call that rock 'n' roll. In my mind set, that doesn't rival Jerry Lee Lewis. That's what my standards are for myself."

Fogerty never forgets the lineage that led to his own place in rock history; it's always there, hovering over his shoulders. Creedence first exploded on the scene in 1968 with Fogerty's interpretation of "Suzie Q," Dale Hawkins' landmark '50s Louisiana rock 'n' roll number. The original featured on guitar a teenage James Burton, who became one of the music's defining instrumentalists.

"When I've got my guitar stuff together now, I think I'm pretty cool," Fogerty said. "I also see James Burton's light way down the track and I go, 'OK, buddy, another 25 years, I'll be down there.' Course, by then he'll be . . . but I'm willing to put the time in. I don't see anybody else standing there doing that."

Sunday Datebook | *May 11, 1997*

CHAPTER 7

Blues and Soul

John Lee Hooker

Charles Brown

Sugar Pie De Santo

Jimmy McCrackin

Mike Bloomfield

Elvin Bishop

Rodger Collins

Booker T.

Taj Mahal

Appreciation

Hooker a true bluesman

I wrote this in the business office of some San Diego motel.
John Lee had been such a part of the scene, a landmark, a tribal
elder, someone who had been part of the landscape since I first
walked on the stage. He was possibly the most unpretentious
man who ever lived. He once interrupted a live radio interview
and put the deejay on hold because he got another call.

THE LAST GUNFIGHTER JUST LEFT TOWN, boot heels first.

Boogie man John Lee Hooker, 83, died in his sleep two nights ago at his Los Altos home. He was the last bluesman of his kind. B.B. King and a handful of lesser figures are still alive, but King and the others represent a different, more urban tradition.

John Lee Hooker played country blues. He sang stump songs, played cotton-patch guitar and growled out his blues like some primordial ooze. He made his name in Detroit in the late '40s, but his music never left his native Clarksdale, Miss.

He lived long enough to see honors heaped upon him and have several new generations hear his music. He leaves behind something like 125 albums, by his own estimate, and an indelible style.

His songs like "Boogie Chillen," "Boom Boom" and "One Bourbon, One Scotch, One Beer," are clearly all poured out of the same spigot. Even when played by other musicians, they were stamped "John Lee Hooker."

As a man, he was a glowing ember, an intuitive master who neither wasted a motion nor suffered fools. He looked as if his face had been carved out of ebony, and he always wore his lucky socks.

As a musician, he played with them all. The Rolling Stones invited him to appear as a special guest at concerts. A raft of rock superstars joined him for a 1990 Madison Square Garden tribute concert. His recent recordings have sold extraordinarily well, thanks largely to guest appearances by the likes of Carlos Santana, Keith Richards and Van Morrison. His duet with Bonnie Raitt, "I'm in the Mood," on 1990's "The Healer," won a Grammy.

For all his success and fame, he remained a plainspoken, simple man. He lent

his name to John Lee Hooker's Boom Boom Room, just because he liked the joint and wanted a place where he could hang out. Van Morrison once hurried down to the Fillmore club after a concert and spent more time singing the blues in the tiny room with Hooker than he had performing for the ticket- holders he left behind on Nob Hill.

Hooker was a man of immense dignity. Like his music, he was rooted deeply in a low, rolling gait that could by turns be ominous and joyous, dark or sensual. He could be expansively warm or sharp and a little scary.

The last time we did an interview, he lay on his bed fully clothed down to the inevitable hat, the door to his bedroom closed and the heat turned on. The room felt like the greenhouse where Philip Marlowe met Gen. Sternwood in "The Big Sleep." He took a couple of phone calls between the soft mumbles that passed for answers to questions and, after about 10 minutes, looked up and ended the meeting.

"I suppose you've got enough now," he said evenly.

He was right. I did.

San Francisco Chronicle | *June 23, 2001*

A Blues Legend Passes

Neglect didn't stop $\mathcal{C}harles\ \mathcal{B}rown$

I loved Charles Brown deeply. We first met when I was 20 years old and he was playing B-3 organ at the Zanzibar Room and living upstairs at the California Hotel. He would sometimes call early in the morning, waking me up, to play me pieces of classical music he was practicing over the phone. His second act – with guitarist Danny Caron – was one of the most satisfying comebacks I ever witnessed.

CHARLES BROWN GOT HIS SECOND CHANCE.

The rhythm and blues pioneer, who died of congestive heart failure at 78 Thursday night in Oakland, had been all but forgotten only 15 years ago. But he lived long enough to see honors heaped on him, to play piano and sing for presidents and kings and to acquaint a new generation of blues fans with the works of a master.

Brown, who was named to the Rock and Roll Hall of Fame only weeks ago, died at Summit Hospital after a battle with heart disease that left him bedridden for the past three months in an East Bay nursing home. Two weeks ago he got out of bed long enough to attend a star-studded, sold-out benefit on his behalf at the Great American Music Hall. It featured such friends and fans as Charlie Musselwhite, Maria Muldaur, Dr. John and Bonnie Raitt. He sat in a wheelchair in the wings, beaming that contagious smile that lighted dark corners wherever he went.

Rock star Raitt, in fact, played a large role in bringing Brown back into the spotlight, taking him on her tours as her supporting act, singing with him on records and generally acting as his unofficial fan club president.

As recently as 15 years ago, he had been reduced to working as a janitor, although he was always careful not to do anything that might jeopardize his fingers because even at his lowest ebb he envisioned a return to the piano.

"To have been able to work and get close to Charles during our dual comebacks this last decade is one of my life's greatest gifts," Raitt said.

And return he did. In 1997 at the White House, President Clinton presented him with the Heritage Fellowship of the National Endowment for the Arts. In 1989

Charles Brown

he received one of the first awards from the Rhythm and Blues Foundation and played a subsequent Kennedy Center concert in Washington, D.C. He won awards all over the country and found himself schmoozing with Clinton during a break at the wedding of Mary Steenburgen and Ted Danson in 1995 at Martha's Vineyard.

The rock world awakened to his return and paid its respects. Eric Clapton asked him to New York for a recording session. Elvis Costello wrote a song especially for him to record. Van Morrison, a fan who turned up at various Brown appearances, used him as a pianist on a John Lee Hooker record Morrison produced.

His first time around, Brown was a king of the segregated black music world. In the days immediately after World War II, he became a phenomenon with the smash hit – "Driftin Blues," with Johnny Moore's Three Blazers, when music business trade magazines still called rhythm and blues records race music.

His smooth, elegant vocal style became a touchstone for young singers, and many black performers such as Ray Charles and Sammy Davis Jr. began their careers doing little more than Charles Brown impersonations.

In 1947 he dashed off a Christmas song and sold the rights for $35. His song, "Merry Christmas Baby," grew to rival "White Christmas" over the next half- century, with versions recorded by Elvis Presley, Chuck Berry, Otis Redding, Bruce Springsteen and others.

'Air to Spare'

"Charles Brown is like Ben Webster on the tenor – they both got air to spare," said

239

record producer Jerry Wexler, who supervised historic sessions with Ray Charles, Aretha Franklin and others.

Brown left Moore in 1948 and quickly established himself as one of the leading solo artists in the burgeoning rhythm and blues field.

His star dimmed through the '50s, although he managed to lodge one more Christmas record, "Please Come Home for Christmas," on the charts in 1961, a song that was later revived by '70s rock superstars the Eagles.

By the time he landed in the East Bay, playing an organ at the basement nightclub in Oakland's then-decrepit California Hotel in 1971, Brown was a forgotten figure. When San Francisco Blues Festival producer Tom Mazzolini booked Brown for his annual event in 1976, the singer was living in a dump in the Western Addition and playing at a small neighborhood bar in Hayes Valley. "Nobody was interested in Charles Brown at all," Mazzolini said. "He turned off to the music business. Charles was just hanging. His career was nowhere."

Just Getting By

And when guitarist Danny Caron heard Brown perform at a small Oakland nightclub in 1987, the singer was living on his Social Security and was musically rusty from inactivity. Caron steered Brown back into a productive and prosperous musical career at a time when most people his age had retired.

He lived in a senior citizens' housing center in downtown Berkeley. When the money started rolling in during the past decade, as he and his band started playing European jazz festivals and prestige nightclub dates around the country, he moved out of his studio apartment and into one of the fancier, one- bedroom units downstairs. He also moved up from the $2 window at Golden Gate Fields, where he could customarily be found every day.

He was a kind, gentle man with a deep, slow-rolling voice, as remarkable in conversation as singing. He had a million stories, a never-ending reservoir of long, involved tales featuring the greats and near- greats of show business. He liked to practice piano in the early moring hours, often playing classical works by Debussy, Ravel or Liszt, whom Brown called "a showoff pianist." He never expressed the slightest bitterness over the harsh treatment life handed him.

"I never think over the mistreatments I've had," he said in an interview 11 years ago. " 'Cause I've had a wonderful life."

San Francisco Chronicle, Saturday | January 23, 1999

The fire killed her husband and destroyed everything

But not Sugar Pie's spirit.

A tough, crazy broad who ran around with Etta James in the Fillmore when they were teenagers – that's Sugar Pie, baby.

TODAY WAS A GOOD DAY FOR SOUL QUEEN Sugar Pie DeSanto. She could laugh a little, even talk about the fire without crying. She may have wakened her manager with a panicked phone call around five that morning, but she was okay for now.

She lit a cigarette and opened the window in the studio apartment the Catholic relief agency found for her in the Satellite Senior Center in downtown Oakland. The small, spotless room has only a few small pieces of inexpensive, brand new furniture. She sits on a folded futon where she sleeps at night, her sheets and blanket neatly folded by the side.

It's been six weeks since she lost everything in an apartment blaze that killed her husband, "the love of my life," the 71 year-old rhythm and blues star says, Jessie Earl Davis, who was married to the singer twice over the course of a 27-year relationship.

"I think he saved my life and gave his own up," she says. "I think he really did. He shoved me down the whole hallway. I think he died trying to save my life."

A petite spitfire of a woman, who is known to the Red Cross, St. Mary's Center and all the other relief organizations as Peylia Davis, she has assiduously listed in a notebook the names of the people who have helped her in the past weeks. She awoke in the middle of the night October 26 to find her living room in flames. Her husband, she says, pushed her out the door wearing nothing but her nightgown. She didn't even have her teeth and she cut her bare foot on the way out.

"They hand me a metal box and his teeth," she says. "My husband's dentures and a box with some papers. That's what I got."

Down at the busy intersection of MacArthur and Telegraph, her burned out third story apartment glares out angrily at the street below. The blackened apartment is a total loss. Her husband was said to have been burned beyond recognition.

"He was my guy," she says, looking away, her eyes brimming with tears.

Davis was a strapping 26 year-old the day his future wife, sitting on her porch, saw him walking down the street in a pair of orange continental slacks, "skin tight to the bone," she says.

"We were together 27 years on and off," she says. "We did divorce for a few moments. Everybody has their problems. This takes the cake for me. I would never marry again. That's my last. I never will. I have to say he was the love of my life."

She is living on assistance, taking anti-depressant medication and sleeping pills at night ("nights are the worst," she says). She hasn't cooked for herself since the fire and says one takeout meal usually lasts her two days. The tiny woman has dropped from 129 pounds to 112.

"My nerves are bad and I'm under great strain," she says.

Some of her colleagues in the music scene have thrown fundraisers, although the Celebrity Ballroom in Daly City is not the scene of rock star benefit concerts. Some of the old-time East Bay R&B guys such as the Dynamic Four or Johnny Talbot and De Thangs got together for an evening that raised more spirits than money. DeSanto herself jumped onstage and belted out some music. "The spirit hit me," she says.

Another old colleague, bluesman Jimmy McCracklin, turned his recent Biscuit and Blues performance into an event for DeSanto and some other local R&B singers such as Maria Muldaur dropped by to pay respects. There was a night at

Kimball's Carnival. But only old-timers remember her now. Although she has been doing more shows in Europe and elsewhere over the past several years, DeSanto has not been a national figure since she returned to live in the Bay Area in 1968.

For the last 35 years, she only made records because of Jim Moore, a retired carpenter for Kaiser Hospital who has been putting out Sugar Pie DeSanto records on his Jasman Records label since 1970 and serves as her manager. Moore knows something about what she is going through. His home burned to the ground in the Oakland hills fire 15 years ago.

She was the oldest girl in a family of ten children who grew up in the Fillmore District. Her father was a Filipino who worked making mattresses. Her mother was a black from Philadelphia. One of her teenage friends was a tough, plump juvenile delinquent who would change her name when she started her own recording career to Etta James. "This was one crazy family," wrote James in her 1995 autobiography. "I liked hanging out with them."

Bandleader Johnny Otis, who discovered and renamed Etta James, also brought young Umpeylia Balinton to Los Angeles to record and gave her the name Sugar Pie (DeSanto came later). Her national career started with the 1960 recording, "I Want To Know," done with her first husband, guitarist Pee Wee Kingsley. Recorded by Oakland R&B pioneer Bob Geddins, the track was sold to Chicago's Chess Records, and DeSanto moved to Chicago, leaving Kingsley behind, where she made records of her own for many years, as well as writing songs for other Chess artists.

She never made the big time. She had a midchart hit in 1964 with "Slip-In Mules," a sexy answer song to "Hi-Heel Sneakers," and another 1964 record, "Soulful Dress," has been revived by Marcia Ball, among others. She is probably best known for a 1966 duet with Etta James, "In the Basement."

After the No. 2 R&B chart success of "I Want To Know," DeSanto toured for two choice years with the James Brown revue. Known for her athletic, acrobatic stage manners, she and Brown would often close their show by jumping off pianos together and landing in splits. Brown, not famous for acknowledging his colleagues, introduced her to a Circle Star Theater audience in the early '80s and brought her up onstage with obvious affection (although Brown admitted in his autobiography that she was the only one of his female vocalists he didn't sleep with).

She also toured Europe in 1964 as the unlikely female vocalist with Sonny Boy Williamson, Lightnin' Hopkins, Howlin' Wolf, Willie Dixon and others on the American Folk Blues tour "I refused all them old goats," she said in a current interview in *Living Blues* magazine.

She is a feisty dynamo, known for turning flips and other more raunchy stage antics. She can be boastful ("I have had quite a life") and, a sentence or two later, turn shyly modest, almost girlish, talking about a social worker driving her to appointments "just like I was somebody truly special."

The Red Cross put her in a motel and gave her food vouchers immediately after the fire. Her sister contacted the Mayor's office in Oakland, who put them in touch with Catholic relief agencies to help find her housing. "I had offers, but I didn't want to stay with my family," she says. "I'm a grown woman and I wanted to cry on my own. I wanted my privacy."

Some of the relief workers recognized her, even without her stage name. "They knew I was Sugar Pie after they saw me on TV," she says. "How can I hide? Hell, I've sung in Oakland for 50 years."

Her booking agent gave her a new electric keyboard, which is carefully poised on one of her few chairs. Another friend knew how much she loved the mink coats she lost and gave her one of hers. She also lost her housecat in the fire. "They let you have pets here," she says, "but you have to ask."

She doesn't have any plans. There are no gigs on her calendar. She really doesn't know what she is going to do.

"I have no living right now," she says, "since all this happened. But I do plan to come back, if I live to do it, one of these days."

She perches on the edge of her sofa, a straw-colored ponytail hanging out the back of a floppy knit cap. She is wearing around her neck a cell phone her brother gave her. She can laugh and talk dirty, but she is still a stunned victim, living in shock. The breeze blows through her hollowed core. Behind her glasses, dark thoughts cloud over her eyes, this spunky old dame who had the stuffing knocked out of her. It's been a long, hard life for Sugar Pie DeSanto, but never any harder than it is now.

San Francisco Chronicle | *December 12, 2006*

Isn't coming back –
he never left

Richmond's Jimmy McCracklin, a top-rank bluesman for many years

Blues great Jimmy McCracklin may embellish and exaggerate some things, but he was the king of Oakland blues, uncontested and unvanquished. That is no exaggeration

Jimmy McCracklin

BACK IN THE '40S, WHEN BLUESMAN JIMMY MC-CRACKLIN first hit town after mustering out of the Navy, Richmond was booming. Shipyard work more than doubled the city's population during World War II and North Richmond was crawling with gin mills and juke joints and that's where the blues lived.

McCracklin, still an ox of a man at 85, lives in a fine house in one of Richmond's remaining nice neighborhoods a few blocks from the massive Hilltop Mall that helped destroy the city's downtown.

"It's not what it used to be," McCracklin says. "It's a whole different ball game. All people care about is shooting, killing, stuff like that."

McCracklin is a very proud man, with good reason to be. Over a career that has spanned seven decades, he says he's written almost a thousand songs and has recorded hundreds of them. He was a contemporary and peer of the greats of his generation, and all of them except B.B. King are dead and gone now.

The top of his piano is littered with awards, plaques and the keys to a couple of cities. Framed photos and memorabilia adorn the mantelpiece, under a painting of his daughter Susie, who lives with McCracklin and his wife of 52 years, Beulah, along with her 14 year-old son, James, McCracklin's 300-pound grandson ("He's a whopper," says his granddad).

McCracklin has written out a list of the performers he has appeared with over the years, printed in careful handwriting on two paper towels, and it is virtual who's who of the blues and R&B world of the '50s and early '60s. He pulls a briefcase out of the front hall closet and extracts a dog-eared computer printout of music publishing information from his massive song catalog. He also fans out a handful of sealed, self-addressed stamped envelopes, sent to himself over the years, a well-known poor man's way of copyrighting songs. The earliest bears a 1948 postmark.

"Once I got to the position where I learned more about how to protect my material, we started going in a different direction," he says.

McCracklin towered over the Oakland and Richmond blues scene in the sunny days that followed the Second World War. Along with Lowell Fulson, who left the Bay Area shortly after he became successful, McCracklin was the biggest name to ever emerge from the Oakland blues scene. His 1958 record, "The Walk," actually landed him in the Top 10 on the pop charts, after more than 10 years of selling records in the black community on a series of small labels.

Somehow, McCracklin got passed over by the blues revival. As the blues went out of fashion in the African American community, McCracklin evolved his music into a tougher, more modern big-band R&B sound. By the time the white audience for the music developed, McCracklin's music was too refined for the tastes of the new audience and an anachronism with his old audience. He slowly faded away through the '70s and '80s, his obscurity only interrupted by a pair of albums he was loath to call comebacks – "I never went anywhere," he says – in the early '90s for the Boston-based blues revivalists at Rounder Records.

Lisa Walters of E.U. Booking in Corte Madera, a boutique agency that specializes in older blues and R&B performers such as the late Ruth Brown, started working with McCracklin two years ago. He didn't have a regular band and hadn't been working much.

"He hadn't played in a long time," she says. "Maybe a festival here and there, but it had been quite a while."

Now McCracklin sports a well-rehearsed nine-piece band with three background vocalists led by his daughter, Susie. He has been playing European festival dates in the summer and already has performances lined up this year in Italy.

He was born in Arkansas in 1921, a date he disputes by 10 years, even though that would make him 14 years old when he first recorded. "They got that wrong, too," McCracklin says. His father was a good friend of the noted '30s barrelhouse pianist Walter Davis from St. Louis, where McCracklin grew up, and McCracklin's early records show him to be a studied disciple of Davis' strong style.

He made his first record, "Miss Mattie Left Me," for the Globe label in Los Angeles in 1945. Two years later in Oakland, he began a mutually antagonistic relationship with record producer Bob Geddins that would last on and off over the next two decades. Geddins, who also made Fulson's first records, was a key figure in the Oakland blues scene, a pioneer even more forgotten than McCracklin these days. Geddins died in 1991 at age 78.

Geddins recorded blues and gospel records around the East Bay on a variety of his own labels, leasing the recordings to larger, national labels if he found some success locally. "All Bob Geddins wanted to do was get two, three hundred dollars in his pocket," McCracklin says. "After that, he didn't care about nothing."

McCracklin recorded "The Walk" with his own band in Chicago, where he found himself stranded, working a dead end gig for pocket change, and took the tape to Chess Records, who released the single. The hit not only had McCracklin rubbing shoulders with the "American Bandstand" set for a brief moment, but blues guitarist Freddy King retooled the song's key lick for his 1961 instrumental hit, "Hide Away."

Years later, the Beatles cut the song as "When Ya Walk" during the "Get Back" sessions, although it never surfaced anywhere except bootlegs. But that didn't stop Christian singer Steven Curtis Chapman from covering the Beatles version on a recent album.

In 1962, following Geddins' strategy, McCracklin recorded "Just Got to Know" for his own Art-Tone label in Oakland and, after the record made No. 2 on the R&B charts in 1961, he leased the master to Imperial Records, where he continued his recording career for a number of years. In 1971, his star dimmed, he cut one last legitimate album for the Memphis soul company, Stax/Volt, although the album barely registered at the time.

McCracklin prides himself on his songwriting. He is a fine pianist and can shout the blues with the best of them, but it is his songcraft that makes McCracklin stand out.

"I was a helluva writer when I was young 'cause I could think better," he says.

His biggest success in the songwriting field came with his song "Tramp," a number he never recorded himself, originally done by Fulson in 1967 and covered the same year by Otis Redding and Carla Thomas, a version that hit the pop charts. Salt-N-Pepa made a hip-hop hit out of the song in 1987. Although Fulson is credited as co-writer of the song, McCracklin said he had nothing to do with the songwriting.

"He was a helluva singer, but he never was a good writer," McCracklin says of Fulson, who died in 1999 at age 77.

McCracklin also maintains that he is the true author of "The Thrill Is Gone," the 1969 hit by B.B. King, perhaps one of the best-selling blues records of all time, which was originally recorded by little-known Oakland blues pianist Roy Hawkins. Hawkins, who also recorded for Geddins and worked the scene at the same time as McCracklin, had a Top 10 R&B hit with the song in 1951. In a 12-minute film made last year for the Regional Oral History Office of UC Berkeley's Bancroft Library, McCracklin visits B.B. King at a casino appearance and the two laugh in the back of King's bus about McCracklin's assertion that he wrote the song.

Rick Darnell, the credited writer of the song, doesn't think McCracklin is funny. "He didn't write a single word of it," Darnell says by phone from his home in Farmville, Va.

Darnell was 22, with songs recorded by Billie Holliday and Charles Brown when, following a performance at Los Angeles' Lincoln Theater, he went back to Hawkins' hotel room where, he says, he wrote the song and its flip side, "Trouble Makin' Woman." Hawkins died in obscurity in the early '70s without ever giving an interview to any blues scholar on the subject. He remains virtually unknown to this day, although jazz great John Handy began his career in Hawkins' band.

McCracklin has a fondness for telling tales. On his mantel there is a frame containing two separate Xerox photos: One looks like McCracklin in boxing trunks and gloves; the other shows light heavyweight champ Archie Moore getting up off the canvas. McCracklin says he fought under the name Jimmy Mackey and lost a decision to Moore, although he knocked him down in the fight.

The only thing is, there is no record of the great Moore ever having fought either Jimmy Mackey or McCracklin. In fact, there is no record of either McCracklin or Mackey fighting anybody in the records kept by the International Boxing Research Organization, although his pugilistic past has been a part of the Mc-Cracklin legend since at least the '50s.

Who knows? Maybe he did write "The Thrill Is Gone." One of those sealed, postmarked self-addressed envelopes in his front hall closet says "The Thrill Is Gone" on the outside. But whether he did or not, McCracklin remains the undisputed heavyweight champion of the Oakland blues.

San Francisco Chronicle | *March 1, 2007*

Mike Bloomfield – Superstar – Had It All and Didn't Know It

What a sad figure Mike Bloomfield was. Running into him backstage was always a pleasure. He was invariably cheerful, talkative, enthusiastic, yet it always seemed like some barely suppressed terror was lurking just out of sight.

"I DECIDED I DIDN'T BELIEVE ALL THAT TORTURED genius crap," Mike Bloomfield, the 30-year-old musician explained, "that somehow there was a corollary between pain and creativity.

"Take Charlie Parker or Billie Holiday or whoever; since they were so completely unhappy and lived such miserable lives, how great their art was doesn't matter – they were failures. You can make all the great art in the world, but if you died a wretch you really punked out."

Rock star Bloomfield sat in his Mill Valley living room and discussed the personal factors that led to his return to the road following three years of sitting around at home, watching television, playing only rare occasions here in the Bay Area.

"Maybe there's a few moments of ecstasy," he continued, "but the price you pay for that is pure daily hell. And it's true, the moments of my greatest creativity came out of intense agony – when I'd been on the road for months, strung out, junk sick.

"But when I see what happens to friends like Duane (Allman, dead at 25 in a motorcycle wreck), I know it's just not worth it. I have to find a balance in comfort and deal with art on a daily, human basis."

So, two years behind in his taxes and one more in his career – with the Michael Bloomfield-Mark Naftalin group – he takes to the road again. Not much yet, just going out on weekends. Still, it's a vast change from those heady days six years ago when Bloomfield was lead guitarist with the Paul Butterfield Blues Band, playing it fast, loose and crazy as one of rock's first top guitarists.

With Jimi Hendrix and Eric Clapton, Bloomfield emerged as one of an elite circle of lead guitarists cast in the role of star. Bloomfield pioneered improvisational lead guitar in rock as surely as Bo Didley invented the rhythm guitar

First as a white musician infiltrating the secret world of black blues in Chicago, to being on hand to add a few licks when folksinger Bob Dylan went electric, to making the debut performance of his own band – Electric Flag – from the stage at the Monterey Pop Festival in 1967, to recording a million-selling album of off-the-wall jams called "Supersession," Bloomfield rode out an eventful four years, witnessing firsthand revolutionary changes in popular music.

Stardom took a unique personal toll on the intellectual and, in some ways, retiring Bloomfield. For the past several years, he has never played out of the area or with a regular group – since Michael Bloomfield and Friends, a loose group that included his longtime friends pianist Mark Naftalin and singer Nick Gravenites.

That band played for nearly a year, establishing their base, North Beach's Keystone Korner, as a rock hot spot overnight. It's been four years since then, however.

One end of his living room is dominated by posters of B.B. King and country singer George Jones. On the opposite wall, his gold record award rests amid a clutter of other memorabilia.

Bloomfield picks up a battered and scratched Gibson acoustic guitar that wasn't all that good when it was new. He explains the strings are extra thick gauge and lifted too high from the fretboard – all to make it more difficult to play. Like a lead bat, he says.

"I'm a compulsive noodler," he admits, "but I have to force myself to practice three hours a day. It takes that long just to get your hands working as fast as your head is thinking."

The albums in his working file – personal selections he listens to from a massive collection – reflect his scholarly bent; in addition to the many rare and classic country and blues albums, there are several LPs by Edith Piaf, an album of mazurkas and even a spoken word record by Evelyn Waugh ("He's one of my favorites"). There is virtually no recent rock. A night table is piled high with books, very few about music.

"I completely ignored school from the third grade on," he says. "I'd just sit in the back of the room, tilt my desk back and read a book."

Son of wealthy parents, Bloomfield bounced in and out of various schools for years. "My one or two friends and myself were always 'the odd guys.' In school, where there were cripples and guys in wheelchairs, we'd be down around there in social status – only we were sound of limb."

Bloomfield started playing guitar at 13 and, two years later, was working his first night club job. "Here I was, 15 years old, from a super rich Jewish suburb,

Mike Bloomfield

straight high school, and I was right in the midst of that milieu I so coveted. The guys in the band were like 50 year-old hillbillies – the very type of guys I worshipped – third-rate Jerry Lee Lewises."

It was a few years before he could gain entrance to Chicago's black clubs. "I had to wait until I at least looked 21. Before then, I just stood around outside and they were very nice about that. But as soon as I got inside, I started trying to cop a gig."

These were the same clubs young Paul Butterfield was beginning to work. "Paul was a novelty, a freak," Bloomfield said. "They'd have a complete show and first would come the shake dancer, then a comedian, then Paul – the white blues player. They always had a picture of him so you could tell he was white."

These were the exciting days when music was still just for fun. The immense success of the Paul Butterfield Band soon catapulted Bloomfield into the public eye.

"I never had it in my mind to 'make it' – never. That just wasn't part of my scheme. When we were with the Butterfield band, we had to be told about that. This limey cat – Derek Taylor – told us 'man, you guys are going to be superstars.' That meant absolutely nothing to us. We didn't understand it.

"It was making those records with Dylan where I first really began to see what this was about. Anthony Scaduto (Dylan biographer) wrote about it very well, but there were all these hanger-on – sychophants – that clung to Dylan and sucked him blind. I was just picking music and never even dreamed of these things.

"Finally, it came to me. This is what all these millions of people are striving for, burning for. I had it all and, when I counted up, they were all deficits.

"I don't even know where any of the money went and I never cared. When I left Butterfield, I had about $6,000 – all saved from salary. When the Flag ended, I was thousands of dollars in debt. I still to this day don't know if I've been ripped off by publishers or not.

"In this industry, they create an image for you. It's a one-sided pre-conception and when you meet someone, you have to wait until they stop deprecating themselves before you can tell them, 'hey man, I'm no different from you.'

"I never felt comfortable with that," he said.

"I just have to take it all day-to-day, I've learned. If I have a job tomorrow, I don't even want to know about it until I get up in the morning."

Sunday Datebook | September 23, 1973

What the Hell Is Going On

For **Elvin Bishop**, *getting back into the musical groove was one tough journey*

Elvin hated this article and I respect him for that. I respect him for so much, but, most of all, for staying true to the spirit that used to send him around North Beach nightclubs in the early '70s, playing with anyone who would have him.

GOOD-TIME GUITARIST ELVIN BISHOP OPENS his new album with an uncharacteristic rant, "What the Hell Is Going On," his vocals processed with digital sandpaper, leaving his singing splintered and raw. The question in the song's title, however, should not come as a surprise from someone whose 22-year-old daughter was brutally murdered in a bizarre, evil extortion scheme.

"I followed my old blues guys' example – Lowell Fulson, Jimmy McCracklin, Percy Mayfield – to write about what's happening in your life," he said. "They just put it out there.

"Having parties, having fun, chasing girls, that's all well and good. It's part of life. But so's the other stuff."

Bishop's new album, "Gettin' My Groove Back," was recorded over the last few years at his home studio in rural Marin County after a series of personal catastrophes left him struggling to find his customary good humor. He finished the CD in time to print up some copies on his own and sell them as concert merchandise last summer when he toured with B.B. King. San Francisco-based blues label, Blind Pig Records, will give the record an official release next week, which Bishop will celebrate with an increasingly rare S.F. nightclub appearance Aug. 19 at the Great American Music Hall.

There was a time when no local nightclub went too long without an Elvin Bishop appearance. When he left the Paul Butterfield Blues Band in 1968, he moved to the Bay Area and launched his solo act on Monday nights at the Keystone Korner, where owner Freddy Herrera served free fried chicken as an added inducement. The Pointer Sisters used to sing background vocals with him back then. When he wasn't playing some club with his band, Bishop could be found prowling the streets and alleys of North Beach with his guitar, looking for a place to jam.

Elvin Bishop

Bishop, 62, has lived for more than 30 years on his three-quarters acre Lagunitas spread, where virtually every inch of the hillside is covered with a labyrinth of vegetables, fruit trees and flowerbeds. He stays up late in bed reading scientific gardening books. One of his most treasured possessions is a 19th century plant encyclopedia. His friends all know to bring him seeds from their world travels. (Harmonica player Norton Buffalo brought back some hot peppers from Brazil that grew six feet tall and yielded hundreds of peppers off every bush.)

"I used to keep a pig, too," he said, "but my neighbors didn't know how hogs are supposed to smell."

Bishop grew up on a farm in southwest Iowa with no running water or electricity. He used to watch television in the window of the furniture store in town. When young Bishop was 11 years old, his father took a job at an aircraft plant and the family moved to Tulsa, Okla., where Bishop began a long- distance love affair with old blues records he conducted over the late night radio airwaves.

That all changed when he received a National Merit Scholarship to attend the

University of Chicago and immersed himself in that city's thriving blues scene. "I knew blues as much as you could from listening to records," he said. "But I didn't really know the life they wrote about. But once I saw that, smelled black cosmetics, tasted the food that went with it, that was the first time I really understood what they were talking about."

As a founding member of the pioneering Butterfield Blues Band, Bishop not only backed up Bob Dylan at his historic Newport Folk Festival electric rock performance, but he also appeared at the Monterey Pop Festival, played the Fillmores on both coasts and jammed with Jimi Hendrix. Leading his own band, Bishop may have reached a certain local peak during the early '70s, packing out clubs with a smoking band that featured his then-girlfriend, an incendiary vocalist, the late Jo Baker. But his greatest national fame came with the 1976 Top Five hit, "Fooled Around and Fell in Love," produced by the same people who were doing the Eagles and sung by Mickey Thomas, future vocalist of Jefferson Starship. His romance with Southern rock, however prosperous, proved short-lived, and Bishop returned to performing and recording blues more than 20 years ago.

His days of doing 200-300 dates a year are through. He goes out almost every weekend, but no longer does extended tours. There is a catfish hole over the hill in Nicasio that rewards regular visits, plus he spends a couple of hours a day tending his garden. He has been busy the past month canning peaches and green beans.

Bishop has been married to his artist wife, Cara, for 19 years and their 17-year-old daughter, Emily, will graduate next year from high school. Their home is crowded with his wife's canvases. A guitar sits in a glassed-in addition, where a cat sleeps on a chair in the sunshine, surrounded by his blooming garden. Cardboard boxes holding the peaches he picked that morning sit on the couch.

His Hog Heaven studio is down a short gravel path under the kiwi tree. Framed photos of a young, straw-hatted Bishop with blues greats such as B.B. King, Albert Collins, Albert King sit in boxes, waiting to be unpacked. His old album collection is stacked on a shelf. Some old posters hang on the wall, but it's not a decorated room, more of a spartan workplace. This is where Bishop retreated in the dark days that followed the grisly murder of his daughter, Selina Bishop. He had already begun work on a new record, but the studio quickly became a haven.

"I was starting to do things and that's when my daughter died," he said. "It was not just one disaster, really. First, my mom died. Then my daughter was murdered. Then my favorite uncle, Uncle Buster, died. And then, Kirby the dog. There was a lot of getting over to do."

One song, "He's a Dog," commemorates the late Kirby, who is also pictured on the back of the CD cover. "What the Hell Is Going On" is less whimsically sentimental. Over an angry, clanging electric guitar boogie, Bishop grinds his voice into electronic anguish: "Bombing and shooting ... raping and killing ... bloody murder ... molesting ... running airplanes into buildings ... what the hell is going on?"

"I had to get the s – out of my system," he said. "So this was pure therapy. I'm usually an upbeat person. But once in awhile, the s – gets so heavy you can't smile about it."

"I'm tired of living in this big old world of hurt," his drummer Bobby Cochran sings on "I'll Be Glad," the song that gave the album its hopeful title.

"Victims' assistance wanted to give me $10,000 to go talk to a shrink or psychiatrist about it," Bishop said. "But I got to thinking about it and realized I got my therapy right here."

Bishop refused to publicly discuss the killing of his daughter, her mother (Bishop's ex-partner), Jennifer Villarin, and three others in August 2000 in an elaborate plot to extort $100,000 out of a wealthy retired Walnut Creek couple. The killers were convicted in a highly publicized trial and sentenced to death. But Bishop never said a word.

"When all the heavy stuff was going on," he said, "the last thing I was thinking about was my commercial career. I was thinking about the rest of the family. You have to deal with what remains. I made a decision not to talk to the media. I decided from now on talking to reporters is not going to help. I was protecting my family, making it easier to heal and it was amazingly effective in keeping the uproar down.

"But I'm very disappointed in the media. They acted like our personal tragedy was their free programming, and they resented the hell of it being withheld."

Bishop sat at a table in the dappled sunlight of his bucolic garden next to Emily's abandoned childhood playhouse. Selina Bishop, who had been living nearby at the time of her murder, grew up far away in Pennsylvania.

"I broke up with her mom when she was 1 year old. But I visualize this happening to the daughter I've lived with all her life ..." He looked away. His throat constricted and his eyes rimmed with red.

"The less we make of this the better," he said.

San Francisco Chronicle | *Wednesday, August 10, 2005*

An authentic contender

One record gave singer Rodger Collins a taste of fame, but no fortune. That was long before he became Hajji Sabrie.

Rodgers Collins looms large in the soul music universe of my mind. "She's Looking Good" ranked with James Brown on local radio and was always a favorite record of mine. I often wondered what became of him.

HAJJI SABRIE HAS OPERATED AN APPLIANCE REPAIR BUSINESS in Oakland for years. The devoted family man and his loving wife of 21 years have two children on the cusp of adulthood. A self-described "very religious" Muslim born in Texas and raised in San Francisco, he is a humble, happy bear of man whose face falls naturally into a deep, radiant smile. He is understandably leery about bringing up the past.

"Hajji Sabrie can move around anywhere he wants," he says. "But with Rodger Collins, things can be difficult."

Rodger Collins is a name from Sabrie's previous life.

During the golden age of soul, Oakland never produced a bigger star than Rodger Collins. When he headlined the Showcase on Telegraph Avenue, he tore up the crowds as much as the other big-name acts that came through the room – Marvin Gaye, the Temptations, Ike and Tina Turner.

And he cut a record that, if the country had heard it, would have made Rodger Collins an authentic contender. "She's Looking Good" was not just another half-baked soul side that never got any further than No. 101, "bubbling under" Billboard's Hot 100. The track was a certified, stone-in-the- groove, drop-dead classic that never got a fair hearing. Where it was played - - including in the Bay Area – the record was a smash. It vied for the top of playlists on local Top 40 stations with the Rolling Stones, the Monkees and Buffalo Springfield in the early weeks of 1967, a heady time for pop music on the radio.

Sabrie, 64, doesn't like to do interviews. His last one, with Britain's Melody Maker magazine more than 20 years ago, did not prove satisfactory. He was news at the time because another one of his old records, "You Sexy Sugar Plum," was

257

Rodger Collins

experiencing a second life – if that can truly be said about a record that essentially arrived stillborn the first time around – on the trendy Northern Soul circuit, where English DJs specialize in reviving obscure American rhythm and blues records.

While speaking with a reporter, he sips a homemade brew of chopped ginger and picks at fresh fruit from a platter on the living room coffee table in his West Oakland home. The scent of spice and flowers wafts through the sunny rooms. A stack of videos beside his television betrays a catholic taste in music – Willie Nelson, Buena Vista Social Club, Lightnin' Hopkins. Long-playing albums and CDs are stacked everywhere.

"I liked performing," Sabrie says. "But I didn't like all these problems with bands, hassling with musicians all the time. By this time, my career was fading. So I retired from show business."

He remembers harmonizing doo-wop in the tiled bathrooms at the Hamilton Recreation Center, where Bobby Freeman, San Francisco's first rock 'n' roll star, would work out with his first vocal group, the Romancers, long before "Do You

Wanna Dance?" As Rodger Collins, he won a talent contest pantomiming a Chuck Berry record and did a wicked Elvis impersonation.

Brook Benton, an older songwriter and recording star ("It's Just a Matter of Time"), counseled the young Collins backstage at Oakland's Paramount Theatre to work up his own act and sing the songs himself, promising to send him some material. Sabrie still has the acetates Benton sent.

He studied drama at the Actor's Laboratory in San Francisco and moved to Los Angeles, where he thought his star would rise, but wound up in a Wilshire Boulevard car wash polishing Rock Hudson's silver Chrysler Imperial.

Back in San Francisco, singing at local clubs, Collins came to the attention of Fantasy Records, which was having some success in the R&B field on its Galaxy subsidiary with blues singer Little Johnny Taylor. The first two Rodger Collins releases came and went without notice, but the third single was "She's Looking Good."

Two blasts from the horns and a snaking bass line lead to the explosive opening verse ("You got that kind of lovin' make a man lose his mind"). By the time the brass section fans out behind the chorus and Collins sinks into the title line, the record is plowing pure pay dirt. Dancing while he sang the song in the studio, Collins spun around and missed the microphone, causing him to memorably stutter the beginning of a verse: "Ma-ma-mama get your mojo ..."

"It hit in spots," Sabrie says. Markets as remote as Shreveport and Pittsburgh played the record. Without concentrated airplay and sales, the single never made the pop charts. But when Wilson Pickett covered the song the next year, changing the groove and utterly lacking the primeval force of Collins' version, he made it all the way to No. 15.

"Fantasy sold Mexican music and jazz," Sabrie says. "They weren't set up to handle a soul record or soul-pop. ... I made more money off Pickett than I did mine."

Soul man Collins cut a singular figure onstage. He was the inventor of the short sleeved suit ("I didn't like people sitting in the audience with suits that looked like my suits"), a fashion innovation that failed to spread. He also liked to wear custom-tailored trousers with different-colored legs. He made nine singles over the years for Galaxy, including the Ike Turner-produced "Get Away From Me" (engineered by Tina Turner). He never released an album. But Rolling Stone noticed his other great classic, the little-known "Foxy Girl in Oakland" ("From every possible aspect, this disc is incredible ...").

All of the guys in Frisco don't do nothing all day but think about the girls in Oakland.

The song was written by a Coast Guard enlisted man stationed at Treasure Island. Joe Crane, a white Texan R&B fan, knew Collins from hearing "She's Looking Good" on the radio and thought the number would be perfect for him. He found Collins listed in the phone book and called him. Since the songwriter was confined to base, Collins drove out to meet him and hear the song.

"I loved Joe Crane," Sabrie says. "I thought, 'If this guy can't get out of Treasure Island, I'm going to where he is, 'cause he sounded so sincere on the telephone.' "

Crane played guitar on the session, and now that he was officially in the music business, mustered out of the service in San Francisco and formed a fabulous but unlucky rock group called the Hoodoo Rhythm Devils, a band he led until his death from leukemia at age 34 in 1980. He and Collins collaborated on one more single, "Your Love, It's Burning," which may have been partially inspired by the gonorrhea epidemic of the day.

Collins began to develop an interest in Islam. He toured with soul singer Joe Tex, himself a Black Muslim minister, and together they visited mosques all over the country. "For a while, that white-man-is-the-devil stuff worked for me," he says. "But while I was saying that, I never gave up my white friends."

Sabrie followed the lead of Imam W. Deen Mohammed, of Black Muslim founder Elijah Muhammad, who took over the sect after his father's death in 1975 and immediately set a more conciliatory course for the church. "Mohammed taught that everybody was equal," Sabrie says. "You may come with a male or female body, but the person inside is a human. The creature inside doesn't have a race."

The more he studied the Koran, the more he grew disenchanted with the music business. His last nightclub engagement was opening for Ike and Tina Turner and Redd Foxx at Las Vegas' Hilton International, playing the lounge while Elvis played the big room, hardly hard-luck, bottom-rung show business. But he was not happy with his career in records and found himself the victim of company politics.

"It discouraged me thinking I would get a fair shake with the record industry," Sabrie says. "But it didn't discourage me to improve myself as a human being. I knew happiness was available."

So, 30 years ago, Rodger Collins retired from show business and changed his name to Hajji Sabrie. With a couple of scarcely noticed exceptions – a nightclub appearance here, a one-off single there – Rodger Collins disappeared as if he'd gone into the witness protection program. "People say, 'Didn't you miss out on a lot?'" Sabrie says. "Everything that happened was supposed to happen. You can't change it. No one can change it."

Sabrie learned the appliance business. He has run his company, Trustworthy Appliance Repair, longer than he was in show business. His youngest entered UC Riverside last fall. Sabrie has made two pilgrimages to Mecca to pray in the holy precincts. He leads a full, happy life with immense dignity.

He still makes music. In a spare bedroom in the midst of some remodeling, he keeps a boom box and some recording equipment. He has some tapes he has been working on for the past couple of years, positive messages set to funky beats, with some powerful singing. Rodger Collins hasn't entirely disappeared off the face of the earth.

"I'm still trying to record," Sabrie says. "But if I never sell it, I'm still successful."

"I'm successful when I wake up in the morning and see my wife and know she's a decent human being and know she lived up to a vow we made when we got married: not to criticize but to improve the other one.

"I do a lot of things that might not be what some other people like to do," Sabrie says. "But it works for me. If I see someone on a path I'm not on, I respect that. I love a lot of people who disagree with me. But there is nothing worthy of worship except the Creator – not the creation, only the Creator."

San Francisco Chronicle | *Tuesday, March 9, 2004*

Booker T. Jones

Technology for a soul great

It's back to school for soul great Booker T. Jones

There isn't anybody in music I admire more than Booker T. Jones, not just for playing on all those incredible Otis Redding records, but for his deeply centered, Buddah-like character. Spending a couple of days with him at ProTools school was one of the reasons I loved writing for the newspaper.

THREE STUDENTS SQUEEZE TOGETHER IN THE DARKENED San Francisco recording studio, looks of intense concentration on their faces. It's a school for digital recording, and they are running an exercise on their own. Two are young amateurs. The third is soul great Booker T. Jones.

He missed class one day last month because he flew down to Los Angeles to produce Willie Nelson singing John Lennon's "Imagine" for an Amnesty International CD. When he returned, his classmates Jonathan Schickman, 23, and Nick Perez, 21, were ahead of him on class work.

"It's challenging when you're behind," said Jones, 60, long ago inducted into the Rock and Roll Hall of Fame as leader of Booker T. and the MGs, the music's greatest instrumental group.

Technology in recording studios has changed over the past 10 years, leaving many veterans like Jones in the dust but creating opportunities for newcomers like Schickman and Perez.

"I outlived the recording medium I was brought up with," said Jones, who began recording as a 16-year-old 10th-grader in 1960 at Stax/Volt studios in Memphis. He scored his first national hit two years later, "Green Onions."

A number of well-known professional musicians, who have installed Pro Tools digital recording systems in their studios, have received private consultations from instructors at Pyramind, said co-owner Matt Donner. But no one has ever before showed up for courses at the studios on Folsom Street, South of Market. Greg Gordon, Donner's partner, taking roll the first day, actually asked out loud "not the Booker T. Jones?"

Jones took the first eight-week program with more than a dozen other students. But the second-level course is a hands-on intensive routine with only the three of them sharing the equipment. Instructor Gordon runs through an endless list of bewildering details in his two-hour lecture/demonstration before leaving the three students on their own to figure out how to work their way through the complicated exercise in the Pro Tools instruction manual. Perez operates the board, while Schickman and Jones try to figure out what to do next.

"I don't know if I'm ever going to be a real operator," said Jones. "But I need to know what a real operator does. If I want to stay in the music business, I need to know this. How can I be the guy in charge and not understand this stuff?"

He could confidently work his way around tape recording (Pro Tools records to a computer drive). He knew how to run analog recording consoles – they call the digital counterpart a control surface – and he could edit tapes with razor blades. He first ran across digital recording a number of years ago, watching a Nashville record producer do some edits in the studio. But working with fellow old-timers Willie Nelson and Neil Young has not required Booker to move into the digital domain.

He sold his own analog recording equipment ("basically gave it away," he said) several years ago and closed the small studio he maintained at Berkeley's Fantasy Records, which quickly installed Pro Tools equipment in his vacated room.

Pyramind is one several schools in the Bay Area offering certification on Pro Tools, which was invented by the Daly City company Digidesign. Gordon and

Donner folded their South of Market production business into an existing Folsom Street studio and slowly began to convert their part of the operation to a training facility. Gordon even took entrepreneur classes at a business school around the corner. They still do business as a recording studio, but Donner said the school now accounts for as much as 80 percent of their business.

With state universities and colleges perennially strapped for cash, only private schools like Pyramind can afford the latest equipment or find the instructors up to speed on the gear. In fact, Jones originally enrolled in the Pro Tools classes at Pyramind through the extension program at San Francisco State University, which had an arrangement with the studio. He plans to take his next level of training at a more intensive program offered by San Jose's Future Rhythm, six days of eight-hour classes at a private training facility with ties to Foothill College.

Jones flew down to Los Angeles last month and supervised a Pro Tools session with Nelson at Henson Studios, formerly A&M. "All their analog machines were out in the hall," he said. Satisfied that he was now qualified to produce the session, Jones ran everything through analog pre-amps in front of the Pro Tools setup to give the sound more warmth. He expressed great pleasure with the results.

"It sounds as good as 'Stardust,'" said Jones, who produced three landmark albums with the great country singer after the two met when they lived in the same Malibu apartment building.

As organist with Booker T. and the MGs, Jones not only put a procession of R&B instrumentals on the charts starting when he was still in high school, but he played a crucial role in the house band at Memphis' Stax/Volt label, where he made classic soul records with Otis Redding, Wilson Pickett, Sam and Dave, and many more. His compositions include "Born Under a Bad Sign," recorded by Albert King and now a blues standard.

Jones spent several years commuting from session work in Memphis to his studies at Indiana University, where he graduated with a music degree. He practically grew up in the recording studio.

He left Memphis and moved to California in 1971, where he not only produced Nelson's immensely successful '70s albums, but also supervised the classic 1971 debut album by soul singer Bill Withers featuring the hits "Ain't No Sunshine" and "Lean On Me." He recorded Booker T. Jones solo albums and played sessions with Carlos Santana, John Fogerty, Bob Dylan and others.

The surviving MGs reunited in the early '90s and they served as house band for the 1992 all-star Bob Dylan tribute at Madison Square Garden. Neil Young used Booker T. and the MGs as backup band for his 1993 tour, and brought Jones onboard the 2002 Crosby, Stills, Nash and Young tour as musical director. Young also has used Jones extensively on recording sessions.

The re-formed MGs still play occasional dates. Jones went back to Memphis last month after finishing the Nelson session in Los Angeles to receive an honor from the University of Memphis and play a rare hometown concert with MGs guitarist Steve Cropper and bassist Donald "Duck" Dunn at the new Pyramid Arena, home of basketball's Memphis Grizzlies. "I saw more people I knew than I knew what to do about," said Jones. "It just didn't stop."

He and his wife, Nan, moved to the Bay Area more than 12 years ago. They live in Tiburon, where they raised three children, two still in high school, the oldest attending UCLA. At a surprise birthday party she threw for her husband at their comfortable home last month, there wasn't a single rock star or show business mogul in attendance, although a number of people had children who played sports with the Jones kids.

He takes the ferry and rides Muni to classes, dragging an attache case on wheels. At Pyramind, he puts on glasses and pulls open a binder. As Pro Tools instructor Gordon goes through the detail of automation and sub-mix control groups, Jones pays close attention and takes careful notes. Then Jones and his two classmates flub and flounder their way through a Pro Tools mix.

Belonging to the Rock and Roll Hall of Fame doesn't help him here. "My experience doesn't mean a whole lot," he said. "Trying to learn all this stuff is a great leveler. Greg's tried to tell them a little and I've told them a few stories, but we concentrate on learning this."

After the bass and most of the drums are mixed, Jones takes his turn at the controls. Schickman hovers over his shoulder and Perez scoots up a chair. Jones finishes the drums and mixes the keyboard parts. All three agree the mix is done and pack up their bags for the day.

Jones puts on his coat and straps his bag to its stroller. He blinks at the afternoon sun on the sidewalk outside the studio and heads off to the bus stop, just another student happy to be out of school and on his way home.

San Francisco Chronicle | *Thursday, December 2, 2004*

The last great bluesman

Taj Mahal cools his heels in Berkeley again,
blending thirst for world's music and its link to the land

Taj Mahal, after all these years, has become what he aspired
to. He is the last great bluesman and another extraordinary
character living his life and playing his music outside the world
of pop music.

TAJ MAHAL IS BACK IN BERKELEY. He stalks the street like a horse, striding down
Shattuck Avenue with a thoroughbred's grace. In other places, this mountain of a
man in white pants, tropical shirt and straw hat might draw some attention, but on
the streets of Berkeley, he doesn't rate a second glance. He dismisses the Berkeley
he finds today with a single word.

"It's Yupsterella-land," he croaks. "You know, like Cinderella, but it's Yupster-
ella."

He slides behind the Formica table of the fluorescent-lit Thai Noodles, where
the cook nods a greeting, and orders up his customary pile of fish cakes, a plate of
eggplant and glass of iced coffee.

"It was Mario Savio got me out here," he says, referring to the charismatic
UC Berkeley '60s student protest leader. "I saw Mario Savio on top of that car in
Sproul Plaza and said 'great google-bee, I'm outta here.' I drove across the country.
I wanted to go somewhere where it looked like the youth knew what time it was.
Every other place, they were so afraid. Out here, it was happening."

After 14 years on the island of Kauai, he has returned to Berkeley, where he
lived throughout the '70s, at the height of his currency on the pop charts and FM
radio, to be around his four now-grown daughters. He is staying with an ex-wife,
Anna DeLeon, mother of one of his daughters, who pulls up with Taj in front of
her downtown Berkeley restaurant and nightclub, Anna's Jazz Island.

In the empty nightclub, he strums a tobacco-colored handmade guitar and
out comes a demented ragtime instrumental that manages to somehow simultaneously evoke cranky bebop jazz and muddy Mississippi Delta blues. He calls it "The
New Black and Crazy Blues." In the course of one song, his music encompasses
several lifetimes. But he is more than a walking musical encyclopedia, a multicul-

266

Taj Mahal

tural experiment in progress, or a grand patriarch of a sprawling family, 12 children in all, so beloved that his 60th birthday party was attended by all his ex-wives.

"He's an amazing man," said David Rubinson, who produced his first six albums. "He's got family all over the world. He runs businesses all over the world. And the most amazing thing of all, the music just keeps getting better."

In May, he received an honorary degree from his alma mater, University of Massachusetts, where he graduated with a degree in animal science in 1963. Earlier in the year, he was named the official blues artist of the Commonwealth of Massachusetts. Next year, he celebrates his 40th anniversary as a recording artist.

"That's 40 years without having to yield to the record companies for how it is and what it is that I do," he says. "I've always done what I wanted to with the music that I want to do."

In the course of a career spanning literally dozens of albums, he has recorded every kind of blues, dabbled in jazz, conducted major cross-cultural experiments. He once did an album with a quartet of tubas. He made children's records, movie soundtracks, Hawaiian music. He does solo acoustic or big band. He has recorded with Miles Davis and the Rolling Stones. He was one of the first major artists to cut songs by Bob Marley. But both his parents, who met in New York City, originally came from the Caribbean island of St. Kitts.

"We were always connected to the Caribbean, all my life, growing up," he says. "Everybody thought 'Oh, you went to Jamaica, you heard Bob Marley, now you play his songs.' That's what you think. No matter how long we say it, you don't understand it. This is cultural. What I am doing is celebrating cultural diversity. I AM cultural diversity, right here.

"My mother's and father's people are from the Caribbean. Because they're both black doesn't mean they're automatically on the same page. They got to work it out just like everybody else. People don't get that. In this country, they don't realize that black is not a culture. Black is a color."

He shaves his head clean down to his eyebrows, although he keeps a crooked mustache across his lip. He wears a gold sailfish on a chain around his neck and a diamond stud in his ear. He is a skilled cook who knows his way around restaurants all over the world; from enchilada parlors in the Mission to more epicurean eateries in capitol cities of Europe, where he has been spending a lot of his touring time over recent years. He hosts his fifth annual fishing tournament in February in Gulfo Dulce off southern Costa Rica and is known to enjoy a good Cuban cigar occasionally.

He checks his Blackberry. He is tracking a wholesale shipment of seeds he is sending to Caribbean farmers with a program called Seeds of Change from New Mexico that specializes in distributing organic seeds. Taj hopes to expand his seed distribution to West Africa.

"Music and agriculture kind of go together," he says. "In the oldest societies in the world, it certainly was a part of it. One of the large inputs to music in the United States came from people in the agrarian sector. That's where all the stuff came from – the work song, this, that and the other thing. They are the components of the music we hear today.

"Also there was a huge disconnect with agriculture. A lot of African American people after slavery were, like, agriculture? You must be kidding. I don't think so. I wear cotton. I ain't picking cotton."

Born Henry St. Claire Fredericks in Harlem, Taj grew up in the New England factory town of Springfield, Mass. His father had been a classically trained jazz pianist, but took the day job to support his family. His mother was a schoolteacher and gospel singer who grew up in South Carolina. His father kept a large record collection and there was always music in the house.

He studied piano and picked up a number of other instruments. But he learned guitar from a neighbor, a nephew of bluesman Arthur "Big Boy" Crudup, recently relocated from the South. His father died in a farm accident when Taj was 13 years old.

While studying animal husbandry at Amherst, he played in a local band and changed his name – the name came to him in a dream. A year after graduation, he moved to Los Angeles, where he put together a band called the Rising Sons (also featuring a young Ry Cooder on guitar), who opened shows at the Whiskey a Go Go for Otis Redding, Sam the Sham and the Temptations. His 1967 Columbia Records solo debut, "Taj Mahal," was an instant classic.

"I'll figure out some way to celebrate this," he says. "I've been a busy man. I'm still doing 125-150 dates a year. I'm lucky. If I wanted to do 300 or 360 dates, I could. I'd like to get it down to that Bocephus thing" – the nickname for country star Hank Williams Jr. – "I like Bocephus. He was talking to Don Imus and he was saying 'Well, Imus, it comes down to this – the bottom line is 25 dates a year.' That would be the bottom line. I'd like to walk that line, I'll tell you what, goll-lee."

Hank Jr., Taj says, told him he and the band like to listen to Taj on their private jet's sound system, flying between shows. "I always liked country music, too," Taj says. "It ain't nothin' but the blues coming up another way."

Now 64, Taj is old enough to have studied at the feet of the masters – not only the country blues guys like Mississippi John Hurt, Sleepy John Estes or Lightnin' Hopkins, but the Chicago blues crowd – Muddy Waters, Jimmy Reed, Junior Wells and Buddy Guy, or, the king of them all, Howlin' Wolf.

"Wolf," he says, "No over it. No under it. No way around it. Got to give him his due."

Even if he sounded like an old soul right from the start, Taj identifies with the white blues musicians of his own generation. He first met the Rolling Stones when the band caught his act at the Whiskey in 1968 and sent him and his band eight round-trip tickets to London to appear in the Rolling Stones' Rock and Roll Circus, a historic concert filmed for a television special that went unreleased until 1996.

But he really first encountered his British counterparts late at night listening to the radio. "Early Van Morrison, Them – what great records those were," he says. "I remember laying up at midnight saying 'who the heck is this guy 'cause he knows where the music is. I can feel it in the back of my neck.' I love Van.

"I was also real crazy about Brian Jones," he says of the late Rolling Stones guitarist. "Those guys jumped over the Elvis syndrome.

"In the United States, because of the politics of race and class, this whole thing about white boys dancing and playing the blues, everybody got stuck at Elvis. The Brits didn't get stuck at Elvis. They jumped over Elvis and said 'Your name is Elmore James and you play slide guitar – cracking.' And that's where they went. But this is where his source was.

"And they were an island culture and they were already stretched out. Hey, you have a different kind of headspace. Everything's coming in from everywhere. Those guys did good."

San Francisco Chronicle | November 27, 2006

CHAPTER 8

Rock Classics

CSNY2K

Neil Young

Captain Beefheart

Mimi Farnia

Linda Ronstadt

Steve Miller

Boz Scaggs

Sammy Hagar

Bonnie Raitt

Nilsson

Deja Vu All Over Again

Crosby, Stills, Nash and Young reuniting for a
new album and their first tour in 25 years

Manufactured press events like this – daylong group interviews
– rarely work, but somehow I came out of this one with a story.

"CSNY2K" IS COMING. The title for the 41-city Crosby, Stills, Nash and Young tour
that starts in January may seem obvious, but it did give the band members an opportunity to crack jokes about possible T-shirt slogans.

"CSNY2K – Ask Your Parents," suggested Neil Young.

"CSNY2K – You're Not Ready," said David Crosby.

The four horsemen ride again. On October 26, CSN&Y will release a new
album, "Looking Forward," an event that happens about as often as a solar eclipse.
Tours are even rarer. Their last tour 25 years ago invented the stadium rock concert, an epochal enterprise that was the biggest-grossing tour at that point in history. The new tour dates, including the Bay Area, will be announced Tuesday.

All four rockers – Young is 53, Stills 54, Nash 57 and Crosby 58 – spent the
better part of the last two days in the General MacArthur Suite at the St. Francis
Hotel, meeting the press two at a time, seated thronelike behind a coffee table covered with plants and candles. Graham Nash, originally not expected to attend, was
cheerful as usual, despite having broken both his legs in a boating accident three
weeks ago in Hanalei Bay in Kauai, where he lives.

"I'm OK from the knees up," he said.

The reunion album was born when Young and Stephen Stills were working together on a box set for their old band Buffalo Springfield, which predates CSN&Y.
Stills asked Young to play on one of his songs that Crosby, Stills and Nash were
recording.

"We didn't plan it," said Crosby. "We didn't talk about it, think about it or do
it. We didn't focus on anything except the music that was in front of us. If we do
that, it works like a charm."

"Those were good days," agreed Young. "We never talked about doing a CSNY
album. It was just obvious that we were.

"I came down," Young continued. "I was just visiting, and the tunes were real good. They were making a record. They started it because they wanted to – not because the label told them it was time or anything like that – and that's a great reason to do it. I could hear that from the first note."

Crosby, Stills and Nash didn't have a record contract and were financing the sessions themselves. The trio, whose first album was released in 1969, has been working steadily since Crosby was released from a Texas jail in 1986, where he served a year on drug charges. While the group remains a concert attraction, its infrequent latter-day recordings have largely been lackluster affairs widely ignored by the public.

With Young on board, the band's commercial prospects brighten considerably. Alone among the four, Young has long established himself as a solo artist, and the Crosby, Stills, Nash and Young configuration echoes the band's glory days in 1970 when the first CSN&Y album, "Deja Vu," was No. 1 and songs like "Teach Your Children," "Ohio" and "Our House" were everywhere. Their 1988 reunion, "American Dream," is not as well remembered.

"We get together whenever we feel like it," said Young. "Obviously it doesn't happen all that often – this is our third record. We're on a roll."

To select the 12 songs that appear on "Looking Forward," the group posted a list of all the songs recorded, and each musician put a check mark beside songs he wanted to include. On the first pass, they chose nine songs unanimously. "The next part took a month," said Stills.

Although the album contains only new originals, the group experimented recording some old songs – "Turn Turn Turn" from Crosby's old group, the Byrds, and the Springfield oldie, "Rock and Roll Woman," with Joe Walsh on guitar.

"We did an old song of mine called 'White Line,'" said Young, "one that I don't recall releasing at all. We did a great version, too. Then the engineer said he also liked the one I did on 'Ragged Glory.' I was shocked. Senior moment No. 58."

"See how much we like you?" said Crosby. "We didn't even rag on you."

The fellows were getting a little giddy after all the questions and cameras. Crosby was apparently still thinking T-shirts when an interviewer asked what he hopes fans will come away from the concerts with.

"Smiles," said Crosby. "And merchandise."

San Francisco Chronicle | October 9, 1999

Lost & Found

A chapter from a collaborative biography of Neil Young that covers the end of the Crosby, Stills, Nash and Young tour to the birth of his son, Ben, the Crazy Horse years, appeared in a special publication by Mojo magazine. Neil's not talking – my specialty.

NEIL YOUNG FIRST MET FRANK SAMPEDRO AT the Chess Records studio in Chicago, where Crazy Horse showed up in December 1974 with the guitarist everybody called Pancho in tow. Young and "Harvest" producer Eliott Mazer were working on an album tentatively titled "Homegrown" and they booked time in Chicago, where Young was trying to contend with both the dissolution of relationship with actress Carrie Snodgrass and the suicide of her mother.

Young and Snodgrass had been falling apart for some time. They had a two year-old son, Zeke, but Young had lately been avoiding his Northern California ranch in La Honda, in part, because of their troubled relationship. After the CSNY tour ended in September in London, rather than go home, he bought an antique Rolls Royce, named it Wembley, after the source of the funds, and took off on an auto tour of Europe with Graham Nash and several members of the road crew.

In November, he and Mazer were recording in Nashville. When Young went to Chicago in a show of support for his child's mother, whose wet-brain alcoholic mother had been threatening suicide for years, he continued to work on the record, if only as link with sanity, and summoned the fellows from Crazy Horse, who brought along their new guitarist.

A mutual friend had introduced Crazy Horse bassist Billy Talbot to Sampedro and they took a trip to Mexico together. "He wanted to go," Talbot said. "I wasn't doing anything, so I went along." The Chicago sessions proved problematic and unproductive, but when Young showed up a few weeks later at Talbot's Echo Park apartment in Los Angeles and Sampedro was there, the jamming took on a new life. They played for a couple of days and Young left his equipment at Talbot's place promising to return.

With a renewed Crazy Horse at his side, over the next four years, Neil Young would reach some of the greatest creative heights of his career. Freed to explore his creativity as an electric guitarist, Young with Crazy Horse would give voice to some of his finest songs and provide him a solid working relationship that he could return to time and again, as he experimented with other ideas and other musicians. For the next four years, as Young wrote and recorded some of his most extraordinary albums, Crazy Horse would be home base.

These were the wilderness years for Young. He lived like a gypsy, flitting from project to project, town to town, restlessly creative, looking for something just beyond the horizon. The enormous commercial success of CSNY continued to hover over his shoulder, but Young took his own path, only occasionally glancing back at the supergroup he left behind. At this point in his life, Neil Young was still a man with something to prove.

In December, Young rejoined Crosby, Stills and Nash for recording sessions at Sausalito's Record Plant. They managed to record two complete songs before Young left at the end of one day and simply never came back. Although Snodgrass and their son Zeke moved out of the ranch, Young still did not return, leery of hangers-on and free-loaders, but instead bought a large beach house outside Malibu once owned by F. Scott Fitzgerald. He called Crazy Horse out to the nearby home of producer David Briggs, where they began recording the tracks that would become "Zuma."

After coming up empty-handed with Crazy Horse at the Chess studios in Chicago, producer Elliott Mazer and Neil continued recording "Homegrown" in Nashville with Levon Helm and Tim Drummond. Young added vocals by Emmylou Harris to "Star Of Bethlehem" in Los Angeles. Mazer found a live recording of CSNY doing "Pushed It Over the End" – "the single best live performance I ever heard them do," Mazer said. He played the finished album – "acoustic, dark and very emotional" according to Mazer – to a number of people. Record company executive Chris Wright called Warner Brothers chairman Mo Ostin to tell him that the album was as good as "Harvest." But "Homegrown" would never be released.

Young played the finished album one night at a party that included Rick Danko of The Band and the guys from Crazy Horse. On the back of the reel of tape was a copy of "Tonight's the Night," the dark, slurry electric rock album Young made two years previously, a gloomy meditation on the drug overdose deaths of roadie Bruce Berry and the original Crazy Horse guitarist, Danny Whitten. The other musicians at the party enthusiastically recommended releasing the older recording and Young shelved "Homegrown" with its many downbeat songs about the breakup with Snodgrass.

He took time out from recording "Zuma" with Crazy Horse in March long enough to play the historic SNACK concert at Kezar Stadium in San Francisco. Producer Bill Graham put on the benefit to raise money for depleted after-school programs in San Francisco and he promised a special guest. When actor Marlon Brando took the stage, most people in the audience assumed that was the mystery guest Graham was talking about. But Brando was followed by a loose group that included Young with Helm, Danko and Garth Hudson from The Band and David Briggs' Malibu neighbor, Bob Dylan, who had been hanging out and tinkling keys on some of the "Zuma" sessions.

A proposed summer tour with Crazy Horse was postponed when Young underwent throat surgery. He was still not talking or singing and was communicating by passing notes when he joined Stephen Stills for a couple of songs at Still's show in July at UC Berkeley's Greek Theater. By the time he joined Stills again in November at UCLA's Pauley Pavilion and Stanford's Maples Pavilion, he was singing and talking. In December, he took out Crazy Horse for an impromptu barnstorming tour of small joints in the remote reaches of the Bay Area, rock clubs in Santa Cruz and Cotati, tiny bars in nearby La Honda and Marshall in western Marin County, places where Young and the band joined the crowd at the bar for drinks after the show, a far cry from playing for stadiums full of screaming fans with CSNY. In honor of Dylan's then-current semi-spontaneous East Coast tour, wags dubbed the Young dates the Rolling Zuma tour. The dates were not advertised. The band simply showed up and played for whoever was there, tiny little, out-of-the-way roadhouses like Cotati's Inn of the Beginning or the Marshall Tavern. "It was exactly the right place to see Crazy Horse," said longtime Young photographer and tape archivist Joel Bernstein.

"Neil was real loose and so were we," said Crazy Horse's Talbot. "The atmosphere to those shows was congenial. They didn't mean anything. We weren't making any money. There weren't any promoters around. There weren't any critics there."

Young celebrated New Year's Eve that year goofing around onstage with Stills at a tiny restaurant near his La Honda home. A few days later, he went to Miami and spent much of January and February 1976 recording with Stephen Stills.

Young and Crazy Horse took March and April to tour Japan and Europe. Crosby and Nash turned up at the continuing Stills and Young sessions in May and added their vocals to a number of the pieces the pair had already recorded, only to learn their vocal parts were later erased and any thoughts of turning the Stills-Young project into the long dreamed third CSNY album vanished. Young departed in June for the abortive tour with Stills.

In October, Young warmed up for a U.S. tour with Crazy Horse by playing another handful of unannounced shows at small local clubs. He flew straight from the last date on the month-long, twelve-city tour in Atlanta, Georgia, back to San Francisco for "The Last Waltz," the all-star finale for his pals, The Band, that would be filmed by Martin Scorcese. Drugs were everywhere that night at Winterland. A room backstage was painted white, decorated with noses cut out of dime store masks with a tape loop of sniffing running in the background. Band guitarist Robbie Robertson could be seen not so discretely passing vials to guests as they left the stage. When the film hit the editing room, special measures had to be taken to remove a large white clump visible in one of Young's nostrils.

Young plunged into recording a new album with Crazy Horse called "Chrome Dreams," another Neil Young masterpiece that would never see the light of day. By March, he and Crazy Horse completed an album – acetates exist – but Young continued to record. In April, Linda Ronstadt brought her 24 year-old friend Nicolette Larson to the ranch to add their distinctive harmony blend to a number of songs. Before long, "Chrome Dreams" devolved into "American Stars and Bars." One side was countrified rock songs with Ronstadt and Larson – dubbed the Saddle Bags for the occasion – and the other side featured various leftovers, including the "Homegrown" outtake, "Star of Bethlehem," and the towering "Like a Hurricane" from the original "Chrome Dreams."

But the strangest wrinkle was yet to come. In June, Young began appearing around Santa Cruz nightclubs as part of a band called the Ducks. Young had long been friends with Jeff Blackburn, whose group Blackburn and Snow shared bills with the Springfield. Blackburn joined a later edition of Moby Grape that played around Santa Cruz and he and Grape bassist Bob Moseley and drummer Johnny "C." Craviotto formed the core of the Ducks, who were looking for a lead guitarist when Young happened along. On the condition the band never appear outside the Santa Cruz city limits, Young joined the group for the summer. He played lead guitar and supplied only some of the songs – he did "Mr. Soul" and "Are You Ready For the Country" alongside new numbers such as "Sail Away," the instrumental "Windward Passage" or "Comes a Time." Moseley and Blackburn sang others. Young rented a house on the beach and all summer long the band played Santa Cruz clubs, either replacing announced acts or under a "phone for details" advertisement.

"These guys play some great music," Young told a local reporter. "Sure, they want to go out and do something, but all I want to do is play some music right now. You see, I haven't lived in a town in eight years. I stayed on my ranch for about four years, and then I started traveling all over, never really staying anywhere. Moving into Santa Cruz is like my re-emergence back into civilization. I like this town. If the situation remains cool, we can do this all summer long."

That fall, Young took five year-old Zeke, by that time diagnosed with cerebral palsy, on a cross-country trip on the tour bus. With long hours on the highway, Young piled up songwriting. When the bus pulled into Nashville, he assembled a team of crack sidemen to accompany him and called Nicolette Larson in Los Angeles to come out and sing harmonies. The two began an affair. After the album was done, Young took the entire twenty-two-piece ensemble, called the Gone With the Wind Orchestra for the occasion, to Miami for an open-air benefit concert for children's hospitals before a crowd of more than a hundred thousand on his 32nd birthday. He ended the show by playing a piece of Lynyrd Skynyrd's "Sweet Home Alabama" – with its famed Neil Young reference – and dedicating the song to "a couple of friends up in the sky." In December, a Rolling Stone reporter found Young and Larson nestled into his Zuma place, looking at the reformed Crosby, Stills and Nash on the cover of People magazine.

"Strange seeing that," he told Cameron Crowe of Rolling Stone. "Those three with Jimmy Carter on the inside…it makes me think. It's good that they're together, but it's also good to be apart too."

By Christmas, however, Young was back in La Honda and Larson was alone at Zuma packing her bags. It was about the same time that Young began seeing a Redwood City neighbor, Pegi Morton, an attractive blonde he'd known for several years who used to waitress at some of his local hangouts.

By the time Young did his famed run at the Boarding House in May 1978, he was already well along in production of his second feature film project, "Human Highway." Shooting the five nights at the three hundred-seat San Francisco club was one part of the unscripted movie that was planned. Appearing solo and acoustic, singing through a newfangled wireless headphone mike, Young sang eleven new songs out of the sixteen songs he performed. The stage was empty except for several six-foot tall wooden Indians. One of the new songs paid tribute to his growing appreciation of the radical punk rock coming out of England that took aim at exactly the kind of crusty traditions Neil Young proudly represented: "Hey, Hey, My My (Into the Black)." All ten shows were filmed.

After the late show on the last night, Young went over to the Mabuhay Gardens, San Francisco's punk rock emporium, where he got onstage with new wave weirdos Devo and bashed out a twisted, demented version of his salute to Johnny Rotten, also duly captured for the movie. He heard Devo chanting their own background vocal refrain to his lyrics – *Rust never sleeps* – not knowing the phrase came from their days working on the Rustoleum account for an ad agency. It stuck with Young.

In August, he married the very pregnant Pegi Morton. During a honeymoon sailing trip in the Bahamas, the ideas for his next tour tumbled into place. As he and Crazy Horse rehearsed for the twenty-five city tour, Young began to envision the show in specifics – the giant amplifiers and microphones, the stage announcements from Woodstock, the "road-eyes" with their costumes borrowed from "Star Wars." From an acoustic set that began when a "sleeping" Young awakes on top of one of the giant amplifiers and carries a giant harmonica down to the stage where he plays "Sugar Mountain," through a turbulent, cataclysmic electric set bookended by "My, My, Hey, Hey" and punched home by a benedictory "Tonight's the Night," the "Rust Never Sleeps" tour was not just one of the highlights of Young's performing career, but one of the peaks of '70s rock tours.

"Some of the best music we ever played," said Talbot, "some of the best music anyone ever played, we played on that tour. That was us at our best."

The night before the tour ended, a fire burned Young's Zuma home to the ground, where only two months before he held his wedding. A month later, his wife gave birth to their son, Ben. The baby arrived home from the hospital bruised and crying. Several months later, doctors were finally able to diagnose his condition. Against incalculable odds, Young's second son also suffered from cerebral palsy. Young retreated to the sanctuary of his ranch and pulled his family around him like covered wagons in a circle. It would be years before he ventured forth again.

Q Classic | August 2005

Captain Beefheart a Success?

Nobody was ever more fun to hang out with than Don Van Vliet. We took a number of dinners over the years, including one especially memorable evening at Sam's Café, where he went off about the mounted deer head and how it needed ticks running around the snout. Not ordinary ticks, mind, but those fancy imported European mechanical ticks. The night of this interview, as I recall, Don decided he could turn anything into an artwork by signing it and we were autographing soji screens in the restaurant, newspaper racks on the sidewalk.

SOME OF THE THINGS CAPTAIN BEEFHEART WOULD like to do if his new album, "Clear Spot," succeeds:

"I'd like a house next to John Paul Getty's for openers. Only I wouldn't have police dogs out front.

"Next thing. I want to paint Hughes Air West aircrafts 'cause I object to the color. I'd paint it by hand and leave in the brush strokes so you could see them.

"Change the traditional shape of the heart. I'm getting tired of it the way it is. Maybe square off the bottom, crimp the end, change places with the triangle. Something, anything.

"Mail every girl who's ever been a bunny an eraser shaped like a nipple.

"Bring back the kind of scissors they give little kids when they don't trust them. You know...stubbies.

"Put a hex on Rexall. Why not?"

Captain Beefheart, known otherwise as Don Van Vliet, age 31, seems an unlikely candidate for top 40 stardom. He once recorded an album called "Trout Mask Replica" with musicians who had never played at all before. He wore lipstick and rouge on stage six years before Alice Cooper. He calls his corporation God's golfball - a sobriquet for earth.

Regardless, Beefheart is heading for the nether world of commercial success through accessibility. The single off the album, "Too Much Time," sounds very much like a Motown-Stax soul record.

"It's definitely AM," the Captain said. "It's the traditional breakfast egg. Really

Wilkinson blade material."

Beefheart started his musical career at a late age (24) only after abandoning a life-long pursuit of sculpting. His parents – thinking artists are all queer – moved out of Glendale when Van Vliet was 13 after he won a scholarship to study abroad. Van Vliet spent the remainder of his adolescent years in Lancaster, a backwater burg 40 miles north of Los Angeles. Frank Zappa was a close friend in Lancaster. (Judy Garland was another Lancaster native.)

Since his first album five years ago, Beefheart has been the subject of much critical acclaim and little record sales. His record companies have often wondered what to do with him.

"Trout Mask Replica," he said matter-of-factly, "was supposed to be the furthest out thing done with words and music. Or at least a number of people have written that."

He described working with the un-tutored musicians as "a conversation without any commas or periods. They do that because they never played before so they're not hung up."

Beefheart still uses the same group, now with the addition of two ex-Mothers, bassist Roy Estrada and drummer Art Tripp. The band has been together three and a half years.

"Now they're ready to play that awful stuff called music," the Captain smiled.

The Captain and his wife of three years, Jane, live in northern California, not far from the Oregon border. He believes nutrition is the key to restoring civilization, that Al Jolson was the greatest and Salvador Dali is a fake.

"You know how I know I'm an artist?" he asked. "Because people keep using my ideas and not mentioning my name."

His patented personal mode of expression makes liberal use of word play, one-liners, abstractions and digressions. If it's sometimes difficult to fully understand what he's saying, his vibes are unmistakable.

"So many poison merchants have used my native tongue, I chose another one," he explained simply.

Van Vliet is a warm, open man; an artist committed to something. ("I have something not to say.")

"I don't want to be Captain Beefheart," he said. "I just want to put my paw in the water and you can't rent an ocean."

As the Captain is fond of saying, "Everybody's colored, otherwise you wouldn't be able to see them.

"I was going to do that on my last album," he continued. "But one of the guys didn't believe it then. He does now, so I'll do it on the next. But do you know why he didn't believe it?" he asked.

"His father is a house painter." He paused. "The connection eludes me too," he admitted.

Sunday Datebook | December 17, 1972

Mimi's New Struggle

Bread and Roses founder who brought music to many is now battling lung cancer

Typical of Mimi, she wouldn't have consented to such a personal interview if she didn't need to sell tickets and she made me apologize for some awkward social misstep she still held against me before she would even start the interview. She was, as someone pointed out to me, someone with so much innate dignity, you just behaved better when you were around her.

MARIN COUNTY – MIMI FARINA SPENT TWO YEARS planning her 25th anniversary Bread and Roses concert. What she didn't plan on was cancer.

This class act on the local celebrity scene learned she had metastasized lung cancer in December, just as she was beginning a $3 million fund-raising campaign for the Marin-based nonprofit organization, which brings musical performances to jails, hospitals and other institutions around the Bay Area.

Jackson Browne, Boz Scaggs, Kris Kristofferson, Pete Seeger and Farina's big sister Joan Baez will appear March 20 at the War Memorial Opera House in a concert that could bring as much as $500,000 to the campaign.

But once Farina, 54, was told she had cancer, her workaholic days at Bread and Roses ended. She has not been back to the office since.

"This will be one of my biggest learnings this time around," she said. "It will provide me with the time to think about what's next in my life. I have to change my lifestyle, and I don't know what's next. In my best moods, I think this is a great time for rebirth."

Sitting last week in the living room of the Mill Valley hilltop cottage where she has lived for more than 25 years, Farina is composed, as always. Federal Express has just delivered a wig from her sister Joanie. Her hair, she says, has started to fall out because of the chemotherapy. She is thinking of shaving her head, wondering whether to go with wigs or hats for the Opera House show.

Farina is no stranger to struggle. That Bread and Roses exists at all is a tribute to her dedication or, some might say, stubbornness. For many years, Bread and Roses seemed to be on the edge of extinction.

"There were really lean years all through the '80s, where we really weren't sure from month to month," said Bread and Roses Executive Director Lana Severn. "It's only been the past couple of years that the organization has been at all stable, able to look beyond a couple of months."

500 concerts

But the shows have always gone on. This year, Bread and Roses will present more than 500 performances – with more than 600 volunteers – at 99 institutions. The staff numbers only nine. Bread and Roses stages shows at prisons, old-age homes, psychiatric facilities, homeless shelters, children's hospitals, AIDS hospices – wherever Farina finds a shut-in population that can use her particular brand of sunlight.

Among the many name entertainers who have volunteered for Bread and Roses are Paul Simon, Joni Mitchell, Herbie Hancock, Huey Lewis, Neil Young and Van Morrison. Bread and Roses recently brought jazz great Jon Hendricks to sing at the Redwoods, a Mill Valley retirement home and presented Willie Nelson to Delancey Street residents last year. Michael Feinstein once stayed on stage at Laguna Honda hospital until he sang every request.

"They're something really outstanding," said Peg McCourt, who lives at Vintage Estates, a Kentfield nursing home. "It's something you really look forward to."

Bread and Roses has long made jails and prisons a specialty. "When Bread and Roses comes in, that whole doom-filled state of mind disappears," said San Francisco Sheriff Michael Hennessey. "And after their programs are over, there's good will for a long time in the halls."

Upscale Contributors

Her sister Joan Baez recently stood in for Farina at one of the preconcert dinners. "I was flabbergasted," said Baez. "I looked around at this roomful of what I call Mr. and Mrs. I. Magnin, and I couldn't believe it. Bread and Roses has reached a status that I'd never dreamed it would. I thought Bread and Roses was a brilliant idea from the start. It just grew. But it never got big and stupid and yucky. It just got big and wonderful."

Bread and Roses gave Farina a purpose. Performing music, she could never escape the shadow of her famous older sister. With Bread and Roses, Farina was no longer somebody's sister, wife or singing partner.

Mimi Farina is the youngest of three daughters, born while their father studied for his doctorate at Stanford. She lived with her family in Baghdad and in Paris, where she met Richard Farina, a half- Irish, half-Cuban beatnik.

They married and moved to the Carmel highlands and pursued a career as a folksinging team. Richard and Mimi Farina recorded two albums, "Reflections in a Crystal Wind" and "Celebration for a Grey Day," and one of their songs, "Pack Up Your Sorrows," was an airplay staple in the early days of underground FM radio.

Richard Farina published a novel, "Been Down So Long It Looks Like Up to Me," in April 1966 and died in a motorcycle crash on his way home from his first book signing. He was 29 years old. Mimi Farina was a widow on her 21st birthday. Her husband's dulcimer still sits in her home.

S.F. Theater Group

She joined the popular San Francisco satirical theater troupe, the Committee, and recorded an album with singer-songwriter Tom Jans in 1971. But Farina was tiring of the music business merry-go-round.

"I suffered from comparing my voice to my sister's," said Farina. "In the end, it was a great relief to stop singing."

She and her sister had attended a show by bluesman B.B. King at New York's Sing Sing prison, but it was a performance she gave at a halfway house for troubled teens that crystallized the idea for Bread and Roses.

"It wasn't inspiring at the moment," she said. "It was hard to get their attention, this roomful of unhappy teens. But I realized I could imagine people who could be really good at this."

Farina raised funds with annual benefits at the Greek Theatre in Berkeley – all-acoustic concerts long before anyone called it "unplugged" – that featured three days of the greats and near- greats of folk, blues and rock. When losses from the sixth annual concert almost put the nonprofit organization under, Farina shifted her focus to corporate and private donors. Her music events – like the more recent Greek Theatre concerts or the series of shows on Alcatraz – now account for no more than one-quarter of the organization's almost $1 million annual operating budget.

Long-term endowment

She and Severn devised the current campaign to create an endowment that would keep Bread and Roses solvent for the next quarter century and would be a means for them to step down.

"We've been planning it for three years," said Severn, who joined Bread and

Roses 17 years ago. "Of course, it took a radical turn once Mimi became ill." Farina has thrown herself into healing with zeal. In addition to conventional medical treatments, she is following the advice of an herbalist and going to a cancer dance-therapy workshop. She took her family to a Native American sweat lodge healing ceremony.

Only a few years ago, Farina beat another life-threatening illness, hepatitis C. "It didn't have the clout cancer does," she said. "Cancer has benefit concerts, stores, wigs, books, support groups."

She said that there are 15 other community groups modeled after Bread and Roses across the country. "It's something I feel every community should have," she said, "like cancer support groups."

San Francisco Chronicle | Saturday, March 4, 2000

Adieu False Heart,

Linda Ronstadt, at 60, is back in San Francisco, raising kids and singing what she wants to sing

Having watched her perform since she belonged to the Stone Poneys, I never thought Linda Ronstadt was ever the slightest bit comfortable onstage. "I'd much rather rehearse," she said, when I made that observation.

LINDA RONSTADT HAD CELEBRATED HER 60TH BIRTHDAY three days earlier – going to see "Pirates of the Caribbean" with her teenage son and having the girlfriends over later that night – and flowers are still everywhere in the sunny upstairs Laurel Heights duplex where she has lived since moving back to San Francisco last fall.

"I think flowers are almost as important as groceries," she says.

Not interested in having her photograph taken, Ronstadt lounges in dishabille – rolled-up jeans, white blouse, pink house slippers – in her third-floor living room with the Golden Gate Bridge outside her window, her bowl-cut hair framing a heart-shaped face. Her eyes sparkle and she is happy, chatty, enthused about a scintillating new acoustic record, "Adieu False Heart," that she's made with Cajun music specialist Ann Savoy. The album is yet another unexpected chapter in a career that has been full of surprises since she was the glamour girl of the '70s Los Angeles music scene, romantically linked with then-Gov. Jerry Brown and filmmaker George Lucas, and red hot on the best-selling charts with a string of glossy pop-rock remakes such as "You're No Good," "When Will I Be Loved" and "Blue Bayou."

"I hated those records," she says. "I never thought of myself as a rock singer. I was interested in songs like 'Heart Like a Wheel' and I liked the others for about 15 minutes. But it wasn't until I found Nelson Riddle that I had music I could live with."

Ronstadt is back on the road this year after taking off much of the past 10 years to watch her two adopted children, ages 12 and 14, grow. She left San Francisco, where she lived across the street from her current residence, in the late '80s and moved back to Tucson, where she grew up in the '50s, a small-town rancher's daughter whose grandfather owned the hardware store. She left Arizona, she says, because she could no longer stand the strip-mall culture and right-wing mentality. Now her kids walk to school and she feels comfortable strolling the shops in her neighborhood. "I feel a sense of community here," she says.

Even if she is working more than she has in a long time, Ronstadt is still without management, a real record deal or even her own Web site. She has no publicity representatives or handlers outside of her crisply efficient personal assistant.

"I fired my manager years ago because he kept trying to get me to work," she says.

In her live shows, she must balance the jazz standards she's become devoted to singing – she did three albums with the Frank Sinatra and Nat King Cole arranger Riddle in the '80s that changed her career – with the pop hits her audience expects to hear. If she initiated the now loathsome cliche of fading rock stars singing standards – "Bolton Swings Sinatra" is only the latest and perhaps most egregious example – Ronstadt long ago moved beyond all that. She talks about working with an ensemble that would include violin and viola but no drums, rearranging everything for the small, flexible group and presenting her songs like chamber music. She likes the idea of singing standards in front of a small combo without having the extra baggage of the full orchestra.

"I sing them as works in progress," she says. "They're so sturdy, so finely constructed. You can't get bored with them. There's always something you can do with them."

Her 2004 release, "Hummin' to Myself," showed off a confident, skillful Ronstadt, not the big-band vocalist in front of the lush orchestrations of Riddle, but a swinging session with Ronstadt riding a tight, hard-bopping small jazz combo.

But she has a long list of accomplishments. She has tackled Gilbert and Sullivan, Appalachian folk music, Mexican canciones. She did "La Boheme," she says, just so she could learn the music. As a record producer – and there are very few female record producers of any note – she not only has done exquisite work on her own recordings but also introduced New Orleans R&B great Aaron Neville to a broad audience, something many others had tried and failed to do. The polished "Hummin' to Myself" went virtually unnoticed, selling a modest 75,000 copies.

"I thought it was a rather good record," she says, "but I didn't know what to do to make it distinguish itself. And I don't know what to do with the Ann record either."

The "Ann record" is an increasingly uncommon labor of love in the unsentimental world of pop music. "Girl music," Ronstadt says it's been called.

"We both made a lot of compromises with boy music over the years," she says.

Ann Savoy has become one of the great exponents of authentic Cajun music.

She is married to Marc Savoy, the master accordion-maker who has run the Savoy Music Store outside Eunice, La., for more than 40 years. As one of the three members of the Savoy-Doucet Band, she has helped spread the iridescent music beyond the Louisiana backwoods. Although she was born and raised in Richmond, Va., since marrying Savoy in 1977, she has become immersed in Cajun culture. She has photographed, written books, collected folklore. She worked with T Bone Burnett on "The Divine Secrets of the Ya-Ya Sisterhood" soundtrack and produced the 2002 collection "Evangeline Made," where she first sang with Ronstadt on a pair of tracks.

"A lot of people said, 'They sing like sisters,'" Ann Savoy says on the phone from Louisiana.

The two women share bonds beyond music. "I love them," says Ronstadt of the Savoys. "I love the way they raised their children. I like what she likes. I go to her house and I see the same teacup we both bought. I love the way they live. I love her taste. She lives in that house – Martha Stewart-really-means-it-and-goes-to-the-swamp."

"Linda called and said, 'Let's just hang around my house and sing some songs,'" Savoy says. "She wanted to play guitar. We switched around harmonies, traded leads. We had the best time."

Staying at an antebellum guesthouse outside Breaux Bridge, La., the ladies went antique hunting during the day, ate barbecue outside by big, roaring fires and played music in the dark, sensuous bayou nights, taking Ronstadt back to her childhood on the ranch singing around the mesquite fires.

"We'd spend the morning in our pajamas," Ronstadt says, "singing and drinking tea. Maybe we'd go to the nursery and pot some plants. Or hang her laundry out on a line – she doesn't have a dryer."

In that part of the country, they make music the old-fashioned way, and Ronstadt knows something about old ways. When she hears Savoy's family talking about a door they built – "I remember the day we cut down that tree" – she recalls the hand-carved door her father made for their home.

Ann Savoy supplied all the material, plumbing the songbooks of Bill Monroe, Edith Piaf, Richard Thompson, even the '60s pop nugget "Walk Away Renee." "That's the magic of it – we love the same music," Savoy says. "She just loved everything."

Says Ronstadt: "Ann is one of the great song finders. I never find songs taking my kid to kindergarten – Ann was so good; I was so happy to see them."

Ronstadt made Savoy sing in English for the first time in her career, and Savoy got Ronstadt to sing in French. They recorded the album in Nashville with acoustic musicians, including Savoy's son Joel Savoy on lead guitar, under producer Steve Buckingham, a friend of Savoy's from their days in the Richmond music scene, long before he made all those Dolly Parton records.

While "Adieu False Heart" may be a sharp departure from other Ronstadt records, a decidedly low-key, folky affair with limited obvious commercial appeal, it is practically a big-budget blockbuster to Ann Savoy, who has spent her career in an arcane, dusty corner of American music.

"I think of it as well-recorded roots music," Savoy says, "maybe with a little more commercial value, not as obscure as all the other stuff I've done. It's something more people in the world can relate to than anything else I've ever done – let's say that."

"When I sing with her," Ronstadt says, "I know I'm doing something we can't do alone. That's the joy of collaboration."

Now Ronstadt puzzles over how to present the material in concert. The duo will play some folk festival dates later this summer and will headline one of the shows at this year's Hardly Strictly Bluegrass Festival in Golden Gate Park in October. But she can't exactly just shoehorn this material into her already schizoid act. "Don Henley says he has trouble slipping one new song into the Eagles show," she says. "I've got 12."

But anyone who posed for those photographs in hot pants and roller skates all those years ago knows something about show business. She chose to pursue her career as a musician, not a celebrity, which probably accounts for her durability as an artist. Long after all the other Geffen girls who were her peers and contemporaries have disappeared, Ronstadt is enjoying a thriving, productive career full of fine work that doesn't depend on the pop charts. She keeps an entire second career in the Spanish language running, in addition to the pop and standards shows she plays. For Ronstadt, music has been a part of her life since she was a little girl on the ranch.

"It's her job," Savoy says. "It's her work. It's her life."

Ronstadt can get under the hood with the songs. She compares folksinger John Jacob Niles with Schubert's 19th century songs, describes Burl Ives' singing as "true bel canto with beautiful breath and all that." She traces the lineage of Aaron Neville's countertenor vocal style to Catholic singing instead of Baptist gospel. She talks about recording a Leonard Cohen song with Emmylou Harris ("It was fun to get in there and experience all that architecture, but I don't think we had anyone jumping up and down when we were done"). And although she's cut a few memorable versions of Randy Newman songs herself, she says only Bonnie Raitt can really sing his songs – "besides Randy," she says.

Meanwhile, she is reconnecting with old Bay Area music friends like Carol McComb, half of the '60s folk duo Kathy and Carol, and trying to adjust to the smaller quarters of an upstairs duplex. Her two dogs have been boarded with friends. She keeps her Tucson place ("It's costing me a fortune, but I can't let it go"), a small house surrounded by an acre of land in the old downtown area, but admits they don't get down there more often than Christmas and Easter yet. She keeps looking for properties around Laurel Heights that might be roomier, at least have a small plot of garden, but real estate prices in that neighborhood have gone through the stratosphere since she moved out more than 15 years ago. And she's a single, working mother with two kids in private school.

"You have no idea how much that costs," she says. "If I put the money I spent to educate them in a trust fund, they'd be rich and wouldn't have to work anyway."

San Francisco Chronicle | *Friday, July 28, 2006*

Steve Miller Band/
King Biscuit Hour

There is no musician I admire more than Steve Miller, who despite his immense success is probably still under-rated. He has become a close friend and I've written a lot of his CD liner notes. This one was only released for a minute.

BACK FROM A YEAR OF CEASELESS TOURING CHASING the Top Ten success of "The Joker," Steve Miller found a rather large royalty check in his mailbox. He called his agent and stupefied the man by telling him he would be taking the next year off.

He bought a home on a remote hilltop in Marin County and installed eight-track recording equipment. With his longtime bass player Lonnie Turner and a drummer he knew from previous sessions, Gary Mallaber, who also played on Van Morrison's "Moondance," Miller went into CBS Studios in San Francisco and, in two weeks, ripped off more than two dozen instrumental tracks.

Miller took the tapes home and scrupulously overdubbed instrumental and vocal parts for many months in his home studio. "The Joker" opened the door. He knew his next album presented a golden opportunity. He had polished the song "Fly Like an Eagle" for years, recording it several times, changing the lyrics, road-testing the number in concerts over the previous three years. But it wasn't until he came up with the burbling synthesizer line in the introduction that all the parts fell together.

He wrote another tune, "Rock'n Me," specifically for the sole performance he did play during his year off – a one-off at England's gigantic Knebworth Castle rock festival with Pink Floyd – a bluesey, driving number he designed with the enormous crowd in mind. "Take the Money and Run" was another song he fiddled with, recording it at first to the tune of "The Joker." He mixed the results in two intense days in Seattle and brought the tapes and a slide of the finished cover to the Capitol Records president.

These were the songs that would make Steve Miller a classic rock hero. Not only was the "Fly Like an Eagle" album itself a multi-platinum success, those songs he recorded in two weeks at CBS in San Francisco would drive sales of his "Greatest Hits" album past the fourteen million mark, a record that has sold steadily

Steve Miller

since its original release almost thirty years ago.

Miller spent the first ten years of his career, in a sense, preparing for this moment. He left the Chicago blues scene, where he was playing rhythm guitar for Buddy Guy, for San Francisco, where he formed the Steve Miller Blues Band and, within weeks, started working the Fillmore and Avalon Ballrooms. The band appeared at the historic 1967 Monterey Pop Festival a mere six months later. Three months after that, his best friend from growing up in Dallas, Texas and going to college in Madison, Wisconsin, showed up and joined the band, Boz Scaggs. The debut album by the renamed Steve Miller Band, "Children of the Future," established the group with the burgeoning FM rock underground radio.

With tracks such as "Living In the U.S.A.," "Space Cowboy," "Going to Mexico" and others, Miller became a staple of underground radio as the phenomenon spread across the country. He worked every small theater and psychedelic dungeon in the country and then worked them again. When "The Joker" finally landed Miller on the best-selling charts and AM radio, he had been on the road doing five shows a week for five years.

With bassist Turner and drummer Mallaber, on the "Fly Like An Eagle" tour, Miller added guitarist David Denny, keyboardist Byron Allred and harmonica player Norton Buffalo, a musician he ran across at a jam session in San Rafael who began a musical association with Miller that continues to this day. It was Miller's first tour with his own sound and lighting. The set design featured a triptych-style rear projection screens and laser effects that drew favorable comparisons with Elton John and Led Zeppelin for state-of-the-art concert production. Without an opening act, the Steve Miller Band played two and a half to three hour shows with one intermission.

The tour started at the small theaters that had been his specialty since his days as underground rock hero and hitless wonder. When the tour rolled into New York's Beacon Theater on June 12, 1976, the first single from the album, "Take the Money and Run," was just starting up the charts. As the singles exploded off the album, one after the other, Miller grew out of the theaters into hockey rinks and basketball arenas. When his record company released "Book of Dreams," the next album originally recorded at the same sessions that produced "Fly Like An Eagle," a short year later, Miller was headed for football stadiums. His opportunity had not been wasted. At the Beacon Theater, the night of the original King Biscuit Flower Hour broadcast, it was all just starting to come true.

February 2006

Boz Scaggs

Boz Sings the Blues

Boz Scaggs' new album is a surprising return to his pre-pop roots

I've heard all the stories, but you can't prove anything by me. In more than thirty years, Boz Scaggs has always been nothing but a scrupulous gentleman with me. He is always wary about letting his guard down, but he opens up talking about misic.

BOZ SCAGGS STILL REMEMBERS THE FIRST TIME he saw Ray Charles. Out of the 3,000 people in the Dallas auditorium, the 15-year-old Scaggs was one of perhaps a half- dozen white faces.

"There was ozone in the air," Scaggs recalled. "It was snapping in that room." With saxophonists David "Fathead" Newman and Hank Crawford fronting the large, brassy band, the genius of soul was, Scaggs said, "at the peak of his dynamism."

295

A woman sitting next to him, caught up in the rapture, innocently took his arm and squeezed. "I was from a segregated little farm town in north Texas," he said. "I had very little contact with Afro-Americans, black people, in my life."

Swept up in the spellbinding charm, the mysterious but encompassing allure of this raw, vital music, Scaggs knew things would never be the same for him. "It gave me some hint, some clue, to what my life might be like if my life was perfect," he said.

When "Come On Home" (Virgin, $16.99) is released on Tuesday, the suave balladeer of "Silk Degrees" makes a surprising return to the bliss of rhythm and blues with a startlingly authentic set of songs originally recorded by Jimmy Reed, Bobby "Blue" Bland and T-Bone Walker. Already radio has picked up on it; it was the album "most added" to playlists in the country last week.

While many rock stars have paid tribute to their roots in this fashion – including the 1994 No. 1 album by Eric Clapton, "From the Cradle" – what makes this album surprising is that Scaggs is customarily associated with sleek pop ballads, not the kind of intensely soulful, richly evocative music on his new album.

"I've always looked to the rhythm and blues as my teacher," Scaggs said in his South of Market studio. "From my first love of the music, I listened to the black stations. As R&B matured, it became more sophisticated. The chord styles became more progressive as the '60s entered the '70s. That's how I learned to write the songs that I write."

In fact, the first record that put the former Steve Miller Band member on the map as a solo artist was an extraordinary, blistering blues song from his unjustly overlooked 1969 solo debut, "Loan Me a Dime," a 12-minute blues epic that featured Duane Allman on lead guitar.

While the album itself sold next to nothing – and isn't even available on CD – that track found its way onto the playlists of the burgeoning FM rock radio stations of the day and has followed Scaggs around like a stray dog ever since, a piece apparently out of synch with everything else that made him famous.

But Scaggs has always been a blues singer at heart. His explosive, tight quintet that played Bay Area clubs in the early '70s was a powerhouse little blues-rock combo, before he headed off in the direction of the highly polished pop productions that led the way to the multimillion-selling 1975 album "Silk Degrees," which made Scaggs a staple of the elegant pop of the era. It is an avenue he continued to pursue with diminishing returns until the 1994 album "Some Change," his first record in six years, reversed this decline.

Ironically, it was "Some Change" – a title that reflected the contents; some change, not necessarily a lot – that led, in part, to his return home to pure rhythm and blues. For the first time in many years, Scaggs pulled out his guitar for those sessions.

"I surprised myself," he said. "I used to pride myself on being a guitar player when I had my band working seven nights a week. I had the dexterity, that magic connection between the brain and the fingers. But at a point in my career, I elected to bring in studio players and played less and less guitar myself. But I love the guitar – it's one of the reasons I took up music in the first place."

Rediscovering the guitar started Scaggs thinking about playing R&B again. "Every once in a while you get to play a wild card if you have a career that's long enough," he said. "If you have enough radio hits, you get to put out a greatest-hits album. If you're any good at live concerts, you get to put out a live album. Or you can do the `Sinatra Sings Gershwin' or `Ella Sings Cole Porter' thing. And this is `Boz Gets to Do His R&B Album.' Ordinarily I just steal all the ideas from the R&B guys and make my own stuff."

He consulted with Harry Duncan, a little-known behind-the- scenes figure in the Bay Area community for the past quarter century. Duncan, who has managed Van Morrison, Captain Beefheart and the Neville Brothers, went to work as the booker at Slim's, the 11th Street nightclub that Scaggs financed, when it opened in 1989. Duncan's weekly Tuesday night KUSF roots radio show, "Treasures Untold," gives him a regular opportunity to flex what Scaggs calls his "encyclopedic knowledge" of the music. "We've had an ongoing music dialogue for many years," Scaggs said. Scaggs was leery of treating the material they selected in an offhand manner. He is notoriously scrupulous with his recordings; he spent a year making "Some Change." And he believed the prospects of recording "classical rhythm and blues" posed unique challenges.

"There's a simplicity to most of these songs that's deceptive," he said. "There's a lot of volatility – it's extremely emotional. If it's not handled correctly, it can become superfluous in a flash, untrue, false. Many people have tried to re-create it and they were deceived by its simplicity. The only way is to make it your own."

Scaggs touches on a variety of blues styles – from the uptown Texas big-band sound of Bland to the New Orleans R&B of Fats Domino, the deep soul of Memphis' Stax/Volt and the Chicago blues of Junior Wells. Every so often the sound of the organ recalls the Memphis soul records of Al Green and Ann Peebles – not surprising, since the overdubs were played by the organist from those sessions,

Charlie Hodges.

Scaggs has already road-tested himself as a bluesman, sneaking off on club dates around Northern California outposts such as Chico, Healdsburg and Eureka with his new blues band and singing nothing but the blues – "The most fun tour I've had in years," he said. He will put together a more formal tour this summer mixing material from the new album, the Scaggs standards and some of the blues he was throwing around with guitarist Steve Freund and harmonica player Apple-jack on these recent dates.

This self-assured blues project is only another sign that Scaggs obviously feels comfortable with himself. His two sons have graduated from high school and are working in the music business. He and his second wife, Dominique, have settled in Napa, although they still maintain their San Francisco home.

Even the record company is enthusiastic about the album. The only suggestion made by label executives was that Scaggs include a couple of original songs alongside the certified R&B classics. He tweaked an old Robert Cray song and managed to eke out a pair of acceptable new songs of his own, leery of how they would stand up against the works of the masters. "They were the hardest songs I've ever written," he said.

But when Scaggs speaks about having to "possess" these songs, he is really talking about the ability to get inside the emotional reality of the compositions. He knows this music rejects the imitators, reveals the phonies and ridicules the poseurs. And Scaggs, a careful, deliberate man, was not about to join their ranks.

"You have to come to possess these songs and they to possess you," he said. "It seems easy to fall into the emotion of them, but it is daunting. Possessing these things is not easy – you can go way off base. There's nothing quite as disappointing to me as hearing someone sing Jimmy Reed badly. It's immoral."

Sunday Datebook | April 6, 1997

Sammy

Post-Van Halen, Hagar's been riding high on his own tequila. Now comes rock enshrinement.

Sammy and I go way back. He moved to San Francisco with a college friend of mine. He once gave out my home phone number to a Van Halen audience – he didn't like the review – and the next time I saw him, he screamed at me across a crowded room "Joel, I need your new home phone number."

SAMMY HAGAR GETS NO RESPECT.

The self-styled Red Rocker is a blue-collar, workingman's rock star from decidedly down-market Fontana, a hardscrabble old Southern California steel town that makes Asbury Park look like the beach resort it once was. He does not summer in the Hamptons visiting the Spielbergs or make the jet-set scene with Mick or Elton. But as of Monday, he will belong to the Rock and Roll Hall of Fame.

"Would you have ever guessed?" he says. "I wouldn't have either. I think I carved out a real stupid career in the sense that I was never loved by the press. I've received some awards with Van Halen. We got a Grammy, an American Music Award, MTV Awards and all that stuff. But Sammy Hagar is not the Bruce Springsteen kind of guy.

"I don't know how I screwed up. I haven't screwed up actually. I always had the reputation as a goofball, no respect as an artist, things like that. I never earned that," he continues. "I told my band when I left Van Halen: 'I'm going to warn you guys about one thing – the venture we are going into now, this party we are throwing, we are never going to get respect from anyone. But the fans are going to love us. The fans are going to flock to us. We're going to be as big as anyone, but no one is going to respect us for doing it.' And, sure enough, I was right."

It is pouring rain outside Hagar's Mill Valley mountaintop home, where he has lived for more than 30 years, and his wife, Kari, is building a fire. But Hagar is wearing shorts and a T-shirt from the cantina he owns in Cabo San Lucas, Cabo Wabo, with a tattoo of the Mexican cantina's logo peeking out under his rolled-up sleeves. "I'm in denial," he says, glaring at the downpour outside.

Tanned, trim and sporting dyed-blond shoulder-length hair and a shaggy goatee, Hagar, 59, speaks in staccato bursts, punctuated by laughter. He radiates maniacal energy and talks quickly, as if he can't quite keep up with his own thoughts.

He only recently returned to the Bay Area after spending a year living in Mexico with his wife and their two young daughters (he has two grown sons from a previous marriage). In May, he celebrates the third anniversary of his second Cabo Wabo at Harrah's in Lake Tahoe. He is building another in Fresno – Fresno? "I've been to Fresno. There's nothing to do. I'm opening a Cabo Wabo. They're going to have something to do." – and is looking at other possible locations, especially beach resort towns. He is also planning a resort of his own in Cabo.

"If I was ever a genius at anything," he says, "I found everything I like to do and where I want to live and I rolled it all together. I got a business. I can play music at my business. I love tequila and that whole lifestyle, the Mexican food. I've got a Mexican restaurant. I have the tequila that goes with it. I have the whole lifestyle rolled into one. I love that Cabo Wabo lifestyle, which is beach all day, party all night."

His Cabo Wabo brand tequila is the No. 2 best-selling premium tequila in the United States. He has made, he says, "way more" in the liquor business than he ever did in music. But Hagar went into the tequila business more an enthusiastic fan than anything. He first tasted the nectar of pure agave during his first visit to the sleepy Baja California fishing village in 1982. He began producing handmade tequila for his bar, which he opened 10 years later, and started importing in 1999. He sold 140,000 cases last year. But tequila is more than booze to Hagar.

"I swear by it," he says. "Tequila's a great high. Every booze has got a different trip. Beer's got a thing. Wine's got a thing. Champagne has a nice bubbly thing, but it's a short window. It's a quick up and down. Tequila, if you maintain it when you're drinking it and you don't get too plastered, get over that crazy edge, and you just keep that good buzz going – wait in between shots, do a couple shots, wait awhile, just sip – you can last the night. It's really an up high. It makes you want to have fun. It makes you want to jump on the table and start dancing.

"And when you play for an audience of 10,000 people that are all on the same drug like the old Fillmore days – where everybody was on acid and smoking dope and they were all in tune; the band would go up and play, everybody went up with them and came down with them – you get on that emotional ride. Tequila is the only one that I think does that and because my brand is so strong with my fans, I get to experience that. So when we play, especially in Cabo, everybody's drunk on tequila, including my band, and it's an awesome experience. It's like wow."

Hagar's tequila got something he never had – good reviews. Cabo Wabo consistently wins awards and blind taste tests, Hagar says. This month, he will introduce a limited edition, Cabo Uno, made from only the heart of the agave plant that will come in a crystal decanter and sell for more than $200.

"No one can do what I do because to everyone else, it's a business," he says. "For me, it's become a business, but originally rock 'n' roll was my business. And so when I made tequila, I could do everything the right way. I could waste product. I could throw a lot away. You drain off the barrel. The bottom of the barrel is worse. You want the middle cut. We've always done it that way.

"For me, it was like a hobby. I had rock 'n' roll money. So I did it as a luxury and that's half the reason why Cabo Wabo is so good and pure because, like I said, I never had to make any money with it. I just got lucky. I didn't have to. I just wanted to make the best tequila in the world – big ego trip. It's like the Rothchilds of wine. Like the Rothchilds need money. They try to make the best frigging wine in the planet. They raised the bar is what they did."

For all his business expansion plans and aspirations to start a charitable foundation for children's charities, Hagar is still all rock 'n' roll. He returned the night before from performing in front of 87,000 NASCAR fans at the California Speedway in Fontana. He played a brief set before NASCAR's Auto Club 500 and Fox TV broadcast him playing "I Can't Drive 55" live before the race. The speedway stands on the site of the former Kaiser Steel plant where Hagar's father worked, the stage right about where the open hearth was, reckoned his brother-in-law, whose father also worked at the plant.

Hagar made it a family day, entertained many nieces and nephews and spent the night in the guest room of a niece in nearby Riverside. He got a thunderous roar from the hometown crowd, larger than either race car driver Dale Earnhardt Jr. or grand marshal Kevin Costner (or any of the other TV and movie stars also appearing, whose names he could not remember the next day).

He keeps a band on salary year-round and rehearses two or three days a week. But he is bowing out of the record wars, after putting a year's work into last year's "Livin' It Up," which lofted three Top 10 radio hits, but still sold only a paltry 57,000 copies. "The record industry sales for a guy like me are over even though my records are as good as they've ever been," he says.

Instead Hagar thinks he'll give away new recordings to fans on the Internet and just keep touring. He envisions a world dotted with Cabo Wabos scattered across his favorite places – Atlantic City, Orlando, Hawaii – where he plays extend-

Sammy Hagar

ed runs. Fans already flock from all over the world to cram into his 1,000-capacity club in Mexico for his notorious annual birthday parties, which last for days, where there is never any admission charge. The city of Cabo San Lucas gave Hagar an award for his contribution to tourism.

"I want more of them, so I can go play those places," he says. "Wouldn't it be great? I can play any of these places as many nights as I want. I can go to town, stay there and play every night until I'm tired of that town and then go back home and then go to another one. That's my concept. That's my retirement instead of playing golf."

Retirement is a long way away; enshrinement comes next week. Hagar will be inducted in the Hall of Fame as a vocalist for Van Halen, who were the most awesome Top of the Pops heavy metal heroes going in 1985 when the group jettisoned vocalist David Lee Roth in favor of Hagar, who had already established a successful solo career following his spell as lead vocalist of '70s heavy metal prototype Montrose. Hagar rode that juggernaut down the backside of the bell curve for 11 years, including four multiplatinum albums. He returned to the fold for one eventful 2004 tour. Otherwise, Van Halen after Hagar has not amounted to much. There was talk of a reunion tour this summer with Roth, who hasn't exactly prospered since leaving the band, but Hagar says that has fallen apart already. He doesn't know if erstwhile band mates Eddie and Alex Van Halen will even attend, but Hagar says he will go to the ceremony with former Van Halen bassist Michael Anthony.

"He's my good buddy," Hagar says. "It's not him and us against the others. He got thrown out of the band, too. I don't think Ed and Al are going. The word I got from our management is that now they said they're not going. Roth'll be there. S – , he's there right now. He's already got a room. I'm fine with him. I'm fine with Ed and Al. I don't talk to Eddie. I'm not mad at Eddie. I still love the guy. He's just hard to get along with.

"When we were all going, when they were gonna do their tour with Roth that just blew out – I could have told you that; I bet money that would never happen. I would love to see it. They owe it to the fans. They should do it. I believe it's the right thing for Van Halen to do is to do a David Lee Roth reunion. Look how long it's been. It's never worked. This is the fourth abortion. There's a lot of fans out there and they've been waiting a long time for this. And it's gotta happen someday. We did it – they should do it. Before it blew out, everybody was going. But the word now was, from Ed and Al, 'we're not playing.' "

The band will be inducted by Velvet Revolver (after Red Hot Chili Peppers were unavailable), who will perform a medley of Van Halen music.

Hagar praised the other 2007 inductees "I'm really happy about Patti Smith," he says. "That's one thing I like about the Hall of Fame. I never expected to be inducted. I really didn't, I knew Van Halen would eventually somehow, someway, but it was still hard for me to imagine Sammy Hagar being part of it. But it is. I'm so honored. But someone like Patti Smith, who really had such a short, intense career. She did it so cool. She really deserves it for being such a rebel and being a girl at that time. She was cool. I think it's cool that they honor those kinds of people. Some awards shows don't. They go with the most commercial. Half the people don't know who Patti Smith is, but I think it's awesome. She was a true artist, a Neil Young kind of artist, where, s – , man, you do it my way or forget it. I like that. I'm almost that kind of artist. For some reason, my art doesn't project that. But I'm that kind of person. I never cop out. I never sell out. I never endorse things. It's so funny. What did I do wrong? Or right?

"R.E.M. – another artsy band. I like R.E.M., they're not my kind of band, but they made some great records. Grandmaster Flash. I don't own a Grandmaster Flash record, but he was really the innovator. I like who they're recognizing this year. The Ronettes. How long have they been waiting? For Sammy Hagar to be a part of that crazy, eclectic group, I like that part of it. If it was Bruce Springsteen, U2 and Sammy Hagar, I'd be this thin, little guy – oh, man, I'm going to get no respect at this thing. But with this eclectic group, I kinda fit in, quirky-wise."

For Hagar, this is a happy ending, unequivocal and undeniable recognition and acknowledgment, permanent vindication, a Get Out of Jail Free card that trumps a lifetime of naysayers and petty bourgeois critics. At long last ... respect.

"This is something that is so etched in stone that when you say I'm a Hall of Famer," Hagar says, "you have to live up to it. I think that every time I step up to a microphone from that day on, I have to live up to it. I think I'm going to have to be a f – Hall of Famer."

San Francisco Chronicle | *Wednesday, March 7, 2007*

A rowdy blues mama

'I Don't Want to Be a Star' Says Blues Singer *Bonnie Raitt*

Years later, I mentioned to Bonnie Raitt that I had conducted an interview with her about her first album among the first few articles I did for the pink section. "Imagine that," she said. "And we both still got our same jobs."

DON'T LET HER LOOKS FOOL YOU. Behind that golden-haired, dimpled face lurks a lusty, rowdy blues mama. So what if she went to Radcliffe, her heart is in the Mississippi delta.

Bonnie Raitt, 23, is the living incarnation of the lady blues singers of the '20s and '30s; the Memphis Minnies that could play and sing the pants off their male counterparts.

For some reason – no blues scholars can satisfactorily explain why – female blues singers have slipped entirely out of the music. Once women like Big Maybelle, Chippie Hill, Sippie Wallace, Victoria Spivey and, of course, Bessie Smith were staples in the blues world. But since World War II few women even recorded, let alone had much of an impact in the blues market.

"I just had a career dumped in my lap," Ms. Raitt said simply. "I fill a vacuum; there aren't any chicks singing blues."

Her two Warners albums have met critical acclaim and the second is steadily climbing the charts. Bonnie, born to a show biz family, is aware and cautious of the pitfalls of stardom.

"I don't want to be a star," she said, straightforward. "The music business works to make you a star and I don't want any part of that. I've seen the whole trip."

Her father, John Raitt, has led a successful career singing in musical comedies as long as she can remember. Her father's profession, however, had no influence on her blues singing.

Her interest in blues and bottleneck guitar playing began academically and developed into a professional casually. All the time she was at Radcliffe, she thought she would be going into African Studies.

One summer vacation she played a few folk clubs, just for the extra money, and on returning to school, found her interest in studies had met a serious decline. She began working, off and on, as opening act as folk clubs around the eastern seaboard and only decided to record when the clubs told her they needed recording acts to open. Like it or not, she had to record.

She chose Warners because they guaranteed her complete artistic control.

Bonnie came to the blues through a route that has to be a modern classic. Raised in Los Angeles, her liberal parents placed her in a semi-Bohemian summer camp while they toured in summer stock circuits. There she discovered folk music of the early sixties: Bob Dylan, John Hammond, Dave Van Ronk.

"I wanted to be a beatnik," she said of growing up in L.A., "and all my friends were going to beach parties."

Broadway beckoned her father and the whole family moved east. There she attended a progressive private school and went on to Radcliffe. "I thought Cambridge would be the hippest place to go."

"In Cambridge," she said, "everyone had intellectual pretensions. Mine was my blues record collection and being able to play every? single Charlie Patton lick."

Bonnie seems earnest in her desire to expose the past masters artists she admires and to that effect has jammed at the Philadelphia Folk Festival with Mississippi Fred McDowell and brought aging Sippie Wallace out of retirement to join her at last year's Ann Arbor Blues Festival. She hopes to use any influence she may gain to "get people on the bill who ordinarily aren't commercial enough."

She refers to her "socialist orientation" when explaining she would like to see promoters charge less for concerts.

"I'm not a flaming, uncompromising radical," she said, "I don't want to play on bills with some folk singer who plays '500 Miles' all his life."

"I'm sorta hoping I don't have a hit record. People like Don McLean and even James Taylor get bad reviews now. I want my following based on years and years of live performances.

"I'm not that good. Or rather, I'm not that excited about what I do. But it's fun. Like getting paid for having a party every night.

"I just want to keep going so I can bet messed up every night for the next 20 years."

Sunday Datebook | December 31, 1972

Bonnie Raitt

Bonnie Raitt: Secure at Heart

We did the interview at a Sausalito sushi restaurant, empty in the middle of a weekday afternoon. She pulled up in a beatup old Toyota she borrowed from singer Pamela Polland.

BONNIE RAITT MAY BE THE BEST-SELLING ARTIST on the Capitol Records roster, but that comes as news to her. In fact, her 1991 release, "Luck of the Draw," sold more than 5 million copies, even more than her 1989 Grammy-winning, popular breakthrough, "Nick of Time."

"They tell me how many records I sell, but it doesn't mean anything to me," she said, sipping green tea last week at a Sausalito sushi bar. "Let me put it this way: When the lights go down at Shoreline, it's the same as New George's. What it means to me is my gig is secure."

Old habits die hard. Raitt, who lives in the same modest Hollywood hills home she has owned for the past 20 years, went record shopping recently and saw the $150 boxed set of Billie Holiday recordings. "I thought, 'I can't afford that,'" she said, laughing.

With her new album, "Longing in Their Hearts," to be released Tuesday, the leadoff track, "Love Sneaking Up on You," was the most added song on three radio formats last week. After a 20-year apprenticeship, Raitt, whose 1971 Warner Bros. debut initially sold a measly 12,000 copies, has become the leading female singer-songwriter in the record business.

She remains the bright, snappy wise guy she always has been, quick with the witty riposte, tooling around Marin County in a friend's borrowed car. Raitt takes her ascension into the rarefied ranks of the industry's best-sellers with a calm equanimity. She may have learned to wear a baseball cap to disguise her trademark white swatch of hair curling over her forehead, to not turn her head at traffic lights and to sit in corners at restaurants, but nothing can shake her commitment to honest, bluesy music.

" 'Nick of Time' was basically a better version of albums I had already been making," she said. "There's no way to alter my taste in music. At the time, I didn't think 'Nick of Time' was anything particularly special."

She found herself astonished to discover the release greeted by a full-page review in Newsweek and a half-page accolade in the New York Times. "Even before the Grammys it had sold nearly a million," she said. "I was surprised."

Some people facing the prospect of recording a multiplatinum album might experience a certain degree of anxiety, but not Raitt. "Piece of cake," she said, when asked how the recording to her latest album went.

"Oh, I suppose I shouldn't say that," she continued. "But making these records has been enjoyable since this unit came together to make `Nick of Time.' The only difficult part was looking for the tunes."

Raitt said she listened to thousands of songs, helped in the process by her longtime associate, Bay Area broadcaster Bonnie Simmons. Driving around in her car auditioning tapes, she tossed the ones she wanted to listen to again behind the passenger seat, the ones she didn't want behind her seat and the ones she wanted to listen to right away in the front seat.

"I went through reams and reams of stuff, the cream of the crop," she said. "I get the best because I sell tons of records now. But it's like fishing – to find a good one is so hard."

With a rhythm section composed of drummer Ricky Fataar and bassist Hutch Hutchinson, the basic session group revolved around keyboardists Scott Thurston from the Jackson Browne band and guitarist George Marinelli from the Bruce-Hornsby group, with Raitt adding occasional slide guitar. Producer Don Was and engineer Ed Cherney complete the crew. A few guests, such as Levon Helm of The Band, David Crosby, guitarist Richard Thompson and blues harp ace Charlie Musselwhite spice up the mix.

"We recorded `Nick of Time' in five days," she said. "This time, the tracks were done in less than a week. Two of the songs were demos I made to play for the band. The agony is all beforehand. I don't know if I'm going to find those tunes or write ones that are going to hold up. All my vocals were live. There was really no pressure – nobody looking down my shirt, er, over my shoulder."

Venerable record producer Jerry Wexler calls Raitt "Little Miss Payback" because she has been scrupulous in sharing her spotlight with performers she admires. She took bluesman Charles Brown along as opening act on the "Nick of Time" tour and used folk singer John Prine on the "Luck of the Draw" dates. Bruce Hornsby will open the U.S. segment of the yearlong tour that starts in Europe in May.

"I'm up on this pedestal," she said, "so it's `C'mon up, Delbert.' That's why I recorded the Richard Thompson tune on the new album. After all this time, people should have found out about him. I thought it would be like, `C'mon in, we're all on the radio again,' but two years later John Hiatt still isn't known. I don't know how to explain how I broke through."

She merrily appears on other people's records, lending her newfound stellar presence to throw a little light on otherwise worthy projects, even though she admits she has had to rein in the duets a little. "I can't be barbecue sauce on everybody's records," she said. "How do I tell Tammy Wynette I can't do her duet because I just did Willie Nelson's? But I am obligated to these people at Capitol and radio will often treat these duets like the new Bonnie Raitt record, where in the old days nobody would have played it anyway."

She also spends a lot of time boosting political causes. "There's a responsibility now that I'm in this position," she said. "I get hit on all the time and I end up not having any time off. But if the choice is between spending a weekend with my father or stopping nuclear power, it really isn't difficult. You have to weigh the private life with the public persona."

Married to actor Michael O'Keefe, who recently landed a regular part in the TV series "Roseanne," Raitt rents a home in Marin County with him for half the year, and they spend as much time as they can in the Bay Area. O'Keefe is also a a poet, and recently finished his first screenplay. "I get first crack at all his poetry," said Raitt, who fashioned the blues-rocker title track of her new album from one of her husband's pieces. "I think he thought it was going to be a ballad, "she said.

Sunday Datebook | March 20, 1994

Nilsson Ratings: Injured, Brilliant

The interview had to wait until we watched the latest episode of the PBS series, "The Ascent of Man." I asked him about the strange single he did with Cher that was produced by Phil Spector. "Have you heard it?" he said. "How is it?"

HARRY NILSSON WORE A SHORT FOREARM CAST on one arm, and had his badly sprained ankle taped tight. The injuries were the results of two separate, unrelated incidents.

He sprained the ankle the night before, dancing drunkenly in his home and falling down. He injured his hand on an over-zealous inebreit in a bar. The forearm cast didn't slow him down at all, but the sprained ankle left him to canes and a wheelchair for personal mobility.

The brilliant vocalist was ensconced in a suite at the Mark Hopkins Hotel on a small jaunt to help promote his latest album, "Duit On Mon Dei (formerly God's Greatest Hits)," his 12th LP for RCA Victor Records.

"How many all-night movie stations are there up here?" he asked as the TV rolled from "The Best of Groucho" into the 1950 Marlon Brando film, "The Men." "I watch between 40 and 80 hours of televisions a week," he said matter-of-factly. "Not so much prime-time shows; mostly movies and game shows."

"There are only four songwriters who can write a line that can really crack you up," Harry said. "I consider myself one, along with Randy Newman, John Lennon and Frank Zappa."

Between television shows (the set was shut down after "Ascent of Man" and not turned on again until "Groucho"), Nilsson discussed his album, his fascinating career, and a few of the multitude of his drunken exploits.

He shook his head and whistled at the thought of listening to one of his old demo tapes. "Whew," he said, "such blazing high notes . . ." His voice trailed off as he reached across the table to knock some ashes off his cigarette, and he muttered lowly, "since donated to whiskey."

Nilsson broke into the recording business as a singer on demo tapes. Song publishers always need fresh singers to cut demonstrations of songs the publishers would like other singers to record.

Since selling the song depends a lot on the strength of the demo tape, the demo singer better have more than a few chops of his own if he expects to work much. Tony Orlando and Carole King are two other artists to come from this area of the record industry.

Nilsson spent seven years working nights at a bank computer center in the San Fernando Valley processing checks from all over southern California, and hustling music business every other day (alternating with sleep).

Despite the enormous success of "Everybody's Talking" – a Fred Neil song Nilsson sung that became a smash following its inclusion as theme of the film "Midnight Cowboy" – Nilsson remained known mostly to connoisseurs until producer Richard Perry and he collaborated for two gold record albums, "Nilsson Schmilsson" and "Son of Schmilsson." The former included the Grammy-winning "Without You" as well as the incredible "Coconut" – both giant hits.

San Francisco Chronicle | *April 13, 1975*

CHAPTER 9

California Classics

Eddie Cochran
Dick Dale
Glen Campbell

Eddie Cochran

When I met Sharon Sheeley, her mantle and walls were still covered with pictures of Eddie, thrity years after the car crash – rock and roll's Miss Havisham. She is without doubt one of the great untold stories – the queen of '50s rock and roll Hollywood.

Eddie Cochran

SHARON SHEELEY MET EDDIE COCHRAN after the Los Angeles date on the tour. The Newport Beach teen and her sister were visiting Don Everly, laid up in his room at the Hollywood Hawaiian with the Asian flu, when somebody knocked on the door. "It's Cochran," the voice announced and in he walked, gun on hip, doing his quick draw routine to cheer up the ailing Everly. He wore a vintage .45 Buntline, the kind of gun Wyatt Earp used at the O.K. Corral, and Cochran was gunfighter fast on the draw. He didn't even seem to notice Sheeley. She was smitten instantly, telling her sister on the ride home that night that she was going to marry him.

Six months later, seventeen year-old Shari Sheeley was the composer of "Poor Little Fool," the next single by Ricky Nelson, the hottest thing in rock and roll this side of Elvis, and Capehart was looking for songs for Cochran. None of the five singles since "Sittin' In The Balcony" had done much – including "Drive-In Show," "Jeannie, Jeannie, Jeannie," or even "Twenty Flight Rock," when it was finally released – and Cochran badly needed a hit. Sheeley had a song Capehart thought might work and he arranged a meeting between songwriter and singer. Sheeley showed up at Cochran's hotel room terrified, awestruck and lovesick. Cochran handed her his guitar and she explained she didn't play. "What do you play?" asked Cochran. "Monopoly," said a shrinking Sheeley. Cochran coaxed her through a version of "Love Again," her voice cracking, and she ran out crying. "You just chased away a million dollars," said Capehart. He went after her and soothed some of her shattered nerves and he did record the song. "Love Again" was the intended A-side of his next release in

June 1958. On the back was a little offhand piece Cochran had been dabbling with for some time called "Summertime Blues."

"Summertime Blues" captured Cochran's personality. It had leaked out on everything he did, but for the first time, one of his records was all Eddie Cochran. The smart-ass smirk, the sarcasm, wiseguy slant – it was all pure Cochran, right down to the Kingfish voice he dropped into on the punch lines to the verses ("...I'd like to help you, son, but you're too young to vote"). He used the same voice when he answered his phone at home ("Hello dere"). But the record not only summed up Cochran's character, it defined rock and roll attitude. It became, almost immediately, one of the cornerstones of the literature.

The record didn't even chart until two months after its release and peaked at number eight six weeks later. But it was more than a hit; it was a career. It was also an annointing anticipated for fully two years, so it hardly came as a surprise. For Cochran, it was business as usual. More than most of his fellow first generation rockers, Cochran was a studio animal who had logged hundreds of hours playing on other people's sessions. He sat in some Gene Vincent sessions that April at Capitol Studios, essentially took charge, rearranged the songs and sang the main background harmony vocal part with the group.

But he was like that. Drummer Earl Palmer remembered that Cochran did not hesitate to take apart an expensive Rene Hall arrangement if he felt like it. His command of his instruments extended to the studio. He was comfortable overdubbing different guitar parts on experimental recordings like his seismic "Eddie's Blues," which anticipates the British blues revival by half a dozen years, or "Fourth Man Theme," his multi-tracked take on the old zither specialty.

He relished collaboration. He loved playing guitar on demo recordings by songwriter Johnny Burnette, who was the first signing to Capehart's Freedom label that Liberty bankrolled in the wake of "Summertime Blues." Cochran sang demos for aspiring songwriter Baker Knight, a down and out Southerner living in the same Hollywood building as Capehart, the Park Sunset. Knight was about to give it all up and go home when Ricky Nelson heard Cochran singing the demo of his song "Lonesome Town."

While in New York for an eleven-night run opening Christmas Day 1958 at Loew's State for impresario Alan Freed appearing with the Everlys, Dion and the Belmonts, Chuck Berry, the Flamingos, Jackie Wilson and others, Cochran shot a song – his next single, "Teenage Heaven" – in his third movie, "Go Johnny Go," a low-budget Freed quickie.

Sheeley flew to New York that Christmas, determined to make Eddie Cochran notice her. He had been friendly when they bumped into one another, but Sheeley wanted him to ring in the New Year with a different perspective. She rummaged madly through her entire wardrobe to find the exact right outfit to attract his attention at the New Year's Eve party after the show that night, before giving up and slipping into her old blue jeans. Into a sea of chiffon and crinoline Sheeley walked, wearing her Levis, and the minute Cochran laid his eyes on Sheeley, he was hers. Cochran asked her to marry him before he ever kissed her.

Connie Smith got married and quit the road. Cochran pulled together a new band, dubbed the Kelly Four, and they backed him on his first single of 1959, "Teenage Heaven." The death of his pal Buddy Holly hit Cochran hard and he went into the studio and cut the mawkish recitation, "Three Stars," a weepy tribute to the dead rockers Holly, Ritchie Valens and the Big Hopper that was never released during his lifetime. Like a lot of rock and roll musicians in that year, Cochran was struggling and searching. His songwriting collaboration with fiance Sheeley, "Somethin' Else," shot through with the trademark Cochran combination of insolence and envy, battled its way up to a mid-chart position. He left a lot of tape on the shelf, like the super macho "My Way" or the formulaic "Weekend," whose writers, Bill and Doree Post of Connie Stevens' "Sixteen Reasons," must have had Cochran in mind when they wrote it. He tried various experiments in the studio, including a number of quirky instrumentals and even a couple of blues sessions (his "Milk Cow Blues" easily outdoes the Elvis version in nuance and detail). Even so, his boisterous, confident cover of Ray Charles, hardly a household name at the time, for his next single, "Hallelujah I Love Her So," must have confused the conservative, narrow-minded label. Liberty sent boy wonder producer Snuff Garrett back into the studio with the tapes and he dumped goopy strings on the top, right over Cochran's guitar solo. Despite his bravura performance, the record didn't even nick the bottom of the charts. America wasn't listening.

In England, producer Jack Good wanted real American rock and roll stars for his new pop program, "Boy Meets Girls." Very few were available. When Vincent arrived in December 1959, Good was surprised to discover he hardly qualified as teen idol material. With bad skin, bad teeth, and bad hair, Vincent was a craggy-faced, almost meek young man in bulky cardigan sweaters who hobbled around with a bum leg injured in a motorcycle crash. He also discovered that Vincent had no prior commitments in the States, that his career had instantly disappeared. "Be Bop a Lula" was a long, long three and a half years before. Good tucked Vincent into a tight black leather suit, hung a large silver medallion around his neck and told him to strike dramatic poses onstage, not to try and move around too much. The British had never seen anything like it. The stage was set for Cochran's arrival in early January.

"Hallelujah I Love Her So" bombed so badly in the States that, before Eddie left for England, Liberty owner Si Waronker insisted on chairing the Goldstar sessions for Cochran's next release, accompanied by his new protege, Snuff Garrett. Backing Cochran were Jerry Allison and Sonny Curtis of the Crickets, along with Connie Smith. Sheeley attended the session, although they were officially "broken up" at the moment. She had threatened to marry the handsome local disc jockey Jimmy O'Neil. "I'll pack a lunch and come see you sometime," Cochran told her. Cochran and the Crickets cut his "Three Steps To Heaven" and covered a country song that Carl Smith had done, "Cut Across Shorty," for his next single. He left for England the next day.

Cochran tore up the crowds on the double-bill tour. Opening with his back to the audience, guitar slung over his shoulder, silhouetted finger snapping over the introduction, Cochran would launch his show with "Hallelujah I Love Her so," released in England to coincide with his appearances. Strutting across the stage in black leather pants and red velvet vest, he had a full orchestra in the pit and a well-schooled English rock band on the stage backing him and he routinely whipped the crowds into a frothing frenzy. He would play his hits. He played "Eddie's Blues." He would do "Milk Cow Blues" and "What'd I Say," a song entirely unheard on British shores at the time. He seethed his way through "Fever." Sometimes he and Vincent would sing George Jones' "White Lightnin'" together. They walked tall. They were stars of the highest magnitude. It was a magical transformation.

Cochran called Sheeley and they patched things up. She flew to England to witness first-hand this extraordinary acclaim and celebrate her twentieth birthday. For the first time, they slept together. Cochran had his affairs. Phil Everly watched in amazement once as Cochran seduced a flight attendant in the back of the plane mid-flight. Women were everywhere on the road. But Cochran didn't see his future wife the same way. He told Sheeley he wanted to take her back to California so they could be married and return to England, where more dates were already waiting for him and Vincent. He told his mother he wouldn't have to go out on the road again after one last tour. He told Capehart he was interested in spending more time producing other artists. These heady, idyllic days for young Eddie Cochran would not last long.

As plucky and good-natured as he may have been, there was also a dark, gloomy side to this Byronic young man. Capehart always remembered later that when he bawled out Cochran for showing up late to what turned out to be his last recording session, Cochran turned uncharacteristically oblique. "Who cares?" he scowled. "It doesn't matter. None of this matters." He may have held secret premonitions of his own death. He inscribed the inside cover of his Bible, right after the words "For God so loved the world that he gave his only begotten son..." "...and Eddie Cochran." Sheeley walked in on him in a hotel room in England, listening to Buddy Holly records, crying and mumbling about seeing Buddy again sometime soon. He always signed his autographs the same way - a plea more than a promise - "Don't Forget Me, Eddie Cochran." It hasn't happened yet.

Eddie Cochran: Legends Of the 20th Century (2000)

Dick Dale

These were supposed to be the liner notes to "Tribal
Thunder," the 1994 comeback by the King of the Surf Guitars
that I co-produced with Scott Mathews

DRIVING DOWN THE BARREN STRETCH OF ROADWAY a few miles south of March
Air Force Base outside Riverside on the edge of the Southern California desert, the
bright yellow sign jumped into view: "DICK DALE'S." Underneath a list of attractions promised Cold Beer, Entertainment Girls, Dancing, Food, Pool...

Such regulation roadhouses were already near extinct even in 1970, but the
whole scene was something out of the past. Bar girls served beers from an elevated
service bar that made them bend over and expose their cleavage. Onstage the band
wore uniforms and did steps. Dick Dale himself fancied stage suits, one black and
white checkerboard number in particular.

This was where the fabled King of the Surf Guitar had come to rest five years
after playing his final Southern California concerts not far away at the Riverside
National Guard Armory. He lived in a trailer in the back and a pen outside held his
exotic animals – a young female lion named Elsa, as friendly as an oversized kitty

cat, a couple of mountain lion cubs and an ocelot.

When the first waves of surf music finally washed up on the shore, Dick Dale split for Hawaii in fitful pique, after an enormous fight with his domineering manager/father, where he counted cocoanuts and thought things over. He married a hula dancer and returned Stateside to work Vegas lounges as a Polynesian revue, playing as many as eighteen instruments in the course of a performance – "Dr. Zhivago" on the accordion, the works.

The bar outside Riverside was a long way from the glory days of the Rendez-vous Ballroom, where Dick Dale reigned supreme beginning in 1960 as the first bonafide rock and roll star of Southern California. His album, "Surfer's Choice," released on his own Del-Tone Records with a cover picture showing the man himself shooting a mean curl, spent eighteen months as the best-selling record in Hollywood's top record store, Wallach's Music City, at the corner of Sunset and Vine, mere blocks from the Capitol Tower. When Capitol signed Dick Dale in 1963, the company paid him a $50,000 advance, eclipsing the previous industry record set in 1956 by Elvis Presley. Dick Dale became a star so early, when he appeared on the "Ed Sullivan Show," one of the other acts that night was the Three Stooges.

Even though he was stuck in Riverside, like a king in exile, playing six nights a week for sometimes fewer than a dozen beer guzzlers, he flashed bits and pieces of pure fire, filtered through a Top 40 repertoire of the day that mixed "Get Back" with "Put a Little Love in Your Heart." But he could strike sparks out of the gold-flaked Fender Stratocaster he played left-handed and backwards that Leo Fender himself built for Dale. He plugged it through a worn, battered amplifier and reverb unit of similar vintage and provenance. He just burst out of the tepid, tame sound of the green underpaid band, a sudden buzzing that cut through the brain deep into the synapses before sinking back into the mire of mediocrity that surrounded it.

At the University of California, Riverside campus a strange ritual every spring takes place called Scot's Week. Classes are ignored and faculty and students alike gather off-campus, and on, for drunken outdoor parties, beer kegs and assorted associated behavior – a perfect time for a Dick Dale concert. Many of the now long-haired hippies attending the college were among his final loyal following as teenagers at the National Guard Armory. Dick accepted my invitation not without certain reservation.

During the previous five years, the earth cooled considerably under the rock world – changes Dick Dale watched from a remote distance. He sat behind the sound board that night on a plastic chair watching the opening act, a pair of Jeff

Beck and Eric Clapton clones from the Hispanic ghetto of nearby Colton who blew molten blues licks around like kids tossing a basketball. Dick sat in silence, soaking in his first contact with the new world of rock. He walked backstage grim-faced and quiet. His wife came out of the dressing room holding up a grass skirt, regulation costume for her Polynesian dancing. "No hula tonight," muttered Dale.

He rocked that cafeteria probably as hard as he ever did anything. He played string-busting, blood-letting, blister-raising guitar that left the stunned audience drop-jawed and mind-blown. He used up every existing rock number in his song-book, dropping to his knees and plowing through the staccato volleys that filled the breaks on his self-celebratory "King of the Surf Guitar," the audience cheering and singing along as the background vocalists chanted "from San Bernardino to RIVERSIDE..."

Shaken, unsure what to do for an encore as the crowd stomped their feet, shrieked and whistled, he looked at me backstage with his color drained, eyes watery and lips tight. He had given all. Nothing was left. "Just go out there and tell them you don't know any more songs," I told him. They cheered that even more. As he walked out of the cafeteria, he could hear the crowd yelling in unison "Dick Dale...Dick Dale...Dick Dale."

Buoyed by this eventful re-entry into the realm of rock, Dick and I rented time at a local studio and cut a timid demo tape of three of the more bluesy songs from his repertoire. A *Variety* columnist picked upon the Dick Dale comeback concert and he introduced me to some screwball currently running the artist and repertoire end of Vanguard Records. It was the first of many meetings, as word of the Dick Dale tape flashed around Hollywood record company offices and I found myself ushered into the darkened chambers of the industry's inner sanctums as an honored guest.

Before long, the prospective record companies were narrowed down to two – one, a label run by Frank Zappa and the other, a big corporation with a couple of old L.A. deejays heading the operation for the time being who remembered Dick Dale from his Top 40 days and thought of him as an oldie but a goodie. Dick felt more comfortable with these cronies than the long-haired Zappa associate with the flashy belt buckle.

Everything came to a head one night in Dick's trailer with Glen Campbell's prime-time variety show on the TV set in the background. He rose early that morning to remove a black panther from his pen and take him to somewhere the ferocious wild animal could be suitably handled. After a forty-five minute battle in the pre-dawn morning, Dick finally managed to get the recalcitrant beast into his van, but he was still quaking from the harrowing experience fourteen hours later. He kept looking at Glen Campbell and snapping off angry comments. "That's what I want to do," he said, pointing at the set. "I used to hire that guy for $80 an hour to play on my records and look at him now."

We had come to a fork in the road. I left Riverside to pursue my college journalism ambitions in San Francisco and Dick Dale signed with the big corporation, who plunked down a modest advance for the privilege. When I visited the following year, he had exchanged his new Cadillac for a Rolls, but was still living in the trailer behind the club and had yet to spin one inch of tape on his new record contract. He never did. I wrote a story about him for Rolling Stone. It never ran.

Twenty-two years later, the manager of a local thrash-punk band with a major label deal called Psychefunkapus called to talk about the coup of the band's new album -- getting the King of the Surf Guitar, Dick Dale himself, to play a solo on a song titled "Surfing On Jupiter." He gave me Dick's phone number and we talked.

Today he lives with his second wife Jill and their baby son, Jimmy, in the sun-swept high desert of Twentynine Palms, about an hour north of Palm Springs. He maintains an eighty-acre sky ranch with two landing strips. The exotic animals are no more, but he keeps horses and rides daily. His father, long reconciled with his only son, lives nearby.

He gave up the twelve-piece show band a couple of years ago and stripped his act down to the bare essentials; bass, drums and Dick Dale. His live performances are grueling workouts. He literally melts guitar picks in his fingers. A *Los Angeles Times* reviewer compared his relationship to his guitar with Thor and his hammer. He doesn't tour, but makes occasional forays into civilization for special performances. In the company of other guitar greats like the Leo Fender memorial concert or the twenty-fifth anniversary celebration of *Guitar Player* magazine, he mows 'em down

Because his career never launched outside of the five Southern California counties and his live appearances have been similarly restricted, Dick Dale has assumed a near-mythic status among other guitar players and fans who have only heard his ancient records. Paul Shaffer of the "David Letterman Show" insisted Dick join Joe Walsh and Joe Satriani on his 1989 solo album. The late Keith Moon of The Who sought Dick out to play on his solo album. Dick earned a Grammy nomination for his 1987 duet with Stevie Ray Vaughan on the film soundtrack for "Back to the Beach."

But his reluctance to leave familiar surroundings, even traveling like a tribe with wife and child everywhere he goes, has rendered Dick Dale a fresh, exciting attraction everywhere he has never played. After our phone call, I put him in touch with the proprietors of a San Francisco nightclub called Slim's and they arranged his first Northern California performance of his career. The club sold out in advance. The audience ranged from old fans from Southern California glory days to young rads in baggy shorts carrying their skateboards. Dick Dale, now fronting a trio of bass, drums and him still playing the same Fender Stratocaster, blew 'em all away.

Suddenly the record we never made loomed large as unfinished business. His last studio recording of new material took place eighteen years earlier. He re-cut his surf hits. He tried out a live album. But Dick Dale had not gone into a studio to record new material since his Capitol Records contract ended around the time a new rock group from England, of all places, was dominating the label's attention.

Scott Mathews is the most talented musician I know. He has drummed with the Beach Boys and Robin Williams. His songs have been recorded by a field as diverse as Barbara Streisand and Dave Edmunds. His collaborations with songwriter Ron Nagle have earned him a worldwide underground following. He has produced artists as disparate as Paul Kantner of the Jefferson Starship and John Hiatt. In addition to drumming, he sings, plays guitar, keyboards, saxophone, toy instruments and anything else he can coax a musical noise out of. He was the first call.

Prairie Prince was the second. Prairie first came to the attention as the drummer for the Tubes, THE razzle-dazzle would-be San Francisco rock stars of the '70s. As a drummer, he is Sandy Nelson, Gene Krupa and Tony Williams rolled into one. A talented artist who lives on the side of Telegraph Hill, he would be a household name in the recording industry if he didn't want to live in San Francisco, where he is known as the town's top drummer. Everybody from Chris Isaak to Todd Rundgren use him.

Bassist Rollie Salley put the thump, thump, thump into the Chris Isaak records from the start and was the perfect choice to complete the little ensemble that assembled in April 1992 at Sausalito's Studio D to cut four songs for starters.

The results went straight to High Tone Records, across the Bay Bridge in Oakland. Any label that could find the common link between bluesman Robert Cray and rockabilly champ Billy Lee Riley, while practically specializing in country music, was first and foremost a music company. High Tone partner Bruce Bromberg also produced one of my all time favorite records, "Happy Hour" by Ted Hawkins, another artist who defies easy categorization other than to say he is damn good.

Dick Dale suffers from a misnomer. He doesn't play surf music. He plays guitar. His style is a product of his own deeply personal vision and if his success in the beach dance halls up and down the Southern California coast may have given the music business the bright idea of marketing something they called surf music, that is not Dick's fault. But it is an albatross that has hung around his neck for thirty years. With "Tribal Thunder" he explodes out beyond marketing department catch-phrases and stakes his claim to be acknowledged for what he is – one of the greatest original voices ever to play rock guitar.

Tribal Thunder | Hightone Records (1993)

Glen Campbell: The Legacy (1961-2002) Box Set Notes

Glen Campbell is exactly the sort of artist no rock critics take seriously, but I jumped at the chance to write the biographical essay for his box set. He may have descended eventually into a morass of pop mediocrity on his own recordings, but he lives forever in my pantheon, if only for the guitar solo on the Beach Boys' "Dance Dance Dance."

WHEN 24 YEAR-OLD GLEN CAMPBELL LEFT Albuquerque, New Mexico for Hollywood in July 1960, he drove off with his new wife, their $300 life savings, a puppy and a four-year old Chevy they still owed money on. He didn't have any family or close friends there. He didn't know what to expect and he didn't have any definite plans. He certainly was not thinking about becoming one of the biggest stars in recording industry history.

But something propelled him to discard the relative prosperity of his steady job at a club called the Hitchin' Post with his band, the Western Wranglers, as well as a daily noontime TV program and a Saturday morning kids cowboy show. He spent five years building his professional standing just to reach that point. He had already rescued himself from the Arkansas dirt-farming poverty in which he grew up in a family of ten, seventh son of a seventh son. He learned to play a four-dollar guitar his father ordered from the Sears and Roebuck catalog and quickly demonstrated a phenomenal aptitude for the instrument. In another place, he would have been called a prodigy.

His uncle Boo took the 15 year-old boy to Wyoming, where the promised jobs as musicians vanished in the prairie wind. But young Glen Campbell returned to Billstown with the knowledge that his life no longer belonged there.

Within a year, he moved to Albuquerque to join a band led by his uncle, Dick Bills, a western swing outfit called the Sandia Mountain Boys. After a couple of years with his uncle's band, he organized his own outfit and covered the latest country and western hits in saloons and bars across the Southwest. He thought of himself as a guitarist who could sing, although he cut a couple of small-time singles that nobody noticed. "I knew I could sing, but I really didn't like the sound of my voice," Campbell said. "That's why I copied other people – Marty Robbins,

Hank Thompson, Sinatra, anybody – 'cause we played everybody's music."

He showed up backstage wearing a green suit at the Dick Clark's Cavalcade of Stars show at the civic auditorium, where he met a young Texan with a record on the radio named Jerry Fuller and another brash, young rock and roller, Dave Burgess, whose instrumental group the Champs had a number one record with "Tequila." He asked them for their autographs. Later, they came by the Hitchin' Post and watched him play. They told him he should come to California. After an initial scouting trip with another Albuquerque music business buddy, deejay Jerry Naylor, Campbell did just that.

It wasn't some rash decision. Campbell had been outgrowing the provincial country and western scene. He discovered the jazz guitar of Django Reinhardt in a fellow musician's record collection and absorbed the Belgian gypsy guitarist's extraordinary style and extensive vocabulary of runs and licks. On his September 1959 honeymoon, Campbell took his newly wedded bride to Las Vegas, where they watched Bobby Darin work one of the casino big rooms. Campbell had never seen the polish and presentation of big time show business before and he was impressed by everything except Darin's guitarist. He thought he could do better.

When he and Jerry Naylor visited Hollywood, Naylor used his disc jockey connections to get them inside a professional recording session. Again, Campbell was awed by the sophistication of the technology, the modern facilities, everything about the session except the guitarist on the date. He decided to make the move.

The Hollywood where Glen Campbell arrived in summer 1960 was, in many ways, still a small town where things could happen.

Campbell hooked up with Jerry Fuller once he arrived in Los Angeles, and Fuller used him to play guitar on a demo version of a song Fuller wrote for Sam Cooke. Fuller supplied percussion by pounding on the back of another guitar and sang the song, complete with requisite "whoa-whoa-whoa's." He took the acetate to Cooke's manager J.W. Alexander, whose Sunset Boulevard offices shared a wall with Imperial Records. Joe Osborn, bass player for Ricky Nelson, heard something of the record through the wall that intrigued him. He went over to Alexander's office and asked if he could hear the "travelin'" song. Alexander retrieved the disc from his wastebasket. "Take it," he said.

Two years earlier, with Elvis in the Army, Ricky Nelson was the biggest-selling rock and roll star in the universe. But the hit records had slowed down since his 1958 number one, "Poor Little Fool," and he needed a song like Fuller's "Travelin' Man" badly. No only did Nelson cut the song, but he inquired about the background vocalists he heard on other Fuller demos – Fuller, Campbell and Dave Burgess – and asked them to replace the Jordanaires, Elvis' former background quartet who were getting too busy in Nashville to make his West Coast record dates.

In less than six months, Campbell had fallen in with rock and roll royalty in Hollywood. Ricky Nelson was not only starring in the long-running TV series featuring his real-life family, "The Adventures of Ozzie and Harriet," but he was suddenly back on top with a two-sided hit of Fuller's "Travelin' Man" and "Hello Mary Lou," a song written by then-unknown Gene Pitney. Campbell, Fuller and Burgess became his new best friends, recording together pseudonymously as the Fleas and putting background vocals on Nelson's records.

Things happened quickly for Campbell once he hit Hollywood. Within a couple of months, he landed a job playing guitar in the Champs, Dave Burgess' group now on the downslide of a short but successful career (Jimmy Seals and Dash Crofts of the future Seals and Crofts also belonged to the Champs). He attracted the attention of Jerry Capehart, former manager of Eddie Cochran, the brilliant young rock and roller who died in a British car crash in April 1960, although his relations with Capehart, his manager since the beginning of his career, had deteriorated over various issues including Cochran's claim that Capehart added his name to Cochran's songwriting credits. Capehart signed Campbell for management and found him a job as a $75 a week staff songwriter at American Music, the music publishing arm of Four Star Music, the show business empire of cowboy star-turned-magnate Gene Autry. He found himself working alongside another ex-Texan who had a brief fling as a rockabilly star, Jimmy Bowen ("I'm Sticking With You"). Every week, the two went into the studio to do the demos. "Glen could hear a damn song once and go out and do it," said Bowen.

After Capehart tested the waters with a single on his own label, he launched Glen as an artist on an American Music house label with a song, "Turn Around, Look At Me," a mid-tempo ballad credited jointly to Capehart and Campbell songwriters ("He just put his name on my song," said Campbell). The record did surprisingly well. Campbell even lip-synched the number on "American Bandstand," before disappearing back into the swollen ranks of artists whose singles died before even making it to the mid-charts. But it was a record with a certain resonance, a faint hint of something not fully realized, a classic entry point. Campbell started thinking more seriously about singing.

Campbell signed with Capitol Records in 1962. His first records for the label

Glen Campbell

were produced by Nik Venet, the young hipster of the Capitol artist and repertoire department whose claim to fame was producing the Lettermen. Campbell nicked the bottom of the charts with ""Too Late To Worry – Too Blue To Cry," which remade the honky-tonk '40s oldie by Al Dexter (best known for the original version of "Pistol Packin' Mama") in the style of the then-popular Ray Charles album, "Modern Sounds In Country and Western." Subsequent singles didn't even do that well.

At the same time, Venet also paired Campbell with the Green River Boys on an album, "Big Bluegrass Special," reluctantly covering songs from the American

328

Music catalog, Campbell wearing a string tie and strumming an arch-top hollow-body on the cover. He cut a pair of Merle Travis songs for another single.

But Campbell was hardly making a living cutting country and western records nobody heard. He started playing in a band that worked a club in the San Fernando Valley called the Crossbow, where he began to circulate among an extraordinary group of musicians, including, fresh from the Tommy Sands band, drummer Hal Blaine, or Oklahoma refugee pianist Leon Russell. "Pretty soon, word was getting out," said drummer Blaine, "and we started getting calls to do demos."

Genius producer Phil Spector anointed this elite squadron when he started regularly using the same loose assemblage of up-and-coming players, Campbell included, to build his trademark Wall of Sound. They quickly became the first-call session players all over town. During 1963, Campbell's singing or guitar playing appeared on more than five hundred recordings. Even Elvis Presley dumped his usual guys to use the new Hollywood hot shots on the "Viva Las Vegas" soundtrack. Campbell went from earning $100 a week to $1000 a day. "The first income tax return I did for him was for $1900," his longtime manager Stan Schneider told VH-1's "Behind the Music." "The next year, it was well into six figures."

He put the searing solo on the Beach Boys' "Dance Dance Dance." He played on countless sessions for Beach Boys songwriter-producer Brian Wilson, including hits such as "Help Me Rhonda" and "Good Vibrations." His playing is all over the celebrated "Pet Sounds" album. He played on imitation Beach Boys records, a cottage industry for the Los Angeles music scene for awhile, with Jan and Dean ("Surf City"), the Hondells ("Little Honda"), surf guitar king Dick Dale and innumerable others.

Jimmy Bowen, his pal from doing demos at American Music, landed a job as staff producer at Warner Brothers Records and he started using Campbell on sessions with old guard pop artists on that label's roster, from Frank Sinatra on down. He played on Dean Martin's 1964 number one smash, "Everybody Loves Somebody." When Bowen needed to put an acoustic guitar part, an electric guitar and three-part vocal harmonies on some tracks for a Buddy Greco "Sings the Beatles" albums, all he had to do was call Campbell. When Campbell, who doesn't read music, laid down the charts for the vocal parts Greco wrote for the session without even looking at them, Greco thought his young producer had lost his mind – until he heard Campbell flawlessly match overdubbed vocal parts.

He made tons of commercials, the most famous possibly being his television jingle for Clairol hair products: "Is it true blondes have more fun?" He wrote an off-the-wall candy bar commercial with Roger Miller before "Dang Me" introduced that remarkable talent to an incredulous world. When British TV producer Jack Good assembled the house band in 1964 for the ultimate live rock and roll TV show, "Shindig!," Campbell was the obvious choice on guitar, where he backed all the great names of the day.

Campbell got the emergency call when Beach Boys mastermind Brian Wilson suffered a nervous breakdown mid-air on his way to a 1964 Christmas Eve show in Dallas,. He joined the group, wore those striped shirts, played bass and sang Brian's high vocal parts on two tours. But he had recording sessions waiting and a small part in the Steve McQueen picture, "Baby the Rain Must Fall." After three months, Campbell was replaced by Bruce Johnston, who, as one-half of Bruce and Terry, had some success with imitation Beach Boys himself.

His recording career at Capitol staggered along. The label tried to capitalize on his newfound session guitar status with a pair of instrumental albums, "The Astounding 12-String Guitar of Glen Campbell" and "The Big, Bad Rock Guitar of Glen Campbell." At one point, when other label executives contemplated dropping Campbell as an artist, longtime Capitol country a&r chief Ken Nelson, who produced hit records with Buck Owens, Sonny James, Merle Haggard and others, said, no, Campbell had talent and insisted he stay. But it was Brian Wilson himself who offered to produce Campbell's next single for the label, a sublime pop confection far from the country sides Campbell had been making.

"Guess I'm Dumb" was a song Wilson co-wrote with Screen Gems staff writer Russ Titelman and originally recorded for the Beach Boys with Campbell on guitar in October 1964. He retooled the song into a vehicle for Campbell the following April (about the same he was working on "California Girls" for the Boys) and Capitol released the single, "produced and arranged by Brian Wilson," in June. The single reached the "Bubbling Under" part of the Billboard charts, but sank before bubbling up.

Saxophonist Steve Douglas, who played next to Campbell on several hundred sessions, went to work in the Capitol a&r department where he used Campbell on Wayne Newton's "Danke Schoen," Bobby Darin records, and other sessions. Producer Douglas put a slight Roger Miller parody, "Queen of the House," by Jody Miller, on the charts and thought he was on a roll when he and Campbell tailored the Buffy St. Marie song (already recorded by the English folksinger Donovan) along the exact lines of Barry McGuire's chart-ascendant "Eve of Destruction," leaning on Campbell's TV exposure as a member of the "Shindig!" house band, the Shindogs. The record returned Campbell to the pop charts for the first time in three years and was a smash hit in many markets.

Teamed now with the junior member of the Capitol a&r team, Al De Lory, a former session pianist who played many of the same dates as Campbell and had produced the 1960 Larry Verne number one novelty record, "Mr. Custer," Campbell returned his attention to the country market. His original, ""Less Of Me," and the Jack Scott oldie, ""Burning Bridges," earned Campbell solid country hits, but nothing on the pop side.

"I told Ken Nelson I just want to record what I want to record," said Campbell. "If you've got a good song and I like it, fine. But I'm not going to do it anymore because you say it's going to be a hit. We went down that road. I'd rather take my chances with what I want to do, singles-wise. Otherwise I can make y'all a helluva lot more money doing studio work. First thing I wanted to do was 'Gentle On My Mind' and Ken had never heard it. I had Doug Dillard in the studio (on banjo) and when Ken heard it, he just flipped out. He didn't even let me finish it. He put out the demo. I was going to put strings on it and probably would have messed it up."

John Hartford was already recognized as one of Nashville's bright young contenders in early 1967 when he released his second album, "Earthwords & Music," containing his original version of "Gentle On My Mind." Hartford's version was making some progress on the country charts when Campbell heard the song on the radio. He straightened out the bluegrass hiccup of Hartford's more idiomatic rhythm tracks and gave a relaxed vocal performance that may have owed something to the fact that Campbell didn't think he was singing a final vocal. "I knew immediately that this was the song that was going to put us on the map," said producer De Lory.

Despite a modest chart performance, "Gentle On My Mind" did turn out to be the definitive record of Campbell's career, the point where he not only took charge of his own artistic destiny but became his own creation. With his hands on the wheel, on the "Gentle On My Mind" album Campbell moved into realms remote from country music of the day, songs by Rod McKuen, Donovan and Harry Nilsson, not to mention his exquisite cover of Roy Orbison's "Cryin." The stage was set for his next record.

Jimmy Webb was born in Oklahoma the son of a Baptist minister and a music major at San Bernardino Valley College when he moved to Hollywood and landed a job as staff writer for Motown Records, where he had little success (the Supremes did cut his "My Christmas Tree"). But his demos found their way into the hands of Johnny Rivers, who signed Webb to a publishing deal and recorded his "By the Time I Get to Phoenix" on his December 1966 album, "Changes." "I cried when I heard it," said Campbell.

Released in October 1967, Campbell's smash hit version spent an extraordinary six months on the charts. In February 1968, he won four Grammys, two for "By the Time I Get to Phoenix" and two for "Gentle On My Mind." John Hartford won another two Grammys himself for "Gentle On My Mind." Glen Campbell had arrived.

His follow-up single, Campbell's cover of the Dorsey Burnette oldie "Hey Little One," faltered on the pop charts, as did the April 1968 release, John D. Loudermilk's "I Wanna Live" (a number one country hit). He cut "The Dreams Of An Everyday Housewife," a song Jerry Fuller found in Nashville by writer Curtis Gantry that Mark Lindsey turned down, but battled his way up to the mid-charts against a competing version by Wayne Newton that doomed both records. Capitol teamed Campbell for an album of duets with the label's other new sensation of the moment, Bobbie Gentry ("Ode To Billie Joe"), although their version of her "Morning Glory" never really took off.

"When are you going to get your hair cut?" asked Glen Campbell, the first time he met "Phoenix" songwriter Webb at recording session for a Chevrolet commercial. Webb wrote the jingle ("Chevy loves the road") and Campbell was going to sing it. Webb not only knew Campbell from singing the hit version of his song, he remembered "Turn Around, Look At Me" from when it was released. De Lory and drummer Hal Blaine visited Webb's bizarre Hollywood home, a former silent movie star's decrepit mansion down the street from Ozzie and Harriet's real-life home that he shared with dozens of other hippies. The grand piano was painted green.

"They asked me if I could write something geographical," Webb said, "a town, a place. They needed a follow-up, another "By the Time I Get To Phoenix," if they could get one. At the end of the day, I don't know if what I've got is any good or even finished, but I've got this song. They liked it a lot."

Campbell visited Webb to work on the song "Wichita Lineman," and Webb showed him a keyboard part on a clunky, old Gullbranson church organ Webb owned. Campbell insisted he play the part for the record on the same organ. The unwieldy organ was duly trucked down to the studio and Webb added the keyboard part to the nearly completed record. But it was while listening back after all the orchestrations had been laid down that Campbell decided to add one final guitar part.

"That's when Glen started tuning down the six-string into that Duane Eddy range," Webb said, "and he played the solo, which was the part of the song I was never able to finish."

Tommy Smothers happened to catch Campbell's guest appearance on "The Joey Bishop Show" and remembered him from recording sessions. He was looking for a host to the summer replacement of the wildly popular "The Smothers Brothers Comedy Hour." Campbell proved so appealing on TV, not only did "Gentle On My Mind" go back on the charts, the Smothers Brothers put together a deal to produce his own CBS variety show. When "The Glen Campbell Goodtime Hour" made its debut January 29, 1969, "Wichita Lineman," released in November 1968, was waiting at the top of the charts.

Campbell simply exploded. Overnight he became the biggest new star in the country. He started setting attendance records wherever he played. "It was real shocking," Campbell said. "I went over to England and when I came back it was 'hey baby.' Everyone wanted to shake my hand. Everyone wanted an autograph. I forgot that I already had two TV shows on and from then on, it seemed like I had no privacy."

In 1969, the last year the band was still in business, Glen Campbell outsold the Beatles. In the year of the Woodstock Festival, Campbell was a fresh-scrubbed, wholesome pop singer, a snug harbor for Nixon's Silent Majority. "He was mom and apple pie," said manager Stan Schneider. "You had this apple-cheeked, blonde guy when a lot of the world was getting grungier and grungier. Of course, there was Vietnam and all that. For middle America, he was the antithesis of the counter-culture. It was a place where it was still their music."

Don Ho appeared on the TV show and mentioned to Campbell that he had recorded a Jimmy Webb song on an album. Ho's version of "Galveston," however, was slow, sung like a ballad. Campbell speeded up the tempo and gave the tale of the Vietnam veteran some melodic drive. "I just wanted to say what was in the song and make it feel good," he said.

"Glen had a take on it, an almost militaristic take on it," said songwriter Webb. "He made it a happy song, made it a marching song. He knew what would play on the radio. He knew what would sell."

"Galveston" was virtually as big a hit as "By The Time I Get To Phoenix," which earned Campbell the Grammy Award for Album Of the Year in March 1969. "Having that raft of Jimmy Webb songs come at us was one of the luckiest things that ever happened," said producer De Lory.

"He wasn't above changing a lyric that he didn't like," said Webb, "and he didn't always feel like making a phone call. We had some surprises. But for me, it's just, oh, so that's the way it goes now."

"I could see where something would sound better," said Campbell. "It wasn't major changes. I think I made them flow better. I didn't change any chords or anything. But I might have skipped over a couple. He had flatted R's in there. He could write, boy."

The Campbell/Webb alliance, one of the all-time great vocalist/composer partnerships in pop music, continued with Webb's "Where's the Playground, Suzie?" In between shooting the television show, Campbell took the time to film a co-starring role next to John Wayne in "True Grit" (Campbell likes to say he made Wayne look so good he won an Oscar) and the title song gave him another single on the radio. He answered the demand for a new album with his first live album recorded July 4, 1969 at the Garden State Arts Center, New Jersey.

As the new singles started to peak in the middle of the pop charts, they stayed Top Ten in country, like "Try a Little Kindness" or Jimmy Webb's "Honey Come Back," a song Webb wrote when he was a teenager working at the Three Bears Coffee Shop in Rubidoux, California. Campbell initially resisted the mawkish spoken opening verse, De Lory said.

In 1970, Campbell released four albums; the soundtrack to "Norwood," his feature film follow-up to "True Grit," and "The Glen Campbell Goodtime Album," with his remake of the Conway Twitty ballad, "It's Only Make Believe." He also continued the recording association with labelmate Bobbie Gentry, charting with a cover of the old Everly Brothers hit, "All I Have To Do Is Dream." The following year, Campbell released three more albums; "The Last Time I Saw Her," including his version of Roy Orbison's "Dream Baby" and the Gordon Lightfoot title track, done in a nearly identical arrangement to the original version, a Christmas album and an album of duets with Anne Murray. "I didn't have time to find the good songs," said Campbell.

Murray was a Canadian country singer Campbell featured on his TV show when her first album was just being released. "Surrounded by writers and producers, sitting with Glen and singing before the first TV show, I saw this gleam in his eye," said Anne Murray, "because I could sing any part he could and so could he. We loved to sing together."

With "Manhattan Kansas," Glen Campbell singles dropped off the Top 100 pop charts for the first time in almost five years, even though the track was a Top

Ten country hit. As he was cooling off on the pop charts, an old pal was drafted to record Campbell for the first time in his career in Nashville. "(Capitol executive) Al Coury called me and said the pop world isn't happening for Glen," said Jimmy Bowen. "My assignment was to take him country."

Bowen made five albums over the next two years with his old American Music buddy. They cut country whimsy ("I Knew Jesus Before He Was a Star") and they tried polished country-pop like "Houston (I'm Coming To See You)," which was written by arranger Marty Paich's son, David Paich of the rock group, Toto. They held sessions with composer Burt Bacharach, but the results were never released. On his own, Campbell knocked off an under-rated album backing up Tennessee Ernie Ford, "Ernie Sings & Glen Picks." They did an album of Hank Williams songs. Bowen supervised the long-awaited studio collaboration of Campbell and Webb, "Reunion."

"That was the craziest damn sessions I ever ran," Bowen said. "Trying to corral them in the studio, I went through a case of Jack Daniels that month just trying to keep up." ("That's probably true," said Campbell.)

Drugs and alcohol had started to interfere with Campbell's high life. His wife was supervising the building of a lavish 17,000 square-foot mansion in the Hollywood hills. Since the TV show went off the air in June 1972, Campbell spent his time on the road, touring the world, increasingly remote from hearth and home. His records slipped off the pop charts altogether, when Campbell stumbled across the song that would change his life.

He heard "Rhinestone Cowboy" on the car radio. A Los Angeles station that broadcast album cuts was playing the version recorded by the song's composer, Larry Weiss, a professional songwriter who had some success with songs covered by Al Martino, Jerry Butler, the American Breed ("Bend Me Shape Me"). Capitol assigned the production to producer-songwriters Dennis Lambert and Brian Potter, Top 40 songsmiths flying high with some post-Motown Four Tops hits ("Keeper Of the Castle") and a mawkish Righteous Brothers comeback track, "Rock and Roll Heaven." Campbell knew he found his career record. His wife dismissed it as a dumb cowboy song and asked for a separation. Campbell's life tumbled into soap opera, as his record career soared back to the top after long lean years. "Rhinestone Cowboy" was his first number one record.

Lambert and Potter fashioned the rest of the album for Campbell, writing "Country Boy (You've Got Your Feet In L.A." specifically for him. By the following year, the pair were reduced to dragging out their 1971 Hamilton, Joe Frank & Reynolds hit, "Don't Pull Your Love Out." "We would have done a couple more albums," said Campbell, "but they went in and did tracks and then tried to write something to the tracks. I told them, 'Boys, you've got to run songs through me – I'm the one that's got to sing them.' We quit right in the middle of an album. I'm a musician and a singer and I know what I want to sing and I know what I want to play."

It was Jimmy Webb who found the next song. He called Campbell and told him to come by his house to hear an album, "Southern Nights" by Allen Toussaint. Webb had been obsessively listening to Little Feat when the Toussaint album crossed his path and took over. Despite a recording career that began in 1958 when he played piano on a Fats Domino record while Fats was off touring, the 1974 release was only the fourth solo album by the long-standing master of New Orleans rhythm and blues.. He wrote and produced his first number one hit, "Mother-In-Law" by Ernie K-Doe, in 1960. Al Hirt made a number one hit out of his instrumental "Java" in 1964 and Herb Alpert didn't do badly with "Whipped Cream." He made uniquely flavored r&b hits out of New Orleans over the years with Irma Thomas, Lee Dorsey, Dr. John and others. He wrote and produced a number one record as recently as 1975, "Lady Marmalade" with Labelle. But his solo albums were strangely produced, almost deliberately sabotaged by the production, his whispery vocals running through echoey Leslie organ speakers. But Campbell didn't have to go past the first track on the album.

In an affair splashed across the front pages of America's tabloids, freshly divorced Campbell married songwriter Mac Davis' ex-wife, Sarah, and she introduced Campbell to producer Gary Klein, who helmed Davis' 1974 hit, "Stop and Smell the Roses." Campbell played a hissy cassette of the Toussaint song over the phone to Klein. "I heard something," said Klein. "It sounded like music in a merry-go-round. I couldn't understand a word. But either you get it or you don't. I told Glen I don't know what he's singing, but I love it – it makes me feel good."

Klein, who was also producing Dolly Parton and Barbra Streisand at the time, said he had to talk Campbell into playing guitar on the track. "I think only he can play it that way," said Klein.

"We just had 'Southern Nights,'" said Campbell. "All of a sudden, it's a hit and we didn't have an album. So we sort of had to rush that one. But that's a great piece of work, 'Southern Nights.' Allen Toussaint, what a writer."

The album rushed out behind the smashing number one success of the single also included Campbell's cover of the Beach Boys' "God Only Knows," Neil Diamond's "Sunflower," a couple of Jimmy Webb songs and two songs from an unknown writer out of Roger Miller's band, "Glen was very high on this guy Michael Smotherman," said Klein. "I expected him to become a major songwriter."

After the 1978 "Live At Royal Festival Hall" album, Campbell devoted his entire next album to the songs of Michael Smotherman, "Basic," co-produced by Campbell himself. "It took two years and cost a fortune," said Stan Schneider, "like a rock and roll project." The cover showed Campbell close-up, weighing about 155 pounds, and it wasn't a pretty picture. Even a "Basic" TV special couldn't help – "Can You Fool," the set's sole single, peaked mid-chart.

But when the record company refused to release "Highwayman," a glistening new Jimmy Webb song strung across crystalline orchestrations by Webb himself, Campbell was disconsolate. Label executives told him they thought the song was too complex for radio. He wanted to leave the label. "He pretty much flipped out about it," said songwriter Webb. "He never forgave them for it. Eight years later, he was still talking about it."

Eight years later, Campbell was visiting a recording session by Willie Nelson, Waylon Jennings, Johnny Cash and Kris Kristofferson and told them he knew a perfect song for them. The fellows liked the song so much, they named their group the Highwaymen, and the song that was too complex lived to become a major hit for them.

Campbell completed his contract with two more albums, with producer Gary Klein back at the helm; the first enlivened by the title track duet with Rita Coolidge, "Something 'Bout You Baby I Like," and, the second, "It's a World Gone Crazy," noteworthy for the Waylon Jennings-Shel Silverstein title track, the Michael Smotherman single, "I Don't Want To Know Your Name," the theme song to the Clint Eastwood film, "Any Which Way You Can," and "Why Don't We Just Sleep On It," a duet with Tanya Tucker, whose red-hot affair with Campbell was lighting up the supermarket weeklies. (Campbell returned the favor, singing the old Bobby Darin song, "Dream Lover," on a Tucker album). "His choice of songs was getting pretty bad," said manager Schneider. "He was losing his commercial eye as to what he could sing. He was unsure of himself."

A goofy single, "I Love My Truck," landed Campbell a new record deal. With his old friend Jerry Fuller producing, Campbell made his first album for the new country division of Atlantic Records. Webb called his "I Was Too Busy Loving You" his "homage to Hank Williams, my father's favorite singer." Campbell made his next album for the new label in Nashville, where he mixed with young bloods such as dobro player Jerry Douglas and vocalist Emmylou Harris, working with

Harold Shedd, the Georgia record producer who came up the ranks with the million-selling country group, Alabama.. "It was a good record," said Schneider, "but there wasn't a hit on it."

Jimmy Bowen, now running MCA Nashville and one of the most powerful producers in Music City, signed Campbell and paired him with Steve Wariner, a Bowen protégé who had a few more hits recently than Campbell, but was not really Campbell's stature at the time. "If These Walls Could Speak" was the highpoint of the second MCA album, dominated by Jimmy Webb songs, a piece subsequently recorded by Shawn Colvin, Nanci Griffith and Amy Grant. "Unconditional Love" was a little-noticed album he made at Liberty Records.

"Then Branson came along," said Schneider. With his career coming alive in other arenas, Campbell felt free to turn his recording career toward his beliefs and started making contemporary Christian albums such as "Show Me Your Way" and "Wings Of Victory." Married to Kimberly Woolen in 1982, Campbell slowly took control of his personal life. He moved to Phoenix, started a new family and stopped drinking and using drugs. His new records reflected his new life. "I was just cutting songs I liked," he said. "I'd gone through a transformation from drinking and drugging. I thought I'd say something positive."

But don't be fooled. Underneath that aw-shucks country boy act is a stealthy, cunning craftsman. All those thousands of hours making other people's records – participating in historic recording sessions from "He's A Rebel" to "Strangers In the Night" to "Today I Started Loving You Again" – wasn't wasted on this gifted musician, anymore than the endless nights banging out country and western in bars and roadhouses across the Southwest or the hundreds of songs he learned growing up singing with his family in Arkansas. Campbell drew on all these resources navigating an artistic path through his distinguished recording career. He carefully cultivated his unique musical personality, a guileless blend of ability, experience and country soul. He may not have known exactly where he was going when he drove off from Albuquerque with his meager possessions and indeterminate dreams, but he trusted his instincts. In the end, it was those instincts that served him better than anything.

The Legacy (1961-2002), July 2003

CHAPTER 10

San Francisco in the '80s

Huey Lewis & the News

Journey

Chris Isaak

Metallica

Joe Satriani

Huey's News:
Local Boy Makes Good

Lewis and gang are now among top American bands

I went from Live Aid in Philadelphia to the tour by Huey Lewis and the News, who were, at the moment, the most popular rock group in America. A crowd of several dozen were waiting outside the hotel when the tour bus pulled up. Guitarist Chris Hayes spied the mob from behind the blinds. "It looks like a job for Lewis," he announced. The always affable vocalist was dispatched ahead of the rest of the band. The crowd swallowed him like white cells surrounding bacteria and the others were able to make their way to the lobby with ease.

NEW HAVEN, CONN. – SOMETHING HAPPENED TO HUEY LEWIS AND THE NEWS between the band's somewhat ordinary second album and the third, "Sports," still going strong after passing the six million mark in sales. "We got better," deadpanned Lewis "We learned how to use the technology in the studio, the drum machines. We learned how to make a record."

Such a simple answer cannot fully explain the amazing quantum leap from 1982's "Picture This" to "Sports, " recorded the following year, but withheld from relase for nine months. If this was simply the result of "getting better, " why couldn't anybody else get that much better?

Lewis struggled again with another explanation that sounded suspiciously like the first and began to look as irritated as the genial rock star gets when the interrogation kept up. "What do you want me to say?" he scowled, "the muse visited us?"

With the exception of Bruce Springsteen, Huey Lewis and the News has become today's most popular American rock band, exclusively on the strength of "Sports," five hit singles from the album and the attendant videos that made Lewis rock video's version of the boy next door.

In the Bay Area, Lewis can still live fairly much like the hometown boy who cut his teeth around small local dives and ran a health food store to support him-

Huey Lewis

self. He can still drop by and jam a little at Corte Madera's Uncle Charlie's, where the band played during its early days as Huey Lewis and the American Express, or stop by Mill Valley's 2 a.m. Club to have a drink and visit his gold record awards.

Elsewhere around the country, it is a different story. As the customized tour bus rolled into New Haven's Park Plaza Hotel, hours ahead of the evening's concert, not only was a flock of teenage girls waiting on the sidewalk, but so was a TV crew, ready to capture the illustrious rock band's arrival in Connecticut

The TV reporter claimed to have gone to prep school with Lewis in nearby Lawrenceville, said he had a gym locker next to Huey. He had already filed a report for that morning's news on their school days together. Lewis did not remember him, but played like he did, cordially answering a few questions while signing autographs for fans on the sidewalk.

"I bet that locker was really down the hall," he smiled, walking into the hotel, "and the over the years, it has moved closer until now it was right next to mine."

When the current 29-date tour ends, getting only as close to the Bay Area as Sacramento's Cal Expo August 16-17, Huey Lewis and the News will go underground for awhile, taking a long-postponed vacation and preparing to record a follow-up to "Sports." "We've got a couple of things ready," said Lewis.

Recording will be slightly different this time around. The last time, the band's record label laid off virtually its entire staff the day the group finished mixing the album that would become "Sports." Consequently, the tape sat on a shelf for nine months, waiting for legal and business problems associated with the record company's situation to get straight. It did, obviously, work out.

Today, riding at the top, things are different. Bob Dylan, whom they met during the "We Are the World" sessions, sent the group a song. Randy Newman, whose "I Love L.A." the band is performing on the current tour, is supposed to be writing a song for them.

Meanwhile, "Power of Love, " one of two cuts Lewis and the News contributed to the sound track to Steven Spielberg's smash hit, "Back to the Future, " is roaring up the charts, looking already like the biggest single in the band's career. Lewis and the group even make a cameo appearance in the movie.

The band also recently produced a single by Nick Lowe of Lowe's old song, "I Knew the Bride" (originally recorded by Dave Edmunds). Lewis clicked the tape into the cassette system on the tour bus, steaming down the highway from the tour's first gig in Springfield, Mass. A wheezing a cappella chorus blared, quickly followed by a pounding drum beat and a playful flick of the wrist from keyboardist Sean Hopper.

As his producer, Lewis gave Lowe the trademark News sound and it fits him like a glove. "I'm mad for it," he told Lewis when he heard the final mixes. But it is no accident that Nick Lowe got to borrow the red-hot sound of the News.

Eight years ago, when Lewis belonged to a band called Clover, Lowe took an interest in the Marin County country-rockers when the band moved to England for a last, desperate chance to make it. He hired the Clover cats to back up an unknown singer Lowe was also producing, Elvis Costello, helped the band get a recording deal in England and generally did his best to boost their career.

Now, the tables have turned and Lowe's record company rejected his finished album because they didn't hear any potential hit singles. Enter Lewis and the News and "I Knew the Bride." Now Lowe's label hears a single and the album is on its way out. Isn't it gratifying to be able to repay old kindnesses? "It sure is," said Lewis, suddenly turning sincere.

On the bus between the first two concerts, the main topic of conversation among the band concerned the Live Aid concerts, which took place the day before and which Lewis and his band decided not to play. For the first time in their career, Lewis and his associates find themselves the subject of controversy.

The only previous, fleeting contact with public feather ruffling the band experienced had been quietly put to rest the week before. Attorneys for Ray Parker Jr. settled the lawsuit Lewis and the News launched, charging Parker's No. 1 record, "Ghostbusters," plagiarized the News smash, "I Want a New Drug."

Even in victory, the band prefers to keep a low profile. "We got a major apology," said manager Bob Brown, demurring on offering even a ballpark figure of the settlement sum. Neither side will be trumpeting the settlement with press releases and such, but Parker's lawyers started out laughing and ended up scrambling to settle, according to Brown.

But the Live Aid controversy just won't go away. The group's stand attracted considerable criticism, even from such customarily calm quarters as Harry Belafonte, who blasted the group in a newspaper interview the day before the concerts.

A number of the other entertainers originally announced as appearing also scotched the date, but only Lewis wondered aloud about where the food was going. It was a legitimate question, since apparently as much as half of the food USA for Africa sent to Ethiopia was rotting on the docks, and Lewis, having made a major contribution to both the "We Are the World" recording session and the subsequent album, felt more comfortable sitting this one out.

"As far as I can tell, Ethiopia is a question mark," said Lewis. Although the European press were clamoring for more explaination from Lewis, he and manager Brown talked about various ways to approach the issue and decided to leave any public statements to Brown, but really hoped the waves would die down. They did not feel apologetic and a phone chat with Live Aid organizer Bob Geldof the day after the show left them convinced they had done the right thing and that Geldof understood their stand.

AT THE sound check before that night's New Haven concert, the band rehearsed "Hope You Love Me Like You Say You Do" with the new three-man horn section, preparing to insert the song in the show. Backstage after, Lewis, drummer Bill Gibson, guitarists Chris Hayes and Johnny Colla did calisthenics together, loosening up for the two-hour performance to come.

"Power of Love" opened the set, followed by "Do You Believe in Love," the band's first hit off the second album. Another couple of older songs preceded the "Sports" section, Lewis introducing a song that, he said, "as Bobby Freeman would say, has been very good to us," launching, "If This Is It."

The last time Lewis and the Newsmen played New Haven, they were working a small club, not an 18, 000 seat hockey rink like the Municipal Auditorium. The "Sports" album was sitting on a shelf, but Lewis and the band nevertheless played many of the unheard songs, opening with "Heart of Rock and Roll, " which, like "Back to the Future," nobody knew at the time.

As after all their concerts, the band members showered in a hurry and took their places behind a table, while backstage guests from local radio, press and record stores lined up, holding post cards of the band, and passed by in a receiving line to get the cards autographed. Even the three new horn members got in line.

These are not typical rock musicians. They remain remarkably unspoiled by success, constantly kidding and teasing each other. Manager Brown thinks they behave more like a baseball team – the spirit of camaraderie and all that – than a rock band. They are starting families (two band members have pregnant wives and Lewis has two young children). Backstage, the personalities fit together in an even balance, even if Lewis bears the brunt of public recognition.

The morning after the New Haven job, Lewis didn't get two consecutive bites of breakfast in his mouth without pausing to cheerfully sign an autograph. One waitress brought a stack of paper – "make this one to Nancy and this one to Kathy . . ." Lewis gave every one a smile and a signature.

One shy young woman approached the table, stuttering and apologizing. Before she could spit out her request, Lewis gave her a charming grin and put her at ease. "You know," he said, "I haven't signed an autograph in awhile. Would you please ask me for an autograph?"

Sunday Datebook | July 28, 1985

"Infinity" liner notes

These would have been the liner notes to the CD reissue of "Infinity," Journey's breakthrough album, except for Steve Perry. Oddly enough, it wasn't my first editorial encounter with the band's fragile lead vocalist; I remember the chilling feeling I got when he told me over the phone he was looking forward to "proofreading" my liner notes to the band's box set. He gutted those – among others, took out the passage about bassist Ross Valory watching the reunion from the sound board that manager Herbie Herbert called "a heart punch" – but, swear to God, I have no idea what his problem is.

JOURNEY'S NEW VOCALIST ROBERT FLEISCHMAN HAD NO IDEA WHO STEVE PERRY WAS. He was introduced to the pint-sized Robert Plant as "Johnny Villaneuva's Portuguese cousin" while he was backstage at concerts. Fleischman, who only joined the band three months earlier, had no idea that the band's Puerto Rican road manager had no Portuguese relatives.

After three albums and incessant touring, Journey was on the verge of being dropped by the label, after the most recent release barely sold more than 100,000 copies. The label pressed for stronger songs and a singer. Denver-based concert producer Barry Fey saw Fleischman sing in Chicago, signed him to a management deal and put together a band to back Fleischman at a showcase gig for labels. Two weeks later, Fleischman was flying to San Francisco at the suggestion of a Columbia Records executive who attended the show. Manager Herbie Herbert drove the new recruit straight from the airport to Studio Instrument Rentals, where the band was rehearsing. "They had played together so long and were so tight," Fleischman recalled, "it was like having rockets in your back pocket."

Before leaving in June 1977 to open the Emerson, Lake and Palmer tour, the band wrote and rehearsed almost an entire new repertoire with Fleischman as vocalist. Diane Valory, wife of Journey bassist Ross Valory, had a poem that included the line "the wheels in my head keep turning," which guitarist Neal Schon changed to "wheel in the sky" – "Whatever that means," he said – and handed off to Fleischman to finish the lyrics. The newly honed vocal skills of the musicians, who had been taking voice lessons, blended behind Fleischman like a little glee club. The Santana overtones and jazz fusion strains were gone. Journey started to sound more like a sleek, new British import. Before leaving town, Journey stepped across the street to the Automatt Studios and recorded demos for the band's fourth album.

Once on the road, Fleischman began to betray disturbing signs of incipient lead singer syndrome. At one point, he made road manager Pat Morrow carry his luggage, a trivial demand that actually might have sealed his fate. But when he insisted the band play two or three songs before he made his grand entrance, issuing an ultimatum to that effect backstage at a Fresno concert, Herbert fired him that night after the show.

But it wasn't entirely Fleischman's attitude that cost him, so much as a tape Herbert heard shortly after the band began the tour with Fleischman. The Alien Project was the culmination of almost ten years of work in the music business for vocalist Steve Perry and the band was close to being signed by Columbia Records when the bass player was killed in a car crash. Depressed and defeated, he was living in the farm town of Visalia in the remote reaches of the Central Valley, his dream over, cleaning out turkey cages for a living when Herbert contacted him.

Perry joined the tour using "the Portuguese cousin" subterfuge. At a sound check in Long Beach, Herbert arranged for Fleischman to be somewhere else and Perry sang one of Fleischman's songs with the band, "For You." The hall was empty, but ushers and concession stand workers stopped what they were doing to listen and burst into applause when the song was over. That was all Herbert needed to hear. Fleischman was gone within days. Guitarist Schon told Herbert he was furious. "Who's going to be the singer?" he demanded. "Not Johnny Villanueva's Portuguese cousin?'

"I wasn't completely sold on Perry," said keyboardist Gregg Rolie. "I don't think anybody was." But backstage at the Swing Auditorium in San Bernardino a few nights later, Perry strapped on a bass and played a song he was nearly finished writing titled "Lights" and the other musicians started harmonizing with him. "It dawned on me right then," said Rolie, "that this could be something great."

In a Denver hotel, where Perry and Schon were sharing a room, the morning after a show, Schon picked up an acoustic guitar and strummed a few chords. Within an hour, he and Perry wrote their first song together, "Patiently."

Perry grew up in a small Central Valley town called Hanford, not unlike the town where George Lucas grew up that inspired "American Graffiti." He played in bands around Sacramento, starting out on drums, but soon concentrating exclusively on vocals. He spent years in Los Angeles, knocking on record business doors, and was once involved in a project with bassist Tim Bogart of Vanilla Fudge, but that, too, came to nothing.

He first heard Neal Schon play when the teenaged guitarist sat in one night with Latin-rockers Azteca at the Kabuki Theater in San Francisco. Ironically, Schon gave Perry and his cousin a ride home that night. Perry didn't see Schon again until many years later, when he visited backstage at a Journey show at the Starwood in Hollywood, although nobody in the band even knew he was a singer at the time.

On October 28, 1977, when the band returned for an encore in a benefit at the 600-seat Old Waldorf in San Francisco, Perry walked out with the other members of Journey. He wore all white and sang two songs, including "Lights." He was timid, slightly awkward, but there was no doubt – this was a new era for Journey.

For the next album, the label insisted on producer Roy Thomas Baker, known at the time for his elaborate, baroque productions of Queen. Sessions began at His Masters Wheels in San Francisco, using the studio's recording console, but recording on a special 40-track machine that Baker owned. After a celebration following a successful guitar solo one night, somebody poured a bottle of beer over Baker's head. He retaliated by grabbing a fire extinguisher and blanketing the room in a chemical fog, which almost instantly settled into a thick, bubbling, corrosive film on the expensive mixing board. The damage turned out to be less than initially feared, but not before the enraged studio owner knocked out Baker, after barring the two of them alone in the control room. With the master tape and Baker's fancy recorder spared in the attack, the sessions continued at Cherokee Studios in Los Angeles.

San Francisco psychedelic poster artists Stanley Mouse and Alton Kelley drew the cover, the same artists who gave the skull and roses to the Grateful Dead. Into a world dominated by "Saturday Night Fever" and "Grease," "Infinity" was released in January 1978. The band proudly unveiled the album in a private listening party back at Studio Instrument Rentals. Concert producer Bill Graham smelled success. He not only came back to the party after his roller skating lessons, but he sent manager Herbert a congratulatory telegram the following morning and called the album " a lovely monster."

Although "Wheel In the Sky" never proved to be the hit single Journey needed, the track became an FM radio staple and the band felt the impact of the airplay at the box office. The aptly named "Infinity" tour opened with a sold out headline show at Chicago's 1100-seat Riviera Theater and criss-crossed the country until Journey had played Chicago three times, at a bigger hall each time. By the end of the year, the band was drawing capacity crowds to hockey rinks and basketball arenas on top of a bill that also featured Montrose and Van Halen. "Infinity" was the first platinum album for Journey, although it never rose higher than No. 21 on the charts. The debut of Steve Perry as the band's vocalist would usher in the golden era of Journey. "Infinity" served notice.

May 2006

Journey May Be Year's Rock Comeback Story

> This story was just the tip of the insanity. In my experience, rock stars are all delusional to one degree or another, but Steve Perry really took the experience to a whole different level.

THE MEMBERS OF JOURNEY HATED EACH OTHER. Lead vocalist Steve Perry could hardly wait for the 1983 tour to end so he could move to Los Angeles, record a solo album and wash his hands of the whole dirty deal. Perry wasn't just sick and tired of the band he belonged to for the previous five years. His mother was dying. His longtime girlfriend had left him. He was worn down from the grind of grueling nine-month tours. He had complaints about the band's management.

Journey had sold millions of records to become one of the country's most popular rock bands, its members rich and famous. But Perry wasn't happy. He secretly quit Journey and only rejoined in exchange for control of the band.

The move appears to have paid off. The first Perry-produced album, "Raised on Radio," released only a month ago, is firmly in the country's top five. The first single from the album, "Be Good to Yourself," is in the top ten. Promoters across the country are clamoring to book the band, and Journey appears headed for the rock comeback story of the year.

But things have not run as smoothly as in the past. Two key band members – bassist Ross Valory and drummer Steve Smith – were jettisoned during the long, arduous recording sessions that produced "Raised on Radio" and, for the past month, a steady procession of some of the country's best known drummers has marched in – and out – of auditions at the band's Oakland rehearsal hall.

Instead of knocking out the new album in a matter of weeks at a budget around $75,000, as the band did with its previous 10 albums, Journey spent $500,000 and more than one agonizing year recording "Raised on Radio," with Perry replacing Kevin Elson, who produced the previous hit Journey albums.

Studio whiz Randy Jackson, whose walloping licks grace Whitney Houston's "How Will I Know," among other hit records, replaced bassist Valory, who belonged to the band for its entire 12-year history but didn't play a single note on "Raised on Radio." Drummer Smith ended up on three tracks of the album,

Journey

while studio veteran Larry Londin, recently named country music drummer of the year, handled the remainder of the album drum work. The start of the band's tour, originally slated for next month, has been rescheduled three times, while the band struggles to find Smith's replacement. The description of the ideal candidate supplied by guitarist Neal Schon – "someone who can play heavy rock and the fusion thing" – sounded suspiciously like Smith himself.

For Perry, the band's battle to make this album is inextricably linked with the death of his mother late last year. An only child raised in a small town outside Fresno, Perry watched his mother's life ebb away for five years. The final year, he helicoptered out of recording sessions every weekend to sit by her bedside and never went far away without a private chartered jet at the ready.

"I promised her everything would be okay," he said. "She could let go. She didn't need to be here for me. She just didn't want to leave me here. It was her fleeting last strength of maternal love. Journey seemed like it was just business. It didn't seem that important to get back together with those people.

"I quit the band," he admitted. "I had my solo album. My mother was dying. I didn't care if I ever saw another problem from the music business or from, I thought, old friends. But something happened. I realized these guys were no different than me. They've got their problems, too. And there are so many people who like what we do . . ." He choked off a sob and wiped tears from his eyes.

When Perry returned, he took command of a band that may have been teetering on the brink of extinction, despite its multi-platinum success. Not only did the band face serious personnel problems, but, in the three years since the group disappeared from the scene, the sound of mainstream rock had moved substantially away from roaring arena rock guitar blitz in which Journey always specialized. The band was in danger of becoming a dinosaur, a relic of the '70s.

The group's slow but inexorable rise to the top during that decade was initially a product of the management strategy to keep Journey on the road, playing as many concerts as possible, gaining exposure the hard way – town to town. Journey was originally formed around two free agents from the first Santana band, keyboardist Gregg Rollie and guitarist Neal Schon. Tubes drummer Prairie Prince played on the original demo sessions, before the band even had a name. Drummer Aynsley Dunbar, British rock veteran of bands by the likes of Frank Zappa and David Bowie, joined before the 1975 debut album.

For the first three albums, the band explored a steely, largely instrumental sound that dabbled in fusion, all roundly ignored by radio and the record-buying public. Perry was brought as a vocalist to increase the band's commercial potential for the fourth album in 1978. "Infinity, " the resulting album, was the group's first million-seller, as songs like "Wheel in the Sky" and "Lights" finally punctured radio resistance. Clearly, Perry made the difference.

But the big breakthrough came two albums later, with the 1981 release, "Escape." The album sold more than six million copies, contained no fewer than three Top 10 hits – "Who's Crying Now," "Don't Stop Believin'" and "Open Arms" – and made Journey one of the biggest bands in the country. The multi-platinum follow-up, "Frontiers, " contained another major hit, "Separate Ways," as Journey swept across the country topping stadium bills, picking up as much as $40 million at the box office on a single nationwide tour. But it had all been too much for Perry and the band members. "Those last two months," said Perry, "we were not getting along very well."

At that point Perry moved to Los Angeles and produced his smash solo album, "Street Talk," with a precise, gleaming polish none of Journey's albums could match. Other Journey members tried their hands at solo projects – Neal Schon teamed with vocalist Sammy Hagar for a disastrous live recording, and Steve

Smith pursued his interest in fusion with his jazz band, Vital Information – but only Perry succeeded. "If it wasn't for the solo album, " said Perry, "there wouldn't be another Journey album. I vented a lot of frustrations. I learned to appreciate what I do with Journey and to appreciate what I do with myself."

Perry claimed it was Journey keyboardist Jon Cain who encouraged him back in the fold and denied he had made a power play. He said it was the power of music that lured him to return, not the bucks. "Getting back together started with writing material," he said. "Music supersedes everything."Departed drummer Steve Smith, however, maintains Perry only returned after the band agreed to his terms. "None of us felt strong enough to carry on without him," admitted Smith. "Basically we gave him all the power. Financially, we needed a hit record. We wanted him to sing on the record. We didn't want to start all over again. We all had house payments, etcetera."

After Perry settled his differences with the band's management, he set about producing the album, using much of the painstaking procedures he picked up making his solo album. After two months of recording, Perry had only three tracks to the songs he wrote with Schon and Cain that he deemed acceptable and re-placed the two band members with studio musicians, for the recording, at least.

"We agreed to let him produce the records," said Smith. "I actually thought he would be a great producer. Then he insisted on using whoever he wanted to play on the record. We reluctantly agreed. I felt I had no other choice than to leave the band. And I felt insecure about being an individual musician outside the cocoon of Journey."

Bassist Valory, who allowed the band made "certain sacrifices, certain conces-sions" to get Perry back, was more philosophical. "I felt it was possible to go on without him," he said, "but that the most direct, least complicated way to come-back was with him and do whatever it took to keep it going."

Progress in the studio was painfully slow. Working at Sausalito's Plant Stu-dios, Journey began the sessions the same day Huey Lewis and the News recorded "Power of Love" next door. Lewis and band wrapped up their song, went to New York to mix the record, took a short tour of Europe and returned home with the single streaking into the Top 10. Back at the Plant, Journey was still mired cutting the same tracks. The album was completely recorded twice and Perry was still not satisfied. "At points, it seemed like this album refuses to happen," said Perry. "Maybe it's just not meant to be. I thought, no, we'll make it happen."

Smith felt the quality of the tracks was fine. "To me, they lived up as band tracks," he said. "But it wasn't up to what Steve Perry wanted as a solo artist. It wasn't a band anymore. What he said went. What I said didn't matter." Counters Perry: "I produced the album, took the heat and lost a good friend. Steve Smith doesn't want to be my friend. He thought I had the insight that, no matter what, I would do the best thing."

"He really hurt me," said Smith, "because he insulted me personally. I can rationalize, understand. I know how I play. But the hurt goes deep because he was my friend. That's what bothers me the most."

Valory claimed to have taken his not playing on the record less personally. "I was anxious to get moving," he said. "There was a lot of waiting." Valory said it eventually became difficult to envision himself continuing as a member only onstage and quit. Smith said he was asked to leave ("His lawyer called my lawyer," he said).

"They had a meltdown," said Perry, explaining their exit. "It was pride and integrity time."

"I have too much integrity to even associate with him now," said Smith.

Smith currently commutes to New York to drum with Steps Ahead, an elite squad of jazz players, and is about to release his third Vital Information album, "Global Beat." Valory has been rehearsing a four-piece band with his cousin Dan Newsom, veteran of the local band scene, which he described as a somewhat improvisational mixing of styles. Whatever may have happened, Perry at least can say he is happy these days. He and his mates, Schon and Cain, separately make the long drive daily from Marin to the Oakland warehouse where Schon used to practice many years ago with Graham Central Station. These days Schon makes the ride in a new, bright red Ferrari, a succulent fruit of his labors.

"After many years of getting along and not getting along," said Perry, "music is what saved us. The muse was still talking to us. We're very proud of the songs we write. It's something that goes way back that only we can do. There are a lot of emulators these days. There were none before us. But we are the only ones who sound like Journey. The others are what I call sloppy seconds.

"It looked bleak until we got back together and mended ourselves," he said, "but the three of us discovered that possibly, in a friendship sense, we have something that runs underneath all this, not just music."

Sunday Datebook | June 8, 1986

Chris Isaak

Still Blue After All These Years

Chris Isaak records a moody new album. Touring without break for three weeks while preparing for the release of `Forever Blue' has left Chris Isaak a little out of breath

Jimmy Wilsey was running around at some club one night, waving the cover for his band's forthcoming debut album. Isaak and his crew have been a constant in my life since them. Chris and Kenney were an inevitable presence at my annual Elvis Presley birthday parties. I have been a big fan of the Chris Isaak Show long before it was on TV.

CHRIS ISAAK SINGS SONGS ABOUT A LONESOME and desolate world. His quavery voice echoes Roy Orbison's as he navigates the slow, painful ballads of lost love and empty hearts, the wreckage of romance gone bad. He plays the proverbial loner.

"This past year I made a conscious effort to make friends," he says. "After I broke up with my girlfriend, I said, `I don't want to ever be this lonely again.' My apartment was just a bunch of rooms filled with empty boxes. But my tendency is to work on my own. I like people, but somehow I just end up being on my own."

Although "Wicked Game" made him a star, Isaak, 38, still lives in the same small Ocean Beach apartment and drives the same '64 Chevy Nova he always did. Tall and handsome with eyes an unearthly blue, Isaak needs only to look out his window at the waves to decide when to hit the surf. He rides the waves almost every day. Surfing, of course, is renowned as the loner's sport.

"The songs themselves are kinda accidental, what they're about," he says, strolling through the residential neighborhood behind the Santa Cruz nightclub where he will play that night. "No matter what, it always ends up being about you. I never sit down to write about my life. I never sit down to write about somebody. I never direct it. That would be like Tin Pan Alley. I just sit down with a guitar for fun and see what comes out.

"I like to write about love," he says, "and the most moving thing you can have is unrequited love or when love goes astray."

Those blue eyes are lightly glazed. He has been going without a break for three

355

weeks, without a day to himself. He and his band drove up from Los Angeles and will leave the following day for Europe. He takes a legal pad back to the hotel room, where he will take one last look at the new video and make some notes. The new album, "Forever Blue," will be released in a couple of weeks and the treadmill has already started. And Isaak is already tired.

Walking through the Santa Cruz streets, he remembers living in the beach town as a teenager fresh out of Stockton, sleeping under a makeshift canvas cover in the back of a pickup truck. He worked as a busboy and showered at the beach. His friends would come to visit and drool over the romantic image his life presented.

Isaak's songs are populated by characters haunted by loss, obsessed with loves they can't have. He says he wrote the stark, plaintive acoustic ballad that gave the new album its title in about 20 minutes, while sitting in his dark apartment. He gave up writing a letter to his ex-girlfriend and turned to his guitar. The song just spilled out. "It was one of those things where I wondered if this was going to sound as good tomorrow," he says. "Forever Blue," his fifth album, will be released this week. But already the leadoff single, "Somebody's Crying," is stirring excitement in advance. Not only have radio stations taken the track to their bosom, but both VH-1 and MTV immediately added the video to their playlists, an unprecedented welcome for an Isaak work. It is an assured, moody album, a confident journey through familiar territory for a veteran traveler.

Since his 1985 debut album, Isaak has steadfastly pursued his singular vision. He and producer Erik Jacobsen, who first earned his spurs cutting hits with the Lovin' Spoonful in the '60s, approach the task of recording with a near-manic compulsiveness. Songs can often be rehearsed for weeks, trying every possible tempo, only to end up being recorded at the original rhythm. Vocals are frequently pieced together, even syllable by syllable, from dozens of multitrack versions. The mere recording of the latest album took five months, not counting mixing the finished product, and that is a short time by Isaak's standards. He says it is not uncommon for Jacobsen to keep working on a song for eight or nine months.

"Erik's detail-oriented," says Isaak. "I love things that happen in a moment. We hardly ever disagree. But if there's some strange-sounding note that just feels right, I'm the guy who says, `Let's keep it.' "

Drummer Kenny Johnson agrees. "Erik has amazing ears," he says. "He hears things you don't, but he's never wrong."

Isaak has been working with drummer Johnson and bassist Rollie Salley for more than 10 years. They are more than musical associates. They are trusty side-kicks who ride the range alongside him. "We've kept a lot of life on these records by working up arrangements with the same people," says Isaak.

"But in the studio, you try to get things to sound perfect," he says, "as though angels done it."

His hair askew from the long van ride, an untucked T-shirt hanging over his pants, Isaak leads his band through a sound check at the Catalyst, his trademark plastic tiki lights hanging from the rafters. They try out a few of the songs from the new album, in between goofing around with saxophonist Johnny Reno playing the rhythm and blues oldie "Honky Tonk," or oozing sultry sensuality on "Harlem Nocturne."

The album contains not a single note of saxophone, although Reno did contribute some background vocals and they find room for the instrument in the live shows.

"He's my friend," says Isaak. "He plays great. He sings great. He adds a lot to the show. And when we go to small towns, they never saw something like Johnny Reno."

New guitarist Herschel Yatovitz practices the whammy bar touch on the solo to "You Owe Me Some Kind of Love." He didn't play on the album and may not even be able to play with the band all the way through the summer tour. On the album, lead guitar chores were shared by Los Angeles studio veteran Mark Goldenberg, who has played with Linda Ronstadt and Jackson Browne, among many others, and Jason Morgan, a 19-year-old unknown Isaak met in a San Francisco guitar store who played his first-ever recording sessions on Isaak's new album.

"On albums, I've always brought in different people on different things," Isaak says. "But they are the grace notes."

After Isaak's first two albums went unnoticed, Warner Bros. stood still for one more album, "Heart Shaped World," released in 1989. Despite his becoming something of an in-house favorite with the label, his situation with the record company remained precarious. He joked while performing at the extravagant company picnic, where employees' children romped with rented animals, "If we don't start moving some records, we're going to have to sell the petting zoo."

"Heart Shaped World" also passed through the market with barely a ripple. In fact, when the sound track to the film "Wild at Heart" was released the following year containing a cut from the Isaak album, that cut also had disappeared shortly after its release.

`Wicked Game' Scores

Then a radio programmer in Atlanta added the Isaak track "Wicked Game" to his play list. It caught fire and burned up the charts. The sexy MTV video cemented Isaak's mushrooming public profile, and a new album, already under way, was put on hold while Isaak and the band hit the road, chasing the serendipitous Top Five success of the single.

When it came time to finally record the next album, Isaak no longer felt any pressure to produce a hit record. "I was free as a bird," he says. "I knew this was the one time they're not going to drop me, no matter what I do."

But before the sessions could even start, his longtime associate and one of the prime architects of his patented sound, guitarist Jimmy Wilsey, left the band. Isaak looks downcast, bringing up the subject. "I haven't seen Jimmy," he says. "I've heard rumors. No one knows where he is. It's more than business. I've known the guy for a long time. I'd just like to know what's going on with him."

Despite his cultivated image as a sexy, remote character, Isaak can brandish a courageous deadpan wit. He once played a lunchtime concert at the Warner Bros. Records lot, coming after Prince on an enormous purple stage. He brought an acoustic guitar and Johnson played a pair of bongo drums. "This proves that Prince isn't all ego," he told the crowd. "He's willing to open for a much bigger act. And another thing I want to know," Isaak continued, "if he doesn't want the name anymore, can I have it?"

Accordion Finale

In his live shows, Isaak has been known to finish an hour's worth of his dark songs by whipping out an accordion and romping through the Louis Jordan oldie, "Caldonia." "The music I take seriously," he says. "But I hope I don't take myself seriously. I don't trust people who don't laugh. You've got to watch out for those disgruntled postal employees."

But Isaak has always been a focused artist, in charge of his own image projection, carefully scrutinizing details like photo sessions, videos, album packaging. "There's always somebody who knows exactly what you should do with your act," he says. "But, like with a video, it might have been a great idea, but if I don't get it, I don't do it. I have to do something I believe in. That way, when it's a flop, I don't have to say, `I know – I didn't get it either.'"

In that same scrupulous manner, Isaak has pursued a sideline career as a film actor, taking unusual, oddball parts – like the crazed killer dressed in a clown outfit in "Married to the Mob" or his brief cameo as a federal agent in "Silence of the Lambs." He recently completed a one-line part as a '50s rock-and-roll musician in an upcoming film by director Allison Anders ("Mi Vida Loca"), in which he encounters a record producer in the studio, played by John Turturro. Isaak spent several months in Nepal filming a major role in "Little Buddha."

"I enjoyed doing a story like that," says Isaak, "rather than a film that has a bunch of guns and car crashes – and I like guns and car crashes. But it was a cool story – it attacked a big subject."

Yet, for all his single-minded intensity about his career, Isaak laughs at the thought that he had an overall plan or strategy.

"I don't have a clue," he says. "I make all these plans. But when the lights go out, I wonder what I'm doing with my life. No matter how much you're focused, everyone's still out there swinging and searching."

Sunday Datebook | May 28, 1995

Kenny Johnson and Chris Isaak

Metallica

Metallica nearly fades to black, but comes back

> They sat me in the studio with one of their engineers and
> made me listen to the whole album before they would do the
> interview. Only way they could have made me do it.

THE DAY AFTER METALLICA OPENED FOR THE ROLLING STONES three years ago at SBC Park, the band came back together at HQ, the group's multimillion-dollar rehearsal hall/business office/nerve center in industrial San Rafael. It was their first time alone together since the making of the documentary "Some Kind of Monster," which captured the band almost breaking up.

"It was a different atmosphere," says drummer Lars Ulrich. "There was no psychiatrist, no film crew. It was just the four of us in that room, getting ready to write and play."

The kingpin hard-rock band's ninth studio album, "Death Magnetic," arrives today in stores. It is not only an album that almost never got made, but also a return to the sound that made Metallica in the first place. "Death Magnetic" is a renaissance orchestrated by famed producer Rick Rubin, a man associated with comeback recordings by the Red Hot Chili Peppers, Johnny Cash and, most recently, Neil Diamond.

"It's like a solar eclipse," says guitarist-vocalist James Hetfield, "every five to 10 years, a Metallica album. Our watches are so slow – until we get onstage. We take our time. We want it to be right. I realize in five years, a lot of bands have come and gone. Our fans are patient. I think they realize the wait was worth it."

Hetfield, dressed for sunny weather in T-shirt, shorts and flip-flops, slouches in a leather couch under a framed movie poster for "Hells Angels '69" in the HQ lounge last week. He is squeezing in an interview and a doctor's appointment early in the morning, beginning a day devoted to promoting the new album. Dave Grohl of the Foo Fighters is expected to show up later, to host a nationwide radio broadcast of the new album. A few dozen fan club contest winners are arriving in the afternoon for a barbecue and will be treated to a short performance in the band's recording studio, where every available space has been fitted with chairs for the intimate show. Ulrich arrives later, two phone interviews already down.

Although Metallica hardly qualifies as a candidate for a comeback – with lifetime sales near 100 million, the band still ranks among the top record-sellers and concert attractions in rock – the previous album, "St. Anger," was forged in the heat of the near collapse of the band, stretching across an 11-month hiatus in the middle of recording while front man Hetfield entered drug and alcohol rehabilitation and put his life back together. Documentary filmmakers painstakingly recorded the entire episode. The resulting album, a collaborative experiment overseen by longtime Metallica producer Bob Rock, was widely viewed as a mixed success.

"A lot of people in the hard-rock world don't think a lot of 'St. Anger,' and I can understand that," says Ulrich. "But without 'St. Anger,' we wouldn't be here. 'St Anger' served its purpose. Some people consider it a failed experiment and I appreciate that, but it was a necessary record."

Return to form

On the new record, however, the band returns purposefully to the riff-rich territory of "Master of Puppets" and "Ride the Lightning," Metallica's landmark 1980s recordings that redefined hard rock, a sound it has carefully avoided ever since. The new album was initially researched and developed in informal jams a half hour before showtime on the "St. Anger" tour.

"We get fragmented on tour," says Hetfield, "so a half hour before we go on, we check each other's faces. Jamming makes the world go away, makes it all good."

Works-in-progress were given titles such as "Caspar," because it came out of a Wyoming backstage, or "Black Squirrel," because the band members saw black squirrels in Montreal, where that jam took place. The band even started performing a couple of unfinished tracks in concerts: "The New Song," which eventually developed into "Death Is Not the End," and "The Other New Song." At the end of the tour, there were 16 CDs full of musical ideas and partly finished songs from the preshow rituals.

Rubin, a longtime friend of the band who currently serves as "co-head" of Columbia Records, continues to produce acts outside the Columbia label. Probably the single most powerful and influential producer in the industry these days, Rubin started out making rap records in his NYU dorm room, where he let the unknown Beastie Boys sleep on the floor. After introducing rap to the mainstream with acts such as LL Cool J on his Def Jam label, Rubin turned his attention to Slayer, an intense thrash-metal band that took more than a few pages from Metallica's book. That was about the time he first met the members of Metallica.

"I always knew we were going to make a record with Rick Rubin," says Ulrich. "I just didn't know which one."

Rubin wanted the songs to be as complete as possible before entering the studio. The 16 CDs were whittled down to 24 songs, which were finally boiled down to the seven on the record. Some of the rejects were turned into what hot-rod enthusiast Hetfield called "parts cars."

Collaborative effort

Rubin also solved the ever-present struggle for power between Hetfield and Ulrich by simply ignoring it. "Rick Rubin had no idea who belonged to what – Lars' idea or my idea," says Hetfield. "He didn't care. He would just say, 'I like this better' and that's all there was."

"He made us feel good about embracing the past, which we've never done," says Ulrich. "We made three or four records in the '80s – 'Masters of Puppets,' 'Go Ride the Lightning' – we felt there was nothing more to say with a thrash/heavy metal record, and we've always shied away from going back to those records."

"Death Magnetic" strips Metallica of all studio effects, leaving the band wailing away ferociously. Riptide rhythms and buzz saw guitars drive the band through Rubin's dry, action-packed soundscape. After the intentionally sololess "St. Anger," guitarist Kirk Hammett is unleashed again and he lays down blistering barrage after blistering barrage. Bassist Robert Trujillo, who replaced Jason Newsted after "St. Anger" was recorded (producer Rock handled bass on the record), makes his first official appearance on a Metallica record.

"Rick Rubin used the word 'essence' – the 'essence' of Metallica," says Hetfield. "We have no idea what that is. We are Metallica. Everything we've done is an essence. Everything has been an adventure. He brought us back to what made us us."

The band ceded unprecedented control to Rubin, such as letting him and his staff mix the record while Metallica toured. Band members limited their input to telephone conferences with all four around a speaker box. But Hetfield says the band is much more comfortable now with their unique personal dynamics.

"Lars and I grew a lot," he says. "We're both still stubborn, both still grabbing at the steering wheel, while the other two sit in the back."

These men have been Metallica since they were young, little more than boys really. They dressed alike and maintained a gang mentality, refusing to jam with any other musicians. They spent five years on the road, working their way up from the bottom of the bill to headline attraction at stadiums. Once they came home, they spent another five years recording four albums, literally closed in dark, windowless rooms for much of the time. Now life is different.

Balancing act

The band tours only one week on, one week off (the group plays the Oracle Arena on Dec. 20). The four musicians have 10 children under age 10 between them – "the Metallica baby factory," Ulrich calls it. They are busy picking up kids at soccer matches. Ulrich can't help relishing some of the irony in the aftermath of the crisis conditions of five years ago. "Not only did we survive it," he says, "but we made our best record."

He leans back and smiles. "I hate to use such non-heavy metal words as 'pleasant' – like 'Everything is pleasant.' Actually I like to say it – 'pleasant.' Everybody gets along. The last two years are the best we've ever had. We found a balance between Metallica and what we need."

San Francisco Chronicle | Friday, September 12, 2008

Guitarist Satriani chases perfect 'rock moment'

Joe Satriani – Satch, to his friends – is such a sweet, earnest gentleman he is practically disqualified as a musician.

WHEN GUITARIST JOE SATRIANI CALLED HIS BAND TOGETHER to begin recording his latest album, he knew what he wanted the other musicians to do.

"I told them, 'What I'm going to ask you to create on this record is what we're going to call a rock moment,'" he says. "I don't care if you miss that accent, if you blow through something. I want you to find the spot in this song where you can play your rock moment.'

Joe Satriani

"'That guidance seemed to help us play a certain way."

Satriani, 47, knows rock moments. His entire adult life has been an exhaustive quest for just such epiphanies on electric guitar. He is rock's leading instrumental artist, and he conscientiously developed his own unique voice on an instrument played by many.

Satriani lives with his wife, Rubina, their 11-year-old son, Z.Z., and a chummy Norwich terrier named Grizz on a shady side street in decidedly upscale Laurel Heights, where one of his neighbors owns the Golden State Warriors and the other is the son of the founder of the Gap. His artist wife, who also used to run antique stores, has decorated the spacious '50s home with old clocks and rough-hewn, custom-built wooden doors. Downstairs, a big, largely empty rumpus room opens to the garden. Off to the side, a small room barely bigger than a large closet is where Satriani spends hours every day chasing those moments.

The walls of the small, windowless studio are covered with framed photographs and posters of rock guitar heroes such as Hendrix and Led Zeppelin, along with Satriani's own gold record awards. A tiny drum kit is squashed into the corner, and a rack holds a surprisingly small group of guitars and a couple of electric basses. Satriani sits on an armless chair in front of a computer playing guitar at car-radio volume in this little room daily for hours at a time – "eight to 10 hours, easily," he says.

He mainly plays the JS Joe Satriani model Ibanez, a wooden electric guitar covered with a veneer of aluminum. With a pair of his trademark wrap- around sunglasses, his gleaming guitar and cleanly shaved head, he is instantly transformed into a rock star. Without the guitar and the glasses, he is a soft, delicate, almost wan gentleman with an easy grin and sharp, intelligent eyes.

Growing up as the youngest of five children in Long Island, he turned 14 in 1970, the year Jimi Hendrix died. He had taken drum lessons earlier, but picked up the guitar. He learned music theory in high school. He loved all of the big dumb blues-rock guitarists of the day, but he found a chord book by jazz guitarist Joe Pass that, he says, "changed my playing forever." He also found his way to a second-floor apartment in a Queens brownstone, where he took music lessons from the famed blind jazz pianist Lennie Tristano, who not only played with Charlie Parker and Dizzy Gillespie but was also known as a teacher to big-name '50s jazz musicians such as saxophonist Lee Konitz.

Tristano, a disciplinarian who could abruptly end a lesson if he heard a mistake, taught Satriani that he had to find his own voice.

"He said suburban kids all suffered from the subjunctive disease," Satriani says, "should have, could have, would have ... He taught me to play only what you want to play, not what other people want you to play."

When Satriani moved out to Berkeley in 1976, sharing a small apartment with two older sisters, he locked himself up for a couple of months and spent 13 hours a day incessantly playing, searching for his voice. "It was like trying to lose an accent," he said.

But Satriani always taught guitar, too, giving his first lessons a year and a half after he started playing. One of his Long Island students, Steve Vai, was becoming well known through his work with Frank Zappa and David Lee Roth and was talking about Satriani in interviews with guitar magazines.

In Berkeley, while he played by night in a new-wave outfit called the Squares, he gave lessons during the day above a Grove Street guitar store to young unknowns such as Kirk Hammett of Metallica, David Bryson of Counting Crows and Larry LaLonde of Primus. He developed enough of a reputation on the local club circuit that when the Greg Kihn Band, riding high behind the hit "Jeopardy," lost its guitar player, Satriani got the job.

All the time, he experimented with instrumental recordings (he issued an EP on his own in 1984), but it was his second album, "Surfing With the Alien," that landed him a job backing Mick Jagger on a solo tour of the Far East and started his solo career. "I had never played instrumental music before an audience before," he said.

His ninth album, "Is There Love in Space?," released today, catches Satriani in rip-snorting improvisational rides, laying searing, stinging leads over thick, grinding rhythm parts. Although he cut the album's basic tracks at the Plant studios in Sausalito with engineer John Cuniberti, who has been twiddling knobs for Satriani since he was sound man for the Squares, many of the album's guitar overdubs were done alone in the downstairs closet (credited as Studio 21 in the liner notes).

Sometimes, Satriani admits, he escapes from his cell and retreats to his bedroom upstairs, where he will play nothing but acoustic guitar for weeks. He practiced "If I Could Fly," a song on the new album, that way. Although Satriani is a notorious perfectionist in the studio, one track on the album, "Searching," is nothing but a 10-minute jam in the studio. At first, Satriani refused to even listen to it. But after returning from tour, he listened and slowly warmed to what he heard.

"At first I thought, that's not professional," he says. "Once I got over that, I started to see that someone would hear a voice that they would identify with me."

But Satriani refuses to get more analytical than that. "That's about as close as I want to go. I don't want to know that part of the secret or mystery. I might feel satisfied or, worse, proud."

Another track on the new album also turned out to be a first-take keeper, "Up in Flames," a piece originally intended for a super-group called Planet Us that was on the drawing boards with Sammy Hagar, who instead decided to rejoin Van Halen. "That was the take that had the grease on it," says Satriani. "It was undisciplined, but it sounded right to my ears. I picked up the guitar, did one pass and I thought, 'This was cool.' But that doesn't mean there weren't some songs I played a million times until I got them right.

"You never know when your rock moment is going to happen," he says. "But you've got to respect it when it does."

San Francisco Chronicle | April 13, 2004

CHAPTER 11

Backstage Secrets

Third Blind Eye

Eddie Money

The Last Waltz

Blind Ambition

Third Eye Blind leader Stephan Jenkins makes sure his band is a success

This took weeks. At the time, everybody wanted to talk about Stephan Jenkins; now nobody cares. The article caught the exact height of the Third Eye Blind bell curve; the week the band's second album, the first one without "Semi-Charmed Life," was released.

STEPHAN JENKINS IS A CLASSIC – A ROCK 'N' ROLL BAD BOY with an angel face and a movie-star girlfriend. He rides around town with his dog on a Triumph motorcycle and lives in a rented room above his manager's office in an unremarkable Cole Valley duplex.

More than just his group's singer, songwriter and record producer, Stephan Jenkins dreamed up the name for the band and wrote many of the songs before there were any other musicians involved. His colleagues are all seasoned, highly skilled rockers, but he is clearly the alpha dog of the pack. The band is a corporation wholly owned by Jenkins. Make no mistake, Jenkins is Third Eye Blind.

Third Eye Blind's 1997 self-titled debut sold more than 3 million copies and lofted three hits into the Top 10, including the No. 1 "Semi-Charmed Life." The release earlier this week of the second album, "Blue," could make 3EB the biggest rock band out of San Francisco in a long, long time. "Anything," the screaming rocker released as the first single, is scorching up modern-rock radio playlists.

But people who have worked with Jenkins, if they will talk at all, don't necessarily have nice things to say about him. He has already settled one lawsuit with an old friend. People accuse him of stealing credits he didn't earn. They call him ambitious, driven – which Jenkins confirms.

"I don't think I owe anyone an apology," said Jenkins, unflinching and unfazed. He's heard it all before.

Lower haight roots

Behind the multiplatinum success of Third Eye Blind lies a tangled path that Jenkins followed. If the first album romanticizes the bohemian decadence so easily found around the lower Haight in the early '90s, it is a subject Jenkins knows firsthand.

Third Eye Blind

Longtime friend and later manager Eric Gotland and Jenkins were always the team. They met in 1990 when they were both living on lower Haight Street. Jenkins was a starving rapper wannabe. Gotland was, by day, a straight-arrow management consultant not even allowed to wear colored shirts at his job. By night, he was a lousy club DJ with a huge record collection.

"That was my 1967, my summer of love," said Jenkins, 35. "So much of the first record is drawn from that time."

Jenkins, who grew up in Palo Alto and graduated with an English degree from the University of California at Berkeley, rented out his room and started sleeping in the closet. He was living on money he stole from his roommates to buy coffee, eating lots of Top Ramen and writing songs. "I had a moral boundary," he said. "I wouldn't take anything larger than a quarter."

He started as one-half of an interracial rap duo that eventually landed a song on a soundtrack.

Jenkins teamed with a reggae musician from Detroit, Herman Anthony Chunn, who had a shaved head and called himself Zen, to form Puck and Natty. Their tape found its way to industry heavyweights such as Clive Davis and Irving Azoff.

A track, "Just Wanna Be Your Friend," landed on a soundtrack album of the hit TV show"Beverly Hills, 90210" in 1992.

"You want me to do a song for your TV show that I've never seen?" Jenkins said."No problem. It was $7,800. I bought groceries."

With a cut on a soundtrack and the label interested in signing the group, Jenkins needed a manager. His brother was in a fraternity at the University of California at Davis with Adam Duritz of Counting Crows. Martin Kirkup and Steve Jensen of Direct Management, who managed the Crows, signed them as Puck and Zen. The duo took the new name after New Age-y duo Tuck and Patti raised objections to Puck and Natty. (Leave it to English major Jenkins to adopt a pseudonym from Shakespeare's most mischievous character.)

The record company never released the Puck and Zen track as a single, but another stepped up to the bar. Jenkins found himself in a meeting with Capitol Records executives – "The whole thing was so not rock," he said – discussing who should produce Puck and Zen. "I told them I don't want a second opinion." Capitol quickly lost interest.

"For Puck and Zen, that was it," Jenkins said. "We couldn't withstand that." Zen would not comment for this article.

All through Puck and Zen, the vision of a rock band was growing in Jenkins' mind. He already had a name – Third Eye Blind. And he had some songs, including a piece he developed out of music written by Zen that came to be called "Semi-Charmed Life," Jenkins' tale of sleazy sex and crystal meth that eventually would propel him to stardom.

"I was telling these guys that I had these ideas," Jenkins said."I wanted a production company. I wanted to write my own rock songs. I was having fun with the Puck and Zen thing, but it was a more immediate thing. `You're unfocused,' everyone said. Except Eric (Gotland)."

He needed a band and some demo recordings.

A trip to skywalker

Jenkins met engineer David Gleeson at a Puck and Zen session. Gleeson took Jenkins and his first edition of Third Eye Blind – including bassist Jason Slater and guitarist George Earth of World Entertainment War – to cut demos in world- class studios at Skywalker Ranch and the Marin County studios of Walter Afanasieff, who had produced Celine Dion and Mariah Carey.

Putting a band together and getting established on the local club scene proved problematic and became a sticking point with his Hollywood managers. Jenkins went through a number of guitarists before finding Kevin Cadogan. Arion Salazar from East Bay punk-funksters Fungo Mungo joined on bass. Many drummers came and went before Steve Bowman, freshly dismissed from Counting Crows, took the drum chair. To get his band its first gig, Jenkins appealed directly to Duritz by letter for an opening slot on the Counting Crows shows at the Fillmore Auditorium in October 1994.

"My managers saw the last two songs," Jenkins said.

Third Eye Blind set about carefully making a mark on the local club scene. One longtime scenester remembered early 3EB shows: "Even opening for some s– band at the Paradise, the guy acted like he was at the Oakland Coliseum." Jenkins: "So? You ought to see me at rehearsal."

Engineer producer Gleeson quit working with the band in a huff. "He and Stephan had a fight, a blowout," Gotland said.

Gleeson, who received a small credit on the first 3EB album, reportedly settled a lawsuit for six figures after the multiplatinum success, Gotland said.

Gleeson would not comment for this article.

Battle of the bands

The real low point came in July 1995 with Cocky Pop I. The event was designed to trumpet the three leading unsigned bands of San Francisco's live rock scene and would star Third Eye Blind. The band rented the Transmission Theater and joined forces with two other comers in the clubs, Protein and Heavy Into Jeff. Record company talent scouts flew in for the event, which turned into a debacle for 3EB.

The band's latest drummer, Michael Urbano, quit shortly before the show. Jenkins was suffering from chronic fatigue syndrome, which left him feverish and nauseous when he wasn't actually onstage. With little draw of their own, the musicians faced a hall filled with Protein fans. At the show, guitarist Cadogan's amp blew out two songs into the set.

"Protein wiped the floor with us," Jenkins said. "They got signed that night. Heavy Into Jeff stomped us."

The band lost the big-time managers, the engineer who had been supervising its recordings and Jenkins' publishing deal. The whole thing was on the verge of falling apart. "It would have been a good time to quit," Jenkins said.

Instead, the band regrouped, pulling together, at last, the winning team. Drummer Brad Hargreaves joined. Gotland finally assumed management. They found a new recording engineer, a crucial player as the band prepared another assault on the record industry.

Recording a demo

Gear hound Slater kept a lot of equipment at a small recording studio in Redwood City run by a musician named Eric Dodd. Dodd, who called himself Eric Valentine, was once half of Hollywood Records rock group T-Ride. Dodd didn't want to front the band time, but he agreed to engineer the sessions once Gotland stepped up with his credit cards.

"Eric threw down and paid for the demos and they were expensive," Jenkins said. "But we had recorded these songs multiple times and, in Eric Dodd, I had an engineer who could do it."

"I guess the stuff came out reasonably well," Dodd said. "There was some interest from record companies. It was a reasonably creative combination."

RCA Victor coughed up money for more recording and then passed. The group auditioned for hit-picker Clive Davis of Arista Records in New York. "He said, `Do you have any more?'" Jenkins recalled.

One label felt strongly enough to arrange a showcase performance at the Viper Room on the Sunset Strip in Hollywood. Among the record industry heavies in the crowd that April 1996 night was Sylvia Rhone, president of Elektra Records, one of the most powerful women in the record business. "Sylvia was in the crowd high-fiving people, like she'd already made the deal," Jenkins said. "We made the deal we wanted."

Signed personally by the president of the label in June 1996, armed with a new publishing deal that the label said was one of the biggest ever given to a new artist, Jenkins was ready to make his major-label debut and was going to produce the record himself. Over the course of the sessions, however, engineer Dodd felt his role shift.

"There was quite a bit of trauma that went down, and I'm not sure how much I'm supposed to talk about," Dodd said. "There came a point where it became obvious that I was doing production work and I was hired as an engineer."

Jenkins said Dodd was given a co-production credit – "He never asked for it," he said – and that he was paid a fair royalty. Still, some observers think Dodd made some substantial contributions to the recording that, in other circumstances, could have made him a full producer, a difference that can mean big money and more work.

"He produced the s– out of that record," Slater said. "I think Stephan even got credit for production, but he didn't produce that record . . . Eric and Stephan didn't get along at all."

Sometime before the release of the album, Gotland cut a deal with Jenkins' old partner, Zen, to sell his interest in a couple of songs, including "Semi-Charmed Life," which became a No. 1 record and 3EB's biggest hit. Gotland said he advised Zen against selling the song.

Jenkins fiercely defended his proprietorship of the song. "He wrote part of the music, part of the riff," Jenkins said. "I kept going until it was my song. I had no idea where that song was going, but I bought him out."

He bought out Zen for $10,000 before the album was released to become the song's sole author.

The song did benefit from a lot of work. Many versions were recorded.

"A lot of people contributed to that song," Dodd said. "It's been around for many years. There are a lot of people who contributed to that tune and didn't get credit."

On the road

After the April 1997 release of the first album, the four musicians spent the next two years on the road. The band started as an opening act for U.K. alt-rockers James but quickly graduated to headline status.

The Third Eye Blind record started to get airplay almost immediately and, as each of the three hit singles – "Semi-Charmed Life," "Jumper" and "How's It Going to Be" – went into MTV rotation and headed up the charts, the crowds grew. The band opened a few dates for U2 and the Rolling Stones. Jenkins got into wars of words in the press with other rock stars. He started getting his name in gossip columns by dating his current girlfriend, actress Charlize Theron.

The band barely paused from the endless tour before entering the studio to start the new album.

Second time around

Behind an anonymous Mission Street storefront facade, Toast Studios was home away from home to Third Eye Blind for five months this year. With the October 15 deadline for delivery of its second album five days away, tapes of some songs were being mixed in two other studios, while Jenkins put down some last-minute vocals on other songs in downtown San Francisco. Salazar's vintage keyboards were stashed in every corner. Guitarist Cadogan had a room piled with cords and equip ment. A poster of '40s burlesque queen Patti Waggins, borrowed from manager Gotland's extensive collection, stared back into the control room from the other side of the glass.

"It's an album we can hold our heads up about," Jenkins said. Later he uses the word"redeeming" to describe it. As soon as he finished the record, he flew off to Savannah, Ga., to visit Theron on location.

Even before release, Jenkins' new record hit a nerve, this one at the top of the corporate ladder at Elektra's parent company, Time Warner. The label asked Jenkins to substitute an instrumental for the full version of"Slow Motion," a song that spoofs violence, written by Jenkins. Label executives were apparently sensitive to the issue since the slaying two years ago of schoolteacher Jonathan Levin, the son of Time Warner Chairman Gerald Levin.

"Miss Jones taught me English/ But I think I just shot her son/ 'Cause he owed me money/ With a bullet in the chest you cannot run," go the lyrics.

The pressure of following up his big hit record, Jenkins said, makes him wake up at 6 in the morning grinding his teeth. Jenkins is not ready to coast.

He declines the laurels because the race isn't won.

"I was possessed," Jenkins said."People thought I was crazy. I probably was. I'm more quiet inside now. There's that whole thing in Western mythology that for a man to feel good he has to have gone out and slayed a dragon. To some extent, I've done that.

"But the journey doesn't stop. There's no sense of arrival with Third Eye Blind. I think we can grow. I don't feel like I've arrived. That doesn't mean I'm not happily inspired by the journey.

"Twenty years from now, I'll be in some studio arguing over whether there's too much cello. It's my life's work, and I'd do it all for free."

Sunday Datebook | November 28, 1999

Eddie Money Fights Back After 'the Accident'

In his first interview since he almost died from a drug overdose, his management representatives were worried I would mention his cane. They shouldn't have bothered. Mahoney waltzed into the photo shoot, swinging the thing around like Maurice Chevalier. Interesting footnote to our discussion; Eddie didn't know you could overdose from smoking heroin until he did it. Oh, well. Live and learn.

EDDIE MONEY COULD HAVE DIED. For a couple of weeks, the odds were 3-2 he would. At the very least, he would be crippled. Doctors told him he would never walk again.

He doesn't like to talk about what happened. He calls it "the accident," although it was hardly accidental he was taking drugs the night he almost lost his life nearly two years ago.

At first, both hospital officials and his management insisted he suffered only from food poisoning. Rumors nevertheless flew and even when an East Bay newspaper reported that he had suffered a drug overdose, both the hospital and his management still denied it.

Erroneous reports that his leg had been amputated prompted his office to release a carefully worded statement: "General fatigue combined with alcohol and unknown drugs contributed to Eddie's blood poisoning." Money himself wasn't talking.

Today, almost two years later, he is back and thriving, perhaps as never before. His new album, "No Control," looks like a winner. He is engaged to be married. A grueling regimen of physical therapy has given him discipline he never had before. He has cut out drink and drugs. Next weekend he returns to the stage for the first time since "the accident."

They took me to the hospital and I swore I wouldn't go/My blood was running much too high and my heart was much too low.
> – "No Control" by Eddie Money

Eddie Mahoney arrived in the Bay Area 13 years ago, tossed out of the Brooklyn police force. His grandfather, father and brother all served with New York's finest, but his own stint in blue came to a sudden end when a carbon copy of a letter he wrote mentioning the use of marijuana was found.

He first emerged on the Berkeley rock scene with a band named the Rockets – calling himself Eddie Spaghetti at the time – that broke up in a fistfight onstage at the Longbranch, a now-defunct, seedy San Pablo Avenue rock club. Shortly thereafter, he changed his name again and began leading bands at the Longbranch under his new moniker, Eddie Money.

The Bill Graham organization signed him for management and CBS Records contracted with him to make albums. His first, "Eddie Money," earned him two Top 10 singles – "Baby Hold On" and "Two Tickets to Paradise" – and sold more than a million copies. The second LP, "Life for the Taking," also sold a million, although it yielded no hit singles. His third album in 1980, "Playing For Keeps," turned out to be an expensive failure, but Money still headlined lucrative concerts across the country. He turned 30 with a half-million dollars in the bank.

"I always wanted a gold record," Money said. "I always wanted to play Madison Square Garden and I always wanted to be a rock-and-roll star. Now I have all that and I almost killed myself."

Last month, Money sat in his suburban Lafayette home, ducks wandering around poolside in his backyard, and talked about his traumas of the past two years. He looked tanned and healthy and as if he had been eating perhaps a little too well. "My mother said she prayed for me to gain weight," he grinned. "Now she says maybe she prayed too much."

His last tour, during the worst of the 1980 gas crunch, played consistently to half-empty houses. He broke up with his girlfriend and came home rather depressed. "I was on the road really for four and a half years," he said. "I was actually a very miserable, rich young man."

On that near-tragic November night, Eddie Money visited some acquaintances in Oakland, looking for something to cheer him up. "I was in there doing some toot," he explained. "I was really drunk and having a good ol' time. Somebody gave me what I thought was cocaine and it was this white synthetic powder that's like a bathtub thing. It's a synthetic barbiturate that they make up for junkies to kick when they can't do junk. But I wasn't a junkie. I was just stoned on toot and booze and they gave me this pure barbiturate. Barbiturates and alcohol – forget it.

"I went out like a light. Nobody woke me up. Nobody tried to walk me around

Eddie Money

the room. The guy who owned the place went to a party. The other guy taking care of the place was trying to make love to my old lady. I woke up 15 hours later and I couldn't believe – 'cause I was straight and all – that this happened to me. I didn't know at the same time that my kidneys went out completely."

Eventually, a trusted friend was summoned and took Money to two East Bay hospitals. Money talked his way out of both, saying he only sprained his leg. Little did he know at the time. He went home to sleep – "which would have been the end of me completely," he said – but his friend, still troubled by his condition, returned.

"So they took me into John Muir Hospital in Walnut Creek and that's the last thing I remember for two days," he recalled. "The next thing I knew I woke up and disconnected my life support units to try and walk out of the place to do a TV show. I'm telling you the truth. And I couldn't get up. It was a horror show. My kidneys were out and I f--ed up. I killed a nerve in my f--ing leg. I had some doctors tell me it was never going to come back and I was flipping out."

The kidneys came back but the road to recovery for his leg was a long, slow, painful one. He used a walker to shuffle around his house. His mother had to lift him into the bathtub. "When I got out of the hospital," he said, his voice turning solemn at the memory, "they gave me this f--ing shoe, this brace. I said this can't be for me and they said oh yeah, it's yours. Mahoney? It's yours."

He killed a nerve in his leg from the top of his thigh to the tip of his toe when he passed out by crossing his legs and blocking circulation. At first, the doctors told him not to expect to walk any more. But they were wrong. First, he got rid of the walker, then the crutches, then the leg brace. Only the cane remains now. He undergoes physical therapy daily – "this guy comes over and twists me up like a pretzel." His limp is barely detectable.

"I went to see a couple specialists who gave me the true lowdown," Money said. "They said look, Money, you'll have 90 percent of your leg back. It's just gonna take, probably, another year. You can't fight science, Money."

At first, the prospect of not walking again had depressed him so, he didn't even want to get out of bed in the morning. His friend Dave Revering, then a baseball player with the Oakland A's, visited Money and gave him a pep talk. When Revering was a sophomore in high school, he told Money, a pickup truck smashed into him, splintered his leg in seven places and landed him in a hospital for seven months. "You gotta get up," Revering exhorted. "You gotta move. You gotta walk."

And walk he did. He began work on an album, a curtain of silence drawn over his medical problems. "When the office said they weren't going to say nothing about the accident," he said, "I just started writing tunes about it, because, basically, the accident happened and I didn't think I could hide it."

Producer Tom Dowd was tabbed to chair the sessions. Dowd, a historic figure in the recording business, was the second employee hired by Atlantic Records and engineered sessions for that label by such immortals as Ray Charles, Aretha Franklin, John Coltrane, Bobby Darin and many others. On his own as a producer over the past decade, Dowd has produced records for such big names in rock as the Allman Brothers, Lynyrd Skynyrd, Eric Clapton and, more to the point in Money's case, Rod Stewart.

With the failure of his previous album and the long layoff following his hospitalization complicating the picture, the pressure on Money to cut a successful record was turned up full blast. Production went very slowly. Dowd stayed in Concord, working with Money a full month prior to his entering a studio. After the basic instrumentals were recorded in Los Angeles, Money went to Miami to finish the album. He expected to stay three weeks but wound up spending four months in Miami. "The tightrope was never tighter," he said, "and it's hard to walk a tightrope with one leg."

He still has mixed feelings about publicly discussing his flirtation with death. One minute, he angrily defended management's decision to keep quiet, and the next, his face was clouded over with remorse as he reflected on the lessons he learned the hard way. Asked why he agreed to the food poisoning story, he simply shrugged his shoulders.

"As they say at CBS," he said, "That's not my department. I think they made a wise move because I didn't think the world should really know about the accident. Even when you came out and started prying around about it, I didn't think it was anybody's business. And, to tell you the truth, I still don't think it's that important. The accident is old news. I came back. I made a great record. Merv Griffin didn't even know I was limping."

But, a tear caught in his throat when it was suggested that his accident was a brick wall he needed to run into. "I can't deny it," he said softly. "It's true. I'm getting married. I'm actually happy. I don't drink as much at all any more. I don't do any really heavy drugs. I have really cleaned up my act. Jesus Christ, I have to. I have no choice.

"This time around, I'm going to make sure my private life and my real friends are more important than Eddie Money and Eddie Money's career. Eddie Money doesn't give a damn about anything but being onstage, seeing them lights, checking out them chicks, and picking up the check in the morning. That has got nothing to do with how I grew up or what I want out of life."

"Eddie Mahoney's back," he laughed. "He's back running Eddie Money's career. Eddie Mahoney's got to take care of Eddie Money 'cause Eddie Money's got to take care of Eddie Mahoney. I don't want to be the guitar player in the Pretenders. I don't want to be the lead singer in the Doors. I don't want to be the drummer in Led Zeppelin. I was almost already one of them people."

Sunday Datebook | August 8, 1982

The day the music lived

*Rereleased 'Last Waltz' documents amazing night
in 1976 when rock's royalty bid farewell to the Band*

The Last Waltz was the single finest evening of live music I
ever attended. I can still remember standing back by the sound
board, entranced, looking over to my right and seeing Neil
Diamond, clearly panicked under those gradient tint aviators
as he contemplated taking the stage following Eric Clapton,
Muddy Waters, Neil Young ...

ROBBIE ROBERTSON OF THE BAND WAS SICK OF THE ROAD. "The Last Waltz" was
his idea. Not everybody in the group agreed with his plan to pull the plug on
the troubled rock band and play one final all-star extravaganza, which would be
filmed and recorded, Thanksgiving night 1976 at Winterland in San Francisco. But
Robertson prevailed.

So it is not surprising that a quarter century later, it would be Robertson,
producer of the film and the original three-disc soundtrack album, who would
spend five grueling months editing, mixing and remixing the original recordings.
He's come up with a new theatrical print featuring six-channel surround sound, a
DVD with 5.1 audio and a four-CD box-set stereo mix of the entire tape, all about
to be released in celebration of the concert's 25th anniversary. The film opens a
weeklong theatrical run tomorrow at the Castro Theatre.

"I knew it was all about the results," Robertson said recently in a phone interview, "to get this movie and all the music ready to pass on."

Director Martin Scorsese supervised the restoration of the 35mm print, and
Robertson put together an audio version that brings that night roaring ferociously
back to life.

One of the most magnificent evenings in rock history, the concert was a sublime sendoff, a celebratory climax to a grand career. At the unforgettable finale,
the Band's Richard Manuel and Bob Dylan sang a duet of "I Shall Be Released,"
flanked by Van Morrison, Neil Young, Joni Mitchell, Neil Diamond, Eric Clapton,
Dr. John, Ronnie Wood and Ringo Starr.

At the same time, it was an evening that will forever be remembered for controversy and conflict. Dylan refused until the last moment to allow his performance to be filmed, and Warner Bros. had financed the seven-camera filming only after being assured Dylan would be in the movie. Hectic backstage negotiations were conducted through the intermission and continued right up until Dylan's entrance. Producer Bill Graham always took credit for twisting Dylan's arm, although Robertson discounted Graham's role.

Graham, who went to extraordinary lengths to give the event its lavish atmosphere, always hated the movie and never felt adequately acknowledged for his role in the concert. Levon Helm of the Band expressed his disgust with the business decisions and events surrounding the concert in his 1993 book "This Wheel's on Fire."

The Band was always more respected and admired than popular. Other musicians loved the long-standing group, which started out playing as the Hawks behind Canadian rock 'n' roller Ronnie Hawkins, long before backing Dylan on his first electric rock tours. The Band's 1968 debut, "Music From Big Pink," never sold many copies, but the clapboard honesty of the music was a revelation to the acid-washed psychedelic blues-rock scene.

By the time Robertson decided, at age 32, that having spent half his life on the road was enough, the group was teetering on the edge of commercial irrelevance. The Band played the 1973 Watkins Glen concert, in front of the biggest rock-concert audience ever, as a supporting act to the Grateful Dead and the Allman Brothers. The group toured baseball parks only as special guests on the 1974 Crosby, Stills, Nash and Young tour.

At the time "The Last Waltz" was announced, only a little more than half the tickets to a pending appearance at Oakland's Paramount Theatre had been sold at $7.50. Those tickets were refunded, and a new Thanksgiving dinner show at Winterland was announced with $25 tickets, which sat almost entirely unsold until Graham leaked the special guest lineup to The Chronicle.

He transformed the seedy old ice rink for the evening. He brought in some potted plants and little hedges, hired a waltz orchestra and professional dancers. He hung chandeliers and rented San Francisco Opera's sets to "La Traviata" for the stage. He served turkey dinners at tables to the capacity crowd of 5,400, uncommonly well dressed for a rock show.

Drugs were everywhere. A room backstage had been painted white and decorated with noses cut off plastic masks while a tape loop of sniffing played in the background. A gauzy haze of cocaine lies over the movie. Never mind the reports that close-ups of Neil Young had to be doctored in post- production to remove incriminating evidence from his nostrils; his jaw- grinding intensity stands in stark contrast to the regal bearing of Muddy Waters.

According to Helm's account, he had to fight to have the enormously dignified Chicago blues immortal on the bill and never understood what Neil Diamond was doing there. Diamond's connection to the Band was through Robertson, who had just finished writing and producing an album with Diamond called "Beautiful Noise" that probably sold more than the entire Band catalog ever did. Robertson offered Helms the tepid explanation that Diamond represented the Tin Pan Alley part of the Band's music.

Fish-out-of-water Diamond, who hadn't performed for an audience that didn't come just to see him since he'd left the package-tour days of "Solitary Man," wandered out from backstage before his performance. He stood by the soundboard at the back of the hall, his face frozen in panic behind those designer aviator shades, as he watched the Band tear up a shuffle with Eric Clapton on guitar.

The film contains a large number of relatively gratuitous shots of producer Robertson, sporting an expensive haircut and a Hollywood-rock-star makeover, waving his guitar as if he were leading the band and singing far away from his microphone, which wasn't turned on anyway. Helm sings like a house on fire on "Up on Cripple Creek," the concert's (but not the movie's) opening song. The other Band members largely disappear into the shadows of the film.

The interspersed interview segments were filmed in the days after the concert at the Band's Malibu studio and headquarters, Shangri-La, and Helm is uncharacteristically tight-lipped. Manuel was so drunk he is barely comprehensible. Bassist and vocalist Rick Danko played interviewer Scorsese a solo recording rather than talk at all.

A quarter century later, Danko and Manuel are dead. Garth Hudson is bankrupt, his home in foreclosure, and Robertson bought everybody but Helm's interest in the group. Also dead are Muddy Waters, Roebuck "Pops" Staples, Paul Butterfield and Bill Graham. Even Winterland itself was torn down long ago. But "The Last Waltz," one of rock's shining moments, lives on.

San Francisco Chronicle | *Thursday, April 4, 2002*

CHAPTER 12

Behind the Scenes

Chris Strachwitz

Warren Hellman

Music Man

Without collector **𝒞𝒽𝓇𝒾𝓈 𝒮𝓉𝓇𝒶𝒸𝒽𝓌𝒾𝓉𝓏**, *there'd be no record of some of America's greatest folk music, from zydeco to the Delta blues*

One of the first articles I ever wrote for the Chronicle was a profile of Chris Strachwitz. He may be the person I most admire among all that I've met in the music business. He introduced me to Lightnin' Hopkins, Mance Lipscomb, Clifton Chenier and another handful of the most interesting musicians I have ever known. After this piece ran in the Sunday magazine, I received an e-mail saying that I failed to identify Strachwitz as Count Christian Von Strachwitz, a titled member of the German aristocracy. I sent Chris a note asking if that was true. "In the old country, I was," he wrote back, "but over here, it doesn't count."

WHEN ACCORDIONIST MARC SAVOY COMES TO TOWN, he stays with Chris Strachwitz in his quiet Berkeley hills home. They've known each other about 45 years. Strachwitz was hunting authentic Cajun music in Eunice, La., and had been directed to telephone Savoy, who had been making accordions in those parts since 1960.

"He said, 'I just ran over a chicken so I'm making gumbo – you might as well come over,'" Strachwitz recalls.

Strachwitz, 76, is a tall, hulking man with graying, sandy-brown hair and a slight accent left over from a childhood spent in Germany. Although he holds no degree, he is America's leading folklorist. He can't speak Spanish, but he single-handedly rescued Mexican American folk music. He brought backwoods Louisiana music out of the swamps and he made hundreds of raw, real records with such great musicians as Texas bluesman Lightnin' Hopkins, Delta blues singer Mississippi Fred McDowell, bayou zydeco king Clifton Chenier and Houston conjunto pioneer Flaco Jimenez.

This particular weekend, the Savoy Family Band was descending on Strachwitz – Marc, his wife, Ann, and their two sons, Joel and Wilson. Strachwitz first recorded Savoy (pronounced Savoir) in the early '70s, back when Cajun music had scarcely been heard outside of Louisiana. Now Savoy is known throughout the world, and his latest group, the Savoy Family Band, has two CDs on Strachwitz's Arhoolie Records.

Ann has become a recognized expert on Cajun music, recording movie soundtracks with T-Bone Burnett and duets with Linda Ronstadt. Their grown sons are continuing the tradition, and not just playing with their parents. Joel, 27, started his own label, Valcour Records, and has been releasing recordings by young Cajun musicians. Wilson, 25, belongs to the Pine Leaf Boys, who record for Strachwitz's label. Strachwitz was going to pick up the Savoys the next day at the airport and drive them on a four-day whirlwind of performances. Chauffeur is not generally part of the duties of record company owners.

Strachwitz started Arhoolie in 1960 – a German public school teacher lugging portable recording equipment around ghetto beer joints in Houston or farms in rural Texas – anywhere he could find people playing country blues or old-time hillbilly music. He was on a hunt for real American music.

He had first gone to Texas the year before, looking for Lightnin' Hopkins. When the teenaged Strachwitz was first plopped down in Reno, Nev., straight from the carnage of World War II, he discovered the blues on late-night radio. Black bluesmen were as estranged from society in this country as Strachwitz felt he was. The blues became an all-consuming fascination for him, and after hearing Hopkins sing in those Houston beer joints, Strachwitz was determined to return the following year with his recording gear, on his first of many tours of the South scouting for the sound of America.

"I would drive sometimes all the way through Mississippi and Alabama and wouldn't find anything," he said. "I remember I was in Alabama one time, I don't remember the name of the town anymore, but I was talking to some people in the plaza or the square shelling peas or some damn thing and asked them were there any musicians around who played some blues. They said 'Well, there's one guy, maybe if you come back after we finish.' And the white guy comes and says, "What are you bothering my hands for? Go away. You got no right to bother my workers.' Then he introduced me to some guy, but he was no damn good anyway."

Although Strachwitz thinks the record business is just about through, he is still readying a few important releases. "Hear Me Howlin': Berkeley in the '60s" will be a four-disc boxed set of his private recordings, previously unissued performances that span a panoply of the Berkeley folk scene; aging country blues legends to incipient folk-rockers barely out of their teens (including the original recording of the Country Joe and the Fish anti-war anthem, "Feel Like I'm Fixin' To Die Rag" that Strachwitz recorded in his living room). He is also pulling together his extensive '70s recordings of Austrian folk songs with liner notes in three languages (Austrian dialect, high German and English).

And he is about to release a collection from sessions he held in New Orleans just before Hurricane Katrina that includes everything from traditional brass bands to street singers, many of the tracks featuring Michael Doucet, the Cajun fiddler Strachwitz first recorded with the Savoy-Doucet Band and, later, in one of his best-sellers (with Arhoolie, "better-sellers" would probably be more accurate), with BeauSoleil, a Cajun group with some electric instruments that Strachwitz refers to as his "rock band."

"He [Doucet] was so turned on that day, it was unbelievable," Strachwitz said. "He hung around and accompanied this intriguing little singer who sings the greatest version of 'Hey La Bas.' Then he also played fiddle with the little string band that had my favorite clarinetist down there, Sammy Rimington. He was in town, and it was sort of a Creole jazz band kind of thing, so Michael enjoyed playing behind that. He also played behind Sun Pie Barnes, who is a really very talented singer when he just plays accordion and harmonica. He's really a folk artist. I know he's trying to be a zydeco musician, but I think his real tour-de-force is being a folk singer. He's an actor, too. He's an amazing guy."

Strachwitz is also producing an as-yet untitled documentary about the New Lost City Ramblers, the bluegrass revivalists who first brought the music to New York City in the '50s, a project he took over ("I got stuck with it," he said) under the auspices of the Arhoolie Foundation, a nonprofit wing of his operation that is also digitizing Strachwitz's collection of 78 RPM Mexican American records, which is probably the most extensive collection in existence, and making the music available through the UCLA folk music library.

Strachwitz is also the subject of a documentary film-in-progress, "No Mouse Music." The movie takes its title from Strachwitz's pat phrase for any kind of music he deems useless – "Mouse music," a contraction of "Mickey Mouse music," which was the '30s jazz musicians' term of disdain for unbearably square bands. Strachwitz's amiable irascibility makes him the perfect foil for documentary filmmakers. They build entire PBS TV series around characters like him.

Around dinnertime the next day, he arrives at Berkeley's Freight and Salvage, where the first Savoy Family show is going to take place. The Savoys awoke before four in the morning in Louisiana to make their flight out of Baton Rouge. After the band conducted their sound check, Strachwitz went next door and brought back a pizza. As the club was filling, he quickly scarfed down a piece before manning the Savoy's merchandise table and selling CDs to the crowd, making change with a fistful of bills stuffed between his fingers and keeping accounts in hen scratches on a piece of paper with a felt-tipped pen.

The Savoys put on a peerless display of delicately filigreed, timeless music – the two boys soaring in harmony on twin fiddles, backed by their father's squeeze box and mother's rhythm guitar. They all switched around instruments – Wilson was especially strong on piano and vocals, closing the set solo, singing his translation into Creole French of "You Don't Know Me." The capacity crowd sat entranced in the lithesome, ethereal spell they wove so effortlessly, the two young men confidently leading the music-making. At one point, Ann Savoy looked over at Strachwitz, who was seated at a table by the wall, smiling broadly at the music he was hearing.

"Why are we here?" she said. "The answer is probably Chris Strachwitz. Thank you, Chris." Strachwitz spoke back like it was a private conversation, but loudly enough for all to hear. "You guys are the ones putting out the music," he said. "I just caught some of it."

For a moment, everybody was sitting in Chris Strachwitz's living room.

He lives by himself in a roomy home above the UC Berkeley campus, his living room walls lined with record shelves, a view of the bay out the window. Over the years, he has recorded a lot of music in this room. Before he started releasing CD collections of old Tex-Mex records, the only way to hear the music was to have Strachwitz play you records from his collection. Ry Cooder sat in that living room one night more than 30 years ago, listening to antique 78 after antique 78 as Strachwitz yelped "yee-haw" to the old corridos until tears ran down his cheeks. Cooder, who would later work with Flaco Jimenez and make records with this conjunto sound, followed Strachwitz and his film crew around when they made the 1976 landmark documentary on Tex-Mex music, "Chulas Fronteras."

"I guess I'm alone in that field, although my Spanish is piss poor," said Strachwitz. "Ever since we made that documentary, 'Chulas Fronteras,' and people are still showing it and they're still enjoying it because it's a milestone. Nobody in the gringo world ever paid attention to this music, except a few guys in Texas, those three huge guys with long beards – yeah, ZZ Top. One of them guys always told me where to find some records. There was a guy in Austin (Texas) who died, killed in an overdose, I forget his name, who was a big collector of this music, but he was

Chris Strachwitz

a musician who wanted to be a rock 'n' roll artist. Doug Sahm and those people were interested in it and he brought this music to the attention of the masses. My stuff never did."

Strachwitz oversees his folklore empire from a storefront complex on San Pablo Avenue, in no-man's-land at the far end of El Cerrito. At the rear of the parking lot, a climate-controlled, earthquake-proof vault holds the 78-record library – not just Tex-Mex, but blues, jazz, country and western, folk, rhythm and blues, American Indian chants, what have you. Upstairs is a large dining room and kitchen, site of mob scene parties twice a year at Christmas and the Fourth of July, which doubles as Strachwitz's birthday party. In a small room off the kitchen, a Spanish-speaking assistant works on the Foundation's digitizing project, painstakingly logging the information from the old records and recording them to computer files.

The record company operates out of the adjoining warehouse, with the shipping department on the ground floor, the executive suite upstairs. At the corner of a collection of desks, the room crowded with file cabinets, piles of papers and boxes, Strachwitz sits in front of a computer looking at a Web site about accordions from Texas. Strachwitz, who steadfastly resisted every important technological innovation in his field for the past 40 years or more, a record executive who drives a car with personalized license plates that read "78s," also sheepishly admits to recently breaking down and buying a cell phone. He had always been more at home with the simple pleasures of backwoods life.

When Strachwitz visits Louisiana, he stays with the Savoys ("He's my best friend, I guess," said Strachwitz). He knew Marc long before he married Ann, who came from Richmond, Va., to Cajun country, and he watched their boys grow up. "I was sitting with Marc at his place," said Strachwitz, "and he said to me 'Chris, you remember those kids when they were just fighting in the mud out there, the little squirts?'"

Nobody has done more to unearth Louisiana's wealth of musical treasures hidden in the swamps and bayous than Strachwitz. From the very beginning of Arhoolie, he was recording old-fashioned Cajun music, the folk music of the French Arcadians. He also is the man most responsible for the spread of zydeco, black music barely heard beyond Lafayette, La., before Strachwitz started recording the late Clifton Chenier. Now they use zydeco on beer commercials.

Chenier was introduced to Strachwitz by Lightnin' Hopkins, the great Houston bluesman, whom Strachwitz first went to Texas to find. Hopkins took Strachwitz to see some accordionists in Houston whom Strachwitz used to record his first zydeco album in 1961.

"When I first got to Houston," he said, "it was still the quaint stuff that I recorded on that first zydeco record that I put out, all these guys playing their squeeze boxes in these beer joints. They all said, 'Oh that Clifton Chenier, he's something special.' But he was just trying to be a rhythm-and-blues artist. That French music was just nowhere. To me, that was one of the most interesting things I guess I did accomplish, because I heard him first playing French in that little beer joint that Lightnin' took me to. He did nothing but sing in French, in that patois, and it was the most lowdown blues, and I loved it. Of course, he came over said, 'You're a record man, let's make a record tomorrow.' And he showed up with a god-damn band. He didn't have just the two pieces that he had in that beer joint. 'Oh Chris, I gotta make a record, it's got to be rock 'n' roll,' he said. I said bulls-. But he refused to play anything real that time."

But when Strachwitz returned to make a full album with Chenier, he negotiated (via first class mail) an agreement from Chenier that at least half the album would be old-fashioned French music some people called zydeco.

"Out of that session," said Strachwitz, "when he did the French stuff, came that amazing thing that I called 'Louisiana Blues.' He rattled off the name to me. He told me the name in French. I asked him how to spell it and he said 'You spell anyway you want to.' I said 'That doesn't help me much – can I call it "Louisiana Blues?" He said 'Go ahead, call it "Louisiana Blues." I think that was the smartest thing I ever did because if I had put that weird French name he first told me on the record, the deejays wouldn't have touched it down home. He had some kind of a name, but 'Louisiana Blues' by Clifton Chenier, they said, 'Oh this gotta be.' And then you put the needle down and that first note hits you like a sledgehammer. It was just lowdown blues. The flip side was 'Zydeco Et Pas Sales.' Both those things helped him both become proud of being Creole and helped him become the King of Zydeco, as he later called himself."

The storefront on the street in El Cerrito, the public end of Arhoolie world headquarters, belongs to his specialty retail record store, Down Home Music, one-stop shopping for everything that can't be found at Borders or Barnes and Nobles (world music, rockabilly, blues, old-time country music, Hungarian mazurkas, et al), now the flagship of a two-store chain. Against what he suspects is his better judgment, but having fallen prey to a determined developer who made offers he ultimately could not resist, Strachwitz opened a second store this fall in the high-end Berkeley shopping district on Fourth Street, where the Savoys were making an afternoon in-store appearance that Sunday.

The sound of fiddles and accordion trickles out to the sidewalk. The Savoy Family Band is squeezed in the nook under the little cupola at the end of the tiny store. A couple dozen curious onlookers are threaded around the CD stacks and listening posts. A pair of intrepid couples dance in the crowded space. Strachwitz is standing against the wall, his face creased with delight.

The night after the Freight and Salvage, he drove the Savoys to a show in Sacramento and back to Berkeley. The next night, he took them to play in Santa Cruz and spent the night before driving back to play the next afternoon at his new store. That night, the band would play for dancers at Berkeley's folk dance center, Ashkenaz, after which Strachwitz would take the Savoys to a motel near the airport for an early morning flight back to Louisiana.

Strachwitz is a man anyone can envy. Ever since he took that fateful trip to Texas with his portable tape recorder on summer vacation in 1960, he has been a man who followed his bliss. He made enough money doing what he wanted, he never bothered doing something he didn't want to do to make money. He has never done a single thing in his career because it would make money and he has done plenty of things knowing they wouldn't. Unlike practically everybody else who wanders into the music business because they love music, Strachwitz never lost touch with that original impulse. All these years later, it's still the music that matters to Strachwitz, the music and the people who make it.

San Francisco Chronicle Magazine | Sunday, January 13, 2008

Financier's love of bluegrass leads to concert

Who knew this goofy gazillionaire was going to start the greatest live music festival of the 21st century? This was so nuts, no way did anybody imagine the first year that it would even take place a second time, let alone every year since. Warren Hellman – what a beaut.

THE MILLIONAIRE FINANCIER STOOD AT HIS DESK in the 12th floor Embarcadero Center corner office, punching keys on his laptop, bringing up a Web site featuring sound clips by his favorite artist. His face twisted into a broad grin as a backwoods drawl crackled through the small computer speakers.

"Cotton is down to a quarter a pound and I'm busted," warbled Hazel Dickens.

"I'm driving everybody crazy with this," said Warren Hellman, co-founder and chairman of Hellman & Friedman LLC, one of the nation's top private investment firms. Hellman is an unorthodox captain of industry – "deviant," he said – who is wearing a well-worn blue denim work shirt, no tie and white socks.

Hellman loves bluegrass music with a grand passion. Especially the music of Hazel Dickens. Like all great zealots, he wants to share his joy, so he is throwing a free concert Saturday at Speedway Meadow in Golden Gate Park, starring Emmylou Harris, Alison Krauss and Union Station and, of course, Dickens.

"I don't know what kind of guy this guy is," said a wary Dickens from her low-rent housing co-op in Washington.

"In one of her songs she sings about the rich man who lives on the hill," said Hellman. "I guess that's me."

Dickens, 66, was born to a poor coal mining family of 11 children in Montcalm, W.Va. She began performing old-time mountain music in public after she moved with her brothers to Baltimore as a teenager. She met Mike Seeger, half-brother of the folksinger, while he was a conscientious objector working as an orderly in a Baltimore hospital where her brother lay dying from black lung, the coal miners' disease.

Dickens writes no-nonsense songs about social issues like labor unions, feminism, the hard life of the miner. Her coal mining songs were featured in the 1976 Oscar-winning documentary "Harlan County, U.S.A." (Dickens herself is the subject of a new documentary, "It's Hard to Tell the Singer From the Song.")

"Disaster at the Mannington Mine" is Hellman's favorite.

"I guess I better put it in the set," said Dickens. "I'll put all them songs in there. I was hesitating because I didn't want to insult the man. Most of my songs are pretty blatant against people like him."

But Hellman, 67, is not like other businessmen. Though he lives in Presidio Heights and says he is worth hundreds of millions, he takes a 12 to 15-mile run through the Presidio every morning before the sun rises. He also rides every year in the Tevis Cup, a grueling 100-mile, 24-hour horse race through precipitous trails over the Sierra. He is an enthusiastic participant in another horse X-game called Ride and Tie, involving a team of two long-distance runners and one very fit horse.

"The people I do that with are loggers, truckers, schoolteachers," Hellman said. "I don't play golf. People who do this are people who like bluegrass."

Hellman said that for years, he had dreamed of throwing a bluegrass wingding in the park for the entire city, but it became reality only after he met the management of Slim's, which is producing the event.

"I am having so much fun you can't imagine," he said.

He has been talking on the phone and corresponding with Dickens – "probably more than she wants," he said. But she didn't sound annoyed. "I just didn't answer his last letter," she said.

Dickens politely refused Hellman's invitation to be his houseguest for her trip to San Francisco. "My place is with the band," she said, "and we'll be rehearsing into the night. I told him, 'You go to bed with the chickens and get up with the roosters. It wouldn't work.' "

San Francisco Chronicle | October 25, 2001

Selvin's Specialty Gumbo

A NOTE FROM THE CHEF: When I called Chris Strachwitz of Arhoolie Records to ask permission to use his Clifton Chenier recordings with the gumbo instructional video, he was outraged. He didn't care that we might pirate his music, but he was furious that I would represent this muddled creation as real gumbo. "It's inauthentic," he sniffed, his voice rich with disdain.

Now Chris Strachwitz knows something about Louisianne culture. He not only produced many records by Clifton Chenier, the Savoy-Doucet Band and all those others, he's logged so much time in the bayous, he practically qualifies as coonass. He's never eaten my gumbo -- many certified Louisiana prawnsuckers have and found it not without merit – but he was unmoved by my arguments.

"It sounds like one of those New Orleans gumbos," he said.

Actually, he recipe I prepare is a jumbled combination of things – and I never said it was authentic. It most definitely isn't. My recipe developed over the years. I stole the idea of grinding the sausage, for instance, from a bowl I ate in a North Beach joint many years ago. Gumbo was on the menu as a daily special because the chef was from Louisiana. I don't know who taught him to grind his sausage.

Strachwitz takes a very harsh view of people messing with regional American folk traditions and I want to support that viewpoint. Although there are many variations on the basic Louisiana gumbo – and, in fact, every pot, to a certain degree, turns out its own way no matter what you do – there are purists.

Call it an homage. Call it an improvisation, a meditation based on the concept of gumbo. Call it anything but late for dinner. – J.S.

Ingredients:

6 cloves garlic, minced

1 large onion, chopped

1 yellow bell pepper, chopped

4 whole scallions, chopped

1 stalk celery, diced

6 chicken thighs, boned and cubed (definitely not skinned – this is not health food)

3/4 lb. andouille sausage, ground

14 oz. canned diced tomatoes

1/3 cup okra, chopped

1/2 lb. shrimp (shelled)

1 cup flour for chicken (seasoned with salt, black, white and red pepper, ground thyme, grated parmesan cheese)

1/2 cup flour for rou

4 cups chicken broth

3-4 tablespoons bacon fat

salt

black pepper

white pepper

red pepper

ground thyme

Instructions: Dredge chicken cubes in seasoned flour. Brown chicken in cast iron Dutch Oven (stick-free surfaces don't make it for gumbo).

Remove chicken. Ladle off some of the chicken fat; add bacon fat, if you've got it (vegetable oil can be used, but bacon fat is especially tasty).

To make the roux, add flour to cooking oils (one part flour for one part oil) and cook briskly at high heat, stirring constantly. The idea is to cook the flour, not burn it, and let it go until the color of the paste moves past milk chocolate to chestnut. Be patient -- this can take quite awhile, but reaching the right color is key to a good roux.

Once roux critical mass is achieved – when it turns to a dark brown chestnut color – dump in the vegetables, which will quickly absorb the roux.

Cook until onions and peppers soften. Coarsely grind sausage in food processor and add to pot. Let cook another five minutes or so. Add tomatoes and okra and cook another five minutes.

Return the chicken and spice to taste with salt, three peppers and thyme (I leave off blasting the dish with red pepper and opt for adding hot sauce after serving -- I think the gumbo should have a slight snap, some authority, but not bite back).

Cover with chicken broth and simmer 40-60 minutes. Add shrimp for the final 15 minutes. (Shrimp are not essential; sometimes I ladle out a panful before adding the shrimp in case somebody is allergic to or doesn't like seafood).

www.sfgate.com

Afterword

Funny thing. In March 2009, after work had already started on "Smart Ass," I left my staff position at The Chronicle after 36 years and change. I was only one of more than 200 editorial employees to leave their jobs at the paper that year, but newspaper staff cuts are hardly news anymore. The Chronicle has been generous in allowing me to continue my dialogue with the readership on a freelance basis and that may well be the future of arts coverage for daily newspapers. I watched the space for arts coverage dwindle, the cultural heft of the pop music world wither, the music itself turn vapid, feckless and got the picture. The age of the rock critic was coming to an end.

Who needs record reviews anymore anyway? Anything you want to hear can be downloaded. And, need them or not, there have never been so many record reviews, even without the bloggers. The cultural dialogue has been diffused and probably for the better. The audience for the music has grown enormously and the expanse of its history is widely appreciated. In the iPod era of pop music, the very notion of rock critics just sounds archaic.

The whole rock critic thing was very much a piece of another era, the rock era. It was David Lee Roth who observed that the reason rock critics liked Elvis Costello so much was that they all looked like him, although that was only partly true. No rock critic, however, was ever as cool as he thought he was. Captured better by actor Jeff Goldblum in a scarcely noticed movie called "Between the Lines" than by Cameron Crowe in his celebrated "Almost Famous," no nerdy, tweedy rock critic ever matched the oily panache and vainglorious pomp of Addison DeWitt, the theater critic in "All About Eve" as portrayed by George

Sanders, who arrives at the cocktail party with Marilyn Monroe on his arm. Now that's a role model.

My stories for the Chronicle all enjoyed the benefit of scrupulous editing; some of it even made the stories better. Thanks to Judy Stone, Pat Luchak, Rob Duvilla, David Kleinberg, Bob Graham, Conrad Silvert, Peter Stack, Mark Lundgren, especially to Liz Lufkin and David Wiegand, and, of course, John L. Wasserman, who gave the kid his shot. There were many others. My whole career has been largely a collaborative effort; as if all these people, for reasons of their own, conspired to prop me up and get my stuff in the paper. Sometimes all I had to do was push the keys. It wasn't always that easy, but I saw it as my duty.

Still the music rings in my ears. It was a glorious time to be on the guest list – The Who, Led Zeppelin, Bob Marley, Springsteen, U2 and so many others. The Last Waltz. Live Aid. It was like having covered the 1927 Yankees or something – at Live Aid in Philadelphia, they were making a modest stir over nude photos in magazines by some gal disco singer playing early in the morning who called herself Madonna. A golden era that lasted far longer than anybody had any right to expect paraded across stages for years in front of anyone who cared to watch. I did. The reports I filed may not have always been more than adequate reading, but I was there. The music I heard could never be fully described. It's almost like I did the whole thing just for my own entertainment.

Rock critic? Yep. I did that. Oh but you know yeah.

PHOTO CREDITS

Photographs of Ralph Gleason, Sly Stone, Grace Slick, Mike Bloomfield by Jim Marshall; Vince Welnick by Jay Blakesberg; Kevin Gilbert by Hugh Brown; Quicksilver Messenger Service by Barry Olivier; Charles Brown by Bob Scheu; Dick Dale by Bruce Henderson; Phil Spector, Grateful Dead, Jerry Garcia, Neil Young, courtesy Warner Bros Records; Jefferson Airplane courtesy RCA Victor Records; Fillmore jam session courtesy Vanguard Records; Steve Miller courtesy Capitol Records; Glen Campbell courtesy Glen Campbell Enterprises.

All other photographs reprinted by permission from the San Francisco Chronicle, copyright © 2011, The Hearst Corporation. All rights reserved.

Special thanks to Steve, Kim, Rick, Mark, the estate of Florence Casaroli and all the folks at Parthenon Books.